Santa Ana

*The People,
the Pueblo,
and the History
of Tamaya*

Santa Ana

Laura Bayer with
Floyd Montoya and the
Pueblo of Santa Ana

University of New Mexico Press
Albuquerque

Funding provided by National Endowment for the
Humanities Grant No. ES-00061-79-0666

Library of Congress Cataloging-in-Publication Data

Bayer, Laura.
Santa Ana : the people, the pueblo, and the history of Tamaya / Laura Bayer with
Floyd Montoya and the pueblo of Santa Ana.—1st ed.
p.   cm.
Includes bibliographical references and index.
ISBN 0-8263-1515-1
1. Pueblo Indians—History.   2. Pueblo Indians—Social life and customs.
3. Santa Ana Pueblo (N.M.)—History.   4. Santa Ana Pueblo (N.M.)—Social life
and customs.   I. Montoya, Floyd, 1940–   II. Title.
E99.P9B377   1994
978.9'57—dc20   93-48899
CIP

Contents

Maps

Photographs

Photographs

Tamaya's Churches

Farming and Ranching

Tamayame

Acknowledgments

The history of Santa Ana Pueblo is recorded in many documents, maps, and photographs, as well as in the oral tradition of Tamaya (the name of the pueblo in the people's language). However, in 1979, when this project began, this history was scattered among dozens of archives, libraries, and collections, with most of the materials located far from the pueblo and difficult for a nonspecialist to use. Little had been done to record the wealth of information known to pueblo elders or to catalog the documents stored in pueblo files. Throughout the project, many people have collaborated to produce a tribal archive, an oral history collection, and a map series, as well as this text. These materials are now readily available, for the first time, to the people most vitally interested in Tamaya's history.

The funding that made this undertaking possible came from the National Endowment for the Humanities Grant no. ES-00061–79-0666 and from Santa Ana Pueblo.

Foremost among the contributors are pueblo members and officials, without whose efforts none of this would have come to be. We owe a great debt to the elders of Tamaya who shared their knowledge in a series of taped interviews. Porfirio Montoya's detailed accounts of Tamaya's origins, land use, traditions, ways, and twentieth-century history enrich this text at many points. Other elders interviewed include Leo Peña, Elijio Montoya, Louis Armijo, Lawrence Montoya, Clyde León, Alfonso García, Albert Montoya, Vincent Armijo, Roy Montoya, Andy León, Donna Pino, Ben Peña, José Ramón Sánchez, Félix García, Eudora Montoya, and Cristo García.

Throughout the project, pueblo officials—including Governors Sam Ar-

Acknowledgments

mijo, Lawrence Montoya, and Clyde León, Lieutenant Governor Roy Montoya, and many others—have reviewed the materials, given researchers access to documents, offered support, and generously volunteered their time and expertise. Floyd Montoya, chosen to serve as the pueblo historian for the project, has contributed in many essential ways: doing initial research in the archives; helping to gather and identify photographs for the collection; participating in interviews; providing translations and reviewing the transcriptions of tapes; developing initial base maps and reviewing revisions as the maps were prepared for the text; cataloging the documents in the tribal offices and adding them to the index; preparing an initial summary of the materials; and above all, helping all of those working on the project to understand what this history has meant to the people of Santa Ana.

Several scholars have generously shared their expertise. Among them, Dr. Ward Alan Minge deserves special recognition. Dr. Minge translated Spanish documents obtained from the archives, provided an outline of Spanish-period history, shared his extensive knowledge of source materials, and offered many useful suggestions for the development of the archives, the map collection, and the manuscript. Dr. Myra Ellen Jenkins (then Archivist of the New Mexico State Records Center and Archives at Santa Fe) also suggested useful sources and approaches, clarified points of confusion, made available both archival materials and her own research, and offered her scholarly advice.

Throughout the project, the American West Center of the University of Utah has provided technical assistance and advice. Dr. Floyd A. O'Neil and Dr. Gregory C. Thompson contributed to the initial research and continually provided advice, direction, and encouragement. The materials collected for the pueblo were indexed by John C. Chanik, under the direction of Laura Bayer, who prepared a user's guide to the archive. Jeannie Young shot a series of Tamaya and Ranchiit'u to supplement the historic photographs collected for the archives. Greg Wight drew the initial maps; the maps that appear here were developed by the authors, drawn by Catherine J. Patillo and reviewed by pueblo officials, with the assistance of Gregory C. Thompson. Additional research was done by John C. Chanik, Laura Bayer and David Rich Lewis. Patiently and expertly, Tammy Taylor and Avis Legler undertook the task of typing and retyping the thousands of pages of transcriptions, index cards, and manuscript drafts.

At archives throughout the country, many individuals generously gave their time to the research for this project. Two deserve special recognition: Dr. Myra Ellen Jenkins, Archivist of the New Mexico State Records Center and Archives, and Richard Crawford of the National Archives. We are no less

Acknowledgments

indebted to the individuals on the staffs of the National Archives, Washington, D.C.; the Federal Records Center, Denver; the New Mexico State Records Center and Archives, Santa Fe; the Bureau of Indian Affairs Office, Southern Pueblo Agency, Albuquerque; the Museum of New Mexico, Santa Fe; the Museum of the American Indian, New York; the Library of Congress Map Division, Alexandria, Virginia; and the libraries of the University of New Mexico, the University of Utah, Brigham Young University, and Utah State University. Although we cannot list the names of individual staff members here, their contributions will be reflected not only in this text, but in the work of scholars who use the Santa Ana Tribal Archive for generations to come.

This manuscript was originally completed in 1983; the copy, which had suffered some degeneration over the years, was revised for publication in 1992. The decision was made at that time not to attempt to update the materials to reflect the intervening years of scholarship and the most recent history of the pueblo, except in the instance of cases recently decided that involved pueblo lands and waters, and recent purchases that have affected the pueblo's current landholdings. Final corrections were completed by Laura Bayer, with the assistance of Dr. Floyd A. O'Neil, now director of the American West Center, and reviewed by pueblo officials. In addition to renewing our thanks to those originally involved, many of whom have moved on to new locations and positions, we would like to extend our thanks to Richard Hughes, attorney for the pueblo of Santa Ana, who graciously shared materials developed by his office, with the assistance of Ward Alan Minge, Myra Ellen Jenkins, and David H. Snow, in connection with the Baca case, and to Winston Erickson, who prepared an additional map showing the Ranchiit'u purchases along the Río Grande.

To all of those who have contributed to the making of this book we extend our thanks and apologies for any errors, oversights, and weaknesses in this manuscript, which should not reflect in any way on their knowledge, scholarship, and generosity.

Preface

This history of a unique people is the direct result of efforts made to impact local communities with tribal histories.

The National Endowment for the Humanities funded a major portion of the research and writing. The tribe also contributed time and money to make certain that the manuscript represented their point of view and interests.

Archival research in many locations included Floyd Montoya who served as the historian for the tribe. Floyd and his father were especially helpful in the gathering of oral history. The father, Porfirio Montoya, was a great font of knowledge from the traditional oral history of the Santa Ana people. He was patient, detailed and encouraging to all who worked on the project.

At the American West Center, University of Utah, it was my pleasure to coordinate the work and to act as liaison between the Pueblo and the Center. At the American West Center, many persons helped; Gregory C. Thompson, John Chanik, Greg Wight, Catherine J. Patillo, Jeannie Young, Winston P. Erickson and several others too numerous to mention. Laura Bayer was always at the center of the effort.

There was never a conflict between the Center and the Pueblo. Many tribal leaders contributed to our efforts. Especially important was the role of the tribal administrator, Roy Montoya. The personnel of the Center leave this project with a deep respect for the leaders and the people of Santa Ana—Tamaya is forever in our hearts.

Floyd A. O'Neil
Director
American West Center
University of Utah

Santa Ana

Introduction

Tamaya, known to outsiders since Spanish times as Santa Ana, is a small pueblo on the Río Jémez, located away from the main routes followed by later travelers through the Southwest. Because of its size and relative isolation, Tamaya has often been overshadowed in the written history of the region by its larger and better known neighbors. Until now, the details of Tamaya's history have been available only in footnotes, unpublished technical reports, and remote archives. Consequently, the Tamayame—the people of Tamaya—have had little access to many of the records of their own past. This book attempts to correct that problem by combining the scattered references in the written history with the rich oral tradition that has preserved Tamaya's own account of its past.

From the first, this book has been intended for the people of Tamaya, and especially for the young people who will carry Tamaya's history into the future. Guided by our belief that this history should be written not just for scholars, but for all who have an interest in it, we have tried to narrate events as simply as possible. Where complex legal, scholarly, or technical issues form an integral part of the history, we have tried to explain these matters so that they will be clear to readers who do not possess an extensive scholarly background. In deciding what the text would cover, we have respected the wishes of pueblo officials. Tamaya chooses not to reveal all of its culture to outsiders, and to honor that decision we have omitted descriptions of the pueblo's religious life, ceremonies, and sacred traditions.

At the same time, however, a simple, undocumented summary of events in the history of Tamaya would be a disservice to the Tamayame as well as to scholars interested in technical details, for the sources of that history have never been identified in any study that is generally available. Without some scholarly apparatus, it would be virtually impossible for readers to trace the sources of all the materials included here or to add to the knowledge of Tamaya's history without repeating the work already accomplished during this project. For these reasons, at the end of the text, we include detailed notes, a map-source essay, and a series of technical appendices; acknowledge our debts to those who have preserved parts of Tamaya's history; indicate problems that need further research; and discuss the questions, assumptions, and issues that provide the basis for the material presented in the text itself. The result, we hope, will address the questions that a scholar might pose and provide a foundation for future historians of Tamaya without impeding the readers for whom the text is designed.

The story of Tamaya begins in the remote past, in the oral traditions that recount how the people came into the upper world and made the long journey that eventually led them to Tamaya. This text presents that story as it has been told in traditional accounts for many generations. More recently, scholars have begun to search for evidence of this early history in the pottery, buildings, and remains of the Ancient Ones, as well as in the modern languages of their descendants. These new explorations may eventually yield a wealth of information about the ancient history of the Southwest, and many of them support parts of Tamaya's tradition that earlier scholars had discounted. For several reasons, however, these archaeological, anthropological, and linguistic theories are not integrated in the text, but discussed in the notes and in an appendix. First, and most important, this book presents the history of Tamaya from the vantage point of the Tamayame, not from the perspectives of those who have had ample opportunities elsewhere to present their interpretations of the history of the pueblos. Second, even among those scholars, the leap from discovering ruins and potsherds to explaining the movements or lives of native peoples is based on many assumptions that not all are prepared to accept. Thus, these theories of Tamaya's early history are both more tentative and more subject to reinterpretation than either the people's own traditions or the documents that provide evidence of their later history. This research has been summarized in Appendix 1 ("Tracing the History of the Tamayame before Tamaya"); the chapter notes include complete references to relevant studies, as well as discussions of the relationships and discrepancies between the scholarly studies, the traditional accounts of Tamaya's history, and the documentary evidence available from the post-contact period.

Tamaya's written history begins with the accounts of Spanish explorers, the first Europeans to meet the people of a pueblo that they named Santa Ana. We can only suggest, however, when and where the first meeting might have occurred and what its nature could have been, for the documents now available do not indicate whether the first explorers visited the Tamayame in their pueblo or met them elsewhere. Nothing in these records identifies where the Tamayame were living when the first Spaniards arrived in 1540, or whether Tamaya had been founded in its modern location. Not until the arrival of Spanish colonists led by Don Juan de Oñate in 1598 did the people of Tamaya enter the written record by name. From that time, the pueblo's history may be traced in greater detail through the records of non-Indian travelers, settlers, traders, explorers, and officials who came to the region, as well as through land records and legal documents. Much of the recorded history is partial, seen through the eyes of outsiders and frequently preserved by chance more than by intent. Unfortunately, it usually reflects the interests, purposes, and values of those who recorded it rather than those of the people whose history it documents. Too often it poses more questions than it answers. Much of Tamaya's past now lies hidden in what the records omit, what scholars have not yet found, and what no earlier observer thought worthy of note. Much of that history may remain buried, but more will surely emerge, for this volume represents only the beginning of the task of tracing the history of Tamaya.

ONE

The Tamayame before Tamaya

Long ago, the tradition says, the Hanu (the People) came into this world from an underworld. They emerged at Shipapu, a place north and west of the land that would come to be known as Tamaya.[1] This upper world, they soon saw, was abundant. When they came into this world, their religious leader spoke to them of the beauty of the land and the sky and what they were to do. The people were to travel over the earth until they found the place that suited them best. There they would make their homes. He gave them instructions for the journey. When he had finished, he blessed all those who chose to remain in the upper world, and the Hanu set out on their journey.

They traveled for a long time, always heading south. Though they passed through many fine lands, they did not settle in any of them. When they grew hungry, they stopped to gather the nourishment earth provided for them: deer and antelope, rabbits, turkeys, buffalo, plants of many kinds, and clear cool water. As soon as the Hanu had renewed their energy, they traveled on as they had been instructed. In this way they journeyed, pausing only long enough to regain their strength, until at last they reached Kashe K'atreti (White House). There, after many years of traveling, they stopped to settle for the first time.

Throughout the journey to Kashe K'atreti, the Hanu had been governed by the instructions of their religious leader. Now, under his direction, the people set up a larger system of government, which would give order to their lives as they continued their journey and, much later, when they settled at Tamaya. At the head of this government was the Tiyamune (Cacique), who was responsible for deciding all matters of importance to the people. To see

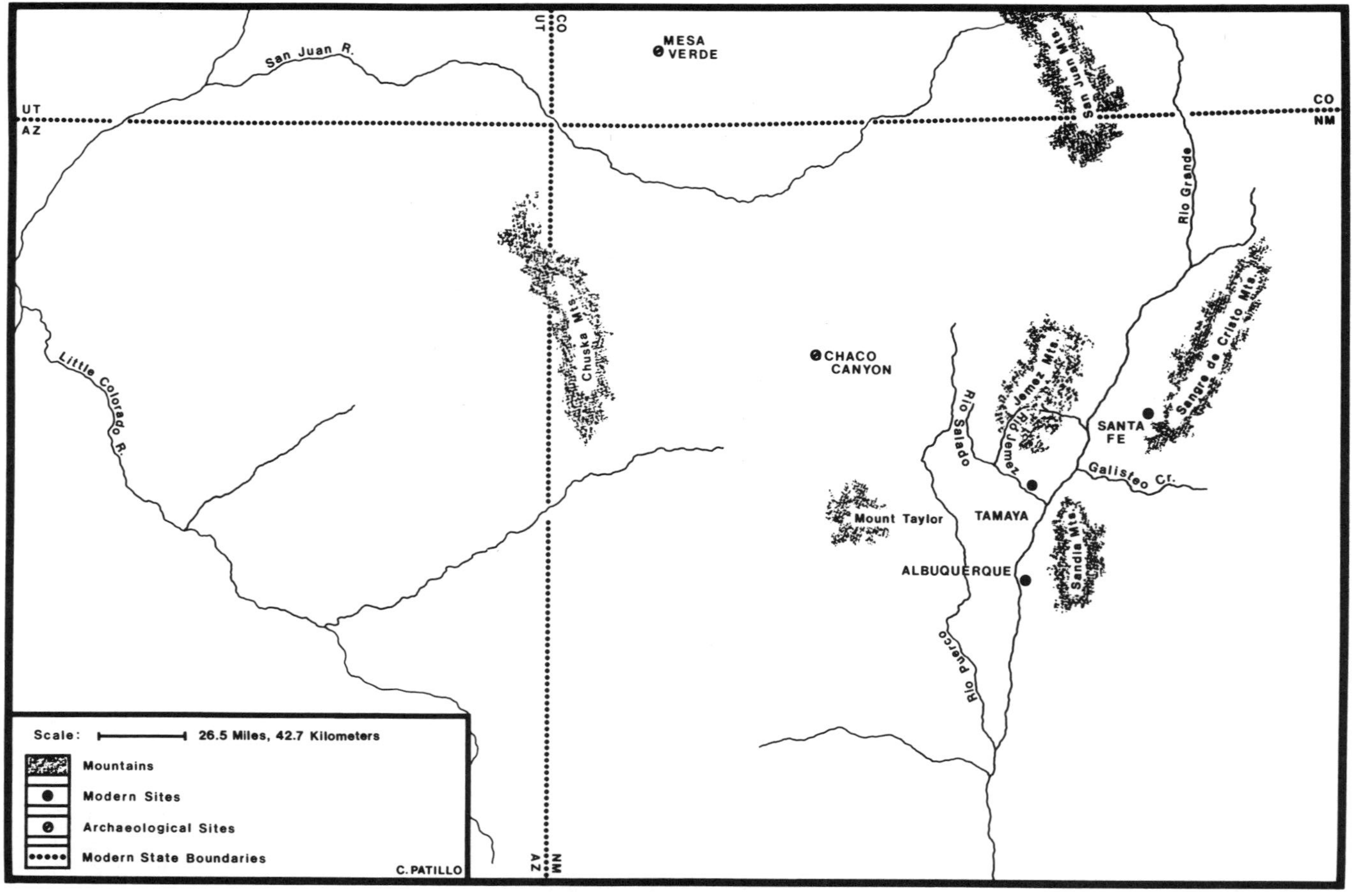

THE UPPER WORLD

Scale: |——| 26.5 Miles, 42.7 Kilometers

Mountains

● Modern Sites

◉ Archaeological Sites

•••• Modern State Boundaries

C. PATILLO

that his decisions were carried out and that all of the things needed for the religious ceremonies were done, the Tiyamune appointed a Mase'ewi (War Chief), an U'uye'ewi (Assistant War Chief), and a number of Kuwachani (Aides). From that time on, the Tiyamune, guided by spiritual inspiration and a council of advisers, was to lead the Hanu.

While the Hanu journeyed, the earth had provided richly for them. Abundant game and the wild plants along the route had met the people's needs. But when they ended their journey, they would no longer rely only on what the earth offered them, for the Hanu were a farming people. Wherever they settled, they planted fields of maize, beans, and squash.

For a farming people, this upper world could be harsh. Without hard work, they would have no harvest, for many places had no water, and untended seeds would wither in the dry ground. When they chose a place to settle, the Hanu had to find a source of water for their crops. Sometimes a river or stream promised a steady supply of water, but often there was no river, or only a small stream that would dry up during the summer when the seedlings most needed water. Rainfall might supply that water, but rain in this land was sparse and unpredictable. To ensure a supply of water for their crops, the Hanu learned to plant their seeds above underground springs, where water would seep up to nourish the young plants. They grew skilled at constructing check dams to capture rainfall and runoff and direct the scarce water to the crops. In the driest summers, the people carried springwater in clay jars to the parched fields.[2]

At Kashe K'atreti, their first settlement, the Hanu built the foundations of their way of life in the upper world. But they were not to remain at Kashe K'atreti, for this was not their homeland. Eventually the time came for them to move on, and they headed south and east once again. After traveling for a long time, they reached the eastern slope of the Sandía Mountains. There, in the high valley west of the San Pedro Arroyo, they settled in the village of Paak'u. This village surrounded by mountain peaks had adobe buildings around a central plaza. As the village grew, more buildings, made first of adobe and later of stone, were added on the west side, leaving the flatlands on the eastern edge of the village free for farming.[3]

The region around Paak'u was rich in resources. A spring provided a dependable supply of water. High in the mountains the hunters could find deer, elk, bear, and bighorn sheep. Bison and pronghorn antelope roamed the valleys and basins. Squirrels, rabbits, chipmunks, mice, bats, and other small animals were also abundant.[4] Piñon, oak, yucca, cactus, and berries grew near the village.[5] The mountains nearby held deposits of lead, turquoise, mica, and other minerals.[6]

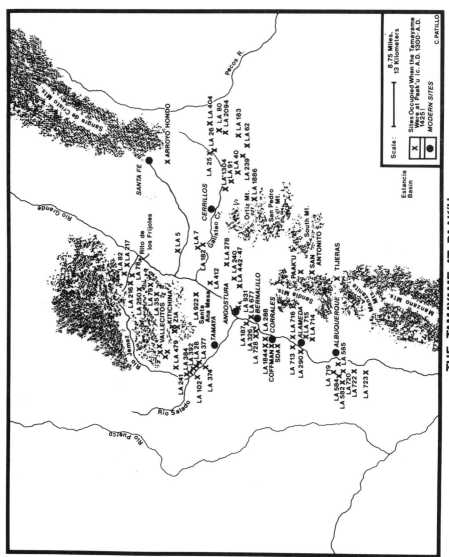

THE TAMAYAME AT PAAK'U

C. PATILLO

Scale: |———| 8.75 Miles,
                13 Kilometers

X Sites Occupied When the Tamayame
   Were at Paak'u ic A.D. 1300–A.D.
   1425 [

● MODERN SITES

With these resources, the people of Paak'u could make all that they needed. The leaves and fiber of yucca and other plants were woven into sandals, baskets, and mats. Wild plants yielded fruits, nuts, greens, and berries for the people's diet.[7] Animals provided both food and a supply of bone that would be used to make a variety of essential tools. Artisans carved and polished the bone to fashion handles, scrapers, punches, and fine awls. Bone could also be worked to make beads and ornaments, game pieces, and musical instruments such as flutes, whistles, and rasps.[8] Using clay tempered with mica, sand, or schist, the potters of Paak'u made both ornate jars, canteens, bowls, and dippers and undecorated cooking pots, jars, bowls, and pitchers. At first the potters used black carbon paint on a white or gray slip to decorate their wares. Then, not long after Paak'u was founded, some potters began to create a red or red-orange pottery, with designs applied in a black glaze paint. Other potters applied this dark glaze to a whitish or yellow slip.[9]

The craftsmen, farmers, and potters of Paak'u were not isolated. Just to the south, in the Sandía Mountains, lay the villages later known as Tijeras and San Antonito. To the east were the villages of the Galisteo Basin. The settlements of the Río Grande were not far away. The people of Paak'u met these neighbors, and perhaps more distant ones as well, for networks of trade and giving brought goods from remote lands to the Sandía village. Although Paak'u was far from any ocean, its residents made beads and ornaments from the sea shells of western Mexico. The people had pottery made by their neighbors to the west, south, and east. Their contacts may well have reached as far as the Plains.[10]

For more than a century, the settlement at Paak'u prospered. The people added new rooms of stone and masonry to the village. Farmers tended their crops in fields on the flats east of the town. Not all of the Hanu remained at Paak'u during this time, however. The tradition recalls that when the people reached Paak'u, they divided into two groups. One group settled in the village on the east slope of the Sandías, while the others set out on a journey that was to take them in a large circle to the west before they returned to Paak'u.

The people who left Paak'u traveled through the Río Grande Valley,[11] where they built a small village on the east bank of the river just across from Katishcha (San Felipe Pueblo). To the Katishchame (San Felipe People) this village was known as Tamaya Kuwasaya (Tamaya Village). The Tamayame (Tamaya People) remained there only a short time before crossing the Río Grande and traveling north and west. When they reached the area south of

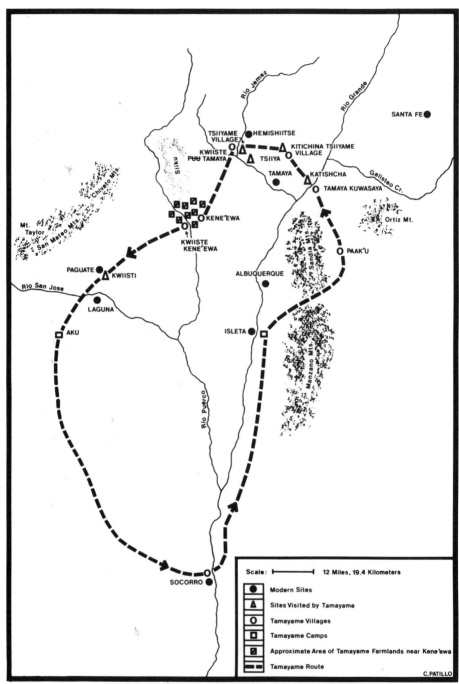

THE TAMAYAME JOURNEY TO THE WEST

Borrego Springs, they settled for a time beside a village of the Kitichina Tsiiyame (Kitichina Zía People). Then, with the Tsiiyame, they traveled west, passing between the pueblos of Tsiiya (Zía) and Hemishiitse (Jémez). Just south of the place where the Río Jémez meets the Río Salado, the Tamayame built a settlement, known as Kwiiste Pʉʉ Tamaya, on the west bank of the Jémez. A Tsiiyame village stood just across the river, on the east bank.

Kwiiste Pʉʉ Tamaya, the tradition says, was blessed with flourishing fields of corn and squash. The women of the Tsiiyame village would cross the river each day to help the Tamayame grind corn. But the stories recall that the men of the Tsiiyame village soon grew jealous because their women were crossing the river, and in their anger, they began to plot against the Tamayame. The men recruited the Nabaju (Navajo), who had recently arrived in the region, to help them attack the Tamayame village.[12]

When the people of Kwiiste Pʉʉ Tamaya learned of the plot, they decided to move on. They gathered food and supplies for the journey, packed all that they could carry, and then set fire to the village. Carrying their belongings, they moved south until they came to Kene'ewa (San Felipe Mesa), just southeast of Siiku (Mesa Prieta) and east of the Río Puerco. On top of the mesa, they sought shelter from their enemies. Later, as the threat of attack became more remote, the Tamayame began to plant corn in the wide valley at the base of Siiku. Then, when the danger had passed, the people moved down from the mesa and built a new village, Kwiiste Kene'ewa, in the valley on the west bank of the Río Puerco near Kene'ewa.

Meanwhile, an old woman and a small boy remained behind at the abandoned village of Kwiiste Pʉʉ Tamaya on the Río Jémez. When the Tamayame fled the village, the woman was too old and tired to make the journey, and her great-grandson, a newborn infant, was much too young to travel. In the smoking ruins of Kwiiste Pʉʉ Tamaya, it fell to the old woman to care for the child. Picking through the charred ruins of the village in search of food, she soon found enough storage jars filled with corn and piñon nuts to feed them both well. She ground the piñon nuts into a milky substance to feed the child until he was old enough to eat solid foods.

As the boy grew, she began to teach him. First he learned the names of the plants and the animals and the birds that filled the land around them. Then, when he was old enough, the old woman showed him how to use the willows that grew by the riverbank to make a strong bow and straight arrows.

As the years passed, the boy learned the people's ways and grew into a strong young man, but his mind was filled with questions. He began to wonder about himself and the old woman, who was by then very old indeed. How had they come to this place, he asked himself, and why did they live alone there? Where had they come from? Who was she? At last, one day, the young man asked the old woman, and she told him the story of the Tamayame.

She explained how the Hanu had come to that place and built the village. She spoke of the Tsiiyame living across the river, recalling how anger had grown among the Tsiiyame men and how the Tamayame had learned of their plan to raid Kwiiste Puu Tamaya. She described the people's preparations for the journey and how, at last, they had set fire to the village and set out to find a new home. Finally, she told him how his mother had left him, her newborn son, in her care.

After hearing what the old woman recounted, the young man grew determined to search for his mother and his people. For several days, he gathered all that he would need for the journey. When he was ready to leave, the old woman gave him instructions to travel south, for that was the way the Tamayame had gone, and to search for the ashes of their campfires, which would guide him along the path they had taken.

When the two had exchanged blessings and farewells, the young man set out from Kwiiste Puu Tamaya. After traveling for many days, searching for signs that might lead him to the Tamayame, he came to a river. As he paused on the bank to drink and refresh himself, two women came down to the river from a village on the opposite bank. Laughing and smiling, they filled their water jars and returned to the village. A short time later, the two women came back to the river and approached the young man, who was still resting on the opposite bank. When they called to him, he replied in their language. Surprised and delighted, they invited him to their village.

That night, after the young man had eaten, one of the women summoned the courage to ask him who he was, where he had come from, and how he had learned to speak the language of the Tamayame. The young man told them of the old woman who had raised him, describing the abandoned village at Kwiiste Puu Tamaya where he had grown up and the old woman who had told him about the Tamayame. Then, as he explained how he had set out to find his mother, the woman who had first spoken to him cried, "I am the one you are seeking, I am your mother." Thus the young man's journey ended and he was reunited with his mother and his people at the village of Kwiiste Kene'ewa on the west bank of the Río Puerco.

For the Tamayame, however, the journey did not end there. When the time came for them to move on, they left Kwiiste Kene'ewa as they had left earlier settlements. Traveling southwest, tradition says, they crossed a small stream

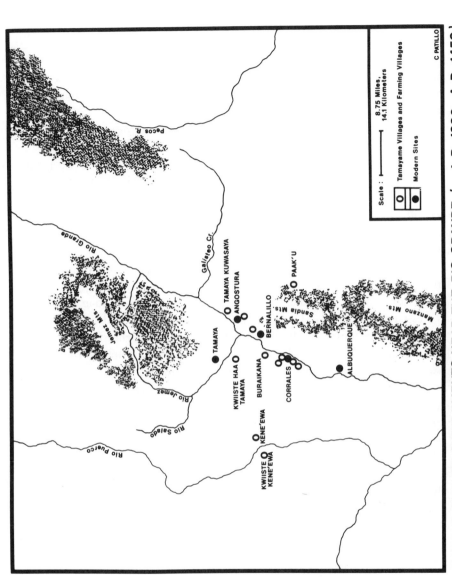

EARLY TAMAYAME SETTLEMENTS NEAR THE RIO GRANDE (c. A.D. 1200 - A.D. 1450)

C PATILLO

Scale: 8.75 Miles,
14.1 Kilometers

○ Tamayame Villages and Farming Villages

● Modern Sites

Pecos R.

Rio Grande

Galisteo Cr.

○ Tamaya Kuwasaya
● Angostura

Jemez Mts.

Sandia Mts.

○ PAAK'U

Rio Jemez

● TAMAYA

○ KWIISTE HAA
TAMAYA

Rio Salado

○ BURAIKANA
● BERNALILLO

Rio Puerco

○○ CORRALES

● ALBUQUERQUE

Manzano Mts.

○ KENE'EWA

○ KWIISTE
KENE'EWA

near the modern settlement of Paguate. As the Tamayame passed their bundles from one person to another across the stream, they called out, "tyiti kwisti." Even today, that place is known as Kwisti.[13]

The Tamayame traveled on, eventually reaching a valley east of the massive stone mesa that was the home of the Acume (Acoma People). Tradition recalls that two of the Hanu climbed to the top of the mesa to speak to the people of Acu (Acoma). Finding that their languages were much alike, one of the two men decided to remain on the mesa, while the other climbed down and returned to his people. The Tamayame reached Acu during a time of drought and, Acume tradition says, they stayed until the rains came. Then, supplied with food for the journey, the Tamayame moved on.[14]

Once again they traveled south, building a village somewhere near the modern city of Socorro. But this settlement, like others along the route, proved to be only a temporary home for the Tamayame, who soon crossed to the east bank of the Río Grande, turned north, and returned to Paak'u.

When these Tamayame rejoined the people of Paak'u, they found that the settlement had changed during their journey. The two sections of the village had expanded until they nearly touched one another. Rows of adobe and stone houses, some of two stories, had spread north, west, and south of the first buildings. The builders had made storerooms, workrooms, living rooms, and special rooms set aside for ceremonial use.[15] As the town had grown, the people of Paak'u had sought new fields and farmlands. Although the Sandía Mountain region was rich in resources and the village of Paak'u drew water from a permanent spring, the area had a short growing season and frost often threatened the crops. Farmers could not depend on the area's unpredictable rainfall, which varied from one field to another.[16] During the journey from Shipapu to Paak'u, the Tamayame had seen the promise of the fertile Río Grande Valley. In the settlement at Paak'u, Tamayame farmers had not forgotten those rich lands. While the first Tamayame group journeyed in the west, the remaining Tamayame had begun to build small farming villages along the Río Grande. From the Corrales region to the Angostura, Tamayame farmers planted and harvested their crops, returning after the harvest to the center at Paak'u.[17]

Soon after all of the Tamayame were reunited, they moved from Paak'u to the lands along the Río Grande, settling in six or more villages that stretched from the area around modern Albuquerque to the Angostura region near the site of modern Bernalillo. The southern villages, in the Corrales area, were grouped on the west bank of the river, while those in the north, near Bernalillo, were built on the east bank. Among the villages was one known as

Buraikana (the Butterfly), which stood south of Bernalillo on the west bank of the Río Grande. This region was also the home of the Tiwa peoples, whose villages often stood across the river from those of the Tamayame.[18]

By A.D. 1425, little more than a century after it was founded, the village at Paak'u was abandoned. Its people moved on, taking most of their belongings with them.[19] The peoples who reoccupied Paak'u a century later found only crumbling walls and broken pottery to identify the Hanu who had once lived there.

For the Tamayame, the journey had not yet come to an end. They settled for a time in the farming villages along the Río Grande, but then, the stories tell, a group of Tamayame traveled north to the west bank of the Río Jémez, where they founded a village known as Kwiiste Haa Tamaya. From this village the people eventually crossed the Río Jémez and traveled north[20] to the place where, after centuries of traveling, the journey ended. There, beside the river and beneath a broad mesa, the Tamayame found the land that they would choose, in accordance with the instructions given to their ancestors, for their home.

TWO

Hanu Meets Kastera

As winter drew to a close along the northern valley of the Río Grande, the people began to think of the year to come. Soon, perhaps within only a month and certainly in no more than two, the rivers would thaw and the snows would begin to melt. Then it would be time for the people to move to the fields, time for the farmers to tend and guard the crops. If all went well, it would be a good year: no frost would destroy the tender seedlings; the rains would come to keep the young plants from withering in dry fields; no enemy would sweep down to carry off the harvest; and, at the end of summer, the storerooms would be filled with maize, beans, and squash enough to keep the people through the next winter and, if need be, the following one as well.

A thousand miles to the south, in the cities and frontier outposts of the land that they had conquered and called New Spain, another group of people also dreamed of the year to come, the year that would be known as 1540 according to their calendar. They too had hopes for a good year, but their dreams were not of gentle rains that would nourish young seedlings or of a plentiful harvest of maize to feed their families in the winter to come. Instead their heads were filled with thoughts of a very different kind of riches. To the north, it was said, the earth held a treasure of gold, silver, and precious stones. Only the year before, one of them had traveled to these lands, and everywhere he went, Indians had told him of the rich kingdoms that lay beyond their villages. He had heard of one kingdom, the Seven Cities of Cíbola, so rich that the doors of its houses were said to be studded with turquoise. Indeed the reports said that he himself had gone far enough to look down upon the first city of this kingdom and had seen that what the

CHAPTER 2

Indians told him was true. It was also true that the residents of Cíbola had not welcomed him and that he and his party had been forced to turn back "with much more fear than food."[1] That fact, however, was not enough to deter those who believed that in Cíbola they might find treasure enough to make them wealthy for the rest of their days, like those of their countrymen who had won both wealth and fame by laying claim to rich lands in the south. As the rumors spread throughout New Spain, many who heard the tales of vast wealth felt that a man would be foolish not to risk his possessions, and even his life, to win such a fortune. By January 1540, when Francisco Vásquez de Coronado was chosen to lead an expedition north to the fabled kingdoms, there was no shortage of men willing to volunteer to accompany him.

When the muster roll for the expedition was completed at Compostela a month later, it listed more than two hundred men with horses and sixty-two who were willing to undertake the journey on foot. Two months later, as the expedition prepared to leave the frontier outpost at Culiacán, their number had grown to more than three hundred Spaniards and as many as a thousand Indian allies. To mount this huge force, to carry its supplies, and to provide meat on the journey, the Spaniards had assembled a herd of more than a thousand horses, mules, and cattle.[2] Fray Marcos de Niza, the man who claimed to have seen the first of the Seven Cities of Cíbola, would guide the expedition, and a number of friars would accompany them, for the land to the north promised heavenly treasures as well as earthly ones. As Christians, the Spaniards believed that they would be blessed with eternal rewards for bringing the word of their god to those who had not yet heard it, peoples such as the residents of these fabled kingdoms, who as yet knew nothing of the religion of Spain and Christian Europe.[3]

In late April, as the snows melted along the Río Grande and pueblo farmers began to tend their crops, Coronado's expedition left Culiacán. Most of this vast army, encumbered with the baggage and supplies, would move slowly north, led by Tristán de Arellano. Coronado himself would lead an advance party, taking only enough cattle and provisions for eighty days so that they could move quickly. With him would go seventy-five mounted men, twenty-five foot soldiers, the friars, and some of the Indian allies.[4]

As the Spaniards moved north, following Indian trails through the land that would come to be known as Arizona, Pueblo farmers tended their fields in the valleys along the Río Grande. Corn grew and ripened; blossoms appeared on the bean bushes; and squash and pumpkin vines spread over the fields. Here and there, in patches blessed with enough water, cotton began to

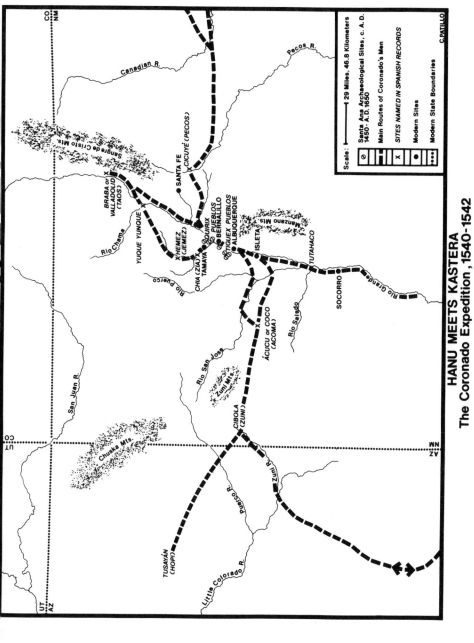

HANU MEETS KASTERA
The Coronado Expedition, 1540-1542

Scale: ⊢——⊣ 29 Miles, 46.8 Kilometers

⊘ Santa Ana Archaeological Sites, c. A.D.
1450 - A.D. 1650

▮▮▮ Main Routes of Coronado's Men

✗ *SITES NAMED IN SPANISH RECORDS*

● Modern Sites

▮▮▮ Modern State Boundaries

C. PATILLO

flower. Women gathered herbs to dry and store for winter. While the men tended the fields, women mixed mortar from charcoal and mud to make plaster for the new rooms that were needed in the pueblos. When the women had finished building and plastering the walls, the men cut roof beams and erected them in the new rooms. The hopes of the winter seemed likely to be fulfilled: it was a good year, and there would be a rich harvest in the multistoried pueblos.[5]

In July, however, before the harvest could be gathered, before the wild piñon nuts had ripened, Coronado approached the first of the fabled cities of Cíbola. This was Hawíkuh, a pueblo of the Zuñi people. Word of his approach had preceded him, and it was not welcome news to the people of Hawíkuh, who had encountered the Marcos de Niza expedition the previous year. One member of that party, Estaban or Estavánico, had made such outrageous demands that the Zuñi had put him to death, and the rest of the party had then fled from the region. Hearing that the Spaniards had returned, the people of Zuñi prepared to defend themselves, but, on July 7, Coronado's men took Hawíkuh by storm.[6]

There, in the town that they believed was the first of the Seven Cities of Cíbola, the hungry Spaniards found something that, at least temporarily, they "prized more than gold or silver, namely much maize, beans, and chickens [turkeys] larger than those of New Spain, and salt better and whiter" than one member of the expedition had ever seen.[7] When that treasure had satisfied their immediate hunger, however, their appetite for mineral riches returned. With it came rage at Fray Marcos, who had led them to this place with tales that could only have been lies about what he had seen or pure invention about what he had not. This village of stone and adobe was no empire, no treasure house; its people possessed no gold or silver or jewels. Instead of the treasures Fray Marcos had described, the residents of Hawíkuh had only some cotton cloth, a few pieces of turquoise, and maize.[8]

Having marched a thousand miles, however, the Spaniards were not willing to give up their dreams of wealth so easily. Although this town that Fray Marcos had called Cíbola was a great disappointment, Indians all along their route had spoken of rich lands to the north, and the Spaniards were still convinced that kingdoms of gold and silver must exist in this land. Making signs and using interpreters from tribes to the south, they asked all of the peoples they met where such kingdoms might be found, and they told the people of Zuñi to send word to their neighbors that the Spaniards had come to seek these fabled lands. Soon the explorers began to hear of other kingdoms that might be the lands for which they searched. To the west were the people of Hopi, but the Spaniards found that they, like the Zuñi, possessed no gold or silver. To the east lay Acu or Acus, but, as Coronado gathered more information, he concluded that this was not a kingdom, as Fray Marcos had claimed, but a single town. Further to the east, he heard, lay "other small kingdoms not far from this settlement and situated on a river."[9] There, perhaps, the Spaniards might find the riches they sought.

Word of the expedition's arrival had soon spread far throughout the region. In August—only a month after Coronado arrived at Hawíkuh—a group of men from Pecos reached Zuñi. In this pueblo far to the east, beyond the Río Grande, the people had already "learned that strange people, bold men who punished those who resisted them and gave good treatment to those who submitted, had come to make their acquaintance and be their friends."[10] The men of Pecos had come to Zuñi to say that if the strange men wished to travel east, the men of Pecos would guide them to the Río Grande, to their own pueblo, and even beyond, to the land of the buffalo.[11]

Coronado accepted their offer, sending Captain Hernando de Alvarado, Fray Juan de Padilla, and twenty Spaniards east with the Pecos guides. Fifteen miles east of Hawíkuh, the trail split, one branch leading northeast to the pueblo of Chia (Zía), the other east to Coco (Acoma). The Spaniards, who chose the second, confirmed Coronado's suspicions: Acoma was not a kingdom but a single village. This pueblo on the high mesa was another disappointment to the Spaniards: it had abundant supplies of maize, turkeys, and cotton cloth, but no gold or silver. Still they would not abandon the dreams that drove them: they traveled on, going north past the Laguna region and then east between the Río San José and the Río Grande.[12]

After three days' travel, Alvarado and his men reached the Río Grande somewhere near Isleta. They camped somewhat farther north, near the region of modern Albuquerque, and sent messengers to all of the pueblos nearby. September 8, the day after the Spaniards' arrival, delegates from twelve pueblos came to their camp with gifts of food, cotton blankets, and hides. In return Alvarado "gave them some small articles."[13] Like the people of Zuñi, Hopi, and Acoma, these Río Grande pueblos brought no gold or silver to offer to the Spaniards, so once again, following Coronado's instructions, the expedition moved on, heading east.

Before the Spaniards left the Río Grande pueblos, however, either Alvarado or Padilla sent news of this area, which they called Tiguex Province, back to Coronado. This letter described a river flowing "through a broad valley planted with fields of maize," with groves of cottonwood trees beside its banks. Near the Spaniards' camp stood twelve pueblos with two-story houses like those of Cíbola, but made of adobe rather than stone. The people were good farmers, with "maize, beans, melons, and chickens [turkeys] in great abundance." Delegates had come from the twelve Tiguex (Tiwa) pueblos and "from the surrounding provinces" to greet the Spaniards. All told, the region had eighty pueblos, all similar to those described in the letter.[14] The prosperous Tiguex region, the explorers suggested, would be a much better place for the expedition to spend the winter than the area around Hawíkuh.[15]

Well-pleased with this report, Coronado sent an advance party, led by García López de Cárdenas, to set up a camp for the entire army along the Río Grande in Tiguex Province. With thirteen or fourteen Spanish horsemen, numbers of the Mexican Indian allies, and several people from Zuñi, Cárdenas followed Alvarado's route east. At their destination, the Spaniards "found the Indians of the province of Tiguex friendly." For a short time, the Spaniards seem to have been careful to maintain good relations with the native peoples. They "began to prepare the lodgings outside of the pueblos in order not to cause hardship to the Indians." Soon after Cárdenas arrived, however, snow began to fall along the Río Grande, and Cárdenas "begged the Indians to clear a pueblo in order that the soldiers might establish their lodgings in it." The Spanish leader suggested that the pueblo's residents "could find homes in the other pueblos." Taking only their food and clothing, the Tiguex people vacated the pueblo of Alcanfor, or Coofor, which stood somewhere near the modern site of Bernalillo.[16] The fourteen Spaniards quickly moved into the pueblo and began to prepare for the arrival of the expedition forces: Coronado and his men; Alvarado's exploration party; the Arellano group; the Mexican Indians; and the large herd of horses and livestock.

Alvarado's men—the first to arrive at the winter camp—brought welcome news: Beyond the lands they had visited, still farther to the east, lay a province known as Quivira, a land so rich that even common bowls there were made of gold. Better still, they brought back an Indian who could guide them to Quivira when spring came.[17] Shortly after Alvarado's arrival, Coronado and thirty other Spaniards reached Alcanfor. On their way, they had circled south to investigate the province of Tutahaco, yet another village of adobe pueblos with no jewels or precious metals.[18]

The Spaniards quickly recognized that the camp along the Río Grande was a much better place to spend the winter than the pueblo of Hawíkuh. The people of the Tiguex Province had greeted them with peace and friendship, offering them food and other gifts. The harvest recently gathered along the Río Grande must have been abundant that year, for one Spaniard wrote that the land was "so fertile that they need to cultivate only once a year, just for planting, for the snow falls and covers the fields and the maize grows under the snow." In a single year, the writer claimed, "they harvest enough for seven years."[19]

Still, Coronado was worried. The winter snows had already begun, and soon the rest of the army and its Mexican Indian allies would arrive. These men, accustomed to the warmer climate of New Spain, would need more clothing to survive the cold winter. They would also need food, because the expedition had used much of its supply during the journey. To survive the coming winter, the Spaniards would have to rely on the pueblos in the region, who had plentiful stores of maize, beans, and squash from their fields, as well as supplies of piñon nuts and other foods they had gathered. Pueblo turkeys were "fatter and finer than those of New Spain." The people had gathered herbs and salt to season their meals, and they had bread made from the fine flour that the women ground from maize. They also had warm clothing for the cold winters. Pueblo cotton had been spun and woven into fine blankets, and the people wore robes woven from feathers or made from finely dressed hides. With resources such as these, the Spaniards could stay warm and well fed through the winter.[20]

When Coronado asked one of the Tiguex leaders to supply the clothing and food that the Spaniards needed, however, the leader replied that what Coronado asked was not in his power to give. No one man, he said, could speak for all of the pueblos. To obtain the things they sought, the Spaniards would have to go to each pueblo individually and make their requests of the leaders who had the authority to grant them. Hearing this, Coronado sent men to the twelve Tiguex pueblos and others in the Río Grande region, with instructions to obtain whatever the Indians were willing to trade. According to Coronado's account, the people of the pueblos "gave everything willingly in exchange for the said articles of barter."[21] Castañeda, principal chronicler of the expedition, in contrast, reported that the Spaniards entered a village, summarily demanded a certain amount of food and clothing, and gave the pueblo residents no time to "discuss or consult about" their requests. There was, he said, "nothing the natives could do except take off their own cloaks and hand them over until the number that the Spaniards had asked for was reached." Not satisfied with what they were given, some soldiers took anything that seemed better, "without any consideration or respect, and without inquiring about the importance of the person they despoiled."[22] A third Spaniard who went on the expedition later wrote that "some of the Indians gave some clothing of their own will, and others against their will, although they were not at all ill-treated on this account."[23]

Although December had not yet ended, the weather had already grown harsh along the Río Grande. The rivers froze over and snow fell steadily. As the days passed, resentment mounted among the people of Tiguex. The strangers had taken their clothing, their blankets, and much of their harvest. Not content with the gifts freely offered to them, the Spaniards seized more by force. They had occupied one entire pueblo. And the people had other grievances. At one pueblo, it was said, a Spaniard had assaulted a man's wife. Several of the men who had offered to guide Alvarado had been held as prisoners, and the Spaniards set dogs upon them to force them to speak about the golden land to the east, a land that did not exist. As the weeks passed, the number of Spaniards taxing the pueblos' hospitality grew ever larger. They used pueblo lands as pasture for their large herds of cattle and horses. They made endless demands that created only hardship for the people of Tiguex. Undoubtedly, news of the strangers' high-handed behavior elsewhere came to the people of the Río Grande from the southern and eastern tribes with whom they traded, from Hawíkuh and the other Zuñi towns, from Hopi, from Acoma, and from their nearer neighbors.[24]

Alvarado, the first Spaniard to reach the Río Grande region, had told Coronado that the people there seemed "good, more given to farming than to war."[25] By the end of December, however, the people of Tiguex had had enough of the strangers' inexhaustible demands. They drove off the horses pastured near Alcanfor, killing one guard and injuring another, and they began to scatter and kill the Spaniards' herds throughout the region. Cárdenas, sent to recover the horses and negotiate with the pueblos, found village after village filled with angry men who had no interest in his offers of peace.[26]

When Cárdenas had made his report, Coronado called the Spaniards together to decide what could be done about this threat. The council of officers and friars voted unanimously to make war on the pueblos if they would not surrender. Cárdenas was sent back to warn the pueblos that the Spaniards would attack them if they did not submit peacefully. He went first to the pueblo of Arenal, one of the centers of the revolt. Its residents refused to surrender, and the Spaniards surrounded the pueblo. By nightfall, they had fought their way up to the "terraces." The next day, they lit "heavy smudge fires" in the first-story rooms to force out the pueblo's inhabitants. Many fled the fire and smoke, surrendering to the Spaniards. But then, either through a misunderstanding or in deliberate violation of the surrender, soldiers began to tie the prisoners to stakes and set them on fire. Before the Spaniards finished, between eighty and two hundred prisoners were burned alive or killed trying to resist.[27]

Hanu Meets Kastera

The day after the Spaniards won this bloody victory at Arenal, the rest of the army completed the journey from Cíbola and joined Coronado at Alcanfor. Although heavy snow hampered their movements, Coronado sent a group of forty horsemen and some foot soldiers to receive the submission of the pueblos in the region. Marching north from Alcanfor to the northern edge of the province, the soldiers found the pueblos deserted. In every pueblo, those who had not already fled abandoned their homes, struggling off through the snow as soon as they saw the Spaniards approach. At the northernmost pueblo, the Spaniards found dead horses; they burned the village "in order to teach the Indians not to kill any more Spaniards or their horses." Throughout the region, when the Spaniards offered peace, the Indians "replied that they would not trust those who did not know how to keep the word they had pledged."[28]

The refugees from the Tiguex pueblos gathered at Moho, a pueblo on the west side of the Río Grande north of Alcanfor, and at another unnamed pueblo half a league farther north. When they refused to submit to the Spaniards, Coronado himself led the attack against Moho. At Moho, however, the Spaniards did not enjoy an easy victory: unable to capture the pueblo, they were forced to besiege it throughout the bitter winter.[29] The defenders held out until March, when their water supplies ran out. Then they tried to slip away. Some succeeded in escaping across the Río Grande, though it was swollen by the spring runoff, but many others were killed in the attempt or captured and held as servants.[30] After the defeat of Moho in March, most of the fighting came to an end in the Tiguex region. The survivors fled to more remote sites, and these pueblos along the Río Grande "were never resettled as long as the army remained in that region, no matter what assurances were given them."[31]

During the long winter, as resentment in Tiguex Province turned to open hostility, the Spaniards were forced to look elsewhere for the food and clothing they needed. Zía, a large pueblo to the northwest, bartered "a certain number of blankets, skins, and quilts" in exchange for Spanish trade goods.[32] After the siege at Moho, Coronado "sent a captain to Chia (Zía), a fine pueblo with a large population." He found the pueblo quiet and left in its care "four bronze cannons which were in bad condition."[33] A Spanish expedition also visited the Quirix (Keres) Province, where they found seven pueblos. The pueblos to the north were wary of the Spaniards. Zía "had sent messages offering submission," and at the first of the Keres pueblos, "which must have contained one hundred residents, the people ran away, not daring to wait" for the Spaniards, who "ran to intercept them and brought them back, fully protected, to their pueblos and homes." From this pueblo, "the Spaniards sent word to the other pueblos in order to restore their confidence," and, Castañeda claimed, "the whole region was gradually reassured."[34]

When spring came at last to the region and the Río Grande, which had been frozen solid, began to thaw, the Spaniards were eager to move on to the rich land of Quivira. The pueblos, no doubt, were also eager to see these treacherous men depart. On May 5, the Spanish army left Tiguex, marching north and east toward Pecos. Within a month, however, Coronado had decided that the entire army could not make the journey to Quivira. He chose a small party to continue eastward and sent the main army, led by Arellano, back to Tiguex to prepare for a second winter.[35]

In mid-July, the larger group reached the Río Grande. They found the Tiguex Province still deserted, as it would remain so long as the Spaniards stayed in the region. Once again the army needed supplies for the coming winter, but this year no delegations from neighboring pueblos welcomed them with gifts of food and turquoise. In the region where they camped, the Spaniards found only the burned ruins of the pueblos that they had destroyed and the gutted, empty rooms of others whose inhabitants had fled destruction. In search of supplies, Arellano sent expeditions to Jémez, Taos, and other northern pueblos; south beyond Tutahaco; and east to Pecos.[36]

In mid-September, the time of harvest along the Río Grande, Coronado led a dejected band of Spaniards back to Tiguex. Once again, the dreams of riches had turned out to be nothing but fantasies. Quivira was not a golden kingdom, but a town of grass houses that had only a little maize, no gold, no silver, and no precious stones. Worse yet, Coronado discovered that the people of Pecos had told their guide "to take the Spaniards out there and lead them astray on the plains," where they "would become so feeble that, upon their return, the people of Cicuyé [Pecos] could kill them easily and so obtain revenge for what the Spaniards had done to them."[37]

It was apparent to the Spaniards that they were no longer welcome guests in pueblo lands, and they had begun to learn that the people of the region, although peaceable by choice, were far from helpless. As soon as Coronado returned to the Río Grande, he "tried to pacify some neighboring pueblos that were restless, and to invite the people of Tiguex to make peace. He tried also to obtain some native clothing, because the soldiers were already naked and in a wretched condition."[38] The winter of 1541–42, like the one that had gone before it, was "intensely cold . . . with snow and heavy frosts" along the Río Grande.[39] Few of the Spaniards still believed that a golden city might be found farther inland; Coronado, injured in a fall from a horse, lost interest in the expedition; and the Spaniards learned that the Indians to the south were in open revolt. As soon as the snows melted in April 1542, the expedition prepared to return to their homes in the south. Only one part of the dream survived the winter: two friars, still hoping to convert the people of Cicuyé [Pecos] and Quivira, chose to stay when the Spaniards left the Río Grande. For their protection, Coronado "ordered the soldiers who had natives in their service to let them go freely to their pueblos or wherever they wished."[40] As soon as these orders were carried out, the army left the way it had come, retracing its steps to Zuñi and south to New Spain.

Spring had always been a time of joy along the Río Grande, and this year the people had an additional reason to rejoice. As the seedlings emerged with the promise of summer's harvest, the men who had brought violence, famine, and treachery to the region departed. This time the word would travel back to the Río Grande that Kastera had truly gone.

During those two long winters, the people of Tamaya must have encountered the people of Kastera, but no record speaks of where, when, and how those meetings occurred. In all of the many reports of the Coronado expedition and all of the volumes that recorded the hearings held in Spain and New Spain to review its conduct, there is not a single reference to the Tamayame as a distinct people. The Spaniards who went to the Río Grande believed that all of the pueblos had, "in general, the same ceremonies and customs."[41] The members of the expedition had neither the curiosity nor the ability to learn a great deal about these peoples. The strangers spoke none of the languages of those who lived in the region, so they learned only what little could be communicated through signs and, less often, through interpreters from neighboring tribes. To Kastera, the pueblos were of little interest except as potential sources of treasure, converts, and food and clothing, or as potential threats to Spanish camps and herds. Thus the records of the Spanish expeditions contain many gaps, gaps in which the histories of Tamaya and the other pueblos lie hidden.

To a large extent, the nature of Tamaya's first meeting with Kastera would have depended upon where the Tamayame were during the autumn of 1540, when the Spaniards came to the Río Grande. If the people of Tamaya were still farming in the villages along the Río Grande between the areas that later came to be known as Albuquerque and Bernalillo, the history of their encounter with Kastera may be intertwined with the story of the region that the Spaniards called the Tiguex Province.[42] If the Tamayame were dwelling in this region during the winter of 1540–41, they, like their Tiwa neighbors, must have suffered greatly. They could have been among those killed or captured by the Spaniards; their storerooms could have been emptied to supply the soldiers with food and clothing; and they might have been forced to flee in the middle of winter to find refuge in more isolated places.

If, on the other hand, the Tamayame had left the Río Grande region by September or October 1540, either to settle permanently elsewhere or to gather at a central pueblo for the winter, Kastera's presence would have been less likely to cause great disruption in their lives. If, as archaeology seems to suggest (see Appendix 1), the people of Tamaya were still farming the fields and living in the villages along the Río Grande at this time, they might still have gathered, after the harvest, to spend the winter at a central pueblo more remote from the area where Coronado's men camped. Or perhaps by 1540 the Tamayame had abandoned the Río Grande villages that they had built when they left Paak'u a century earlier. They could, by that time, already have made the journey to Kwiiste Haa Tamaya that is told of in the oral tradition. They may have moved north, across the Río Jémez, to found Tamaya itself or to settle in a village on the other side of the Río Jémez at the southern end of the mesa. They might have lived in a village on top of the Black Mesa, or in some other place away from Río Grande.[43] In any of those areas, distance would have sheltered the people from the full impact of the Spanish presence. Unlike their Tiwa neighbors, they would not have encountered Kastera in battle, and probably few if any of the people would have been killed or captured.

Wherever the people of Tamaya were living in 1540, however, they would almost certainly have been visited by Spaniards seeking food and clothing, and they would have heard of the things that the Spaniards had done elsewhere. It is possible that the first of the Keres pueblos described by Cárdenas was the home of the Tamayame, and that they were the people who fled when the Spaniards approached. In exchange for their food and clothing, the people of Tamaya may have received a few of Coronado's jingling bells, trinkets, and trade goods. They may have watched as a friar exhorted them, with signs and strange words, to accept the god of the Spaniards. Perhaps, too, they saw, or even acquired, some of the horses and livestock from the Spanish herds. If so, the Spanish explorers did not record it.

Nor do the documents reveal what was said when the Tiyamune and the elders met, as they must have, to decide what the Tamayame should do. Kastera's letters and reports preserve no accounts of the messages that must have passed among the Tamayame and the rest of the Hanu. Not a single document describes the worries that must have been in the minds of the women grinding corn, the children playing in the village, or the hunters who went to the mountains and mesas in search of game. No member of Coronado's expedition recorded that, when spring arrived in 1542, the Tamayame went, as their fathers and grandfathers had, to tend the fields. And no Spaniard wrote that, as the people of Tamaya waited anxiously for the clouds that would bring rain to their seedlings that summer, they must also, after those two long winters, have watched with apprehension for the clouds of dust raised by horses and marching men, clouds that would bring not life-giving water but disaster.

THREE

Kastera Returns

Forty times spring came again to the fields along the Río Grande, and Kastera had not returned. Each year in the adobe pueblos, the women mixed the plaster to repair old rooms and to build new ones. Hunters went to the mountains and came back, bringing deer and rabbits. After searching for just the right clay, women shaped bowls, mugs, and jars. These would be fired and painted with glaze so that they would be strong and beautiful. When the crops had been gathered and snow covered the fields, the men spun the cotton they had raised and then wove it into fine blankets and clothing. Traders came and went. From the plains and basins beyond pueblo lands came men with hides, furs, buffalo meat, and other goods to exchange for the cotton cloth, painted hides, and corn that their peoples did not have. Most came in peace. Sometimes, though, as the corn began to ripen in the field, a raiding party came to seize the harvest.[1]

Each harvest was precious, for it had been a dry time in the lands along the Río Grande. As the years passed, the rains no longer came as often as they had. Many years, the winter snows were no longer as deep as they had once been. By midsummer, no matter what the people did, the crops began to wither in the fields.[2] In some years, only the food stored from an earlier and better year kept the people through the winter. To a farming people, drought was a matter of the greatest concern, and to the pueblo farmers along the Río Grande, it must have been more troubling than the stories of strangers who had appeared one summer long before. For Kastera had come and gone when most of those who tended the fields in 1580 had not yet been born.

Far to the south, the Spaniards themselves had almost forgotten the men who had marched north with Coronado. They had brought no treasure back from their journey, but other men had found fortunes in the mines of New Spain; for nearly four decades, the stories had told of the treasures of Santa Bárbara and Zacatecas, not the lands of Cíbola, Tiguex, or Quivira. Those who remembered the tales of fabled cities to the north were gone. Even if the tales of treasure to the north had been told once again, the laws of Spain no longer allowed a man to lead a huge army beyond the frontier to conquer Indian kingdoms. Explorers, by law, had to go in peace. They could not seek slaves and plunder in the lands beyond their own. But if explorers no longer dreamed of vast treasures and golden kingdoms to the north, Kastera had not lost all interest in its peoples. As Spaniards settled in the northern reaches of New Spain, they heard, from the peoples there, of others who lived even farther north in large houses.

As Christians, the Spaniards believed that they had a duty to spread the word of God to unbelievers. Their laws supported this duty by permitting friars and priests to travel to new lands and preach to the Indians. And, since a friar would surely risk death by going alone to a strange land, the law also allowed soldiers to escort the missionaries. In this way, although a man could no longer lead an expedition as Coronado had, he might still search for rich lands: he had only to go with friars who had permission to travel. If he had the good fortune to find a rich land, he could, as its discoverer, still hope to claim the right to settle it, to work its mines, and to exact tribute and labor from its peoples.[3]

So, for a second time, dreams of wealth and hopes of converts led Kastera north to pueblo lands. In 1581, forty years after Coronado's first winter in Tiguex, a group of friars and soldiers prepared to leave New Spain. Compared to Coronado's expedition, they were a small force. Three friars, led by Fray Agustín Rodríguez, would travel north to spread the gospel; nine soldiers under the leadership of Captain Francisco Sánchez Chamuscado would escort them and nineteen Indian servants would accompany them. Like Coronado, they assembled a herd of cattle for food, horses to ride, and mules to pack their belongings and the goods they brought to trade.[4]

As this small group moved into the unknown land beyond the borders of New Spain, they began to hear about the people they were seeking. They met Indians who told them that "farther on, very far from there, they had heard that there were many brave people with many houses." These people, the Indians said, had "an abundance of corn, beans, and calabashes [squash or pumpkins],"[5] grew cotton "which they spun, wove, and made into blankets,"[6] and "lived in large houses three and four stories high."[7]

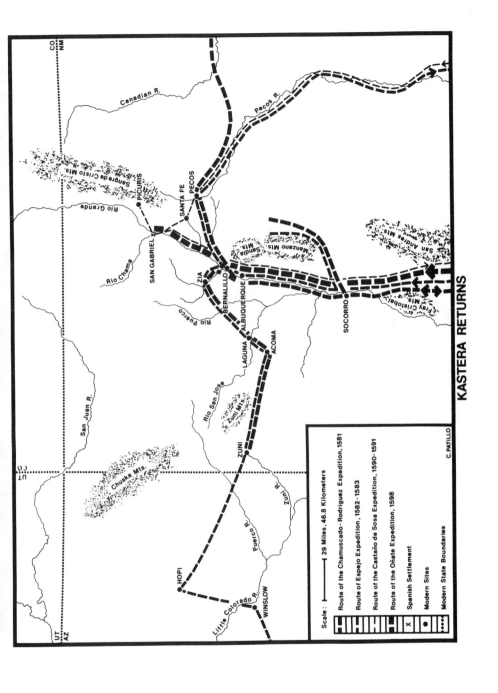

KASTERA RETURNS

Scale: ⊢——⊣ 29 Miles, 46.8 Kilometers

Route of the Chamuscado - Rodriguez Expedition, 1581

Route of Espejo Expedition, 1582 - 1583

Route of the Castaño de Sosa Expedition, 1590-1591

Route of the Oñate Expedition, 1598

Spanish Settlement

Modern Sites

Modern State Boundaries

C. PATILLO

CHAPTER 3

The expedition made its way up the west side of the Río Grande, and by midsummer, as the corn began to ripen, the Spaniards had seen the pueblos for themselves. When Coronado and his men reached the Tiguex area along the Río Grande forty years earlier, they had been disappointed: expecting golden cities, they found only adobe pueblos. By contrast, the Rodríguez-Chamuscado party, which had not hoped to find such fabled kingdoms, reported with pleasure on what they had found in the region. The people, they wrote, were "handsome," "very industrious," "very clean," and "very intelligent."[8] The pueblo women made pottery that would "equal, and even surpass the pottery made in Portugal."[9] They were, as the Spaniards had heard, a farming people who tended fields of corn, beans, and squash. They also raised turkeys, and many men had "corrals" large enough to hold "a flock of one hundred birds." Many of the towns had "large cotton fields."[10] With this cotton, the people made "hand painted and embroidered" clothing that the Spaniards found "very pleasing."[11] The friars, who had sighted as many as one hundred pueblo villages, considered this a promising land, a land where, they believed, the people would readily accept the teachings of Christianity.[12]

From the Río Grande region where Coronado had set up his camp, the group went north to Keres lands. There they were welcomed by people who lived in "well-built houses of four or five stories." These pueblos had "passageways and rooms twenty-four feet long by thirteen feet wide, whitewashed and painted," with "very fine plazas" and "streets between the buildings."[13] At a pueblo that they named "Castilleja," the Spaniards found "forty houses of two and three stories." Beside this town ran "a stream of water with which the natives irrigate their cornfields." Beyond this pueblo, on a "stream" that emptied into the Río Grande, the Spaniards found four more pueblo villages.[14] The land of the Keres peoples, they wrote, was "more highly developed" than any of the provinces they had yet seen.[15]

In September 1581, the Rodríguez-Chamuscado group left the Keres lands along the Río Grande. They traveled east to the pueblos of the Galisteo Basin, and then, like Coronado before them, on to the Plains, the land of the buffalo.[16] On their return journey, they stopped at one of the easternmost pueblos. Badly in need of food, the Spaniards first requested supplies and then, when the pueblo refused to meet their demands, used force to obtain provisions. Throughout the rest of their journey back to the Río Grande, they reported that they were offered food at each pueblo where they stopped. One of the Spaniards, Hernán Gallegos, wrote that "the news had spread throughout the province" that the soldiers had taken "nine loads of flour" from the first pueblo to the east. As they moved on, they "were given exactly the same amount, no more and no less, at the other pueblos."[17]

Although Gallegos hoped that the pueblos would become accustomed to "giving such tribute," he admitted that they offered food out of "fear rather than from any desire to befriend us."[18] As the Spaniards marched west through the Galisteo Basin to the Río Grande, they grew ever more aware that the pueblos resented their demands. By late fall the Spaniards "realized clearly" that the pueblos "wanted to kill" them and "that the people of the entire region were gathering for this purpose."[19] They decided that, under the circumstances, little would be gained by staying. They had already explored the region and reported on it. Clearly their presence was unwelcome, and the friars "could not reap any harvest there at the moment without an interpreter."[20] By January 1582 Chamuscado's men had decided to return to New Spain. Two friars, however, chose to stay behind with some of the Indian servants, to begin their work at Puaray, a pueblo beside the Río Grande near the modern site of Bernalillo.[21]

The soldiers reached Mexico City in May 1582. Soon news and rumors of the northern lands began to spread throughout New Spain. They told of the prosperous pueblo fields and fine plazas, and of the plains rich in buffalo. And they reported that this region had promising "mining areas."[22] While the pueblos along the Río Grande tended their crops, gathered the harvest, and made ready for winter, the tales spread throughout New Spain. Once again the men of Kastera heard that the land to the north was an abundant place, where a man could find "many mines . . . since the region is rich in them, as well as in woods, pastures, and water."[23]

By midsummer, one of the Indian servants who had stayed in Puaray made his way south with disturbing news: he himself had seen one of the friars killed, and he believed that "the other friar and the Indian boys who remained there" were also dead.[24] The Franciscan Order, which had sent the friars north, urged Spanish leaders to take action. Someone, they said, should go north to learn what had happened to the friars and to help them should they still be alive. Antonio de Espéjo volunteered to make the journey and received permission to organize a small expedition. With Fray Bernardino Beltrán and fourteen soldiers, he set out for the north in November 1582.[25]

As Espéjo and his men traveled up the Río Grande, they were told that the friars were dead. With confirmation of the friars' fate, their mission was fulfilled, but they did not return to New Spain. Eager to explore the northern lands, they traveled on, reaching the region near Puaray in February 1583.[26] Fearing that Kastera had come to punish them for the death of the friars, the pueblos "fled to the sierra." Although the midwinter cold caused great suffering among "their women and children,"[27] the people remained in the mountains as long as the Spaniards were in the area. Espéjo's men followed them and asked them, "in a friendly way," to return to their homes. While waiting near Puaray for the pueblos to return, the Spaniards "inspected some pueblos," finding "large quantities of corn, beans, green and sun-dried calabashes, and other vegetables"; turkeys; a great deal of pottery;[28] and "many ores of different colors."[29] The explorers helped themselves to food and supplies, and they also received "presents of turkeys" from the northern pueblos. Still the people of Puaray "were very frightened and for this reason would not come down" from the mountains.[30] At last, after waiting for a week, Kastera moved on.

Traveling north, the Spaniards entered the lands of the Keres peoples. These peoples, similar to those of Puaray "in their dress and other respects," had also "been present at the death of the friars."[31] Within the region, the Spaniards learned, stood five pueblos housing as many as fifteen thousand people. Nearby the people cultivated "many fields of corn."[32] The pueblos were "governed by caciques," but none of these leaders had "authority beyond his own pueblo." Espéjo and his men visited several pueblos near this area, including one that they named La Milpa Llana. At San Felipe the people gave them "corn, tortillas, turkeys, and pinole" and traded some "very fine buffalo hides" for "sleigh bells and small iron articles."[33]

Next the Spaniards visited Zía, a pueblo with "five large plazas." Zía was also a Keres pueblo, but Espéjo believed that it was the center of a separate province. The Spaniards first "raised the flag in the name of his Majesty and took possession" of the pueblo and then put up a cross and explained "its meaning" to the Zía people.[34] "Near a sierra in this province," Espéjo's group met "large numbers of people" who gave the Spaniards "cotton blankets and ample supplies of corn, turkeys, and bread made of corn flour." The explorers were "told of another province to northwest" and of "mines near by, in the sierra."[35]

From the valley of the Río Jémez, Espéjo's group went west to Zuñi and Hopi, stopping at Zuñi a second time on their return journey. There they held a council and all but nine of the Spaniards voted to return to New Spain, since they had learned the fate of Fray Rodríguez and the others, which was what they had been sent to do. Espéjo, however, still wanted to search for mines and refused to end the expedition. He led the remaining soldiers east toward the Río Grande.[36] As they traveled, they heard that "all the provinces were waiting to kill" them.[37] Along the Río Grande south of Puaray, the

Indians refused to give them any food, and no women or children could be seen in any of the pueblos. Some of the men "scoffed at" the Spaniards as they passed.[38] At Puaray, all but thirty of the residents had fled to the mountains. Those who remained "mocked" the Spaniards from the roof of the pueblo and would not come down. Angered by this resistance, Espéjo's men attacked the pueblo. They seized "those natives who showed themselves," and, when some of the Indians evaded capture, they set fire to "the big pueblo of Puala [Puaray]." The soldiers killed sixteen prisoners, in addition to those who died in the fire. Other captives, "who did not seem to belong to Puala," were released.[39]

After destroying Puaray, Espéjo's men marched back to Keres lands, where they were "well received." They soon learned that "news of what had happened at Puala [had] spread throughout the provinces. . . ." Having heard how Kastera had treated Puaray, the other pueblos "were very much afraid and all served and regaled" the soldiers.[40] Espéjo and his contingent, however, did not remain in pueblo lands long after the destruction of Puaray. At the end of June, they left San Felipe, traveling east to the Pecos River, where they headed south out of the region.[41]

Back in New Spain, Espéjo spoke enthusiastically about the land he had explored. Its people, he said, were "healthy," "intelligent," and "orderly." They lived in "attractive pueblos with plazas and well-arranged houses," and their lands had "an abundance of game animals: rabbits, hares, deer, buffaloes, ducks, geese, cranes, and pheasants and other birds." Near the pueblos were "fine wooded mountains with trees of all kinds, salines, and rivers containing a great variety of fish." Farmers and ranchers would find "good pastures for cattle as well as lands suitable for vegetables or grain crops." Best of all, Espéjo claimed, the region had "many rich mines."[42]

The news spread quickly: in the unknown lands to the north, riches were to be had. Spanish law, however, provided that no Spaniard could explore those lands or settle in them without a contract approved by the king of Spain. To win such a contract, a man had to recruit potential colonists and soldiers, and to provide, with his own funds, almost everything that the group would need for the journey. It was an enormous and uncertain undertaking, but one that many were willing to make in the hope of finding great wealth. A few were willing to take even greater risks by going north immediately, without waiting for an official contract.[43]

The first of these was Gaspar Castaño de Sosa, who took 170 colonists north in 1590 to build a settlement in New Mexico. Following the Pecos River, by December they had reached the pueblo of Pecos.[44] In January 1591, they moved west to the Río Grande. Late in the month, they arrived in a valley, somewhere in Keres lands, where four pueblos stood within sight of each other. There Castaño de Sosa raised a cross and asked the people to pledge their "obedience to his majesty." In this Keres town, as in many of the pueblos he visited, he "appointed a governor, an alcalde, and an aguacil."[45]

After conducting this ceremony, the Spaniards left the Keres region for a time, but by early March they had returned from the Galisteo Basin and set up a camp at Santo Domingo, where the people gave them a "very friendly reception."[46] Most of the colonists stayed in this camp, but a small group accompanied Castaño de Sosa on a search for mines, which took them to the region near Puaray. Wherever the explorers went in this region, the people of the pueblos fled as soon as they saw Kastera approach. Near Puaray, many tried to cross the Río Grande, even though the river was swollen by runoff.[47] Others left their homes and "sought refuge in the mountains or in other pueblos."[48]

Castaño de Sosa's party did not stay long in the region: hearing that a group of Spaniards had reached the camp at Santo Domingo, they turned back. When they reached the camp, they found, not the additional colonists their leader had hoped for,[49] but "forty well-equipped soldiers" led by Captain Juan Morlete, who had come to arrest Castaño de Sosa and escort the settlers back to New Spain.[50] Before the Spaniards left, Morlete tried to reassure the pueblos in the region, but he found it difficult to convey his message because these pueblos spoke "many different languages" and he had no "interpreters who would enable" him "to talk to the people."[51]

Although Castaño de Sosa was taken back to New Spain, tried, found guilty, and punished, the lure of the land to the north remained strong. While many men waited in the hope of receiving an official contract, a second group went north without permission in 1593. Little is known of their journey, for, unlike those who had gone before them, the men led by Francisco Leyva de Bonilla and Antonio Gutiérrez de Umaña never returned to New Spain. Years later, it would be learned that they had traveled through pueblo lands, camped near San Ildefonso, and then gone east to the Plains, where they died.[52]

At last, after years of delay, the king of Spain awarded a contract for the settlement of New Mexico. Juan de Oñate received that contract in September 1595, but more than two years passed before his expedition received final approval to leave for the north. By January 1598, Oñate had assembled his colonists and supplies for a final inspection. One hundred twenty-nine men, many accompanied by wives, children, and servants, were prepared for the journey. Eight friars and two lay missionaries would join the colonists. As the contract required, Oñate had obtained wheat, corn, and large herds of cattle, sheep, goats, mules, and horses for the expedition. In addition to iron tools, lead, powder, seed, and medicines for the colony, Oñate had bought a variety of goods for trade with the Indians: colored glass beads, necklaces, earrings, rings, thimbles, needles, scissors, thread, yarn, buttons, knives, combs, medals, hats, clay whistles, bells, and children's flutes and trumpets. Among these trade goods were rosaries, paintings, tin images, and other items that would help the friars explain their religion to the peoples of New Mexico. After reviewing the colonists, livestock, and supplies, the inspector gave his approval: all was in order, and Oñate's group could go north.[53]

Like those who had preceded them, Oñate's recruits hoped to find rich mines and fertile lands, to explore unknown territories, and to bring the word of their god to the native peoples. Although they shared the hopes of those who had gone before them, this group differed from earlier Spanish expeditions to New Mexico in two major ways: they went, not to visit the lands to the north, but to settle them, and they had a mandate from their government to do so in the name of the Spanish king. To demonstrate that mandate, in the manner of their countrymen, they held ceremonies wherever they went, declaring in the name of their god and their king that these lands belonged to Spain. On April 30, 1598, Oñate claimed "all of New Mexico, of its kingdoms and provinces, and those adjacent and neighboring" in the name of "the king our lord."[54] His claim included all that was within in those lands, "without exception and without limitation." Spain's holdings would encompass everything "from the leaves of the trees in the forests to the stones and sands of the river."[55] According to the laws of Christian Europe, Oñate's act guaranteed Spain the rights to the land and resources of New Mexico.

Oñate and the colonists moved north along the Río Grande. By late June 1598 they had reached the region where Coronado had spent two winters nearly sixty years earlier, a region where they passed "many pueblos, farms, and planted fields on both banks of the river, most of them abandoned on account of fear."[56] They traveled northeast to San Felipe and Santo Domingo. In early July, Oñate summoned the region's leaders to a meeting at Santo Domingo. On July 7, delegates from many pueblos gathered to meet the men of Kastera. Among them the Spaniards reported a Keres leader named Pamo, who represented "the seven pueblos named Tamy, Acotziya, Cachichi, Yatez, Tipoti, Cochiti, and Quigui, which is this pueblo of Santo Domingo."[57] Other leaders came from the Tiwa pueblos along the Río Grande, the Jémez towns, Zía, San Felipe, and other pueblos.[58]

CHAPTER 3

When all the leaders had gathered, Oñate began to speak. He had been sent to their land, he said, "by the most powerful king and ruler in the world, Don Philip, king of Spain," who wanted to save their souls from "cruel and everlasting torment" and to "protect and bring justice to them." To do so, the king had sent a man to govern them, friars to teach them, and settlers to live among them. The pueblos could become subjects of this powerful king, Oñate said, but to do so they would have to accept the authority of his representatives in all matters and observe the "will, orders, and laws" of the governor and friars. If they became subjects of the king and then failed to follow his laws, they would be "severely punished." Knowing all this, Oñate asked, did they wish to become subjects of Spain? If they did, they "should fall on their knees," and then "kiss the hand of the father commissary, in the name of God, and that of his lordship, in the name of his majesty."

The colonists reported that, when Oñate finished this speech, pueblo leaders discussed the matter, but the Spanish writers did not record what the pueblo leaders said. Nor did they describe how the men of Kastera explained these foreign concepts so that they could be understood by a group of peoples who spoke at least three different languages and many dialects. The pueblos clearly recognized Kastera's intent: Oñate wanted them to kneel and kiss the hands of two of Kastera's men. Whether or not they understood anything more of what Oñate had said, they did what he asked—eagerly, according to the Spaniards who chronicled the event.[59]

The Spaniards called this ceremony an "act of obedience," or an "act of submission." To them, it meant that the pueblos had freely chosen to become subjects of the Spanish Crown and were thus legally bound to honor the laws of Spain. Oñate repeated this ceremony throughout the region, until leaders of the Río Grande pueblos, Acoma, Hopi, and Zuñi had all knelt before him and the friars.[60]

To people who knew nothing of European laws and customs and surely understood little of what Oñate said, this must have seemed a strange request. But the pueblos had heard, and many had learned firsthand, what Kastera did when its demands—however strange or unreasonable—were not met. Compared to demands for all of a pueblo's food and clothing in the harshest part of winter, this request may have seemed insignificant. Knowing the danger of ignoring Kastera's whims, the leaders would have hesitated to risk the people's lives over so trivial a matter. What harm, many must have argued, could come from doing what Oñate asked? They could not have known or imagined that the men of Kastera would believe that by performing such a simple act the pueblos had renounced their government, religion, and rights.

Convinced that the pueblos had happily agreed to do just that, Oñate's group set up its headquarters along the Río Grande. By August, the last of the colonists had reached San Gabriel, and, while the pueblos gathered their harvest, the Spaniards built a church.[61] When the church was completed, Oñate invited pueblo leaders to attend another ceremony. They came from the pueblos of Pecos, Taos, Picurís, Puaray, and Zía, and from the provinces of the Tiwa, Tewa, and Keres. Once again, on September 9, Oñate again asked the pueblos to perform a formal "act of obedience." Then he told each group that a friar would come to teach them. Fray Juan de Rozas would preach to the Keres, in pueblos along the Río Grande and in the Galisteo Basin. Among the pueblos he was assigned in the Galisteo Basin was one that the Spaniards named Santa Ana. Fray Andrés Corchado was assigned to a vast area that included the pueblos of Hopi, Zuñi, and Acoma, the Zía province, and "the pueblos of Tamaya, Yacco, Toxagua, and Pelcheu."[62] When Oñate had read the friars' assignments, he told the pueblos that "each nation and province should kiss the hand of the priest chosen for it and take charge of him." This they did, the Spaniards reported, "with demonstrations of joy."[63]

The colonists' reports were filled with hope. All had gone well for them in their first months in the north. The pueblos had met them with peace, friendship, and, it seemed, eagerness to learn the word of the Spaniards' god. As winter approached, the colonists traveled throughout the region. While Oñate held ceremonies at those pueblos that had not yet sworn obedience to Spain, other Spanish groups searched for mines, explored the surrounding region, and went east to the buffalo country.[64] What they saw pleased them: the pueblos were "excellent and intelligent farmers, who were also much given to commerce, taking from one province to another the fruits of their labor." Near the Hopi pueblos the Spaniards found what they believed were "rich mineral deposits." In their journeys they saw sources of fine white salt and abundant buffalo. In such a land, the colonists wrote enthusiastically to comrades in Spain and New Spain, surely their settlement would prosper.[65] Throughout the region, however, signs less promising for Kastera had begun to appear. As the Spaniards moved throughout the land to demand food and tribute, resentment grew among the pueblos. At Acoma, in December 1598, that resentment became open resistance. When the Spaniards demanded food, the people of Acoma offered them "some flour and maize." What they offered, however, did not satisfy the Spaniards, who pressed them to give more. Instead the people of Acoma resisted, and thirteen Spaniards were killed in the conflict. Oñate reacted swiftly. The people of Acoma, he said, had sworn obedience to Spain. Having disobeyed Spanish law, they must be punished. Seventy soldiers marched to Acoma, captured and burned the pueblo, and took more than five hundred prisoners back to Santo Domingo for trial. The verdict came quickly, and the punishment was brutal. For their crime, the pueblo's women and young men would lose their freedom for twenty years. In addition to this term of servitude to the Spaniards, each man over the age of twenty-five would have one foot cut off. The pueblo's children would not be held responsible, but they would be taken from their homes and placed as wards among the Spaniards so that they could "attain the knowledge of God and the salvation of their souls." Two men from Hopi who had been taken among the prisoners would have their right hands cut off and be sent back to their people so that the pueblos would know what happened to those who disobeyed Kastera.[66] As Oñate had hoped, this harsh punishment discouraged further revolt: in the years that followed, the pueblos' resentment of Kastera, however great, never showed itself openly.

Open resistance to Oñate came instead from the colonists themselves. As the years passed, the settlers grew increasingly unhappy with both New Mexico and the man who had led them there. The land was dry, farming and ranching were difficult, food ran short, the mines yielded no riches, and the friars made few converts. Many of the Spaniards claimed that Oñate ruled too harshly. In 1601 the unhappy settlers and friars saw their chance to leave New Mexico. While Oñate was exploring the plains to the east, almost all of those at San Gabriel decided to leave the colony.[67]

When the colonists of San Gabriel reached New Spain, they added their complaints to a growing list of charges against Oñate. In stark contrast to the optimistic reports that he and his supporters had submitted, the former colonists said that the land was "inclement" and poor.[68] There was little, if any, hope of finding rich mines there, and the native peoples of the region did not use gold, silver, or any other metal.[69] No Spaniard, the colonists said, would stay of his own free will in this land where food and supplies were so scarce that "any Spaniard who gets his fill of tortillas . . . feels as if he has obtained a grant of nobility."[70] After years of providing tribute to the Spaniards and several dry seasons along the Río Grande, the pueblos had no more food for the taking. The colonists had eaten "all the corn that the Indians had saved during the preceding six years," until the pueblos, like the settlers, were reduced to "famine."[71] Oñate had brought the settlement to ruin. If Kastera was to stay in New Mexico, Spain would have to supply the settlement with "provisions, clothing, and other things." Even if Oñate were replaced by a man fit to govern, a colony in New Mexico could not "be maintained without great cost to his majesty. . . ."[72]

Even more serious to those who had sent the colonists north was the charge that the expedition had failed its mission to convert the Indians, a failure that the friars blamed on the conduct of the settlers and their governor. Oñate had reported that the pueblos welcomed the friars and would "readily and willingly help" the colonists, giving them "the supplies they ask for."[73] When the friars made few converts, Oñate's supporters argued that the friars had failed because they did not learn to preach in pueblo languages.[74] The settlers and friars who had deserted the colony, however, told another story.

The Spaniards' demands for tribute, they said, had placed a heavy burden on the pueblos. Every month, Oñate had sent men to the pueblos to demand maize, and the people were "required to contribute one blanket, a skin, or buckskin per house each year." The people of the pueblos soon found that it was of no use "to say that they had nothing but what they had on," for the armed Spaniards would seize the blankets "by force, sometimes even when it is snowing."[75] If a room in the pueblo the Spaniards had occupied at San Gabriel needed repair, Oñate sent for a pueblo woman to plaster it. All of these things had been taken "without payment or giving anything in trade."[76] In this way, Oñate's men "took away from them by force all the food that they had gathered for many years, without leaving them any for the support of themselves and their children. . . ." The Spaniards "robbed them of the scanty clothing they had to protect themselves . . . and took many other valuables from their homes."[77] Oñate had allowed the horses to run loose, causing "the Indians no small damage, for as the cornfields are near the river, the horses trampled and destroyed them."[78] Indians had been "stabbed and knifed" when their food and clothing were taken from them. There had been complaints about the Spaniards' "treatment of the Indian women."[79]

Those who had returned from the colony urged officials not to believe Oñate's claims that the peoples of New Mexico submitted willingly to this treatment. Their "feelings . . . against" giving up their food, said one Spaniard, "cannot be exaggerated."[80] The taking of tribute "by threats and force of arms"[81] had resulted in conflict at Acoma and resentment throughout the region. One of those who had left the colony added: "your lordship may well imagine how this treatment . . . will incline them toward us and toward accepting baptism and our holy Catholic faith."[82] The pueblos, another reported, "said that if we who are Christians caused so much harm and violence, why should they become Christians."[83]

To the leaders of Spain and New Spain, these were serious charges indeed. True, many of them were made by men who had no love for Oñate. But even if things were not as bad as they were said to be, the settlement had certainly been plagued with problems. It had not been profitable and showed few signs of becoming so;[84] even Oñate himself said that he would need more money, men, and supplies to maintain it.[85] Whether the blame should be placed on the friars' laziness or the colonists' behavior, there was no disputing the fact the friars had made few converts.[86] The region's mineral deposits had not lived up to the explorers' expectations: the ores that Oñate had sent back to New Spain contained only a little copper, not even a trace of gold or silver.[87] When Oñate resigned as governor of New Mexico in August 1607,[88] Spain had still made no decision about the fate of the colony. While Spanish leaders debated, a friar and eight soldiers went north to visit the settlement and inspect the region. They brought provisions to the colonists and ordered Oñate and the remaining settlers to stay in New Mexico at least until December 1609.[89]

Their report settled the matter. It was true, they said, that New Mexico did not seem to be a promising land, and that the colony had not prospered under Oñate's leadership. The friars, however, had baptized seven thousand Indians, who would be lost to the Christian faith if Spain left New Mexico. In distant Spain, the king issued a ruling that a Christian nation could not abandon those it had baptized, and so it was decided. Oñate would be recalled, and Spain would sponsor no more large expeditions to search for treasure in New Mexico, but a colony would remain to continue the conversion of the Indians. The king would send a new governor, twelve friars, and fifty married soldiers to the province.[90] Thousands of miles from New Mexico, a decision had been made that would change the history of the Tamayame and of all the Río Grande peoples: Kastera had come to stay.

Although records of the events leading to that decision fill many volumes, the documents provide only occasional glimpses of the peoples whose lives Kastera changed. The records do not say how, when, or where the people of Tamaya met the people of Kastera, or what happened when they did meet. Clues to that history lie hidden in the documents. To piece the clues together, however, scholars must first resolve two questions: exactly where each expedition went, and exactly where the Tamayame were when the Spaniards passed through the region. Neither question can be answered easily.

The expeditions' reports outline the general route that each one followed to reach New Mexico, but the explorers did not always describe their paths in any detail. Even if their location is clearly named or described, it may still be difficult to tell what place is meant, for many of the places described by the Spaniards are known today by different names, while others lie in ruins. Because, to Kastera, any pueblo seemed much like all of the others, the descriptions are often so general that they could refer to almost any pueblo.

For a people like the Tamayame, who are rarely mentioned by name in Kastera's records, the problem is even more difficult. Not one of the documents indicates their location during the years from 1580 to 1609. Pottery found along the Río Grande seems to suggest that the people of Tamaya were still using the farming villages in the area between the modern sites of Albuquerque and Bernalillo when Kastera returned in 1581.[91] By that time, however, they could have made the journey to the village known as Kwiiste Haa Tamaya, told of in their oral tradition. They could have been living in a village at the southern tip of Santa Ana Mesa.[92] They could already have established Tamaya somewhere near its modern site.[93] They could have settled in a village on top of the Santa Ana Mesa.[94] When Kastera returned, the Tamayame could have been living in several of these places or in others of which no record has yet been found.

Most of Kastera's expeditions visited all of these areas, and their reports describe several pueblos that might have belonged to the Tamayame. The Rodríguez-Chamuscado party saw a number of Keres pueblos along the Río Grande and the Río Jémez. Among them was one the Spaniards called "Castilleja," a pueblo that may have stood on the southern end of the Santa Ana Mesa[95] and could once have belonged to the Tamayame.[96] The next Spanish group, led by Espéjo, traveled through the same region. Their journals noted that Keres-speaking people had been "present" in the region near Puaray where the friars were killed. Espéjo's expedition named five pueblos to the north in the Keres province, three of which can be identified: "Catiete" was San Felipe; "Gigue" was a Santo Domingo settlement; and "Cochita" was Cochití.[97] The other two—"Sieheran" and "Tipoliti"—cannot be directly connected with their modern counterparts. Sieheran may have been either a Zía town or the old pueblo of San Felipe.[98] If the five settlements in this list correspond to the modern Keres pueblos in the region, Tipoliti, "by the process of elimination," would have to be Santa Ana.[99] But some scholars believe that Tipoliti was the pueblo of Gipuy (LA 182). If so, the pueblo that Espéjo named La Milpa Llana might have belonged to the people of Tamaya.[100] Or perhaps the pueblo that Espéjo saw "near a sierra" in the Zía region was the home of the Tamayame in the 1580s.[101] The journals of Castaño de Sosa and Morlete add little that would help to locate the people of Tamaya. Bonilla and Umaña left no records, though they may have passed through the area.

Not until the Oñate expedition do the Tamayame appear by name in Kastera's reports, and even then the records do not locate the sites of Tamayame villages. A leader who represented "Tamy" was among those present at

Santo Domingo in July 1598.[102] Two months later, when Oñate assigned friars to each pueblo, both a pueblo named "Tamaya" and a pueblo named "Santa Ana" appear in the documents. Among the pueblos assigned to Fray Andrés Corchado was one named "Tamaya." At the same time, Fray Juan de Rozas became responsible for a pueblo that the Spaniards called "Santa Ana," which was included in a list of Keres pueblos in the Galisteo Basin.[103] Two months before, in July 1598, Oñate's men had given the name "Santa Ana" to a pueblo in the Galisteo Basin.[104] By 1602, however, Kastera had begun to use the name "Santa Ana" for a pueblo north of the Río Grande on the west bank of the Río Jémez.[105]

What happened when the Tamayame met Kastera would have depended, in some ways, on where the meeting took place. In the late sixteenth century, as in Coronado's time, violence and fear often characterized the contacts between the Spaniards and the pueblo peoples along the Río Grande in the region between the modern sites of Albuquerque and Bernalillo. To the north, in the Keres lands along the Río Grande and Río Jémez, the meetings seem to have been more peaceful. If conflicts occurred in these Keres villages, Kastera did not consider them serious enough to record. The peoples of this region, unlike their neighbors to the south, had not endured the experience of having a large Spanish camp, like Coronado's, in their midst, and usually they did not flee when the men of Kastera approached.

In other ways, however, the effects of Kastera's return would have been the same for the Tamayame no matter where they were living in 1581. Whether their pueblos lay along the Río Grande near Puaray, farther north on the Santa Ana Mesa, or to the northwest along the Río Jémez, the Tamayame were surely visited by Spaniards seeking food, blankets, and clothing. The people of Tamaya may have received some of the glass beads, hats, and iron tools that Kastera had brought to trade. But these were cold and dry years throughout the region. Frost came early in the fall and threatened the crops even in late spring.[106] Drought visited the fields in summer. In such a time, no trade goods could have compensated for the loss of food and blankets that the people needed. Their storerooms emptied by years of drought and tribute, the Tamayame, like many of their neighbors, must have suffered when the men of Kastera came to make their demands.

By this time, though, wherever they were living, the Tamayame would have learned that it was wise to give the Spaniards what they wanted. All around them, their neighbors had seen that the men of Kastera would take food and clothing by force if a pueblo could not, or did not, meet their demands. The explorers themselves noted how rapidly news of their actions traveled from tribe to tribe and pueblo to pueblo throughout the Southwest. Probably the Tamayame were among those who heard that Rodríguez and Chamuscado had demanded food from a pueblo to the east, and that the strangers would be satisfied with nine loads of flour. Perhaps the Tamayame also gathered up just that much flour to give to the men of Kastera, as many of their neighbors did. Whether they were living along the Río Grande or in more remote locations, the Tamayame would surely have learned how Espéjo destroyed the "big pueblo" at Puaray, killed and captured many of its residents, and helped himself to the supplies in nearby pueblos. From their kinsmen at Acoma and Santo Domingo, the Tamayame must have heard about the cruel ways in which Oñate punished those who resisted Kastera's demands. Long before any of the Spanish groups, traveling up the Río Grande or the Pecos River, reached Keres lands, the Tamayame would have received word of their approach.

Wherever the Tamayame made their homes in this region, they would also have seen some of Kastera's ceremonies during this time, although they could not have known that by these actions the men of Kastera believed that they had established a claim to pueblo lands and acquired the right to impose the laws, rulers, and beliefs of Spain on the pueblos. Perhaps Gaspar Castaño de Sosa appointed officials at a Tamayame settlement, as he did at several places in Keres lands. Probably the people of Tamaya watched more than one friar raise a wooden cross and try to explain its meaning to puzzled onlookers. At Santo Domingo in 1598, a Tamayame leader looked on as Oñate asked the pueblos if they wanted to become subjects of the Spanish king.

To the people of Tamaya, however, these events could not have meant what they meant to Kastera. The Tamayame already had a government, developed long before, at Kashe K'atreti (White House). Since that time they had been governed by Tiyamune, whose decisions were their laws. For all of the generations that had passed since the Hanu entered the upper world, the people had preserved their beliefs and seen that the proper ceremonies were carried out. Long speeches in a language that none of the Tamayame spoke, the raising of two crossed sticks of wood or metal, and the strange marks these newcomers made on sheets of paper would have done nothing to change the beliefs the Hanu had brought into this world.

For the people of Tamaya, Kastera could not have been more than an occasional and unpredictable visitor, coming much as a late frost or a flood came now and then, bringing a time of loss and hardship. Like a sudden storm, Kastera may have swept into Tamayame lands with little warning, bringing destruction. Perhaps this storm did its damage to neighboring

Tamaya, 1903. Photograph by George H. Pepper, courtesy of the Museum of the American Indian, Heye Foundation.

Houses at Tamaya, 1903. Photograph by George H. Pepper, courtesy of the Museum of the American Indian, Heye Foundation.

Oven and chimneys at Tamaya, 1903. Photograph by George H. Pepper, courtesy of the Museum of the American Indian, Heye Foundation.

House with chimney, 1903. Photograph by George H. Pepper, courtesy of the Museum of the American Indian, Heye Foundation.

Drawing of Tamaya, c. 1920. Courtesy of the Museum of New Mexico (neg. no. 4094).

Postcard of pueblo women fetching water, c. 1925. Photograph from the Arkansas History Commission Collection, courtesy of the New Mexico State Records Center and Archives.

Homes at Tamaya, c. 1935. Photograph by T. Harmon Parkhurst, courtesy of the Museum of New Mexico (neg. no. 4097).

Kiva, oven, wagon, and corral at Tamaya, c. 1935. Photograph by T. Harmon Parkhurst, courtesy of the Museum of New Mexico (neg. no. 4859).

Tamaya, c. 1935. Courtesy of the Museum of New Mexico (neg. no. 42707).

Tamaya, 1948. Photograph from the Dietrich Collection, courtesy of the New Mexico State Records Center and Archives.

Aerial view of Tamaya, c. 1948. Photograph by Stanley Stubbs, courtesy of the Museum of New Mexico (neg. no. 4095).

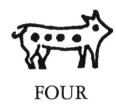

FOUR

Hanu Resists Kastera

In the pueblos along the Río Grande, only the oldest of the elders could remember the time when the people had not known of Kastera. Seventy years had passed since Coronado and his men came to pueblo lands in search of gold and silver. For some, Kastera had brought disaster: several of the thriving villages that had welcomed Coronado in 1540 were charred and empty ruins by 1610; others, like Acoma, still stood but bore the scars of Kastera's violence. Yet in most of the pueblos that had survived, there was little to show that Kastera had come and gone for seven decades.

Only a few small signs, here and there, would have revealed that Kastera had come to the Río Grande. Some pueblo farmers planted Kastera's wheat, chilies, or onions beside the traditional pueblo crops of corn and beans. Peach and apple trees blossomed in the spring, and grapes and watermelons ripened on vines in some villages. In the fields, sheep, goats, cattle, and horses grazed. Some of the pueblos had built small, domed outdoor ovens like those used in Spain. Some pueblo residents chose to use metal knives, axes, and needles, or wore colorful hats obtained from Kastera. A few weavers had begun to work with Spanish wool and flax, as well as native cotton. But, although individuals welcomed Kastera's useful and desirable goods, these things made no great change in pueblo life.[1] Still pueblo farmers tended their crops as their ancestors had done hundreds of years before. Still the women ground corn into fine meal as their mothers and grandmothers had taught them. As always each pueblo, guided by its leader, performed the ceremonies that the people had brought into this upper world.

For seventy years, Spaniards had come and gone, demanding food, clothing, and shelter, sometimes offering their goods in gift or trade, sometimes preaching the word of their god or trying to explain the ways of their countrymen. Most of the strangers hoped and believed that the pueblos would, in time, come to live as Kastera did, but they had done little to force the people to change their ways of life. Almost all of these Spaniards had come as explorers, and few had seen any reason to stay in a land that had no gold or silver and often, in those dry years, little food. As long as the pueblos gave them corn and blankets on demand and listened in peace to their speeches, they had asked little more.

When Kastera returned in the seventeenth century, however, tribute would no longer suffice. The Spaniards who went north in these years came with instructions, not to search for riches, but to bring their way of life to the region. Colonists and friars who came to stay replaced the explorers who had soon moved on. The new arrivals brought Spain's laws, Spain's religion, and Spain's customs, and they expected the pueblos to welcome them. Having heard from those who had gone before that the pueblos were a peaceful, intelligent, and orderly people, they assumed that, with proper instruction, such a people would be eager to embrace all that Kastera had to teach. Although many of Kastera's leaders recognized that the pueblos had not yet adopted Kastera's way of life, Oñate's failure had not altered Kastera's assumptions: where the first colony had failed, the new governor, friars, and colonists were expected to succeed. If the settlers gave a good example, Kastera believed, little time would pass before the pueblos abandoned their old ways and began to live as Kastera did.

Oñate's successor, Pedro de Peralta, received orders from the Spanish king that clearly outlined these expectations.[2] Appointed in 1609, Peralta was told to go north as soon as possible and to "make secure what [had] been discovered" in New Mexico. This time, the governor and the colonists were not to neglect the pueblos in their "greed for what is out of reach." Until the colony was secure, the new governor was not to "permit any exploring trips anywhere." His first responsibility was to build a city that would be the center of the colony, to appoint judges and officials who would bring Kastera's law to the region, and to work with the friars to teach the pueblos the Spanish language. This foundation would enable the colonists to teach the pueblos Kastera's religion, laws, and way of life.[3]

The first Spaniards, who had come primarily to explore, had assembled men, horses, and a supply of food, clothing, weapons, tools, medicines, and trade goods for the journey north. Each expedition had had a leader, a man who could speak for Spain and settle disputes. These exploring parties, however, brought only what they would need to travel through the region in search of riches. Requiring no elaborate systems to govern the lands through which they traveled, they made no provisions to establish them. Needing only a base camp from which to search for riches, they had neither planned nor built large cities. They had little reason to plow farmlands to plant crops that they would not remain to harvest, and their herds were only large enough to support them on the journey. Even the largest of their settlements, Oñate's capital at San Gabriel, had been little more than a temporary camp.

Those who came to settle, however, went north with tools to build homes, seeds and cuttings to plant crops, and breeding animals to establish herds. They loaded their pack mules with clothing, tools, and supplies to sustain them for years in the colony, and they carried plans for establishing towns, building churches, and administering a vast region in the name of Spain's king and Spain's church. Soon after Peralta's group arrived, these systems were put in place.

The new governor immediately began to build the city of Santa Fe, which would serve as the capital of the colony, the center of Kastera's government in New Mexico. Networks reaching out from this first small town linked settlements, missions, and pueblos throughout the vast region. The governor divided the region into *alcaldías,* or districts, and chose a man to represent him in each district. That man, known as the *alcalde mayor,* or *alcalde,* was given authority over the colonists and charged with the responsibility of seeing that they obeyed the governor's orders and the laws of Spain. It was also the alcalde's duty to represent the governor in Kastera's dealings with the Indians. He was to meet with pueblo leaders, to hear and resolve any disputes that arose, and to collect any tribute the law required. The alcalde thus became the first link in a chain of government that stretched from the towns of the Río Grande to the governor and lieutenant governor in Santa Fe, and, through them, to the leaders of New Spain and Spain, and ultimately to the Spanish king himself.[4]

Beside this civil government, the friars established their own rule in seventeenth-century New Mexico. Each friar answered to the head of the mission in New Mexico, a man who was known until about 1616 as the "father commissary," and afterward as the "custodian." He, in turn, reported to his superiors in New Spain, and, through them, to the Franciscan order in Spain, to the king, and finally, to the head of the church, the Pope. While the colonists set up the civil government in Santa Fe, the friars established their headquarters at Santo Domingo Pueblo. They too divided the region into districts, sending a friar to each with instructions to build a mission church, school, and convent. Usually the friar chose to live and establish the central mission at the largest pueblo in his district. The smaller pueblos rarely had their own church buildings or clergy in the early years of the colony. Instead friars from the central missions traveled to outlying pueblos from time to time so that their residents could hear the word of God, attend Mass, and be baptized, married, and buried as Christians. Thus the pueblos without a resident friar came to be known as *visitas.*[5]

The systems that New Spain's governors and friars set up in New Mexico were based on laws established in Spain and Christian Europe long before Coronado marched north to New Mexico. They included a body of laws set forth by the Second Audiencia, the ruling body of New Spain, between 1530 and 1535 to govern Spanish relations with the native peoples of the New World. These decrees, issued before any of the pueblos had encountered Kastera, later came to have great importance for the peoples of the Río Grande. Most significant among them was a ruling that stated that native peoples had the right to choose their own officials and to govern their own affairs.[6]

Not long after Peralta set up the new Spanish government in New Mexico, it became clear that the laws and systems Kastera had brought to the region were not sufficient to resolve the problems created by Spanish settlement. Conflicts soon arose among the pueblos, the non-pueblo Indians, the friars, the settlers, and the officials of New Mexico. The existing laws did not address many of these problems and, even when they did, laws were easily abused in a colony so far from the courts of Spain and New Spain. To resolve these difficulties, the viceroy of New Spain, with authority from the Spanish king, wrote a new decree in 1620. Copies of the new laws were sent to New Mexico's Governor, Juan de Eulate, and to the Custodian, Fray EstevÁn de Perea.[7]

This decree set forth many new laws to establish the duties and govern the behavior of Kastera's colonists, particularly those who held grants. The governor of New Mexico was allowed to give grants, or *encomiendas,* to the settlers. Such a grant gave the recipient, or *encomendero,* the right to work a piece of land and to collect some tribute in the form of goods or services from the native peoples who lived within its boundaries. In return, the encomendero owed the government some services and was required to help the friars convert the Indians. To fulfill his duty, he might build a church, teach the Indians to speak Spanish, or explain the doctrines of Christianity to them. Under the laws of 1620, encomenderos also had to provide "military escort for mission supply trains" and to escort "friars going to administer the sacraments in frontier pueblos."[8] For Tamaya, as for most of the pueblos, these laws had little impact. Tamaya did not fall within an encomienda grant, and the Tamayame answered only to the governor or his agent, not to any encomendero. Only if an encomendero came to the pueblo with a visiting friar or supply train would the Tamayame have seen the effects of these new regulations.

Other sections of the decree, however, touched the pueblos more directly. One of the most important sections guaranteed the pueblos' right to select leaders of their choice to fill positions recognized by Kastera's government. Although the pueblos were still governed by the people's religious leaders and their assistants, as they had been since the Hanu entered this upper world, by the 1620s most pueblos also chose at least two new leaders each year: a governor, who would represent the pueblo in affairs that involved New Mexico's civil authorities, and a *fiscal,* who would deal with the friars. To guarantee that each pueblo would be free to choose these office-holders without Spanish interference, the laws of 1620 said that no Spaniards could enter the pueblos "on the days of the annual pueblo elections." The new laws also responded to frequent pueblo complaints about the behavior of the colonists in pueblo lands. Because Kastera's settlers had damaged pueblo crops, the new decree stated that Spaniards could no longer pasture their "stock within three leagues of the pueblos," and the governor was forbidden to "graze herds of livestock for his own account." To protect the rights of pueblo workers, the laws specified how friars and colonists could and could not use Indian labor and established the wages that Spaniards had to pay Indian workers who did not live within an *encomienda* grant. So that the Indians could fulfill the Christian duties required by the friars without having to travel far from their homes, the friars were ordered to visit all of the pueblos on each Christian feast day. In response to a frequent pueblo complaint, the friars were forbidden to cut "the hair of Indians" as punishment "for minor offenses."[9]

Spanish officials hoped, through this new decree, to resolve the problems that had filled reports from the northern colony. But New Mexico was far from the lands where these rulers lived and these policies were decided. More than a thousand miles lay between the colony and the nearest officials who could speak for Spain's rulers, and only a fragile link connected the two lands. That link was the mission supply caravan, which made its way north from New Spain every three years.[10]

The caravan brought welcome goods to the distant colony. Saddle bags, boxes, and wagons were packed with things that Spanish settlers and friars could not find or make in New Mexico: iron kettles, anvils, bridles, saddles, paper, gunpowder, shoes, thread, nails, and tools to make and repair homes, wagons, and fences; missals, books, vestments, incense, bells, rosaries, and paintings for the churches. And with these necessities came small luxuries for the men and women who had settled in the distant colony: familiar spices, wine, olive oil, and cuttings to start peach trees and grapevines like those they had known in their homelands.[11]

With the caravan traveled new settlers, friars, and soldiers, sometimes joined by new governors or by representatives who came to inspect New Mexico's towns and missions. The newcomers carried messages, orders, instructions, and copies of new laws to the governor and the friars. They brought welcome news of events in Spain and New Spain, and, for the fortunate, letters or word of family and friends they had left behind.[12]

When the caravan headed back to New Spain, the horses and mules were loaded with New Mexico's goods, including many things, like hides and piñon nuts, obtained from the Indians. Often the caravan also carried a human cargo on its return journey: Indian captives to serve as slaves in the mines or as servants in the homes of New Spain. With the caravan traveled Spaniards leaving the colony for varied reasons: messengers from the governor and the friars to their superiors, discouraged colonists returning to their homelands, officials who had been recalled, friars sent to missions elsewhere, and inspectors whose investigations were completed. In this way reports, letters, messages, and official papers from the colony reached New Spain. But New Spain was itself a colony, and any important matters required the attention of the rulers of Spain and the leaders of the Christian Church. To reach those who had authority to resolve a problem or make a decision, the information then had to travel by ship to distant Spain. Word of any decision had to retrace this long and difficult route to reach New Mexico. Thus years might elapse before new leaders and new policies reached the remote colony, for New Mexico had no regular contact with Spain or New Spain from the time when one caravan left until the time when the next arrived, three years later.[13]

The Spaniards who remained in New Mexico when the caravans left were a small group in a vast land. In 1610 Spain's force in New Mexico consisted of a governor, twelve friars, fifty soldiers with their wives and children, and the servants they had brought with them.[14] The colony grew slowly: twenty years later, it numbered only three hundred Spaniards (among them forty friars and thirty-five encomenderos) and seven hundred servants, nearly all living in or near the single town that the Spaniards had built at Santa Fe. Only the friars, who had set up missions at many pueblos, and a few ranchers, who ventured into outlying areas in search of rich land and plentiful water, had settled outside the capital.[15]

The arrival of a comparatively small group of newcomers was, in itself, nothing new to the region. For centuries, small groups of people had made their ways to this land. Some, like the Tamayame, had traveled on long journeys through the region, stopping many times before they settled permanently. Each group had come with its own way of life, its own religion, its own language, and its own government. Each brought its familiar types of household goods, its ways of building homes, its own tools and containers and clothing. For many generations, groups of newcomers had found their homelands among the peoples who had already settled in the region.

Those who had come before had settled, built their towns, planted their crops, and gone about their lives. They met their neighbors and traded with them, sharing their knowledge of the surrounding lands and exchanging the beautiful, useful, and desirable things that they made, gathered, and used. If need be, they joined as allies to fight common enemies.

As the first of Kastera's settlers built their town, they may have seemed little different from those who had gone before. Like them they built their homes and cultivated their fields, keeping the traditions they had brought with them to this new land. Like other newcomers, they spoke a different language and brought unfamiliar ways. Their clothing, tools, and crops differed from those of their neighbors, but they soon learned to eat the foods of New Mexico, to keep their seedlings alive with its precious water, and to adopt some of the useful goods and ways of their neighbors. Yet despite these similarities with the peoples of the region, the men and women of Kastera, it quickly became apparent, were profoundly different from those who had come before them.

Until Kastera arrived, each new group in turn had come in search of a land where the people could live in their own ways, honoring their own leaders and traditions. None, before Kastera, had tried to impose its rules or its ways upon its neighbors. The Spaniards, however, came with the intent to make the region's other peoples adopt Kastera's ways and beliefs, by choice if possible, by force if necessary. They were armed, not only with formidable weapons, but also with elaborate systems designed to allow a few men to enforce their way of life rapidly on peoples far more numerous, living in a vast land. Thus, in only twenty years, a few hundred Spaniards, led by a still smaller group of officials and friars, set up a network of government that reached from Taos to Zuñi, supervised the construction of churches in many of the pueblos, saw that the people of those pueblos followed Kastera's forms of worship, and established the Spanish language as one all of the region's people must learn. With a force no larger than most pueblo groups, and much smaller than some, Kastera had an impact far beyond its numbers, and far different from those who had come before.

Although the men of Kastera rarely recorded their contacts with the Tamayame in these first years of settlement, it is certain that Kastera's systems were imposed upon the Tamayame, as upon their neighbors, in these years. In the first decades of the seventeenth century, an alcalde mayor was certainly chosen for the lands near Tamaya. By this time, if they had not done so earlier, the Tamayame would have begun to choose officials in the Spanish pattern to represent them before Kastera's governor and friars. Because Tamayame lands were not part of an encomienda, Kastera's governor in Santa Fe would have assumed direct authority over the Tamayame. The people would have dealt with the governor's agent, the alcalde mayor, when he came to collect any tribute required of the pueblos and to meet with pueblo officials. If the Tamayame had complaints about the actions of Kastera's settlers or the friars assigned to them, they must have presented them to the alcalde mayor. No records, however, have been found to speak of the contacts between Tamaya and the governor's agents in these years.

Kastera's friars, however, did leave a record of their contacts with the Tamayame in these decades. At first, the friar from the mission at Jémez or Zía seems to have had responsibility for the Tamayame. Fray Zarate Salmerón, stationed in New Mexico from 1618 to 1626, spent much of that time as the missionary at Jémez. While serving there, he also went to Santa Ana Pueblo to preach and baptize pueblo residents.[16] Fray Alonso de Benavides, who came to New Mexico in the late 1620s, wrote a long report to persuade officials in Spain to support the church's work in New Mexico. In that report, published in 1630 and revised in 1634, he spoke of the Keres lands near the Río Grande. The region, he said, was abundant, with fertile soil and a river filled with fish. The people, he added, were "in a docile mood." In seven Keres pueblos, there were "more than four thousand souls, all baptized." The friars had set up three full missions "with churches and convents" in the district, "in addition to the one in each pueblo." Benavides described the friar assigned to the Keres, Cristóbal de Quirós, as "a great minister versed in the difficult language of this nation" and "a friar of great ardor." According to the report, this friar had "taught and trained the Indians well" in both Kastera's forms of worship and what Benavides called the "ways of civilization, such as reading, writing, and singing, as well as playing all kinds of musical instruments."[17]

The Keres pueblos taught by this "friar of great ardor" probably included the Tamayame, who may, as Benavides' report implies, have had a church building in their pueblo as early as the late 1620s. It seems unlikely, however, that a church had been built this early, because Tamaya remained a visita of a larger mission throughout this period; it was still described as a visita of Zía in 1641 and again in 1663.[18] Benavides, writing to gain support for the missions, may have exaggerated the extent of the friars' work. Perhaps when he said that each of the Keres pueblos had a church, he meant only that a friar went to each pueblo regularly. But, whether the Tamayame heard friars preach beneath the roof of a church building or in the plaza outside their homes, they surely heard them during this time. Their own tradition says that, when the friars first came, the people told them that they did not want to become Christians, for they had their own religion.[19] Like many other pueblos who had no interest in Kastera's religion, however, they were probably counted in Benavides' optimistic estimate of the number of converts the Spanish friars had made.

During these years, most of the reports that reached New Spain and Spain described the efforts of the missions and the colony as a success. The governor and the friars had brought Kastera's systems to all of the pueblos—even, by 1630, to the distant Hopi—and the colony had grown substantially. In these reports it seemed that, after only twenty years, Kastera's goals were within reach: soon the pueblos would adopt Kastera's ways and beliefs, the settlement would prosper, and the friars and the settlers would be rewarded for their efforts.

The calm surface mirrored in these early reports, however, was a more accurate reflection of Kastera's hopes and assumptions than of the actual conditions in New Mexico. Letters that reached New Spain in the following decades gradually revealed the actual state of the small colony. New Mexico, it soon became apparent, was beset by problems from within and without, problems arising from flaws in Kastera's own systems, from the attempt to impose Kastera's ways on the peoples of New Mexico, and from nature, which was not subject to Kastera's rule.

The soldiers, settlers, and friars who made the journey to New Mexico had, from the first, carried with them the seeds of internal dissent—diverse goals and irreconcilable priorities. In the first years of the colony, all had worked together, for their common fears and needs were greater than their differences. As the separate church and state systems became established, however, reports of harmony and progress gave way to angry charges and counter-charges. The friars claimed that the governors worked against the aims of the

CHAPTER 4

Church; the governors replied that the friars were scheming to take control of the colony. Each argued that the other took too much of the pueblos' time, collected too much tribute, and required too much labor. As it became clear that the pueblos were not becoming ardent Christians, each faction blamed the other for Kastera's failure to convert them.

With each year, that failure became more apparent. Since 1540, Kastera had waited patiently for the pueblos to accept the word of God. After a hundred years had passed without the conversions they had anticipated, the friars lost their patience. They had worked long and hard and preached with great ardor, but still the pueblos held back. There could be, the friars decided, only one explanation: the pueblos' old beliefs kept them from hearing the word of God. That being the case, the solution appeared simple: the old ways must be destroyed, so that the pueblos would welcome the new. Thus the missionaries began a campaign to eliminate every part of pueblo religion. They punished and imprisoned the pueblos' religious leaders; seized and destroyed anything used in traditional pueblo ceremonies; and did all that they could to keep the people from holding and participating in the ceremonies. They fought bitterly against those governors who had allowed the pueblos to practice their own religions.[20]

No longer could the people gather in the plazas to hold the ancient ceremonies, to keep the traditions they had brought into this upper world. Yet it was a time when the people needed spiritual guidance more than ever, for many troubles had come to the land. Each year Kastera's numbers, and Kastera's demands, increased. With the strangers came disease, violence, and hunger. And in these years when hardship came in abundance, the people watched in vain for the summer rains that had watered their seedlings in years past.

Soon the men of Kastera seemed to be everywhere, and still more arrived each year. In 1610 only fifty Spanish soldiers had been in pueblo lands; by 1680 three times that many had settled there. In 1610 twelve friars had come in peace to speak to the pueblos; in the years that followed, as many as fifty at once spread throughout pueblo lands, demanding that the peoples give up their beliefs and punishing all who kept to the old ways. As more Spaniards arrived, ranchers began to move away from the settlement at Santa Fe to find more fertile lands. They claimed the best lands and took the scarce water for their crops and stock, and they demanded tribute and labor from the nearby pueblos. Pueblo farmers, forced to leave their own fields to work for Kastera's friars, settlers, and governor, complained that, although they presented their claims to the governor as the law provided, they were not always paid for their labor.[21]

Among the claims in Kastera's files were those of Tamayame workers. Those documents show that in the 1650s the Tamayame, with people from Zía and Jémez, built wagons for Spanish settlers near Puaray. Skilled painters, the Tamayame were often hired to decorate leather door hangings for Spanish homes. Tamaya was also known for fine work with hide and leather. One Tamayame, Francisco Cuaxin, sent a bill to Governor Bernardo López de Mendizabal for 38 doublets, 10 leather jackets, and 40 pair of shoes. The Tamayame also requested compensation for 160 days of labor, time spent washing 80 hides for Kastera.[22]

Just as the Spaniards welcomed fine Tamayame hides and paintings, the Tamayame were pleased to obtain Kastera's iron tools and some of the other goods the Spaniards had to offer. Not all of the unfamiliar things Kastera brought were welcome in the pueblos, however. With metal tools and grapevine cuttings, Kastera also brought new diseases such as measles and smallpox, which proved to be deadly to the pueblos. Because people of New Mexico had no resistance to these illnesses, the diseases spread rapidly and did great harm. In 1640 and again in the 1660s, epidemics swept through the pueblos, killing many people.[23]

Disaster also came to the pueblos as a result of Kastera's expeditions into Ute, Navajo, and Apache lands. The Spaniards undertook these forays for a variety of reasons. Soldiers were sent to punish the tribes when livestock disappeared from Kastera's towns and ranches. Spanish expeditions also visited these peoples to take captives as slaves or servants for the settlements of New Mexico and New Spain. Angered by these raids, Ute, Navajo, and Apache warriors retaliated against Kastera's settlements and ranches—and against the pueblos among whom Kastera had settled. In the years since Kastera's arrival, these neighboring tribes had grown larger and more powerful. Mounted on Spanish horses, armed with Spanish guns, and outraged by Spanish actions, they became deadly enemies, and each year they traveled farther within pueblo lands to raid.[24]

With all of these plagues brought by Kastera came a hardship that had been part of pueblo life long before Coronado arrived. Once again, in the 1660s, the dry years returned. Crops withered in the fields, and streams shrank and disappeared in the summer heat. The people emptied their storerooms, and the new harvests were too small to refill them.[25]

Together, these things brought havoc to many pueblos. Throughout the region, the pueblo population dwindled, perhaps by as much as one-half.[26] Many smaller pueblo settlements were abandoned, and rooms that had once been filled with laughter, music, and the sounds of corn being ground fell

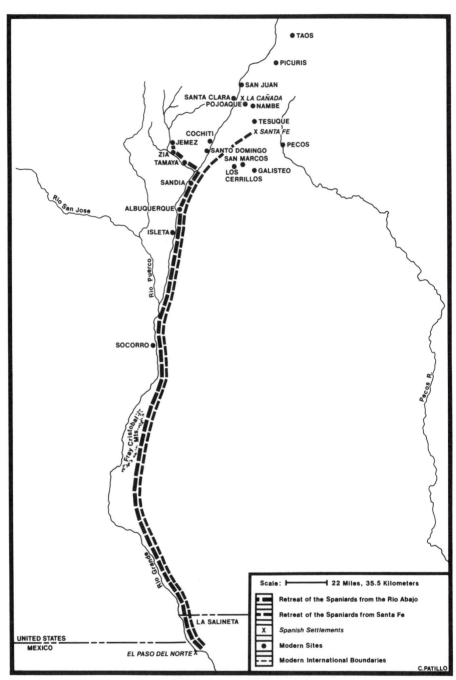

● TAOS

● PICURIS

● SAN JUAN

SANTA CLARA ●   X *LA CAÑADA*
POJOAQUE ●   ● NAMBE

● TESUQUE

COCHITI   X *SANTA FE*
● JEMEZ

ZIA ●   ● SANTO DOMINGO   ● PECOS
TAMAYA ●   SAN MARCOS

SANDIA ●   LOS   ● GALISTEO
CERRILLOS

Rio San Jose

ALBUQUERQUE ●

ISLETA ●

Rio Puerco

SOCORRO ●

Fray Cristobal Mts.

Pecos R.

Rio Grande

Scale: ├————————┤ 22 Miles, 35.5 Kilometers

▊ Retreat of the Spaniards from the Rio Abajo

▊ Retreat of the Spaniards from Santa Fe

LA SALINETA   X   *Spanish Settlements*

UNITED STATES   ● Modern Sites
MEXICO

EL PASO DEL NORTE X   ▬ ▬ Modern International Boundaries

C.PATILLO

THE PUEBLO REVOLT OF 1680

silent.[27] Kastera, however, seemed blind to this devastation. Friars buried the dead and baptized the living; governors submitted their reports; inspectors arrived and departed; and the caravan, loaded with supplies, made its way north. The reports sent to New Spain rarely mentioned the pueblos that had tried to drive Kastera away, but often recounted the numbers of pueblos who had been baptized and the friars' hopes for still greater success in the missions.[28]

No records from this time remain to speak of where the Tamayame were living, or whether Kastera's ranchers had settled in the fertile Río Grande farmlands long used by Tamayame. No documents indicate whether daring Navajo raiders threatened the people in their homes and fields. If smallpox came to Tamaya and the people suffered and died, no Spaniards wrote about it. No journal mentions that the Tamayame were ever paid for the hides they had washed or the clothing they had made for Kastera. If Tamayame leaders were among those imprisoned for keeping the old ways, their names were not recorded. If the friars punished Tamayame who did not attend Mass, no account remains to tell of it. But the records do show that, by August 1680, the Tamayame had joined their neighbors in a plan to drive Kastera from their lands.[29]

For decades, individual pueblos had risen up against Kastera, but the soldiers had put down all of these revolts. This time, the pueblos united in an effort to destroy the Spaniards. They were led by several men, including Popé, originally from San Juan Pueblo and one of those who had been imprisoned by the Spaniards. They laid their plans carefully. Messengers were sent to inform each pueblo of the plans. When the appointed time came, 11 August 1680, all of the pueblos together would attack Kastera. Word spread from the north: a knotted cord, sent from pueblo to pueblo, would be carried "by the swiftest youths under penalty of death if they revealed the secret." When the knots had all been untied, one each day, the revolt would begin. Before the appointed day arrived, however, on August 9, Governor Otermín learned of the plans from two Indian prisoners. As soon as pueblo leaders heard that the two had been captured, they sent out a new message: the revolt would begin immediately, before Kastera had time to prepare.[30]

By noon the next day, August 10, word had reached Jémez. Captain Luis Granillo, the alcalde mayor of the Jémez and Keres district, learned "that all of the natives of the kingdom wished to rebel." Lorenzo Musa, or Muza, a Jémez man, told Granillo that a messenger had come;[31] the rebellion, Granillo wrote, seemed to be "general."[32] Fighting had begun in the pueblos from Santa Fe to Taos and at Cochití, Santo Domingo, and San Felipe. According to the messenger's account, Santa Fe had fallen, and the governor and all of the Spaniards in the north were dead. Now was the time for the pueblos of the Río Abajo to rise up.[33] Granillo quickly sent for help, stating that the people of Jémez "had already proclaimed the rebellion and taken up arms."[34] Fearing for their lives, Granillo, Fray Francisco Muñoz, and three soldiers rode out of the pueblo, pursued by the people of Jémez.[35] Then, after midnight, the requested help arrived: two leagues from Jémez, Alonso García and four soldiers joined the fleeing Spaniards. Seeing these soldiers join the small Spanish group, the pueblos abandoned their pursuit.[36]

Some time after midnight, the ten Spaniards reached Zía, where they found Fray Nicolás Hurtado and three other Spaniards "fortified in the strongest part of the convent, with the beasts shut up inside." Gathering up these men, the group "escaped with great danger and much effort," fleeing toward Tamaya.[37] There, they found "no Indians . . . except some women." When the soldiers "asked them where the men were . . . they replied very volubly and bold[ly] that they had gone to kill all the Spaniards."[38]

Leaving Tamaya, the small group of Spaniards rode south along the Río Grande, gathering up survivors from that region. Everywhere, they found the settler's ranches abandoned, and again and again they heard that "the señor governor and captain-general and the people of the village are dead, as well as every one . . . from Sandía to Los Taos, which is the greater part of the territory of the kingdom."[39] At last they reached Isleta, but they "found it as disturbed as the rest." Seeing this, the survivors from the Río Abajo decided to follow "the route down the river" until they had left "the province of the rebellious Indians."[40]

The rumors that had reached the Río Abajo were, however, only partly true. As the reports said, Kastera had been unable to put down the revolt in the north; it was not true, however, that the governor and most of the Spaniards were dead. They had taken refuge at Santa Fe, where a pueblo delegate brought "two banners, one white and the other red." The white one, the delegate explained to Governor Otermín, "signified peace and the red one war." If Kastera "wished to choose the white," the Spaniards must agree "to leave the country." Should Kastera choose the red, the messenger warned, it would surely mean death, for Santa Fe was surrounded by many pueblo men prepared to fight.[41]

On Tuesday, August 13, Kastera's governor spurned the offer of peace. On Thursday night, men from Taos, Picurís, Jémez, and the Keres towns joined those surrounding Santa Fe. By Friday, August 14, "more than 2,500 Indians" were besieging the city. Kastera chose to fight this force, killing as many as three hundred of the pueblo warriors. By Monday, however, after two more days of siege, Governor Otermín decided that Kastera would have to abandon the city. The people had little food, much of Santa Fe was destroyed, and most of the survivors were women and children. Like their kinsmen to the south, they had heard that all of the other Spaniards were dead, so they had no hope of receiving help. With only "a few sheep, goats, and cows" for food, the survivors fled south.[42]

On August 25 and 26, the ragged group passed through San Felipe and the Río Grande villages south of Tamaya. From Santo Domingo to Sandía, the pueblos were empty. The Indians had gone to the mesas nearby, taking the horses and cattle with them.[43] As the Spaniards straggled southward, they saw the pueblos "watching the march and the camp from the highest points." One survivor wrote that the pueblos "remained quiet" as the Spaniards passed;[44] another recalled that the pueblos had been "verbally mocking and insulting" them.[45] Learning from a captive that the other Spaniards had gathered at Isleta and, from there, had gone south, Governor Otermín's group followed them.[46]

At El Paso del Norte, at the very edge of New Mexico, the survivors camped to count their losses. Twenty-one missionaries and more than three hundred soldiers, settlers, and servants were dead. Those who had made the long, slow journey south had no food and little clothing, having left behind all that they owned when they fled. Their few horses were in miserable condition. If the pueblos had not allowed them to leave, few could have survived.[47] With their homes and ranches, they had also lost their dreams and their illusions. The pueblos, they learned, had resented them from the start. Far from being willing converts, the Indians had only waited for a chance to drive Kastera away. They had been planning the revolt "constantly." The "resentment . . . in their hearts" had "been too strong from the time this kingdom was discovered." One captive told the Spaniards that "he had heard this resentment spoken of since he was of an age to understand." Though Kastera forbade it, the pueblos had "inherited . . . from their old men the things pertaining to their ancient customs."[48] Their anger had grown because "of the work they had to do for the Spaniards and the religious . . . [who] did not allow them to plant or do other things for their own needs."[49] Until the revolt, Kastera had neither seen nor imagined how great and widespread this resentment had been.

To the north, the pueblos rejoiced. At last they had driven Kastera from their lands. When spring came in 1681, there would be, for the first time since 1598, no Spaniards along the Río Grande. No crops planted that year would be taken in tribute to Kastera. No farmers would be forced to leave their own fields to work for Kastera. The hides carefully washed and cut and painted would hang in the pueblos, not in Spanish homes. Most important, the ancient ceremonies could once again be held openly. The people could meet in the plazas without fear. No friar would cut their hair or whip them or imprison their leaders, and their children would learn the people's ways without fear of Kastera's punishments. When the crops were harvested in 1681, it must have been a joyous time in the pueblos along the Río Grande and the Río Jémez.

Not long after the corn was gathered, however, ominous news began to travel north. Rapidly, the word spread from pueblo to pueblo. Kastera was coming back.

Even as they fled south, the Spaniards had not given up the hope of returning to New Mexico. Almost as soon as they reached El Paso, they had made the first plans to recapture the colony. From their defeat, they had learned the strength of pueblo resentment and the necessity for careful plans. There were, one Spaniard estimated, more than sixteen thousand rebels in the pueblos, and they could rely on support from an untold number of non-Pueblo Indian allies who also wanted to keep Kastera from "returning and making settlements." Many of the rebels were "skillful on horseback, and able to manage firearms as well as any Spaniard."[50] Although some Spaniards still hoped that all but a few rebels would be happy to see Kastera return to New Mexico, most had begun to realize that returning Spaniards would not be welcome in the pueblos. That recognition, however, did not deter Kastera. If the pueblos would not accept Spanish rule peacefully, then they must be "subjected and their allies intimidated by the authority of His Majesty."[51] When the governor sent word of the revolt to New Spain and Spain, he also described what would be needed to retake the region. Although the survivors were prepared to attempt the reconquest, additional soldiers and settlers would be required to vanquish the rebels and reestablish Kastera's authority. They would need cannons and a man to repair their armor. To replace property lost in the revolt, the settlers would require food, livestock, plows, hoes, axes, and tools. To prevent future losses, they should have padlocks to protect their property. In case the Indians had destroyed Kastera's records, the expedition would have to take copies of the laws that governed the kingdom.[52] By late 1681, the king of Spain had granted permission for the reconquest, and the necessary supplies had been assembled. The colony's women and children would remain at El Paso, while the soldiers completed their task.[53]

Once again, Kastera marched north along Río Grande. By December 1681,

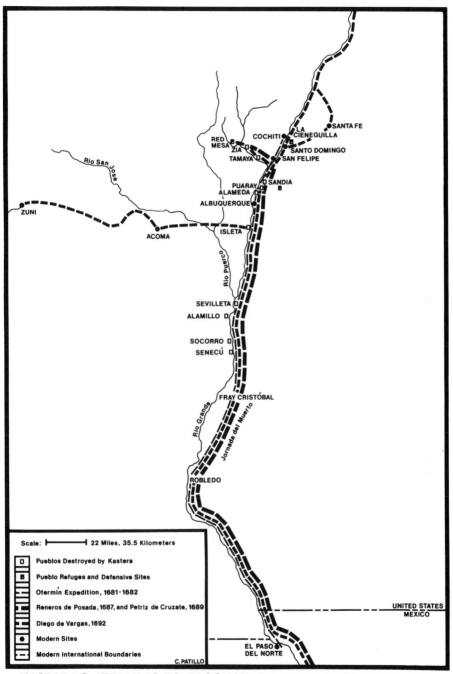

Scale: |———| 22 Miles, 35.5 Kilometers

□ Pueblos Destroyed by Kastera

▣ Pueblo Refuges and Defensive Sites

Otermín Expedition, 1681-1682

Reneros de Posada, 1687, and Petriz de Cruzate, 1689

Diego de Vargas, 1692

● Modern Sites

Modern International Boundaries

C. PATILLO

KASTERA'S ATTEMPTS TO RECONQUER THE PUEBLOS, 1680 - 1692

CHAPTER 4

Otermín's force had reached Isleta.[54] The main group camped there, while Juan Domingo de Mendoza led sixty soldiers north, with orders to investigate the region, burn all of the kivas, sack any abandoned pueblos, and recover the settlers' property.[55] All along the Río Grande, the soldiers found that the people had deserted their homes as soon as they learned of Kastera's approach. Taking their livestock, the pueblos had moved to more secure locations in the mountains and mesas. The people of San Felipe, Santo Domingo, and Cochití had gone to the mountains above Cieneguilla. The Tamayame had sought shelter with the people of Jémez and Zía on Red Mesa, near Jémez. People from all of the other pueblos except the distant Hopi assembled in these mountain and mesa camps.[56]

Mendoza camped near Cochití, ignoring the orders he had received to sack the vacant pueblos. From his camp, he sent word to the pueblo leaders in the mountains that Kastera had come to make peace. For the good of their souls, he told them, the pueblos should allow the friars to return. If they did so, Kastera would forgive them, and they would not be punished. Their women and children would be safe from harm. As a sign that they chose to accept Mendoza's offer of peace, the pueblos were instructed to set up crosses in their pueblos and along the roads.[57]

In their mountain camps, the pueblos debated. Some sent messengers to Mendoza's camp with the request that Mendoza send a letter to their leaders to confirm that the offer they had heard was genuine. While the pueblos waited for Kastera's reply, they continued to discuss what they should do. Some argued that it would be best to make peace with Kastera and return to their homes, for the weather had been cold and their supplies were running short. If Kastera truly meant to offer peace, they were ready to accept. Others, however, had heard that Kastera had already destroyed Isleta and killed its people. Some concluded that Kastera's offer of peace was nothing but a trap. Others said that the pueblos should spurn the offer, even if it proved to be genuine, whether or not Isleta had been destroyed. They had fought and their people had died to drive Kastera out, and if necessary, they would fight again; no matter what promises Kastera's leaders made, the Spaniards should not be allowed to return.[58]

Those who opposed Kastera's return, including many of the younger men, began to make their own plans. They decided to tell Mendoza that they had accepted his offer. Later, while they feasted and entertained the Spaniards, others would surround the camp. At a signal from one of their leaders, Catiti, they would attack the soldiers. A second group, led by Don Luis and El Ollita, would drive away Kastera's horses.[59]

Unaware of these plans, Mendoza waited for word from the pueblos whose delegates had promised to return to his camp. On December 16, word arrived from Tamaya and Zía. The governor of Santa Ana, a man known to Kastera as El Pupiste, or El Cupiste, came to meet with Mendoza. The Tamayame "in the sierras of Los Jémez," he said, "had received a letter" in which peace terms were offered. They were "suffering from the snow and cold of winter and wanted to return to their pueblos." If Kastera truly meant to offer peace, the governor would accept on behalf of the pueblos of Santa Ana and Zía. Assuring El Pupiste that Kastera indeed wanted peace, Mendoza told him to return to his people and instruct them to "erect arches" as a sign that they accepted Kastera's offer and to prepare to receive the Spaniards. Mendoza himself would come to visit them soon. The next morning, El Pupiste returned to the mesa camp with this message.[60]

Waiting for the pueblos' response, some of Kastera's soldiers grew suspicious. Several Indians had obtained gunpowder and horses from the Spaniards, promising to return, but they had not done so. Although some pueblo leaders had agreed to the peace, none of the people had yet come down from the mountain camps. When Mendoza asked the leaders to explain this, they replied "that the time he gave them was short, and that they could not do it within that time."[61] Some of the Spaniards suspected that this "was all deceit and cunning,"[62] and their doubts were confirmed the morning that El Pupiste left Kastera's camp, when a messenger came to warn them "that the peace had been false, and that the Indians desired to entrap the Spaniards under its security in order to kill them."[63] After remaining "under arms all night," Mendoza's force marched south to rejoin Otermín, without "setting fire to" the "pueblos of Cochiti, San Felipe, San Ildefonso, Santa Ana, and Zía" or taking the "large amount of grain and other provisions" in them.[64]

Reviewing the reports of Mendoza and his men, and questioning both Indian prisoners and Indians who came to give information, Governor Otermín began to piece together the complex events that followed the revolt in New Mexico. Some reports, encouraging to the Spaniards, suggested that all was not well among the pueblos and that, as hardships increased, the union forged in 1680 had begun to dissolve. The people disagreed about what should be done, and the bonds that had united them were weakening. Still it was also clear from the reports that, however divided the pueblos may have been about the proper course of action, they had little desire to give up their way of life or encourage Kastera's return. Most had stayed in the mountain camps, "preferring the rigor of the weather and the Apache enemies" to Kastera's overtures. In spite of the hardships, they remained "very well content with the life they [were] living, for they have always desired it."[65] Neither the "labors of the many" friars nor "the punishments inflicted by the various governors and ministers over a period of more than forty years" had led them to reject that way of life or to desire any other.[66] Some of Kastera's force had hoped that opposition would come only from the leaders of the revolt, not from the people in general, but they found that no promises and no arguments could persuade the people to come down from the mountains.[67] Although it had been "snowing on them for at least fourteen days in the heights of the sierras," and the pueblo people were suffering from the cold, they had "resolved to die rather than submit." One Spaniard suggested that "not even a punishment twice as severe as that of the weather would be sufficient" to force them out of the mountains while Kastera remained.[68]

The soldiers had not forgotten how strong the pueblos had been the previous year, and the leaders no longer underestimated the task before them. The Spaniards were a small group with few supplies, and already their horses were so weak that it was unlikely they would survive the winter. Otermín concluded that they did not have the force to attempt the reconquest, and that it would be wisest to return to El Paso del Norte for the time being.[69]

The first of January 1682, the day before the soldiers left Isleta, a Tiwa Indian from Puaray came to their camp "from the sierra of Los Jémez." There, he said, he had "left assembled and united the people of the pueblos of Alameda, Puaray, Sandía, Santa Ana, [and] Zía, and farther on the natives of the pueblo of Los Jémez." The people, he told Otermín, were "very happy without religious or Spaniards." The Tiwa pueblos, whose towns had been burned, planned to settle at another site to "be together and in a strong defensive position." The Tamayame would join the people of Zía. The people of San Felipe and Santo Domingo intended to settle at Cochití.[70] With this discouraging news, Kastera left the region for a second time.

It would be, however, only a temporary retreat. Kastera had not abandoned the hope of reconquering New Mexico, and Spanish forces would return again and again until they succeeded. In Domingo Jironza Petriz de Cruzate's first term as governor, Kastera made as many as seventeen forays into the north without achieving its goal.[71] Then, in 1687, another major expedition was sent to pueblo lands. Its target was Tamaya.[72]

The records do not show where the Tamayame were living when Pedro Reneros de Posada led Kastera north to attack them. Perhaps they were still on the mesa near Jémez where they had found refuge in 1681. Perhaps, as they had planned, they had joined the people of Zía. They may have settled in a pueblo on Black Mesa during this time. They could have gathered at Tamaya itself or a settlement near it on the Río Jémez. Perhaps the pueblo Posada attacked was one of the smaller farming settlements on the Río Grande.[73] The documents state only that Reneros de Posada laid siege to the home of the Tamayame, and that his soldiers "leveled the tiny pueblo of Santa Ana,"[74] and then moved on to mount an unsuccessful attack on Zía.[75]

Two years later, according to the Spanish records, Domingo Jironza Petriz de Cruzate, serving a second term as governor, led Kastera north to Zía again. The Spaniards burned the pueblo to the ground August 26, 1689, killing six hundred Zía people and their allies and taking others as prisoners.[76]

Only a few sentences in Kastera's documents record the fate of the Tamayame and their Zía neighbors. Tamayame tradition, however, recalls the events in greater detail. Once again, the tradition recounts, Kastera came to make the people Christian, and once again the people of Tamaya told Kastera that they had their own religion and wanted no other. Then the soldiers, with a man from Cochití, devised a plan: the man from Cochití would call the men of Tamaya, Tsiiya, and Hemishiitse together for an antelope hunt, telling them to be sure to bring all of the boys of ten years and older. This he did, and all of the men and boys left for the hunt, leaving only old men, women, and small children on the mesa. When the men had left, Kastera's soldiers marched into the settlement and captured all of the children who were about six years old.[77]

Seeing a signal from the pueblos, the men of Tamaya, Jémez, and Zía quickly returned, to learn the sad news from the weeping women. They met together to decide what to do. Then they tried to surround Kastera's camp, but as soon as they approached, the soldiers put the pueblo children forward, so that the men could not attack without the risk of harming them. For three or four days, the people stayed near Kastera's camp, trying to find a way to rescue their children, without success. At last, a Zía man who spoke Spanish said that since there was no way to save the children, he would go with them. Wherever Kastera took them, he would watch and learn all that the Spaniards taught them. Then he would return to the pueblos with news of the children. Having no other choice, the pueblos agreed, and the Zía man went to Kastera's camp. The next day, the soldiers left, taking the children with them.[78]

The stories recall that later, perhaps "a year or so" after the children were taken away, the Zía man returned. He told the Tamayame that "the children were all doing well and growing up and learning to speak Spanish and learning whatever they were taught to learn. Then he went back again, saying that he was going to return, but he never returned."[79]

CHAPTER 4

The people of Tamaya and Zía had suffered greatly. Their homes were destroyed; many of their people were dead; the survivors had been forced to flee to the mountain camps, where they suffered from cold and hunger. Worst of all, their children were gone, taken by Kastera. When the Spaniards returned in 1692, the Tamayame, still in the mountain camps, would take no further part in the fighting. Diego de Vargas came with word that Kastera had come to pardon them and to save their souls.[80] At last, reluctantly, the Tamayame agreed to accept Kastera's religion. With the people of Jémez, they gathered at Zía. There, in the plaza, they and their neighbors were baptized, and Kastera declared that Zía would be the center of the three kingdoms. Then the Spaniards ordered the people to return to their pueblos and begin the process of rebuilding.[81] After this ceremony at Zía, the Tamayame soon began constructing houses and a church.[82] In January 1694, when Fray Juan Alapuente arrived in Tamaya, the church was not yet finished, so the people gathered in the plaza to hear the friar say Mass.[83] Thus the revolt came to an end at Tamaya.

Around the pueblo, the fighting was to continue for some years before Kastera reconquered the region. For the Tamayame, however, hope of driving Kastera from their lands had vanished with their children. Acknowledging that this time Kastera would remain, the people turned their attention to rebuilding their homes and their lives. Once again, it would be necessary to hold the ceremonies in secret. But they would be held, as they had been since the days at Kashe K'atreti. The children would be taught Kastera's language and Kastera's religion, but they would also learn the ways of their own people, as Tamayame children had learned these things long before the first of Kastera's friars came to teach them. The pueblo would select officers to fill the positions Kastera named, and Kastera would recognize these men as Tamaya's leaders, but the Tamayame would still be governed, as they always had been, by the Tiyamune, the Mase'ewi, the U'uye'ewi, and their assistants. On that ancient foundation, a new pueblo would be built from the burned ruins that Kastera had left.

Tamaya in a Changing World

From the first, the Tamayame had found the upper world to be a place of change. Many peoples moved through this world, some searching for their homelands as the Tamayame had done on their long journey, others moving from place to place to gather food as the seasons changed. Some came to the villages to trade, others to raid the fields and storerooms of farming peoples like the Tamayame. Aware that their journeys were not yet finished, old neighbors left their homes, and new ones took their places. Directed by their leaders, the people would leave old farming villages to build new ones. They learned to know and use not only the familiar lands near their homes and fields, but also more distant places. They traveled to the mountains to hunt antelope and ventured out onto the distant plains in search of buffalo and salt. As time passed, they came to make and use new things and to remake the old in new ways. Even the land itself was constantly changing: rivers cut new channels, floods swept over the fields, and, layer by layer, hills were built up or washed away. So it had always been in this world.

Into this changing world, Kastera came as many peoples had come before, bringing strange ways, a new language, and unfamiliar goods. Slowly, as had so often happened in the past, some of these things became a part of life along the Río Grande. Some men planted peaches or grapes beside their corn and squash. Others learned to value metal hoes and knives. Women began to bake wheat bread in dome-shaped ovens like those Kastera used. Families acquired sheep, cows, or horses. Those who found Kastera's clothing, tools, animals, and foods useful or desirable made these things a part of their lives; those who did not welcome these new goods were free to ignore them.

Not all of what Kastera brought, however, was something that a pueblo could choose to accept or reject as a farmer might decide to plant or not to plant the unfamiliar seeds. The actions of Kastera's officials and the rule of Kastera's law would affect all of the people, no matter whether they accepted them, fought them, or ignored them. If one of Kastera's friars was evicted, another would be sent to take his place. Should one settler be forced off pueblo land, another Spaniard, seeing its promise, would soon claim it. Kastera had scarcely been driven from the region before word traveled north that the Spaniards planned to return. And return they did, bringing with them the beliefs, laws, and ways of using the land that had already caused such harm in the region, dangers that would multiply with Kastera's numbers in the coming years.

When the Hanu first came into the upper world, they soon discovered its perils. Farmers began to store harvests during the good years so that the people could survive the dry years that might follow. The people learned to build homes that would stand strong and secure through storms and raids. They came to know where they could find the things they needed. From generation to generation, this knowledge was passed on. Fathers taught their sons to lay the foundations of the pueblo firmly. Girls learned from their mothers to plaster the walls smoothly and evenly. That knowledge had kept the people secure from the familiar dangers. In the years after Kastera returned to reconquer the pueblos, however, these safeguards were no longer sufficient to protect the people. In this time, the Tamayame and their neighbors faced new dangers, perils that their ancestors could not have imagined. If Tamaya was to survive, the people would have to learn to counter the threats created by Kastera's laws, Kastera's settlers, and Kastera's way of life.

In the past, the land and water of this upper world had always been ample to provide for those who sought a home. On their journeys, the people found many places with resources enough to support them. If a people outgrew their pueblo, they could select new land on which to farm or build homes. If a spring failed or a stream dried up or floods covered the soil with sand, farmers could plant new fields in another location. For some of the pueblos, this had changed almost as soon as Kastera arrived. The newcomers built a town, and the farmers and ranchers demanded land and water. In these early years, some farmers and ranchers—like the families who settled near the modern site of Bernalillo—moved on or near to pueblo lands, and their livestock sometimes strayed into pueblo fields. Before 1680, however, Kastera's settlers and ranchers were relatively few, and the threat they posed to

Tamaya and many of the pueblos remote from Santa Fe seems to have been comparatively limited.

By the 1690s, however, for reasons unknown to the pueblos, Kastera's interests in the region had changed. Through the sixteenth and seventeenth centuries, Kastera and its European neighbors had raced to claim the lands of what they called the New World. As Oñate had done when he led the first of Kastera's settlers north to New Mexico, other Europeans had held ceremonies claiming vast regions in the names of their countries. These explorers, however, had little interest in settling the lands they claimed, particularly in regions that seemed unlikely to yield treasures of gold and silver, bales of fur, or rich harvests of valuable crops. In the vast unexplored areas of North America, all of the Europeans hoped to find golden lands, like those that Kastera had discovered in the south.

As the years passed, the search brought other Europeans ever closer to the land that Kastera claimed. French traders, priests, explorers, and trappers reached the Mississippi River and the Plains; Great Britain's colonists moved slowly westward, while its fur trappers and traders moved rapidly inland in search of beaver; far to the north, the Russians had begun to explore the Pacific Coast. Each of these expeditions, it seemed to Kastera's worried officials, brought outsiders closer to the rich mines of New Spain. At the same time, raiders from surrounding tribes began to threaten Kastera's settlements.[1]

These dangers suggested that New Mexico might take on a new role in Kastera's empire, acting as a buffer to protect the valuable southern colonies from the other Europeans and to control the Indian raiders attacking New Spain from the north. To fulfill that role, however, a much larger settlement would be required. In 1609, when New Mexico was a remote region of no interest to other Europeans, a few friars, a governor, and fifty soldiers, with only a few missions and a single town, had been sufficient to allow Kastera to maintain its claim. To secure the northern frontier in the century following the reconquest, Kastera needed a colony many times that size. By 1799, nearly nineteen thousand Spaniards, not counting those in El Paso, had settled in New Mexico.[2] Spaniards had spread throughout the Río Grande area, building towns at Santa Fe, Abiquiu, Santa Cruz de la Cañada, Albuquerque, Bernalillo, Tomé, Socorro, and San Miguel del Bado, with ranches and smaller settlements between the larger towns.[3]

Such rapid growth required vast amounts of land and water. Even as early as the 1690s, it was clear that the unclaimed lands and water of New Mexico might not be sufficient to meet the needs of the new towns and forts, the farmers, and the herds of livestock that would need extensive pastures. Thus, when Kastera decided to reoccupy New Mexico in the 1690s, officials were sent north with a body of regulations to determine how land and water would be assigned. These laws, established to govern land and water use in Spanish colonies throughout the New World, had been compiled in 1680 in a large volume known as the *Recopilación*.

Among this body of laws was one that set forth the rights of the native peoples: all Indians living within Kastera's colonies should "be left in possession of all the lands belonging to them, either individually or in communities, with the waters and irrigation streams and the lands which they shall have drained or otherwise improved."[4] In 1687, as Reneros de Posada marched north to destroy Tamaya, it was decided that each pueblo in New Mexico would be granted the lands that it used. If a pueblo needed more land than the customary grant of the square league around its town, it was to be given more. Under the new regulations, the governor of New Mexico, acting for the King of Spain, would give each pueblo a paper that confirmed its title to the granted lands. When these grants had been guaranteed to the pueblos, the governor would also have the authority to assign lands to Kastera's settlers and towns.[5]

Tamayame tradition recalls that such a grant was "made by the King of Spain to the Pueblo of Santa Ana the same as the other pueblos in the country."[6] This grant, however, included only the square of land around Tamaya itself, not all of the lands that the Tamayame used. According to tradition, the Tamayame were given a paper describing their lands, but because "it was frequently necessary to produce it in settling questions or disputes," the paper "at length got mislaid."[7] That grant, based on both the laws of the *Recopilación* and the 1687 decree, protected the land around the pueblo, the core of the Tamayame homeland.

The land protected by this grant, however, was only a small part of the land the Tamayame used. The square around the pueblo, where the peoples' homes were built, had been used for dry farming,[8] but it alone could not feed all of the Tamayame. Farming within the square was "really dependent on rains." Even for dry farming, this grant land was not ideal; a visiting friar later explained that the "uneven site" would "not permit the formation of pools to quicken and fertilize the plants."[9] According to one account, the Río Jémez often went dry or became too salty for farming. Floods frequently carried away the crops, leaving the fields covered with sand.[10] Tamayame farmers had never relied on the Río Jémez area alone to provide enough food for the people.[11] To obtain what they needed, they cultivated many sites more distant from Tamaya.

Farming villages and fields lay near the Río Grande—at Railroad Tamaya; at a site west of the place where the Jémez Dam would later stand; at Ranchiit'u; at East Point; at Buraikana; and at several places near Corrales. The Tamayame also farmed lands to the west, toward Zía.[12] These Tamayame farmlands, not protected by Tamaya's grant, did not long remain safe from Kastera. Even before the Pueblo Revolt, many Spaniards had settled in this area. By 1698, only six years after de Vargas led the first Spaniards back to New Mexico, Bernalillo had become an important Spanish center where soldiers were stationed. Old settlers returned and new ones arrived to claim the rich Río Grande lands that the Tamayame had farmed.[13] Spanish law should have protected these lands long used by the Tamayame, but Governor de Vargas instead awarded them to Spanish settlers, with priority going to those who had claimed the lands before the Revolt, or to their heirs.[14] Without the papers that Kastera respected, Tamaya's ancient claim to these lands was not considered, and it is unlikely that, in the first years of the eighteenth century, any Tamayame understood the Spanish laws that should have guaranteed Tamaya's rights to the lands and waters the pueblo needed. Thus it was Kastera's grant papers, rather than the Tamayame's long use of the lands, that came to be respected as proof of ownership.

If Tamaya was not to lose its farmlands forever, something had to be done quickly. Since it seemed that the only way for the Tamayame to regain these vital lands was to buy them back from the Spaniards who claimed them, the Tamayame began to do just that. They waited patiently, and whenever a Spaniard was willing to sell land in the area, the Tamayame asked Kastera's governor for permission to buy it. Each sale involved a complicated process. All parties had to agree on the land's boundaries, its price, and the terms of the sale; then, Kastera's governor had to approve it. Only then would Tamaya receive papers for the land. Some of the sales were quickly made and approved, but others required years of negotiation. Even after the grant was issued, a vague boundary description or a legal question could result in lawsuits over Tamaya's rights to the land.

Tamaya's first land purchase was approved in 1709, when nine Tamayame bought a site at the mouth of the Río Jémez from Manuel Baca. The land was bounded on the north "by the table-land; on the south by the river itself; on the west by the lands of the Pueblo of Santa Ana on the other bank."[15] The east boundary "constituted largely the bend in the Río Grande" (see map, page 218).[16]

Between 1709 and 1720, the Tamayame also bought a small plot from Captain Juan González, who had earlier purchased the land from Captain

Diego Montoya. This land was "a parcel bounded on the east by the Estero, or lagoon, along the Río Grande (prior to its westward avulsion, which apparently occurred about 1739), on the south by a line running along the north side of the house of Baltazar Perea, on the north by the lands of Javier Miranda, and on the west by the *ceja* (divide) of the Rio Puerco."[17]

Another purchase may have occurred between 1735 and 1741. According to some commentators, Tamaya bought land in the Ancón de Bernalillo from Juan Márquez, who was acting for his wife, Magdalena Baca, but no deed of sale was signed at the time because no paper was available. Nearly thirty years later, the sons of Magdalena Baca's first husband, Diego Montoya, brought suit against Antonio Baca, claiming that he had sold the land to Tamaya illegally. The decision allowed Tamaya to keep the lands.[18]

In 1742, the Tamayame bought land from Josefa Baca, the daughter of the Captain Baca who had made the first sale to the Tamayame. This parcel, for which Tamaya paid 900 pesos, had boundaries overlapping the tract the pueblo had purchased from Manuel Baca: it ran "along the west side of the river 'on the north at the river crossing [Salida] to Angostura where there is a tree which the Indians cut down, to the east the Rio del Norte [Rio Grande], on the south where the two rivers [Jémez and Río Grande] join, and to the west the lands of the same Pueblo.' The last referred to the Spanish league grant boundary." Seventy years later, the Tamayame asked their alcalde to make clean copies of these papers, which had become "torn and badly used."[19]

Purchase of the parcel known as the Rancho Viejo took more than twenty years to complete. Baltasar Romero had agreed to sell some land "on the other side of the river" to the Tamayame, but in 1734 Kastera's governor ruled that Romero could not do so because the land in question belonged to "Bernalillo, a very ancient settlement of Spaniards." If Romero wanted to sell his land, he would have to offer it to a Spaniard, not to the Tamayame, whose own settlements in the area were far more ancient.[20] In 1739, Romero's son Pedro signed a deed to Javier Miranda, confirming that his father had sold Miranda a tract of land near Bernalillo and a grove of trees, once part of the site, that had been cut off when the river changed course. Miranda included this parcel in his daughter's dowry, and in 1763, she, with the permission of Kastera's governor, empowered her husband, Alejandro Mora, to sell the land to Tamaya for 739 pesos. The deed was signed May 24, 1753; four days later, Kastera's governor approved the sale of the land, then known as Rancho Viejo, and ordered that a copy of the deed "be given to the Indians to serve them as an evidence of their title." The payment was made, as nearly all transactions were in New Mexico at the time, in goods rather than in cash. Thirty-five Tamayame "contributed to the purchase of the ranch with cows, oxen, horses," and other possessions. Two years later, Mora signed a receipt for the payment, and Antonio Baca ordered that the "receipt be attached to the Indians' documents."[21]

These purchases allowed the Tamayame to recover a significant portion of their traditional lands. Together they made up "a large area on the west side of the Río Grande north and south of the point where it is joined by the Jémez River. On the north, the lands purchased went as far as the Salida de Angostura, and on the south to a line through the Baltazar Perea house. The lands were bordered on the east by the river, and extended west to the boundaries of the Santa Ana Grant and beyond to the ceja of the Rio Puerco."[22] Acquiring these lands—which came to be known as the Rincon de Bernalillo—helped to resolve Tamaya's critical shortage of farmland and water, a shortage that had forced many Tamayame to leave the pueblo in search of farming lands. Some traveled south and west to lands at the Black Site (west of modern Alameda) and the Whipple site (inside modern Albuquerque), while others went farther west to the land along the Río Puerco south of Siiku (Mesa Prieta) near the area farmed by the Hanu during their long journey.[23] Even with these first purchases, the pueblo did not have enough land that could be irrigated effectively. As soon as they had acquired the new lands, the Tamayame began trying to irrigate the lands, but, after many hours of effort, they found that the lay of the land made it impossible to build a ditch that would carry water to the fields.[24]

In July 1763, the governor, cacique, and war chief of Tamaya, "with all the elderly and chief Indians of this Republic of the said Pueblo of Santa Ana," visited the alcalde in their district, Bernardo Miera y Pacheco, to explain to Kastera once again that they urgently needed land and water. They hoped to buy a large ranch north of Bernalillo whose owners—Quiteria Contreras (the widow of Cristóbal Martínez Gallego) and her son, Mariano Martínez—were willing to sell to them. Alcalde Mayor Miera y Pacheco presented their request to Kastera's governor, Tomás Vélez Cachupín, who gave his permission. The alcalde took charge of the proceedings, and the Tamayame and the Spanish landowners each chose an appraiser to study the land and decide on a fair price. The ranch comprised three tracts purchased by Gallego, who was known as "El Cojo," or "the Cripple," and held lands in and around Bernalillo in addition to those his widow was willing to sell. The first of these parcels Gallego had purchased for 1,700 pesos June 3, 1733, from Captain Manuel Baca, who had purchased it in 1706 from Don Fernando Duran y Chavez. Its boundaries were "on the north a cross which divides one half of the said Angostura. . . . ; on the south, the land of Captain Juan Gonzales Bernal; on the west the river, and on the east, the Sandía Mountain." Gallego acquired the second tract from Dona Josefa Baca, who had purchased it from Captain Juan Gonzales Bas in 1713. The deed executed in 1713 described this as land "for farming and the pasturage of cattle and sheep"; it located the tract generally on the east side of the Río Grande, "in front of" Bernalillo. Juan Gonzales Bas, the document noted, had acquired the land "by donation from Juan Domingues de Mendoza and Lucero de Godoy, and by new grant from the Admiral Marquis de la Penuela Don Jose Chacon." Gallego's deed included a more precise description of the property, which lay north of Bernalillo:

> A tract of land at the place of Bernalillo upon the other side of the
> river which has been commonly called that of Francisco Domingues,
> that its boundaries are upon the East as far as the Sandías, and upon
> the North below the house of Dona Anna, where there grows a
> spreading "Alamo"[cottonwood] nearby upon the south is a willow, in
> front of the house of old Montoya, right there is a lagoon ["Estero"],
> the Rio del Norte [Rio Grande] upon the west. . . .

Gallego bought the third parcel, "a piece of land [by] the house of Analla," from Antonio Baca February 8, 1849. Together these plots made up "a sizable ranch on the east side of the Rio Grande, directly across from the by then substantial holdings of Santa Ana and far more susceptible of irrigation than Santa Ana's land."[25]

On July 7, 1763, all of the people involved in the sale met at the ranch and agreed to a price of three thousand pesos, to be paid in livestock and other goods—an enormous amount, given that most land sales in the area at the time amounted to only a few hundred pesos. One by one, Tamaya's officers, the heads of Tamayame families, and other members of the pueblo brought forward their shares of the payment. The alcalde and the Spanish witnesses sat beneath a cottonwood tree, listing each of the items. All told, the Tamayame turned over 67 cows, "many with calves not counted"; 29 oxen; 8 bulls; 74 goats; 50 sheep; 3 mules; 8 horses, 1 mare, and 1 colt; 2 new bridles, 4 blankets, and 1 pot. The owners of the ranch agreed that this was a fair payment, and two days later Kastera's governor approved the sale. The Tamayame then received title to the land "bounded on the west by the Rio Del Norte [Río Grande], on the east by the foot of the Sierra de Sandía, on the north by the middle of the Angostura where is placed a cross and bounded with the property of the Pueblo of San Felipe, and on the south by the three cottonwoods" that stood near Gallego's former home. As Kastera measured it, this land covered 4,340 Castilian varas, or approximately 12,000 feet, north to south. Covering 12,000 or more acres, it made up the largest portion of the claim that would later be recognized as the Ranchiit'u.[26]

With title to these lands, many Tamayame were no longer forced to move away from Tamaya to find a way to support themselves. Yet each day during the spring, summer, and early fall, the farmers still had to make the journey to the Río Grande fields. The men and boys chosen to take care of the crops and the ditches set out early each morning, walking down the Río Jémez to Huuchaniitse, on the top of the hill, and then passing by Tuyuna on their way to the west bank of the Río Grande. To reach the Ranchiit'u fields, they had to cross the river. Sometimes they went across by holding to the tails of their oxen, but usually they made the crossing in boats made of logs from the Jémez mountains tied with rawhide and sealed with a mixture of piñon pitch and crushed bark. Each week the governor of the pueblo selected a K'anuwa— one man, or sometimes several—to take care of the boats, which were tied to huge cottonwood trees on the east bank of the Río Grande. When the Tamayame farmers reached the west bank, they called across the river to the K'anuwa, who untied a boat and paddled sideways across the river to pick them up. When they reached the east bank, they unloaded their burros and tools and went to their jobs. In the spring and early summer, some worked on the irrigation ditches, while others planted the corn and squash in the damp ground. Later in the year, they cultivated and watered the plants. When harvest time arrived, they gathered the crops and carried them back to Tamaya for the winter. Near the fields, the farmers built small huts of cottonwood in which they stored their tools and supplies. There, if need be, they could stay overnight, but most usually returned to Tamaya by nightfall.[27]

In these farmlands that the Tamayame had first seen on their long journey and later returned to, the farmers' labor soon brought rewards. In 1776, only thirteen years after the large purchase, one of Kastera's friars, Fray Francisco Atanasio Domínguez, watched the Tamayame working in the "good and fertile level sites" of the Ranchiit'u. By the time of his visit, these fields had "permanent irrigation" from the Río Grande, and Tamayame farmers were reaping "many good harvests of everything they plant."[28] Another friar, Juan Agustín de Morfi, who traveled through the region a few years later, saw that the need to use "canoes to cross" the Río Grande "when tilling is necessary" caused the Tamayame "much delay." At this time the people farmed a third of the Ranchiit'u and used the remainder of the purchase, which was covered with "poplars," for "pasture."[29]

The need for pastureland had become almost as critical as the need for

TAMAYAME LANDS IN 1766

Scale: |——————| 25 Miles, 40.3 Kilometers

Tamaya's Original Grant
(As Surveyed in 1876)

Ojo del Espiritu Santo Grant to Tamaya, Zia, and
Jemez, 1766 (As Surveyed in 1877)

Ranchii'u Purchases, 1709 - 1763
(Approximate Boundaries)

Santa Ana Archaeological Sites, c. 1600 - 1750
(Approximate Locations)

MODERN SITES

SPANISH SETTLEMENTS

C. PATILLO

Pecos R.

Galisteo Cr.

SAN FELIPE PUEBLO

ANGOSTURA

BERNALILLO GRANT

X BERNALILLO

Santa Ana Mesa

Rio Jemez

JEMEZ PUEBLO

ZIA PUEBLO

TAMAYA

Sandia Mts.

X ALAMEDA

X ALBUQUERUE

Rio Grande

X LA VENTANA

Ojo del Espiritu Santo

Rio Salado

San Felipe Mesa

Mesa Prieta

X NUESTRA SEÑORA DE LA LUZ DE LAS LAGUNITAS

Rio Puerco

farmland, for Tamaya's herds had grown rapidly, and the Tamayame had become caballeros as well as farmers. In the years after Kastera returned, the people used livestock to pay for many of the land purchases. Horses, oxen, and burros hauled their goods and tools to the farmlands, carried the crops back to Tamaya, and brought wood from the mountains to the pueblo. The herds also provided meat and hides for the Tamayame. Taking care of livestock had become a part of pueblo life: individuals herded their own cattle and sheep, but the horses were the responsibility of the pueblo as a whole, and men were assigned to care for them under the direction of the Mase'ewi and the Kuwachani.[30]

As their herds grew, the Tamayame needed additional grazing lands; the pasture available in the square grant and the Ranchiit'u could not support large herds. Tamayame herdsmen spread into the hills east of Ranchiit'u and the land on the mesa, and they shared an area to the west with the herdsmen of Zía and Jémez. This land included the valley of the Ojo del Espiritu Santo on the north, extended south to Mu'uwi (the volcanic peaks west of Albuquerque), and was bounded on the west by the lands at the base of Kene'ewa. The Tamayame, who had settled in this region for a time during their long journey, returned there to hunt antelope and to build farming villages after they settled at Tamaya. As their herds increased, they began to rely on this area for grazing.[31] According to one source, Kastera may have recognized the pueblos' use of this land, which included the "whole valley of the Holy Ghost Spring," as early as June 1713, in a grant made by Governor Juan Ignacio Flores Mogollon to the pueblos of Jémez, Zía, and Santa Ana. The three pueblos, however, apparently received no grant papers at that time; more than fifty years were to pass before they took "official possession" of this 382,849-acre grant.[32]

By the 1760s, Kastera's ranchers had moved into this land that Tamaya shared with two other pueblos. Just three years after Tamaya made its last large purchase in the Ranchiit'u, Spanish ranchers applied for grants to the Ojo del Espiritu Santo area.[33] With the people of Zía and Jémez, the Tamayame sent a petition to explain to Kastera's governor that they had long used this land to the west. Giving title to these lands to Spanish ranchers would result, they explained, in "very great injury" to the three pueblos, since none had "any other place to pasture" their herds. In addition to their own animals, they maintained "considerable cattle, sheep, goats, and horses for the royal service." Hoping to protect their grazing lands, the three pueblos asked Kastera's governor to deny the Spaniards' applications and to award the land to the pueblos that used it.[34]

Kastera's governor agreed, and in 1766 the three pueblos received a joint grant that included "the whole valley of the Ojo del Espiritu Santo." The grant boundaries ran "from north to south from the place Ventan [La Ventana] to the stone ford of the Puerco River, the boundaries also of the citizens of San Fernando de Nuestra Señora de la Luz; and from east to west from the pueblo of Zía to the eastern bank of the Puerco River."[35] It seemed that Kastera, as the law specified, had at last honored the pueblo's right to obtain title to lands the Tamayame needed and had long used.

Within a short time, however, the grant papers and deeds of sale would become ragged from handling, and the Tamayame would soon learn that papers alone could not protect a pueblo from trespassers who ignored the law. Possession of a deed of sale would not prevent disputes about who owned the land and water or where the boundaries lay. Again and again, the Tamayame would be forced to produce their papers as proof of their rights to a fraction of the lands their ancestors had used. What the two grants and the series of purchases did do, though, was to establish a firm legal foundation that would enable the Tamayame to defend their rights under Kastera's law.

Meanwhile, as the people dealt with Kastera's threat to their lands, they had to meet other challenges as well. Kastera's return brought the friars to Tamaya, no longer as visitors but as residents. In the early years of Kastera's rule, when converting the Indians was one of the principal justifications for Kastera's presence in New Mexico, the friars had had great importance in the colony as a whole, but little impact in the home of the Tamayame. Friars had visited the Tamayame to preach and baptize, and they had counted the Tamayame among the faithful in their optimistic reports, in spite of the fact that the people of Tamaya had told them again and again that they had neither need nor desire for Kastera's religion. Only when Tamaya lay in ruins, the pueblo's children held captive in Kastera's lands, did the Tamayame agree to accept Christianity. Tradition recalls that they went to Zía for baptism. When they returned to Tamaya to begin rebuilding their homes, they also began to construct a church for the friars that Kastera promised to send.[36]

In the years following the Reconquest, the friars were to play a comparatively minor role in the affairs of New Mexico, but a major one in the lives of the Tamayame. The first resident friar came to live at Tamaya in 1694. Twelve years later, a small church had been completed and furnished with a "a bell and one of the ornaments which his majesty gave, and a very old frontal." A friar visiting Tamaya counted "about three hundred and forty Christian Indians."[37]

No one friar had charge of Santa Ana for very long in these early years. Six friars served at the pueblo between 1700 and 1714; responsibility for the pueblo changed at least nine times in the following nine years.[38] Not all of these friars lived at Tamaya, however: sometimes the mission at Zía had charge of the Tamayame, and one friar, Fray Domingo de Araos, assigned to Tamaya in 1718, again in 1719, and from 1726 to 1729, lived in Bernalillo.[39] Visiting in 1744, Fray Miguel de Menchero noted that Tamaya's friar also taught "some of the Indians of the Navajo nation."[40] Tamaya's church grew slowly; additions to the original building were completed in 1712 and from 1715 to 1717. In 1716 a visitor praised Fray Pedro Montano for building a convent at Tamaya, as well as rebuilding the Bernalillo church.[41]

Accounts of the friars' activities at Tamaya in these years come largely from the reports of visiting churchmen sent to inspect Kastera's missions[42] and from the orders sent to the missionaries. These records hint at some of the challenges the friars faced. Perhaps the greatest obstacle was the language barrier: few of the friars spoke any Indian language, and, in the early years of the missions, the Tamayame and their neighbors understood little, if any, Spanish. The friars were repeatedly criticized for their inability to speak the peoples' languages. In 1730 a visiting bishop complained that since the Reconquest there had "not been, and is not, any minister who understands the languages of the Indians" in New Mexico. In 1741 Fray Juan José Padilla, who had served at Acoma and Laguna and knew the Keres language, received orders to write "a vocabulary" for the Keres. Twenty years later, the missionary at San Felipe had not yet fulfilled his commission to write a "guide to confession and catechism for the Keres."[43]

By the late 1720s and 1730s, numerous criticisms of the friars appeared in official reports. The friars were instructed not to leave their missions or go to Santa Fe without permission. They received orders not to bear arms or take part in the Indian trade. They were criticized because the settlers, instead of providing a model of Kastera's ways, had shown an interest in "Indian superstitions." Some friars were also charged with using Indian labor in ways prohibited by Kastera's laws and making illegal demands for Indian goods. In 1731 a new order proclaimed at Zía and Jémez stipulated that, to quiet the "malice and passion that reigns here," the friars should not "send Indians to any work outside the missions" or "accept even voluntary offerings for any sacraments."[44]

The reports suggest that these were difficult years at Tamaya. In 1728 the Tamayame left Tamaya and moved to the hills with the people of Jémez, Zía, and Cochití.[45] Two years later, when Bishop Crespo came to Tamaya to celebrate confirmations, they had returned to their homes,[46] but their complaints had not been resolved. The following year, officials heard testimony that the friar with responsibility for Tamaya, Fray Domingo de Araos, was guilty of neglecting and abusing the pueblos in his charge. Like most of the friars, Domingo de Araos was unable to speak the people's language. Later that year, he died at Santa Ana, "possibly from poison."[47]

In spite of the problems, the church, and the many foreign things that came with it, slowly became a part of Tamaya. Throughout this period, the friars directed periodic renovations and additions to the church buildings. During the time of Fray Diego Arias de Espinosa, who stayed at Tamaya from 1731 to 1734, the church was rebuilt with the help of woodworkers hired for the project. The new church was dedicated "in the time of Father Menchero," who visited Tamaya in 1731 and 1746.[48] During the tenure of Fray Juan Sanz de Lesaun, who came to Tamaya in 1750, the Tamayame added to the church again.[49] The Tamayame were required not only to maintain the buildings, but also to care for the friar. In 1754 Fray Trigo Istacalco described the services that the Tamayame provided:

> The Indians are few but they do a good deal, for they not only pro-vide for the convent with the weekly services of bell-ringer, porter, cook, two boys for the cell, and two grinding women with their two woodmen, but they all come as well to sow for the minister two *fan-egas* of wheat and one *almud* of corn, thus assuring him of subsistence for the year. The minister has to provide himself with sheep, wine, and wax, the staples which he needs without allowing for incidental necessities, for the Indians do not pay parochial dues.[50]

In 1760 Bishop Pedro Tamarón y Romerol visited Tamaya and reported that he had preached to "104 Indian families, with 404 persons," and cele-brated 178 confirmations.[51] By 1776, when Fray Francisco Atanasio Domín-guez traveled to New Mexico to make a complete report on the pueblos and missions, the church was clearly a part of Tamayame life. In Kastera's eyes, the Tamayame had become the people of Santa Ana, whose portrait hung on the church walls. At the very center of the pueblo, with four house blocks to one side and five to the other, stood the large adobe church with its adobe buttresses. To the north, just touching the front of the church, a convent had been built to provide cells, storerooms, a kitchen, and a courtyard for the friars. The buildings were filled with things that Kastera had brought or sent to Tamaya, including oil paintings in the church of Saint Anne, Saint Francis, Saint Dominic, and others—some "so old that they are indistinguishable."

The king of Spain had sent an altar stone and brass candlesticks, as well as the oil painting of Saint Anne. The friars, who wore vestments of "mother-of-pearl Madrid silk," damask "trimmed with fine gold galloon," and purple satin, had prayerbooks, ledgers, chalices, and vials of holy oil from Europe.[52]

With these unfamiliar objects came new duties. Each year Tamaya chose an officer, known as the chief fiscal, to serve the mission and to represent the people before the friars. "Eight sacristans and a chief sacristan" were appointed to care for the church, and each week the fiscal, two of the sacristans, two cooks, four bakers, and "two big girls to carry water" were assigned to serve the mission at Santa Ana.[53] Tamayame women plastered the church walls once a year,[54] and Tamayame herdsmen took "turns weekly as caretakers of the sheep, cows, hens, pigs, and horses" belonging to the mission.[55] Farmers planted "wheat and maize" on a plot east of the Río Grande, in the Ranchiit'u, that had been "assigned to the convent."[56] Until the Río Jémez flooded, the convent had also had a "good large kitchen garden on the same bank where it stands, below near the river."[57] The Tamayame had learned to speak Kastera's language, though "brokenly,"[58] and they celebrated the feast of Saint Anne each summer.

To Kastera, these things meant that the Tamayame had become the people of Santa Ana. Yet even the friars' own reports also make it clear that they were still the people of Tamaya. If the church had become part of their lives, the Tamayame had also had an influence on the church. Beside the Spanish missals, the oil paintings, the king's altar stone, and the lavish vestments stood the things of Tamaya—a "small buffalo skin carpet" and an adobe altar. The church itself, like the houses around it, was built of adobes made by the Tamayame. Kastera's church bell had gone "to pieces"; the adobe arch that once held the bell stood empty, and a pueblo "war drum" summoned the people to church services.[59] At least one of the friars had left the church largely in the hands of the Tamayame, for Fray Abadiano was told "not to leave the things pertaining to the church in the care of the Indians alone, but, in so far as he is able, to examine and care personally for what pertains to divine worship."[60]

Most important, though the friars' reports did not mention it, was the fact that the Tamayame had not forsaken their own beliefs. They chose the new officers, built the new church, and held the new ceremonies, but, still guided by their traditional religious leader, they also saw to it that the duties and ceremonies given to the Hanu when they entered this upper world were not neglected. They could no longer hold the ceremonies in the plaza or teach their children openly about these ways, but they had not forgotten them.

CHAPTER 5

As Kastera's church slowly became a part of the people's lives, so too did the system of government Kastera had established at Tamaya and the other pueblos. Once a year, Tamaya chose a group of officers to represent the people before Kastera's officials. Although the traditional leaders still governed the pueblo, Kastera would recognize only these new officers. As a sign of their authority, these men were given canes of office, duplicates of those carried by Spanish officials. Each year, soon after they took office, the new leaders might travel to Santa Fe, where Kastera's governor would formally recognize them as the pueblo's representatives.[61]

The pueblo's new leaders would speak to Kastera's officials on behalf of Tamaya in matters both large and small. It was their responsibility to care for the pueblo's grant papers and documents. When Tamaya needed to obtain additional lands, the pueblo's governor would present the people's petition to Kastera's governor. If Spaniards trespassed on Tamaya's land or violated the people's rights, the governor would deliver Tamaya's protest to Spanish officials. It was also the governor's responsibility to see that the pueblo paid taxes or tithes according to Kastera's laws. Because, under Kastera's government, no one could travel out of the region without permission, Tamaya's officers had to request a special pass when any Tamayame planned to join a salt-gathering expedition, go to the Plains to hunt buffalo, or leave the area for any other reason. Word came to the pueblo's officers whenever Kastera needed pueblo men to serve in the militia, to join the settlers' salt caravans, or to provide some service to the government.[62]

Compared to the pueblo governments, Kastera's government was a vast system, but the pueblos dealt directly with only a small part of that system. Most of their contacts were with the alcalde mayor who was chosen to represent New Mexico's governor in their district. Typically an alcalde's district included one or more pueblos, at least one Spanish town or settlement, and the ranches between them. The number of *alcaldías,* or districts, in New Mexico varied, but in the late eighteenth century there were eight. Tamaya was assigned to the Alcaldía of the Queres (Keres), which included the pueblos of Tamaya, Jémez, and Zía, and the nearby Spanish ranches and settlements. The alcalde made his headquarters upriver at Jémez.[63]

The man who served as alcalde mayor had broad powers within the district. It was his duty to supervise land matters, have copies of official papers drawn up, investigate and resolve disputes, and present the pueblos' requests for land to Kastera's governor. He sent notices of taxes, tithes, militia campaigns, salt caravans, and other official business to the pueblo governors. He informed the pueblos of orders and laws that affected them, granted permission for those who traveled outside their own lands, and made sure Kastera's government paid pueblo workers for their services.[64]

With these broad powers, a worthy alcalde could protect a pueblo from trespass and abuse, explain the pueblo's concerns to Kastera's government, see to it that nearby ranchers did not allow their stock to wander onto pueblo land, make sure that the pueblo was not charged an unfair price for lands it purchased, mark the boundaries of pueblo lands accurately, and provide copies of the necessary official papers.

If an honest alcalde could do a great deal to assist a pueblo, a dishonest or disinterested one could also do great harm. Such a man could allow settlers to trespass on pueblo lands or look the other way when the ranchers' stock grazed in pueblo fields. He could permit a land sale or grant that damaged the pueblo's interest, or mark the boundary so that it would benefit a Spanish rancher at the pueblo's expense. A powerful alcalde who chose to ignore the law could force pueblo people to work without pay for the Spaniards or even confiscate pueblo property.

A pueblo could be injured even by the most conscientious alcalde, for each alcalde had responsibility for several pueblos, as well as the neighboring Spanish towns and ranches. When their interests conflicted, as often happened, no alcalde could represent all of the parties fairly. His decision, no matter how thoughtful, might well benefit one group at the expense of the others. Those whose problems he knew best or those whose interests he shared might obtain his attention and his sympathy, though others also had valid claims.

Among the alcaldes who served in Tamaya's district, at least two were generally sympathetic to the pueblo's interests: Bernardo Miera y Pacheco, known to history for the maps he made of the region; and Ignacio María Sánchez Vergara, later appointed as the Protector of the Indians of New Mexico.[65] Both men explained Tamaya's concerns to Kastera's governors. Understanding Tamaya's need for farmlands, Miera y Pacheco helped the Tamayame to make the large purchase in the Ranchiit'u and kept careful records of it. Other alcaldes also defended Tamaya's interest. Some took care to see that the Tamayame were paid and supplied with the horses they needed for government services. When the friars neglected Tamaya and the other pueblos in the region, alcaldes from the surrounding districts joined in protest.[66]

Unfortunately not all of the alcaldes served Tamaya so well. The most strident criticism of the officials came from the friars, whose interests, in the eighteenth century as in earlier times, often differed from those of the settlers and officials. This rivalry resulted in many charges of abuse on both sides, some, no doubt, founded on little more than the conflict of interests.[67] As a result of conflicting Spanish interests, however, specific pueblo complaints were also recorded in Kastera's documents. Fray Ruiz, the missionary at Jémez from 1769 to 1778, declared that he "found it necessary to carry on a war with" Alcalde José Miguel de la Pena, who was responsible for the Jémez district that included Tamaya. Fray Ruiz charged that the alcalde "set out to skin the Indians, demanding sheep, pregnant cows, maize, etc., in the governor's name" and laid "such a burden on the six pueblos under his command that the Indians cried out."[68] Like many of the friars who complained about Kastera's officials, Ruiz believed that the alcalde's actions interfered with the work of the church in the pueblos.[69] Other Spaniards agreed, describing José Miguel de la Pena as among the "worst of the gang" of alcaldes.[70]

This dual system of officials and friars gave the Tamayame some recourse against abuses. Tamayame could enlist the friar to complain to his superiors about the alcalde or the governor. At the same time, Tamaya could also pursue formal complaints through civil channels. Like the Spaniards in the region, they had the right to make a formal appeal to the governor in Santa Fe if they were dissatisfied with an alcalde's decision. Then, if the governor of New Mexico did not resolve the problem, they could bring the matter before the Royal Audiencia in Guadalajara. From time to time, Kastera appointed a man to serve as Protector of the Indians of New Mexico, giving the pueblos another opportunity to protest abuses.[71] Resolving a problem in this way, however, involved a long and difficult process with no guarantee of a favorable outcome.

By the late 1700s, the Tamayame were involved in a boundary dispute with San Felipe over the lands Tamaya had purchased. The sources of the conflict were twofold: first, the Río Grande, which had marked the boundary of Tamaya's first purchases west of the river, had shifted its course to the west, probably by about 1739; second, San Felipe had begun to sell lands in the Angostura region to Spaniards—lands that belonged, not to San Felipe, but to Tamaya. The first sales occurred as early as 1782, when Tamaya's leaders protested to the alcalde that the Tamayame had been doubly injured: first, when the river damaged Tamayame lands by moving to the west; and then when San Felipe sold some of the land near the river, land that rightfully belonged to Tamaya. In 1797 Tamaya's alcalde, Nerio Antonio Montoya, worked out a compromise in which the pueblos agreed to redraw the border down the middle of the old riverbed. San Felipe people, however, continued to sell land in this region. Eleven years later, Tamaya complained once again, this time to Kastera's governor. Once again, Kastera's officials did nothing to protect Tamaya's rights.[72]

At last, in 1813, Tamaya appealed directly to the Protector of the Indians, Felipe Sandoval. Tamaya's governor, Eusevio or Eusebio Mairo, sent a petition to Sandoval on May 5, explaining that, although Tamaya had continually protested to the alcalde and the governor, San Felipes had continued selling Tamayame land to Spaniards. Governor Mairo also charged that San Felipes "had been destroying the timber" on these Angostura lands. Tamaya's governor suggested that "if there should be much more delay in the matter all the timber would be destroyed before a decision could be had."[73] Already, more than thirty years had passed and the problem had not been resolved.

This time, Tamaya's appeal was not ignored. Within five days, the acting governor of New Mexico, Lieutenant Colonel José Manrique, told Alcalde José Pino of Albuquerque to investigate the problem.[74] Pino contacted Felipe Sandoval and the alcaldes of the Keres (Jémez) and Alameda districts to which Tamaya and San Felipe belonged. Three days later, May 13, officials from both pueblos, the two alcaldes, and Alcalde Pino met at the site of the disputed lands. Tamaya's leaders showed Pino the title to their Ranchiit'u lands, a title which placed the boundaries of Tamayame land at the "salida de Angostura," in a location once marked by a tree trunk known to all of the Indians. The south boundary of the tract lay at the junction of the Río Grande and the Río Jémez. To the west, the boundary line adjoined the boundary of Tamaya's "Spanish league" grant. All of the parties agreed that the eastern boundary in the northern section of the purchase had been defined by the Río Grande.[75]

After studying the deeds, inspecting the area, and hearing testimony on May 14 about the changing boundaries of the river, Alcalde Pino issued his decisions on both the northern boundary and the eastern boundary of the northernmost parcel of Tamaya's land. The tree that had once marked the northern border had long since been cut down, and with the approval of everyone involved, Alcalde Pino set up a pile of stones to mark the Salida of the Angostura as the north boundary. He could not find the markers on the eastern boundary of the northern section, where the river had changed course, so he suggested that the eastern line be redrawn to run along Tamaya's irrigation ditch. The Tamayame would retain title to all of the land west of the new line; San Felipe would be given the land east of the line. San Felipe would have to repay the Spaniards to whom they had sold pieces of Tamaya's land. The Spaniards, who had used the nearby woods and pastures "to the injury of both pueblos," would have to give up the land, but would receive compensation from San Felipe. All parties seemed, at the time, to be satisfied with this decision.[76]

After studying the matter, however, the people of San Felipe decided not to accept Pino's decision, and within a week, they sent a protest to the Protector of the Indians.[77] As a result, Protector Sandoval faced a dilemma: by law, he was responsible for the welfare of all Indians in New Mexico, but in this matter he could not represent the interests of both pueblos at the same time. His first petition had outlined Tamaya's problems. His second asked the governor, on behalf of San Felipe, to reject Pino's decision and draw a new straight line between the two pueblos.[78]

Unwilling to decide the matter on the basis of these conflicting reports, Acting Governor Manrique ordered an officer of the Santa Fe Presidial Company to inspect the matter again and prepare another report. That officer, José María de Arze, met with the two pueblos, their alcaldes, Alcalde Pino, and Protector Sandoval June 5 and 6. The following day, he sent reports to Manrique. After studying the documents, he found that San Felipe had not produced a single paper describing the boundary they claimed; instead that pueblo's land grant papers clearly showed that San Felipe was trespassing on the lands bought by Santa Ana.[79] First Arze marked the northern boundary at the Salida of the Angostura, where Tamaya's papers placed it. Then he studied the descriptions of the troublesome eastern boundary, read the accounts of the 1797 compromise, and tried to find the markers Alcalde Montoya had placed at that time. At last, he found one of them in the old bed of the Río Grande, near the hills to the east. Using that marker as a guide, Arze calculated where the river had run and then placed new markers along the eastern line (see map on page 218).[80]

When Arze had redrawn the border, he met with leaders of both pueblos to read an "account of the establishment of the boundary along the center of the old river bed, by Don Nerio Antonio Montoya." After hearing this account, the leaders agreed to reestablish the border as Arze had marked it. Then the leaders had to resolve what would happen to the lands that had been divided according to Pino's compromise. The Tamayame had planted crops on the land assigned to them by Alcalde Pino, some of which would fall to San Felipe under the new agreement. San Felipe's leaders agreed that the Tamayame could harvest the crops they had already planted that year. The Spaniards who had bought the disputed lands would return them to Tamaya, and San Felipe would settle their complaints by returning the purchase price or offering them other lands in exchange. Arze reviewed the terms one last time, asking all of the participants if they could accept this agreement. He had a copy of the account of Montoya's compromise made for San Felipe. Then he reminded the people of Tamaya and San Felipe to see that the markers remained in place so that they would be able to find the border even if the river changed course again. After reading Arze's reports, Acting Governor Manrique approved his decision June 18, 1813.[81]

After more than thirty years of protesting to the alcalde and to Kastera's governor, it seemed that the Tamayame had at last obtained justice by appealing to the Protector of the Indians. Complaints continued, however, so the governor sent the case on to the Royal Audiencia at Guadalajara for review. It published its decision on April 19, 1817. Nearly a year later, apparently in response to another appeal from the Protector of the Indians, the Audiencia approved a request to "restore the lands in question to their rightful owners, and to give a hearing to the persons who had bought them with a view to providing other lands for them on the royal domain and entirely separated from the lands of the Indians." By May 1818 a message had been sent to inform New Mexico's governor of the decree. Because no response was received from New Mexico, the Audiencia's secretary prepared a copy of the proceedings January 14, 1819, in Guadalajara. This copy of the decree, directing the return of Santa Ana lands and the compensation of Spaniards who had been sold the lands, reached Santa Fe by March or April of that year.[82]

Fully two years after the Audiencia's decision, the alcalde at Albuquerque, Jose or Josef Mariano de la Peña, received orders to carry out its rulings. May 7, 1819, Peña inspected the area with Governor Juan Jose El Cuate of Santa Ana and Governor Juan de Jesus Martin of San Felipe. Later Peña reported that he had visited the lands with the Protector of the Indians, Ignacio María Sánchez Vergara, and, having studied the matter carefully, he believed that the border should be redrawn to compensate Santa Ana for the damage caused when the Río Grande changed course in the Angostura. He recommended drawing the new line at the eastern edge of the old riverbed rather than down its center, as Arze had proposed.[83]

The alcalde then notified the Spaniards who had bought Tamaya's land from San Felipe people between 1782 and 1816—Juan Estavan Pino of Santa Fe, Pablo Montoya of los Golondrianas, Jose Garcia, Alonso Garcia, Diego Chavez, Juan Domingo Archibeque, Pablo or Lallo Archibeque, Francisco Gutiérrez, and Fray Geronimo Riega. He met with the purchasers at the Rancho Anaya May 8. Not all of the Spaniards attended: some were absent, some were ill, and some were represented by individuals who used, but did not own, the lands. All were told that they must restore the lands that they had purchased in the Angostura area to Santa Ana, the rightful owner, but that they would either be paid in full or be given other lands from the royal domain near Socorro or between San Felipe and Santo Domingo to compensate them for the loss. At the Spaniards' request, the alcalde asked Governor Facundo Melgares to give them permission to plant the Angostura lands that year, since it would be too late for them to irrigate new lands and put in crops. Governor Melgares, however, replied that he had no authority to grant the request; he told the Spaniards that only the Tamayame, who were the rightful owners of the land, could give permission for anyone to use it.[84]

A few weeks later, Protector of the Indians Sánchez Vergara informed Governor Melgares that San Felipe was selling land near Algodones to the Spaniards. According to one account, Sánchez Vergara urged that Tamaya be allowed to buy this land, since it appeared that San Felipe had no need of it. He explained that the Tamayame desperately needed additional lands and hoped to buy these parcels so that they could move near to the Río Grande, where they already had farmlands.[85] In the end, however, it was determined that the Algodones lands would be given to the Spaniards in compensation, a proposal that received the approval of Governor Manrique and, despite his earlier recommendation, the Protector of the Indians. Thus, from August 5 to August 12, 1819, Alcalde Pena met with the Spanish claimants and awarded lands at Algodones to Juan Domingo Archibeque, Juan Pablo Archibeque, Francisco Gutiérrez, Jose and Alonso Garcia, and Bles Chavez. The same month, Peña drew up his final report. After visiting San Felipe and inspecting the pueblo's deed to the Angostura lands, he felt confident that he had decided the matter correctly. He concluded that the disputed land clearly belonged to Santa Ana, not to San Felipe.[86] The Protector of the Indians reported that, by October, the alcalde had "turned over to the Santa Ana Indians the lands which belonged to them but had been sold by the Indians of San Felipe." Sánchez Vergara had drawn up a "document for the protection of the Santa Ana people, who were to keep it in their possession" as proof of their title to the Angostura lands. The original document was to remain in the Protector's office.[87]

The Royal Audiencia at Guadalajara was notified, and at last the matter seemed to be settled. For nearly forty years, the Tamayame had lost the use of these lands and the valuable timber taken from them. They would receive no compensation for the losses they had already incurred during the long process of appeals. The pueblo, however, had received papers intended to protect its title to these lands, and the border had been clearly marked to prevent further disputes.

Within only three years, however, the Tamayame would be required to produce the pueblo's documents "in regard to a number of suits between the Indians of San Felipe and those of Santa Ana, which arose from the fact that the former had sold a piece of land which belonged to the latter."[88] Once again, officials would go to the Angostura to investigate, study the history of the lands, question pueblo officials about the problem, and submit reports on the matter. But when the question arose again in 1822, it would not be Kastera's officials who would decide it, for, after nearly three hundred years in New Mexico, Kastera's rule was coming to an end.

In little more than a century, the world around Tamaya had changed greatly, and already other strangers were moving toward the Río Grande, with ways and expectations that would prove to be as foreign as those of Kastera. The homeland that the Hanu had chosen was no longer as it had once been. Some things told of in the tradition were gone forever, like the children who would never return to Tamaya. Things once foreign to Tamaya, like the church that stood in the center of the pueblo and the horses that grazed on the mesa, had grown familiar.

But if this world had changed, it had not changed beyond all recognition. Still the Tamayame performed the ceremonies they had learned when they first came into the upper world. As their fathers and grandfathers had done before them, the farmers would plant their seeds in the damp ground near the river when spring arrived and tend the fields through the summer, until the ripe corn could be harvested and carried to pueblo storerooms. In new tasks and old, the Tamayame were guided by their traditional leaders. And still, in the center of the homeland they had chosen, in the land where the journey had come to an end, Tamaya stood secure.

SIX

Tamaya Besieged

By the early nineteenth century, signs of the great changes that had taken place could be seen throughout Tamayame lands. Ferried by the K'anuwa, Tamayame farmers crossed the river to the Ranchiit'u fields to tend their crops. Herdsmen traveled to the mesa in the Ranchiit'u and to the Espiritu Santo lands to the west to find pasture for the pueblo's cows, sheep, and horses. The children of Tamaya grew up learning two ways of life: the traditions of the Hanu, passed on by their elders, and the religion, language, and ways of Kastera, taught by the friars. When the *fiscal* called the people to the adobe church at the center of Tamaya, they might pray for rain along the Río Grande or give thanks for the birth of a child in Spain's royal family.[1] At midsummer the pueblo celebrated the feasts of Kastera's Santiago and Santa Ana in the plaza, but throughout the year, out of the friars' sight, the Tamayame held the ancient ceremonies of the Hanu.

In the governor's keeping were the land papers and a silver-tipped cane, signs of Tamaya's standing in Kastera's world. A hundred years after the first resident friar had come to the pueblo, that world was no longer a remote kingdom with only a few representatives in New Mexico. Soon after Kastera's calendar marked the beginning of a new century, the records showed that 458 Spaniards had made their homes in the district that included Tamaya, Zía, and Jémez. Nearly 1,500 lived in the district of Alameda, Sandía, San Felipe, and Cochití, and 4,000 had settled in and around Albuquerque.[2] To the west, at the edge of the Espiritu Santo lands, the people of Tamaya, Zía, and Jémez shared a boundary with the town of Nuestra Señora de la Luz. Near Tamaya's Ranchiit'u lands stood the settlements of Bernalillo and Algodones, where the Spaniards would soon be granted a license to build a chapel.[3] Southwest of Tamaya, near Tamayame farmlands, the Spaniards had built settlements at Corrales and Alameda. Tamayame lands stood like islands in the midst of Kastera's settlements.

Tamaya's neighbors had not been left untouched by these events, and the changes that came to them also came, like ripples, toward Tamaya. A hundred years after Kastera's return, those ripples were gathering into swift currents that would alter the contours of the world along the Río Grande.

When Kastera came to the Río Grande, the Tamayame had shared this land with many peoples. Nearest to Tamaya were the homes and fields of other farming peoples who lived much as they did, building pueblos, tending their crops, making distinctive types of pottery. Among them were the speakers of Keres languages, most closely related to the Tamayame. Once their ancestors had all shared a common language. As they traveled through the upper world, however, they split into smaller groups, each going its own way and finding its own homeland. Some of the people settled at Acoma and Laguna, in the west. Others traveled east to the Galisteo Basin, as the Tamayame did; some ended their journey there, while the Tamayame moved on in search of their homeland. Other Keres groups moved into the lands along the Río Grande and the Río Jémez, where they built the pueblos of Zía, San Felipe, Santo Domingo, and Cochití. As their journeys took them apart from one another, their languages began to change, but they remained similar enough that the relationship among them was clear.

Still other pueblo peoples, who shared a similar way of life but spoke completely different languages, also settled in the region. North and east of Tamaya, along the Río Grande, were the Tiwa peoples of Taos and Picurís and the Tewa peoples of San Juan, Nambé, Pojoaque, Tesuque, Santa Clara, and San Ildefonso. The Towa peoples built pueblos at Jémez and Pecos. The Tanos settled in the Galisteo Basin and in the valley of the Santa Fe River to the east. Along the Río Grande, from its junction with the Río Jémez south to Isleta, Southern Tiwa groups built pueblos, some of which stood across from Tamayame farm villages and fields on the opposite bank. Still farther south lay the pueblos of the Piro and Tompiro peoples. To the west, beyond Acoma, the peoples of Zuñi and Hopi found their homes.[4]

While these peoples settled their homelands, other peoples began to move into the mountains, basins, and plains beyond, bringing ways of life very different from those of the Tamayame and their neighbors. These newcomers did not settle in large permanent villages, and, though some had learned to farm on their journeys, none cultivated fields as the pueblos did. Instead, they traveled through a wide area as the seasons changed to gather and hunt what they needed. Moving regularly on this seasonal round, they used brush, hide, and wood to build homes they could carry with them or temporary shelters they could leave behind. They lived and traveled, not in villages with hundreds or thousands of residents, but in small family groups or bands, each with its own leaders. While these bands might meet with other related groups throughout the year, they remained independent, recognizing no common leaders such as Tamaya's Mase'ewi, U'uye'ewi, and Kuwachani.

Like the pueblo peoples, these peoples shared a general way of life but spoke many languages and came from many places. From the far north came the Athapascan-speaking peoples who, after Kastera reached the Río Grande, came to be known as the Navajos and Apaches. In small groups, they moved slowly into the lands north and west of the Río Grande.[5] Some may have reached the lands west of Tamaya while the Tamayame were making the circular journey that took them from Paak'u to Acu, for tradition recalls that the Tsiiyame asked Navajos to help them attack the Tamayame village at Kwiiste Puu Tamaya.[6] While the Navajos settled north of the pueblos, near Gobernador Canyon, in a homeland they called the Dinétah, Apache groups moved into the lands north and east of the Río Grande.[7]

From the west came speakers of Uto-Aztecan languages, whose descendants would become known as the Ute, Shoshone, Paiute, and Comanche peoples. They too lived by following the seasonal round, traveling in small groups. As the Anasazi pueblos of the San Juan region were being abandoned, the first of these peoples moved into the Great Basin lands of Nevada and Utah. Northern Paiute bands found homelands throughout Nevada and the region to the north, while southern Paiutes moved into the desert and basin lands of Utah and Nevada. Utes spread through Utah and into the mountain parks of Colorado. Shoshones moved north and east through Nevada to the lands drained by the Snake, Yellowstone, Upper Platte, and Missouri rivers. In the seventeenth century, the people who became the Comanches split from these Shoshone bands and began to move south though the Rocky Mountains.[8]

To all of these peoples, Kastera's presence brought great changes. The pueblos, in whose lands Kastera settled, were the first to suffer from contact with the region's most recent arrivals. When Kastera reached the Río Grande in the sixteenth century, eighty or more pueblo villages stood in the region between the Hopi towns in the west and Pecos in the east, from Taos in the north to the lands south and east of Socorro. By 1692, when de Vargas led Kastera north again, fewer than thirty of those pueblos remained. As the Spanish population grew, years of drought, conflict, and disease took a great

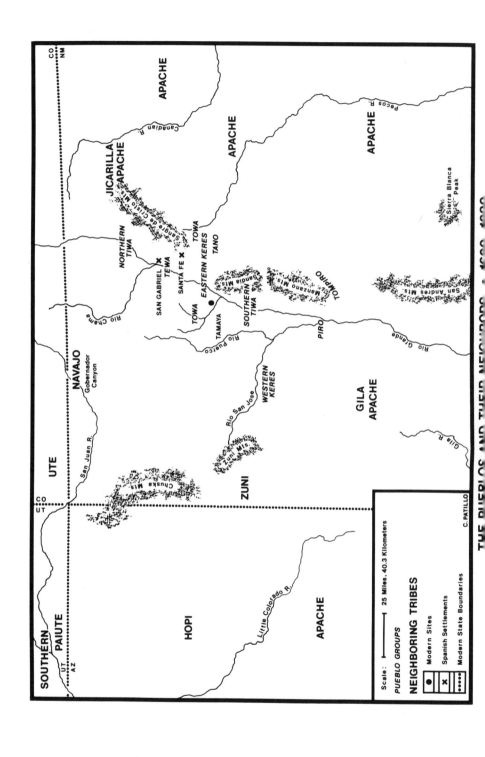

THE PUEBLOS AND THEIR NEIGHBORS, c. 1680–1880

SOUTHERN PAIUTE

UTE

NAVAJO

HOPI

APACHE

ZUNI

WESTERN KERES

GILA APACHE

APACHE

JICARILLA APACHE

NORTHERN TIWA

TEWA

SAN GABRIEL

SANTA FE

TOWA

EASTERN KERES

TANO

TOWA

TAMAYA

SOUTHERN TIWA

TOMPIRO

PIRO

Rio Grande

APACHE

APACHE

Pecos R.

Canadian R.

Sierra Blanca Peak

San Andres Mts.

Manzano Mts.

Sandia Mts.

Sangre de Cristo Mts.

Chuska Mts.

Zuni Mts.

Rio San Jose

Rio Puerco

Rio Chama

San Juan R.

Gobernador Canyon

Little Colorado R.

Gila R.

CO / NM

CO / UT

UT / AZ

C. PATILLO

Scale: 25 Miles, 40.3 Kilometers

PUEBLO GROUPS

NEIGHBORING TRIBES

● Modern Sites

✕ Spanish Settlements

•••• Modern State Boundaries

toll on the pueblos. All but a few moved at least once as a result of Spanish pressure.[9]

Conflict with Kastera brought a time of great movements along the Río Grande, as refugees fled from the pueblos to seek safety in more remote locations. Some Río Grande pueblo people joined the more isolated western pueblos, while others sought shelter with the Apaches to the east or the Navajos to the west. Many Río Grande pueblos left their old towns and fields to join other peoples in self-defense, at least for a time. Some pueblos, like Tamaya and Zía, built new towns in more sheltered locations, but returned to the old pueblos when the danger diminished. Beyond the central Río Grande, however, many pueblo towns were abandoned and never resettled. From Isleta south, the old Piro and Tompiro pueblos stood empty when de Vargas marched north. The remnants of their peoples had fled south with the Spaniards, settling the pueblo of Isleta del Sur near Kastera's town of El Paso del Norte.[10]

Kastera's presence also changed the relations among many of Tamaya's neighbors. Common opposition to the Spaniards had created a broad alliance that united all of the pueblos, as well as some non-pueblo bands, at the time of the revolt. That union, formed to drive Kastera out, dissolved soon after its goal had been achieved. By the last years of the seventeenth century, the question of how to deal with Kastera had become a wedge between old allies. Some pueblos had prospered in the years after the revolt, but others, like Tamaya, had suffered heavy losses to the Spanish troops led by Reneros de Posada and Petriz de Cruzate. With their people killed, their children taken, and their homes, crops, and fields destroyed, the Tamayame and their Keres relatives at Zía and San Felipe were no longer in a position to resist Kastera with arms. Many of their neighbors, however, having survived the period without such heavy losses, still hoped to defeat Kastera by force, and some continued to fight throughout the 1690s.

By the beginning of the new century, however, Kastera had put down the revolt, convincing even those who had resisted most bitterly that guns and bows would not evict the Spaniards. To protect pueblo peoples and pueblo homelands from the Spaniards, the people would have to use Kastera's laws and papers. When they accepted Kastera's peace, the Río Grande pueblos no longer needed to fear that Kastera's soldiers would seize or burn their homes and crops, and kill or capture their people.

This peace, however, did not end the fear of violence throughout the region. Instead, Spanish and pueblo settlements alike were threatened by new invaders—groups of Navajo, Apache, Ute, and Comanche raiders. As these peoples had moved into the regions beyond pueblo lands, occasional raiders had been drawn to the rich settlements along the Río Grande, hoping to seize desirable pueblo goods like corn, squash, pottery, feathers, colored stones, and cotton cloth. The Tamayame and their neighbors had sometimes suffered from these attacks, but until Kastera settled the Río Grande, raiders came infrequently and did comparatively little damage. A small group of enemies, coming and going on foot, might surprise pueblo farmers in their fields, but they could do no great harm to the large, secure pueblos, and the newcomers soon learned that it was far easier to obtain what they wanted in trade than to attack a well-defended pueblo. The pueblos would willingly exchange their desirable goods for resources that the Utes, Navajos, and Apaches had in abundance—furs, hides, meats, skins, pine pitch, and piñon nuts—and for goods that the Athapascan and Shoshonean peoples could acquire in a vast trade network. In this way, shells from the Pacific Coast and other exotic items might reach the pueblos. In turn, pueblo goods would be welcome as they passed in trade from tribe to tribe until they reached distant lands.[11] Such trade often led to friendship and alliances.

The arrival of Kastera and other Europeans, however, disrupted that network and created new and compelling incentives for raiders. Like others who had come before, the Europeans had strange new goods, and at first it seemed that they would participate in the trade. Traders carried knives, clothing, tools, and beads to many of the Indian groups, and Kastera invited the Indian peoples to yearly trade fairs at Taos. Like the pueblos, the Spaniards were interested in obtaining the furs, hides, and other goods that the Navajos, Apaches, Comanches, and Utes had to offer in trade. Few Europeans, however, would agree to any trade that involved the most valuable and desirable of their own goods—guns, powder, ammunition, and horses. Knives and kettles might be useful, but the peoples beyond the pueblos quickly recognized that owning guns and horses could give them power, a more reliable food supply, and wealth. Horses would enable a band to control a much larger territory and cover greater distances in much less time, and, by allowing the people to transport more supplies and gain access to more resources, permit them to live together in larger groups. If powder and ammunition were available, guns could increase this new power enormously. As some of these bands acquired guns and horses, obtaining them became a matter not just of power, but of survival, for those around them. A band that could not acquire guns and horses would soon be at the mercy of its newly powerful neighbors. Armed with Kastera's guns, mounted Utes soon began to put pressure on the Navajos, who moved south and east to escape the raids. Comanches, attacked by the Utes on the west and by the Blackfoot and other tribes to the north and east, moved south. They, in turn, forced many Apache groups farther south. Thus, from the north, northwest, and northeast, mounted raiders moved closer to the pueblos and settlements of the Río Grande.[12]

They came for many reasons. Some, lured by Kastera's goods, came to obtain in raids what they could not acquire in trade. Others raided in anger, for like the pueblos they had been touched by Kastera's violence. Many first learned of the danger from pueblo refugees, but they soon experienced it first-hand. As Spanish soldiers moved throughout the region to punish raiders and those who had joined in the pueblo revolt, all of the bands adjacent to the pueblos were at risk. Although these peoples recognized no overall leaders and each band acted independently, Kastera's soldiers often considered all Indians who spoke one language to be responsible for any act committed by another speaker of that language. Thus those who had not participated in raids sometimes fell victim to Spaniards intent on punishing those who had. They, in turn, might be drawn to Kastera's settlements to avenge the deaths of their innocent people. Others came filled with rage because the Spaniards had taken their children captive. Some found raiding the quickest way to obtain wealth and power, while many found it the only way to obtain the means to defend themselves against other groups, newly equipped with European weapons and horses, who were vying for their lands. Regardless of the reasons that brought them, all of the Navajo, Apache, Comanche, and Ute bands posed a deadly threat to the pueblos and towns along the Río Grande. Mounted and armed, these raiders could attack the largest settlements, carry off property and livestock, and retreat quickly to lands that they knew better than anyone else.[13]

Tamaya itself, surrounded by other pueblos and towns, was sheltered from direct attack, but Tamayame crops and livestock on the Ranchiit'u, south of Siiku, and in the Espiritu Santo lands were vulnerable, and the Tamayame knew that they could be attacked as they traveled to their fields and grazing lands or west to hunt antelope. Those who went farther, to the salines in the south or the buffalo plains in the east, found themselves in even greater danger.

Tamaya shared this vulnerability with both pueblo and Spanish neighbors, whose villages, towns, ranches, and fields attracted the raiders. To raise a force large enough to pursue a raiding group, any one town or pueblo had to leave its fields and flocks untended, its homes unprotected, its children at risk. This common danger brought forth a new alliance: Kastera, so long the enemy, joined with the pueblos to defend the Río Grande villages. The alcaldes, under orders from Kastera's governor, would recruit men from pueblos and towns alike to form a defense force when raiders threatened the area. Notified by the alcalde, a pueblo would organize a force led by its war chief. As soon as possible, this group would join those from other pueblos and from Kastera's settlements at a central meeting place. If any of Kastera's few professional soldiers could be spared, they would join the militia. Volunteers who did not have their own horses and weapons would be provided with mounts and guns for the expedition. At the end of the campaign, the troops would return to a central location to disband. The volunteers—pueblo and Spanish alike—might simply recover the property their people had lost in raids, or they might be paid for their services.[14]

When Diego de Vargas met with the Tamayame and their Keres neighbors on the mesa of Cerro Colorado in 1692, the Apache already posed a threat to the region. De Vargas recommended that his superiors send fifty settlers to build a Spanish town near the old pueblo of Santa Ana, "to close the way to the enemy Apache."[15] In 1704, when Apaches raided Bernalillo and la Cieneguilla, volunteers from Tamaya, Zía, and Jémez joined forces from the Spanish towns and nearby pueblos, meeting at Bernalillo and pursuing the Apaches south into the Sandía Mountains.[16] Two years later, Navajo raiders struck at San Ildefonso, Santa Clara, and San Juan.[17] In 1707, just before Governor Cuervo y Valdés left office, he held a ceremony to honor the men from Tamaya and the other pueblos who had served in many campaigns during his term. Pueblo governors, caciques, war captains, and other leaders were invited to Santa Fe for the occasion. During the ceremonies, Kastera's governor also recognized the newly selected pueblo leaders, presenting the governors with "shoes and suits of fine Mexican cloth." In turn, the pueblo governors praised Cuervo y Valdés for bringing peace to their lands.[18]

In these years, however, peace rarely lasted very long. The same year that Governor Cuervo y Valdés honored the pueblos, at least five campaigns were organized to deal with Navajos who had raided Jémez and Santa Clara.[19] The Comanches, first seen at the Taos trade fair in 1706, returned with Utes the following year to attack Spanish, pueblo, and Jicarilla Apache groups near Taos and Cochití.[20] The regions near Galisteo, Pecos, Taos, la Cañada, Albuquerque, and Bernalillo suffered from Apache attacks.[21] By 1730 Navajos had settled throughout the region from Santa Ana to Santa Clara, just west of Tamaya and the Ranchiit'u.[22]

With raiders all around, no one could venture far without protection. Throughout the eighteenth century, Kastera's governor organized annual caravans that enabled both pueblos and Spaniards to gather salt safely. In the

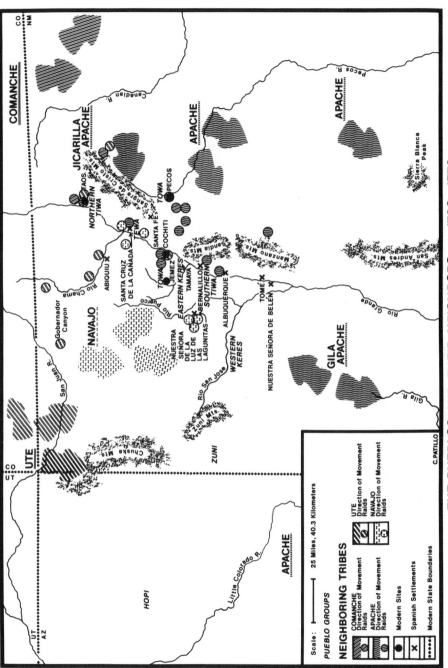

THE PUEBLOS AND THEIR NEIGHBORS, c. 1700 - 1770

Scale: |———| 25 Miles, 40.3 Kilometers

NEIGHBORING TRIBES

| | COMANCHE Direction of Movement Raids |
| | APACHE Direction of Movement Raids |

PUEBLO GROUPS

| | UTE Direction of Movement Raids |
| | NAVAJO Direction of Movement Raids |

●	Modern Sites
X	Spanish Settlements
·····	Modern State Boundaries

C. PATILLO

spring or summer, the alcaldes received word that the caravan was forming and notified the pueblos in their district. Those who wanted salt traveled to Galisteo to join the caravan, which would set out for the salines south and east of the Manzano Mountains as soon as a group large enough to provide protection from Comanche and Apache raiders had assembled. The Tamayame were listed among those who joined the caravans in 1716, 1732, and 1742; they probably joined many other pueblo caravans, of which no records remain, and they may also have formed part of the escort when Kastera's settlers went to gather salt.[23] A century later, New Mexico's settlers formed annual caravans to hunt buffalo. Some buffalo expeditions took place from June to the end of summer; the largest began in October, after the harvest. The hunters would return with thousands of buffalo, enough to provide meat and hides throughout the winter.[24]

As the years passed, the Comanches posed an increasing threat to eastern New Mexico and, indirectly, to the Río Grande settlements. Armed with guns acquired from French traders farther east, Comanche groups swept into New Mexico, pushing the Apache bands south and west.[25] As a result of growing Comanche pressure to the east in the 1740s and 1750s, Apache raids increased in the Río Abajo. In 1744, the Tamayame joined their neighbors in a campaign against Apaches who had taken a great deal of livestock from the area around Albuquerque and Bernalillo.[26] Throughout much of the 1750s, Kastera's governor "maintained a continuous summer patrol of forty Indians from the six Keres pueblos" to protect the region. The patrol, augmented by Spanish soldiers when possible, traveled through the region south of the Río Grande settlements, going as far as Quarai, east of the Manzano Mountains. Through their efforts, one of the major Apache attack routes was closed off, but Apaches could still reach the Albuquerque area by traveling up the Río Puerco from the west.[27]

Meanwhile Navajo raids continued near Tamaya. For a time, Navajo raiding forced Spaniards living in and around Nuestra Señora de la Luz to abandon their claims, until this town and others along the Río Puerco "became ghost villages."[28] When these towns were abandoned, Tamaya's adjacent Espiritu Santo lands became the Navajo frontier. Although there is no record of individual campaigns, the people of Tamaya, Zía, and Jémez must have participated in many efforts to repel the raiders during this period. In 1766, when they petitioned for a formal grant to the Espiritu Santo lands, the pueblos noted that, in addition to their own stock, they maintained large herds "for the royal service."[29]

Briefly, Governor Tomás Velez Cachupín brought peace by persuading the

Comanches, the Utes, and some Apaches to join the Spanish-Pueblo alliance. In 1767, however, when Cachupín's second term ended, this larger alliance dissolved. The new governor, Pedro Fermín de Mendinueta, renewed the campaigns against the Comanches, and Tamayame volunteers were among those who joined the troops.[30] Men from the Keres pueblos also joined forces pursuing Navajo and Apache raiders. In 1773 and 1774, Navajos raiders in the area near Albuquerque took six lives, wounded two, and carried off or killed livestock. Three of the four Spanish/pueblo campaigns against these raiders succeeded in overtaking the Navajos and recovering the stolen property. But raiding bands struck from every direction, and the defense forces could not always protect all of the pueblos and settlements. Once, while the militia was pursuing Navajo raiders, nearly one hundred Comanches attacked near Albuquerque. As soon as the pueblo force returned, they went, with the alcalde of the Keres, in pursuit of the Comanches, but the raiders had disappeared.[31] In 1775 a Tamayame was killed by Comanche raiders at Sandía, where Comanche attacks remained a threat in the following years.[32]

Until the mid-1780s, Navajo and Apache raiders remained a familiar menace to the fields and flocks of the Río Abajo. Gradually, however, the Navajo bands were persuaded to join the alliance, and by 1786 the Navajos were no longer considered a threat. When unknown raiders attacked in June 1785, the alcalde, the interpreter, and the justices of Alameda, the Keres, la Cañada, and Albuquerque all stated that the Navajos had not broken the peace in their lands. The Apaches, however, continued to raid. In 1785 the Spanish government sent two hundred guns, four hundred horses, twenty mules, and money for supplies to assist New Mexico in a campaign against the Gila Apache. Supplies were to be distributed to "the militia, settlers," and Navajo allies; the horses were provided for the use of "the settlers and Indian auxiliaries both Pueblos and heathens . . . for the period of campaigns."[33] Three years later, in another campaign against the Apaches, the militia included a unit composed of 117 Tamayame led by a Tamayame captain and lieutenant.[34]

Meanwhile, the Tamayame, besieged by raiders, fell victim to another deadly foe: European disease. After Kastera reached the Río Grande early in the sixteenth century, epidemics of European diseases like measles, cholera, and smallpox became a familiar threat. In the late 1720s, measles—or a disease like it—killed 109 Indians in and around Jémez. Smallpox broke out in the region five years later[35] and struck again at Pecos in 1738.[36] But the most severe epidemics came in the last decades of the eighteenth century. A major outbreak of smallpox erupted in the spring of 1780, killing thirty-one

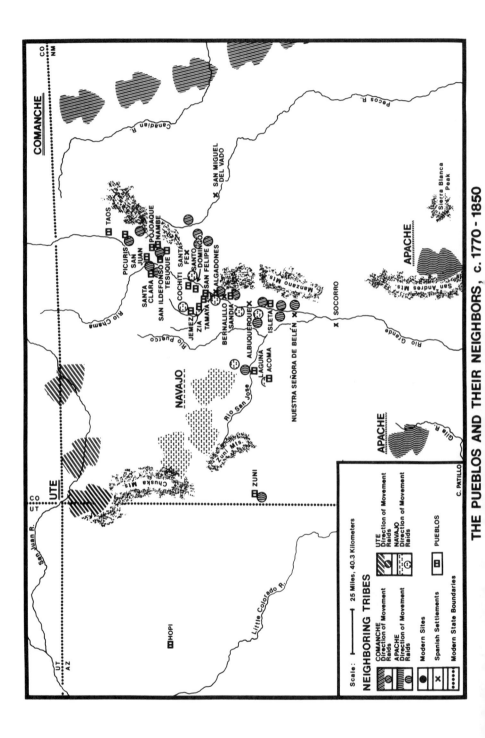

THE PUEBLOS AND THEIR NEIGHBORS, c. 1770 - 1850

NEIGHBORING TRIBES

COMANCHE Direction of Movement Raids		UTE Direction of Movement Raids
APACHE Direction of Movement Raids		NAVAJO Direction of Movement Raids
Modern Sites	●	PUEBLOS
Spanish Settlements	✕	
Modern State Boundaries	•••••	

Scale: |——| 25 Miles, 40.3 Kilometers

C. PATILLO

people in Albuquerque; the following January and February, smallpox took 161 lives in Albuquerque and Santa Fe.[37] The disease spread rapidly, striking the regions around Sandía, Bernalillo, Corrales, and Alameda.[38] Between February 4 and March 9, more than 230 Indians died at Santo Domingo alone.[39] By December, smallpox had broken out at Santa Clara.[40] The epidemic took a great toll in pueblos already weakened by raiding.

Nothing could be done to prevent the spread of the disease until a smallpox vaccine was discovered in 1799. Within six years, Kastera's officials had set up a vaccination program for New Mexico;[41] friars received orders to implement the new program in 1805.[42] The annual supply caravan would bring children who had been exposed to the disease and could be used to vaccinate the peoples of New Mexico. By November 1805, more than three thousand children had been vaccinated in New Mexico; only the children of Zuñi, Acoma, Laguna, and Cebolleta had not yet been protected. For the next ten years, yearly vaccinations helped to reduce the threat of smallpox.[43]

Throughout the eighteenth century, Tamaya's greatest problems were raiding, disease, and the protection of land and water rights. For Kastera, however, these concerns diminished in importance as Spain's hold on the New World began to crumble. By mid-century, the Comanches who came to trade at Taos brought goods obtained from French traders to the east. French men soon followed French goods to New Mexico, just as Kastera's officials had feared they would.[44] By obtaining the vast Louisiana territory in 1763, Spain ended the threat of French intrusion for a time. That, however, did not stop the westward advance of Anglo-American traders, and by 1803 the newly independent United States had acquired the Louisiana territory. Three years later, Zebulon Pike entered New Mexico on an expedition sent to explore the Louisiana Purchase lands.[45] To the west, Russian, British, and American traders and trappers moved toward Spain's California settlements. As the Apaches were pushed farther and farther south, raiding increased along the northern frontier of New Spain, disrupting the trail to New Mexico, delaying mails, and causing friars to postpone their visitations.[46]

Focusing on these external threats, Kastera tried to regain control of its New World holdings by keeping foreigners out of New Mexico, organizing the colonies to provide better defense, and mounting campaigns against Indian raiders. Again and again in the last decades of the century officials appealed to "all free subjects in the colonies, including Indians" to contribute to the defense.[47] Although Tamaya and the other pueblos were exempt from many of Kastera's taxes, they were asked to send men and money to support Spanish troops on campaigns in New Mexico and even in distant European wars. Like their neighbors, the Tamayame probably paid these levies in blankets, crops, and other goods, as well as in cash.[48]

For a time these efforts preserved Kastera's claims. Outsiders soon learned that if they entered Santa Fe, they might be arrested and their goods would almost certainly be confiscated. Negotiations brought at least temporary truces with the Apache, Navajo, Ute, and Comanche raiders. In the end, however, it was neither European rivals nor Indian raiders that brought an end to Kastera's New World empire. The death blow came not from without, as Kastera had feared, but from within, when the peoples of New Spain rebelled against Kastera's rule. The treaty signed in 1821 to conclude this revolution brought an end to Spain's rule over New Spain and its colonies to the north. By the terms of this treaty, Mexico gained independence—and jurisdiction over New Mexico and Kastera's other northern holdings. With the stroke of a pen, Tamaya and the other pueblos were transferred to the legal authority of a new nation.[49]

When word of the change reached the Río Grande, "the people of the surrounding country," including delegates from the pueblos, went to Santa Fe. For five days, while New Mexico celebrated, "the square was covered with Spaniards and Indians from every part of the province." Among those who arrived on the second day to join in the dancing were a group of men and women from San Felipe, wearing jewelry and "cotton cloth of their own weaving."[50] The friars, who two years earlier had been told to celebrate oaths of loyalty to the Spanish Monarchical Constitution, now led the people in masses of thanksgiving for the proclamation of Agustín de Iturbide as emperor of Mexico.[51]

At first these celebrations were the only sign of change in New Mexico, which remained as remote from Mexico's government as it had been from Spain's. The settlers gave their loyalty—and their taxes—to a new government, but they were the same men and women who had lived beside the pueblos for many years. Even the old Spanish governor, Facundo Melgares, held his office for three years after Mexico declared independence,[52] and the same alcaldes, in the same districts, administered the affairs of New Mexico. To Tamaya and the other pueblos, the Hispanic peoples of New Mexico were still the people of Kastera. Ten years after the changeover, New Mexican Antonio Barriero wrote that pueblo ceremonies and councils were "always closed to the Spaniards, for so they call us."[53]

Slowly, Mexican rule brought change to New Mexico. Under the treaty giving Mexico independence, Indians became citizens of Mexico, and the new government instructed New Mexican friars that citizens should not be listed by race or blood origin in parish records and official documents.[54] The new leaders recognized pueblo governments and gave new canes of office to pueblo officials.[55] Although the New Mexican government underwent several reorganizations, Tamaya remained under the jurisdiction of the alcalde at Jémez until 1837; then the districts were redrawn, and the prefect at Algodones was given responsibility for the pueblo. In spite of these reorganizations, most of the old Spanish laws remained in force, and officials followed custom in deciding the questions that came before them.[56]

The reorganization of the church had a more immediate impact on the pueblos. As Franciscan friars were replaced by secular clergymen and the number of priests sent to New Mexico declined, the missions were combined and recombined. In 1815 Tamaya had been under the care of the mission at Zía,[57] and in the years immediately following Mexican independence, Tamaya had a resident friar. In 1824, however, a visiting friar performed multiple baptisms at Tamaya.[58] Two years later, a vicar was appointed for the Río Abajo district.[59] In 1828, Father Muro was transferred from Picurís to take charge of Cochití, Santo Domingo, San Felipe, Sandía, and Tamaya.[60] A year later, Tamaya and Sandía were placed under the care of the friar at San Felipe, Fray Manuel Antonio García del Valle, who had charge of them until 1833.[61] Some secular clergymen, like Mariano de Jesús Lucero, who served at Tamaya from 1841 to 1844, came to replace the friars as they died or moved on to missions elsewhere.[62] The few secular clergy who made the journey, however, could not hope to serve the vast area, and soon the church's role in the pueblos and settlements declined. Schools, formerly maintained by the friars, closed, and mission and church buildings fell into disrepair. Visiting churchmen reported a chronic shortage of clergymen.[63] As New Mexico's clergy dwindled, some pueblos began once again to hold their traditional ceremonies openly in the plazas. As Barriero noted in 1833, the pueblos had not forgotten the "teachings which have been handed down to them by tradition," and they were "careful scrupulously to teach" these traditions "to their descendants."[64] Once again they were free to honor these traditions without fear of Kastera's punishment.

For Tamaya and the other pueblos, however, the most significant effects of Mexico's revolution came, not from the departure of the friars, government reorganization, or new policies, but from decades of chaos. In the years leading up to the revolution, the governments of Spain and New Spain had been preoccupied with the problems that led to their downfall. Inheriting many of these problems, the newly independent Mexican government also had to face the difficulties of setting up a new state. As a result, the problems of the remote colony in New Mexico received less and less attention from the government. Word of policies and decisions made in the south reached New Mexico slowly and erratically. Often it was the old laws and customs, rather than new policies, that held force in New Mexico. Funds for the colony, never lavish under Spanish rule, ran shorter than ever during the years of turmoil as Mexican rule was established. As the Spanish alliances collapsed, Indian raiding increased once again.

The leaders of New Mexico, who could expect little from the distant government to which they owed allegiance, focused their attention on the colony's most immediate concerns. In some of these matters, the interests of the pueblos and the settlers coincided. Pueblo and Hispanic farmers, ranchers, and settlers alike hoped to control the raids that damaged their homes and endangered their people. Everyone—pueblo and non-pueblo alike—benefitted when American traders were allowed into the region, bringing necessary and desirable goods not available in New Mexico.

In other areas, however, the interests of the pueblos inevitably conflicted with those of their non-Indian neighbors. New Mexico no longer had sufficient unclaimed land and water to provide for all of its residents, and some non-Indians took advantage of the governmental disarray to trespass on pueblo lands and divert pueblo water. When unscrupulous colonists had attempted to take pueblo resources in the past, the pueblos had been able to seek the assistance of the friars, the Protector of the Indians, outside inspectors, officials sent from New Spain, and the Royal Audiencia to defend their rights under Kastera's law. During the Mexican period, most of these advocates for pueblo rights disappeared. The friars dwindled, and the infrequent church inspectors were preoccupied with the decay of the missions and the disorder of the church. Protecting the rights of pueblos in the distant colony was not a matter of great concern to Mexico's officials. Local officials, born and raised in the non-Indian communities of New Mexico, would hear the claims and resolve the disputes between the pueblos and their non-Indian neighbors. Rarely checked by any outside review, these officials were far less likely than their predecessors to support the pueblos' causes in disputes that involved their own non-Indian relatives, neighbors, colleagues, and friends. Thus, as the pueblos faced ever greater threats to their land and water, they lost many of the avenues of recourse that they had learned to use, during Kastera's tenure, to protect their rights.[65]

Threats came with little warning, to lands and waters that had long been protected by Kastera's law. Although the Mexican government had agreed to uphold and protect the land rights recognized by Spain, many of those rights were soon questioned. In February 1821, José García and Pablo Montoya raised the issue of land ownership in the Angostura.[66] Not long after the peoples of New Mexico had gathered in Santa Fe to celebrate Mexican Independence, the Tamayame were "summoned to appear at Angostura, where the alcaldes of Jémez and Alameda and the protector of the Indians ordered them to deliver up the land that had been given to them by the decision of the royal authorities . . . ." The officials asked the people of Tamaya "if they were satisfied" with this order; they should not have been surprised that the Tamayame, whose claim to the lands had already been upheld by the highest authority in New Spain, "replied that they were not . . . ." The officials responded that the people of Tamaya might "appeal the matter to whomsoever they saw fit; whereupon they appealed to the governor of New Mexico, asking that justice be done to them." The same year, Andrés Maygua submitted a petition "on behalf of the Indians of Santa Ana, in regard to a number of suits between the Indians of San Felipe and those of Santa Ana, which arose from the fact that the former had sold a piece of land which belonged to the latter."[67] Only three years after Tamaya's repeated appeals had at last brought justice from Kastera, the Tamayame would have to begin the process of seeking recognition for their rights under foreign laws once again.

In May 1822, New Mexico's governor began to review the matter. It seems that no official records remained of the previous decision, for the governor asked the Protector of the Indians to "explain his connection with the matter." He also asked the alcalde of Alameda, who had responsibility for San Felipe, to "state what proceedings had been had in the matter" and to send "all documents throwing light on the subject." San Felipe's alcalde replied that he had been present in February, when the Tamayame were told they would have to give up the lands, and he had heard no complaints about the decision. If Governor Melgares also consulted Tamaya's alcalde or the Tamayame themselves, no record remains. Nor is there any evidence that the Protector of the Indians sent Melgares a copy of the document he had drawn up, three years earlier, "for the protection of the Santa Ana people." The record is silent about what, if any, decisions the governor made, but the number of suits involving the Angostura lands in the following years clearly demonstrates that the Tamayame did not receive the justice they sought.[68] During these years, San Felipes continued to sell land in the Angostura region to Spaniards. In 1822 the principal men of San Felipe appeared before Protector of the Indians Ignacio Maria Sanchez Vergara, testifying that they had voluntarily given land in this area to Pablo Montoya. The following year Montoya made an additional series of six purchases, for a total of 58 pesos and

677 sheep and lambs, of lands south and east of the main Santa Ana ditch, a tract in the arroyo that ran from the Río de las Huertas, and another parcel adjacent to land owned by a Santa Ana.[69] During the same period, yet another change in the course of the Río Grande seems to have created or exacerbated a boundary dispute in the Ranchiit'u, near Bernalillo. When Don Alvino Chacón, alcalde of Santa Fe, held hearings to resolve the dispute in April and May 1846, the Pueblo of Santa Ana had been protesting against trespass by Ramón Gurule for twenty years. Tamaya's governor testified that the "river had originally formed the boundary between the two properties, both legally acquired, but that it had changed its course . . ." after a flood in 1828. In 1846, and again in 1848, at the pueblo's request, a series of witnesses from the surrounding pueblos and towns testified that the river had moved to the east in that flood, and that a number of old houses, which may have defined part of the boundary, had been swept away in it. May 20, 1848, an order was issued in Algodones "to allow the claim of the Pueblo of Santa Ana" and to fix the boundary in the middle of the river.[70]

Tamaya's water, as well as Tamaya's land, was at risk in these years. Led by the Montoya family, non-Indian settlers in the Angostura tried to appropriate Tamaya's water. Year after year, between 1824 and 1838, Pablo Montoya and other Angostura residents requested, and received, permission to use water from Tamaya's ditch, arguing not that they had any legal rights to the water, but simply that they needed it to raise their crops. In 1824 the alcalde of Alameda was told that both the Tamayame and the non-Indians should be allowed to use Tamaya's ditch "with the same limits as . . . last year, so that in this way the crops will not be damaged." Five years later, Pablo Montoya was awarded rights as a cotenant in the ditch; he was ordered to help maintain it, but not required to prove that he had any legal right to the water. In 1838 the official who had jurisdiction over Santa Ana was ordered to allow Montoya to use the water "until he presented his documented rights" to it. The Tamayame were informed that, if Montoya could not provide legal justification for the claim that he had already asserted, without any legal proof, for 17 years or more, any necessary adjustments would be made later.[71]

Although obtaining justice through Kastera's system had often been a long and difficult process, those who reviewed the complaints had at least tried to consider both the law and the pueblo's needs when they made their decisions. In the years after 1821, New Mexico's officials frequently disregarded both. Ignoring the law that bound them to uphold the land rights that Kastera had recognized, officials allowed outsiders to use Tamaya's lands and water without presenting any proof that they had a legal right to do so. They recorded the outsiders' needs, but made no mention of Tamaya's.

Tamaya's complaints appear only occasionally in the records of these troubled times. From the last years of Kastera's tenure through the decades of Mexico's rule, Tamaya's most frequent protests involved the attempts to take the pueblo's land and water in the Angostura. But there were other complaints as well. In 1801 a friar writing from Santa Ana reported to his superior "about Father Rubi unjustly taking crops from [an] Indian."[72] In a suit heard in July and August 1808, the Tamayame charged their alcalde, Ignacio Sánchez Vergara, with illegally demanding "forced personal service."[73] Five years later, the people of Tamaya presented a "complaint through Deputy Bautista Gonzales of damages received at the hands of the citizens of Bernalillo and Angostura."[74] The next year, a churchman mentioned "injustices at Santa Ana" among other problems.[75]

In the last years of Mexican rule, Tamaya once again faced three familiar plagues: disease, drought, and raiding. Smallpox, controlled for a time by Kastera's vaccination program, broke out again in the 1830s. From 1837 to 1840, epidemics killed as much as 10 percent of New Mexico's population; the losses at Tamaya may well have been as high or higher. From 1797 to 1808, population estimates for Santa Ana ranged between 430 and 634 people; by 1850, the official count had fallen to 399. Although it is difficult to evaluate the accuracy of these early population figures, they do reflect significant decreases in two major periods when epidemics devastated the region, falling from 634 in 1797 to 430 in 1805, and declining from 550 in 1809 to 471 in 1821 and 399 in 1850.[76]

With the epidemics came years of drought. One trader wrote that rains came to New Mexico only in June and July, and land with a reliable water supply could be sold for a hundred dollars an acre.[77] In 1829, 1830, and 1837, friars at New Mexico's missions were asked to lead prayers for rain.[78] As another American trader explained, because the American trading caravans reached Santa Fe between July and October, in the midst of the rainy season, their arrival became a sign that the rains would soon come. In the 1840s, when drought was widespread, the traders received an eager welcome among the pueblos of New Mexico.[79]

As the drought made crops ever more precious in the pueblos, Indian raiders returned to the Río Grande. By the early nineteenth century, Comanche, Ute, and Apache raiders rarely troubled the lands near Tamaya, but the Navajos posed a major threat to the pueblo. For the first time, raiders struck at Tamaya itself. In early August 1821, Navajo raiders stole four horses from the Tamayame, who chased them as far as Cabezón Peak, north of Siiku.[80] Four years later, friars led prayers for the success of a campaign against the Navajos and Apaches.[81] In the 1830s, the alcalde at Jémez reported that the people of Tamaya, Zía, and Jémez were all "very poor and demoralized because of Navajo raids."[82] Once again Tamayame volunteers joined campaigns against the raiders. In 1839, when Governor Manuel Armijo told New Mexicans that they would "be called upon to support the wars against the numerous tribes of the Navajo," men from the districts of Jémez, Cochití, and Santo Domingo reported for duty.[83] Occasionally, the government paid compensation to those who had lost property in the raids; in 1839, for example, a Jémez man received thirty-six yards of linen because his mule had been stolen by raiders.[84] Six years later, Navajo raiders struck at Tamaya again. The Tamayame pursued them, hoping to recover their property, and two Navajos were killed during the chase. The Navajo leader Cuero demanded that Tamaya pay for their deaths, but New Mexico's officials told him that if he wanted to complain, he would have to go to Santa Fe and discuss the treaties his people had broken.[85]

As Mexico's rule in New Mexico drew to an end, Tamaya still stood on the legal foundations established by Kastera, but the Tamayame were threatened on all sides. Intruders eyed the pueblo's land and water; raiders preyed on its flocks and fields; disease swept through one family after another; and drought withered the seedlings while farmers waited in vain for the summer rains. As the farmers worked in their fields; as the K'anuwa tended the boats; as the herdsmen watched the pueblo's stock; as the hunters went to the mountains and plains in search of antelope, deer, and buffalo; as the salt-gatherers journeyed to the salines; as the women dug the clay for their pottery; as the governor traveled to Santa Fe to speak for the people; even in the streets of Tamaya itself, as the children played—wherever they went and whatever they did, the Tamayame, in this troubled time, knew that they must be watchful. Swift as the spread of disease or interminable as the workings of a foreign legal system, danger in its many forms waited constantly below the mesa and amidst the fields.

Housing at old Santa Ana, 1980. Photograph by Jeannie Young.

Community center at Santa Ana, 1980. Photograph by Jeannie Young.

Tamaya, 1980. Photograph by Jeannie Young.

Santa Ana Mission, 1899. Photograph by Adam C. Vroman, courtesy of the Museum of New Mexico (neg. no. 12431).

Santa Ana Mission, 1903. Photograph by George H. Pepper, courtesy of the Museum of the American Indian, Heye Foundation.

Carlos Vierra's painting of the Santa Ana Mission, c. 1910. Photograph from the Trent Thomas Collection, courtesy of the New Mexico State Records Center and Archives.

Santa Ana Mission, c. 1935. Courtesy of the Museum of New Mexico (neg. no. 21228).

Church interior, c. 1935. Courtesy of the Museum of New Mexico (neg. no. 4072).

Santa Ana Mission, 1980. Photograph by Jeannie Young.

St. Anthony's Church at Ranchiit'u, 1980. Photograph by Jeannie Young.

SEVEN

Tamaya Meets Merikaana

While first Spain's officials, and then Mexico's, turned their attention to matters that had little to do with Tamaya, the familiar patterns of life were repeated each year along the Río Grande. As the first signs of spring appeared, the men and boys went to the Ranchiit'u and the other Tamayame farmlands to prepare the fields. The ditches had to be repaired. Stock had to be moved from one pasture to another. Tender seedlings had to be watched and, if the rains did not come, watered. Before the rainy season, the houses had to be replastered. Potters had to gather the materials they would need throughout the summer to make the fine pots for which the pueblo was recognized throughout the region. After adding sand to strengthen the orange-red clay, they would shape it, cover it with a cream-colored slip, and decorate it with the bold black and red designs for which Tamaya was known.[1] Each year, the families of Tamaya would need new bowls, cooking pots, and jars to replace those broken or worn out, as well as pots to trade with their neighbors. That trade, which had long been a part of Tamayame life, expanded in the early nineteenth century, because the residents of Kastera's towns, like nearby San Miguel del Vado, relied on pueblo potters for their supply of dishes, cooking vessels, bowls, and jars.[2]

At midsummer, the potters stopped their work, the farmers left the Ranchiit'u fields, and all the people returned to Tamaya to celebrate the feasts of Santiago and Santa Ana. After the summer ceremonies came a time of anxious waiting. This was the time when the rains should come, when the year's crops would be saved or lost, when Kastera's ranchers eyed the pueblo's precious water most greedily. It was also the time when Navajo and Apache raiders were most likely to attack Tamayame herds and herdsmen in the summer pastures on the mesa near Siiku, Tamayame patrols on the trails, Tamayame farmers in the Ranchiit'u, and even, as the raiders grew more daring, the women and children at Tamaya itself.

As the days grew shorter and the farmers kept their vigil for rain, Tamaya began to prepare for the joyous time when the people would return to the pueblo to celebrate the harvest. Those who needed sickles would obtain them from Kastera's blacksmith, who also supplied them with metal plows, axes, and brands. Either the blacksmith or a Tamayame man who had learned from him would build the wooden-wheeled ox carts that would carry the grain to the threshing ground and back to Tamaya. North on the mesa, at Homayah, the Tamayame cartmaker would find the large piñons used to make the cart wheels. Other Tamayame selected a high spot, where water would not stand, and began to prepare the threshing ground. They soaked the soil with water, covered it with clay, and smoothed and flattened the surface with rocks. The men cut trees, six or seven feet tall, and placed them in a circle around the prepared ground.[3]

At last, when all was ready for harvest, the Tamayame cut the wheat, stacked it in carts lined with rawhide so that they would not lose any grain, carried it to the threshing place, and piled it inside until it stood as high as a house. Horses were led into the threshing ground and tied to the posts with strips of twisted rawhide, to trot around the circle again and again until the pile had been flattened. Then the horses were led out so that the threshers could stir the pile, placing any large pieces back at the center. Again the horses were led in, to pound the pile with their hooves until all the wheat had been flattened. Then a group of the men stirred the pile with forks made of tree branches, throwing the wheat into the air so that the breeze would separate the grassy stems from the heavier seed kernels. As the grain fell onto the pile, a woman brushed away any weeds and chaff that had fallen with it. At last, when all the grain had been threshed and cleaned, the people loaded it back onto the rawhide-lined carts for the journey to their homes and storerooms.[4]

In the fall, after the corn and wheat had been gathered, all of the people began to return to Tamaya for the winter. The farmers gathered up their tools and left the fields of Ranchiit'u, sometimes paying one of their Hispanic neighbors to watch the fields through the winter.[5] Those who had spent the summer near Siiku, farming and herding their stock, gathered up their corn, squash, and melons to take back to Tamaya.[6] The summer patrols sent to guard the trails and protect the fields from Apache and Navajo raiders disbanded.[7] The buffalo hunters who had traveled to the Plains returned with fine thick hides and a supply of meat.[8] Before winter arrived, the Tamayame would hold a rabbit hunt for the women. In November, men traveled north and west to hunt deer.[9] Then came the time of the winter ceremonies. Just after Christmas, as the new year began, the governor, teniente, fiscal, and other officers were installed. Then, after the ceremonies of January and February, it was time once again for the farmers to go to the fields.[10]

In the years after Mexico took control of the region, a new event became part of this annual routine. In late summer or early fall, just before the time of the harvest, farmers in the Ranchiit'u fields could have seen groups of strangers moving down the Río Grande with horses, mules, oxen, and large canvas-covered wagons unlike any seen before in New Mexico. From signal points on the mesa, the Tamayame might have sent word to the peoples of Zía and Jémez, or received word from San Felipe, that the strangers were approaching.[11]

These strangers did not come, as Kastera had nearly three hundred years earlier, to conquer and claim the Río Grande in the name of a foreign government, to convert its peoples to their religion, or to search for fabled treasures in the mountains and mesas of New Mexico. They came, not as representatives of a distant power, but as individuals. They had a vision of riches to be obtained not by plundering gold and silver mines or working fertile farmlands, but by offering goods for trade in a land that was known to be far from any markets and poorly supplied.[12]

And the goods they brought were indeed welcome to the peoples of New Mexico, far from the markets of New Spain to the south. As long as Kastera ruled New Mexico, however, the traders themselves were not welcome. Those few who, like Zebulon Pike, reached New Mexico, were confronted by anxious Spanish officials convinced that Merikaana planned to take the lands Kastera claimed. Traders who reached Santa Fe were immediately arrested, questioned, and often expelled from the colony. In spite of this unfriendly reception, many returned and others followed, willing to risk the loss of their goods in the hope that New Mexico's policies would change and they would be the first to take advantage of this promising market.[13]

Their hopes were realized suddenly, when the Mexican government replaced the Spanish one and officials opened the markets of New Mexico to outsiders. The few American traders nearby soon sold all their goods and returned to Missouri for more, bringing tales of huge profits to be made from the trade. Word of their success spread quickly in Merikaana, and many soon followed them to New Mexico. In the two years after Mexico became independent, 120 Americans brought 27,000 dollars worth of goods to Santa Fe. The third year's trade was valued at 35,000 dollars, and within ten years the annual trade volume had grown to 250,000 dollars. In 1831, more than 300 traders, with 130 wagons full of goods, arrived in Santa Fe.[14]

Merikaana's traders carried items that had long been scarce or unavailable along the Río Grande, and the peoples of New Mexico, just as the traders had hoped, proved eager to buy these goods. Each year, when the first of the caravans reached Santa Fe in July, the traders found people from all parts of Mexico and New Mexico waiting to meet them in the capital, which took on "a very festive appearance."[15] As soon as the goods cleared customs, the traders laid out their wares. They brought thread, and cloth of every kind from durable flannel, muslin, broadcloth, and calico to luxurious taffeta, velveteen, and silk. They carried metal goods like knives, guns, hoes, kettles, and nails—all scarce in New Mexico. To tempt buyers, they offered many items that were luxuries in the isolated colony: jewelry, crucifixes, window glass, silk shawls, looking glasses, coffee mills, paper, and books.[16]

Unlike Kastera's first explorers, Merikaana's first traders found the riches of their dreams. Those who followed them, however, were doomed to disappointment, for the New Mexicans simply did not have enough to trade for the wagonloads of goods that arrived each year. The very conditions that made Merikaana's goods desirable also made it impossible for New Mexicans to pay for them: in this remote colony, the prosperous had the food and livestock they needed to survive, but little else. There were few industries except those that made essential tools, clothing, and shelter, things that were not in demand in Merikaana. Only a few New Mexicans had gold, taken from placer mines near Santa Fe; the majority possessed no currency to exchange for Merikaana's goods. New Mexico's furs, hides, and mules found willing buyers in Missouri, and Merikaana's traders could find markets for "small quantities" of "coarse Mexican blankets" on Merikaana's borders, but most of New Mexico's cloth was coarser and more expensive than that available in the East. As more and more traders came to Santa Fe, New Mexico's stock of items valuable to Merikaana's traders was quickly exhausted. After the first years of the trade, fewer and fewer traders were able to sell or exchange their wares at a profit. When the time came for the return trip to Missouri, some sold out at a loss and returned to their homes disappointed. Some remained in New Mexico to trap for beaver. Many, however, began to travel further south, to the more promising markets of Mexico, where American and European goods were in as much demand as they were along the Río Grande, but the towns were much larger and richer than Santa Fe, and the mines provided an ample supply of silver. By 1843 almost three-fourths of the goods brought by Merikaana's traders went to the markets of Chihuahua and other Mexican cities; in that year alone, the traders made three hundred thousand dollars in Mexico.[17]

The southbound traders traveled over an old route that passed through or near Tamaya's Ranchiit'u lands. Oñate had used much the same route in 1598. Throughout the seventeenth century, mission supply caravans had come and gone by this path. Since Kastera came to New Mexico, the mails had traveled along this trail; it had carried colonists, soldiers, officials, and churchmen to and from the Río Grande, as well as New Mexican ranchers driving their sheep south to market.[18] This well-worn route was not, in fact, one path, but several, all leading south and west from Santa Fe toward the Río Grande. One trail reached the river near Albuquerque; another cut over to the river near Santo Domingo, following the east bank through San Felipe, Algodones, and Bernalillo, then heading south to Albuquerque. By either route, it took "about ten days' drive" to travel from Santa Fe to Socorro. From there the trail headed south through El Paso del Norte to Chihuahua and other Mexican cities.[19]

This route soon carried Merikaana's traders through the thickly settled Río Grande region that was home to the Tamayame and many other pueblos. Many of the travelers kept journals, from which Merikaana would first learn of the peoples of New Mexico. The traders often joined forces before they went south, for Indian raids still posed a threat along the Río Abajo.[20] Because there were no inns along the route, the larger groups often camped outside towns like Algodones and Bernalillo, while smaller groups might stop near the homes of settlers, like the Delgado Ranch, located sixteen miles from Santa Fe, and the Perea ranch in Bernalillo.[21] New Mexicans offered the travelers "hospitality,"[22] and among Merikaana's traders, the pueblos soon became "famous for hospitality and industry."[23] Pueblo vineyards and herds impressed many of the travelers,[24] as did the pueblo peoples. Although most of the pueblos still spoke "their native language among themselves," traders like Josiah Gregg found that they also knew Spanish well enough to deal with the Mexicans.[25] The pueblos were friendly, curious, and eager to trade with the newcomers; wherever a trading party stopped, pueblo people appeared with fresh foods to trade. At a camp south of Albuquerque, pueblo traders offered melons, eggs, tortillas, and grapes in exchange for the empty black glass bottles the traders carried. All along the river, Susan Shelby Magoffin, the first woman from Merikaana to make the trip, found herself surrounded by curious pueblo people. They were most interested, she wrote in her journal, to learn "how some things about the carriage and my clothes are made."[26]

Thus Tamaya's first meetings with Merikaana would have been informal contacts with some of the many parties that passed through or near the Ranchiit'u. Many travelers described this region, often mentioning Bernalillo and the home of the Perea family, wealthy Hispanic settlers who soon began to send their own trading expeditions east to St. Louis.[27] Some travelers described the vineyards along the river, like those James Ohio Pattie saw near San Felipe,[28] while others visited Algodones, which was to become one of the two major stopping points on the trail from Santa Fe to Albuquerque.[29] At a town that he called "Elgidonis," Pattie saw cattle grazing along the river banks and "small huts of the shepherds, who attend them."[30] One American traveler, a doctor named Lyman, was arrested there and bribed the local alcalde to obtain his release.[31] The travelers, who set up camps all along this trail and stopped to buy fresh fruit and vegetables from the area's farmers, must surely have met some Tamayame, and some of the pueblo fields and herds they described were probably within the Ranchiit'u, although none of the journals mentions the people or the lands of Tamaya by name.

Merikaana's traders were individuals who came to sell their goods, as people had come from other pueblos and tribes to trade with their neighbors long before Kastera's arrival. These traders did not speak for Merikaana's government as the first Spaniards had represented Kastera's rulers. Their business was with those who wanted to trade, not with the leaders of the pueblos, and they made no speeches and conducted no ceremonies. Still they were not unaware of the organization and government of the lands through which they passed, and some, like Josiah Gregg, who wrote the most famous account of the trade, described the pueblos' ancient traditions of government. Gregg explained to his readers that, although the pueblos fell "nominally under the jurisdiction of the federal government, as Mexican citizens," they kept "many features of their ancient customs . . . as well in their civil rule as in their religion." Each had "a cacique or gobernadorcillo, chosen from among their own sages, and commissioned by the governor of New Mexico." Pueblo leaders, with the cacique, conducted the pueblo's business and saw to it that order was kept in the village. Kastera played no part in these meetings; Gregg reported that "no Mexican" was ever "admitted to these councils."[32] From the 1820s through the 1840s, as Merikaana's traders moved along the Río Grande each year, people from the pueblos met people from

Merikaana, but Tamaya and the other pueblos had no contact with Merikaana's leaders, and those leaders knew little of the men who governed the pueblos. These informal relations, however, were to change, and hints of the change soon appeared as the caravans came and went along the Río Grande. At first, Mexico had welcomed Merikaana's traders, for their trade brought goods, and the duties and taxes imposed upon it brought currency to the remote colony. Before long, however, the intrusion that Spain had feared became a reality for Mexico. As the United States grew, its people began to look west, to the little known lands beyond their borders, lands whose riches attracted settlers, miners, and trappers. To many Americans it soon came to seem that it was their destiny to move into those lands, to extend their way of life from one coast of North America to the other. Within that range, however, lay vast territories that the people of Mexico believed were theirs by right. Thus, in spring 1846, just as traders began to load their wagons for the trip to Santa Fe and the south, the United States declared war on Mexico.

That year, Merikaana's soldiers as well as Merikaana's traders would march into Santa Fe. In August, Stephen Watts Kearny led 2,700 American soldiers into New Mexico, claiming the region in the name of Merikaana. The last Mexican governor of New Mexico, Manuel Armijo, fled, and Kearny announced that Merikaana would "provide for New Mexico a free government, with the least possible delay, similar to those in the United States." Merikaana would respect the rights, property, and Christian religions of New Mexicans, and Merikaana's government would "protect the persons and property of all quiet and peaceable inhabitants within its boundaries" against the raids of Utes, Navajos, and other hostile tribes.[33] The war between the United States and Mexico was to continue for two years after Kearny marched into Santa Fe, but for Tamaya and her neighbors, Kearny's arrival marked the beginning of a new era. Along the Río Grande, Kastera gave way to Merikaana.

As word of the change spread, pueblo leaders met to debate the matter. There were many questions to be raised. No one knew what sort of officials Merikaana would have, or how a pueblo might deal with them. These men would arrive knowing nothing of the many problems in the pueblos. Merikaana would, no doubt, be as powerless to stop the drought as Kastera had been. But in matters a government could resolve, the new officials might bring a change for the better. Perhaps Merikaana could bring an end to the raids that had caused such great hardship along the Río Grande. Perhaps Merikaana's leaders would take the time to understand, and then resolve, the land and water disputes that had gone unsettled under Mexico's government. Perhaps Merikaana's soldiers and officials would evict the Mexican settlers and ranchers who had moved onto pueblo lands and taken pueblo water. For every hope, however, there was also a fear. Would Merikaana recognize the pueblos, as Kastera had? Would the men in authority be able and willing to redress the wrongs done to the pueblos? Or would they, like their Mexican predecessors, hear only the complaints and understand only the needs of the region's non-Indian residents? Would Merikaana try, as Kastera had, to disrupt the peoples' ancient ceremonies and traditions? Some had already heard rumors that Merikaana planned to take the pueblos' land and perhaps even attempt to move the pueblo peoples from their homes. For two years, as the distant war between Merikaana and Mexico continued, doubts and expectations multiplied along the Río Grande.

Merikaana too had many questions. From the accounts of traders and travelers, Merikaana's leaders had learned something of this vast land and its peoples, but not enough to enable them to govern a large region so different from other parts of their country. The soldiers who marched west to take over the region also had orders to explore it and provide information to distant leaders. After taking Santa Fe in August 1846, Merikaana's soldiers pushed farther into the lands Mexico still claimed, heading south toward Mexico and west, through the Navajo country, toward California.

Like the traders who preceded them, the troops followed the well-used paths along the Río Grande from Santa Fe to Albuquerque. The first group set out in early September. Some of the soldiers left the "main route" to visit Santo Domingo, where pueblo elders, "two of them carrying gold-headed canes with tassels," came out to meet Merikaana.[34] Pueblo warriors put on a display for the troops; in return, one of Merikaana's officers made a speech. Then the soldiers marched on, camping that night in a cottonwood grove near San Felipe.[35] The next day, they traveled through Algodones and Bernalillo. One of them, a Captain Turner, wrote that in this region he found "everything to present a more cheerful and civilized appearance." Like many of the travelers who had come before them, the soldiers were impressed by the wealth and hospitality of the Perea family in Bernalillo. Along the route they saw "sand hills . . . on either side of the river," but, like the traders, they complained that they could find "little or no timber" near the Río Grande and often had to "go to the distance of several miles" from the river to gather wood. They also learned of the threat that raiders posed to the Río Abajo; at a camp about twenty miles north of Socorro, they heard that Navajos had just struck twelve miles to the south.[36]

Almost a month later, a second group of Merikaana's soldiers marched down the Río Grande to Albuquerque. On the night of October 21, they camped about eleven miles from Bernalillo. Some of the men were sent out in search of wood and food, and an interpreter returned with "twenty-four bushels of corn" he had managed to buy. The next day, the troops, many of whom had influenza, reached Bernalillo and set up camp near some recently harvested corn fields. The weather had been "hot and dusty" until that day, when the soldiers complained of "wind and some rain."[37] Their journals described the small town of Bernalillo as "one of the best built" the troops had seen, a village surrounded by peach orchards and vineyards with adobe walls "covered with prickly cactus" at the top to protect the grapes from raiders.[38]

These first of Merikaana's troops, marching toward distant lands, only glimpsed the region around Tamaya on their way to Albuquerque. Others, however, soon received orders to explore New Mexico. Two lieutenants— William G. Peck and James W. Abert—led a group responsible for surveying the region and preparing a detailed report about it. Even before they left Santa Fe, they began to describe the pueblos. Peck, who had seen pueblo orchards of peach, apricot, and plum trees north of the city, explained that the Indians raised "almost all the fruit that is grown in the country."[39] Many brought their produce to the markets of Santa Fe, arriving with "great quantities of peaches" or driving carts "loaded with little crates filled with grapes." Pueblo produce was displayed among the red and green chilies, onions, watermelons, eggs, cheese, cornhusks, tobacco, piñon nuts, bread, and meat spread out for sale in the capital.[40]

The two surveyors left Santa Fe in October, setting out along the familiar route down the Río Grande. The night of October 10, they stopped at San Felipe, where the people brought melons, corn, and pumpkins to their camp. They found that the bridge at the river there, described by Pike in 1806, had washed away. Throughout the next day's journey, they heard of the damage caused by Navajo raids, first from a rancher at Cubero and from the people near Santo Domingo. That night, from their camp near that pueblo, they saw a "fertile valley" and the large mesa beyond, but the residents told them that Navajo raids kept the region's people from "enjoying" those fertile lands.[41]

The next day brought them to Tamayame lands. Many of Merikaana's soldiers and traders had passed through this section of the trail, but Peck and Abert were the first to identify Tamaya and the Ranchiit'u by name and describe them in detail. After traveling through Algodones and Angostura, they reached the mouth of the Río Jémez, where they "got entangled among the 'acequias,' which were then full of water. . . ." With the help of "some Indians," they extricated themselves from the ditches and "visited 'Ranchito,' where they saw great piles of corn, the best [they] had yet noticed." Then, unlike those who had preceded them, they left the path toward Albuquerque to explore the lands along the Río Jémez.[42]

After crossing the Río Grande, Peck and Abert traveled along the Río Jémez toward Tamaya. As they moved through the "very sandy" valley, with black volcanic rock above, they observed that the river had "a dark red color" and ran in a bed three-fourths of a mile wide, but had, "in many places, no water." That night, they camped five miles up the valley, near Tamaya. They found the pueblo "almost entirely deserted, all the inhabitants being engaged at Ranchito, gathering their corn." They could discover "no grass . . . anywhere in the vicinity," and they had "much trouble" finding enough wood for their fires and fodder for their mules. The following morning, Peck climbed to the top of the mesa with "a Spanish school master, who teaches the children of the Indians in St. Ana." The priest told the surveyors about the gold mines at the head of the Río Jémez and explained that the Indians farmed extensively on the mesa above Tamaya, but Abert, who was unfamiliar with pueblo dry farming, doubted his report, believing that farming could not be possible in an area that could not be irrigated.[43]

After visiting Tamaya, Peck and Abert retraced their route down the Río Jémez to the Río Grande, where they "crossed the river, which was full of wild geese," and passed through Ranchiit'u a second time. From Bernalillo they set out for Albuquerque, planning to travel west through the Río Puerco Valley. When local residents learned of their plans, however, they warned the soldiers to avoid that route, explaining that "the war trail of the Navajoes runs through the valley of the Puerco." Residents urged caution: at least, if the expedition insisted on going that way, they should move "with great circumspection, and not . . . make any fires at night."[44] Under orders to report on the unexplored lands of New Mexico, Peck and Abert decided to continue west as they had planned in spite of the warnings.

As they neared the Río Puerco, they found themselves in a "wide and flat" valley "overgrown with varieties of artemisias [sagebrush] and coarse grass"— land that Abert concluded was "fit only for sheep and goats."[45] When they reached the river, they decided not to follow the main path west toward Cebolleta, but to turn north and follow the Río Puerco "far enough to fix its course." They moved north slowly the next day, for the path was often covered with dense sagebrush and five to six inches of sand. In late afternoon, they stopped near a field of corn and pumpkins and allowed their exhausted mules to graze on the corn, having decided that the field must be abandoned because they saw no houses nearby. Later that day they passed a "conical hut," made of light poles and mud, with a corral nearby, but they met no one in the area. Crossing the river to explore a high bluff on the east bank, they found a group of ruins "built of flat stones plastered with clay." At the top of the bluff, protected on one side by a 180-foot perpendicular rock face, stood the remains of a round building ten feet in diameter and three feet high; an elliptical building that once had possessed high walls; and "many rectangular shaped structures." Peck and Abert were baffled; they could not imagine who had erected these buildings or why they had been built in such a remote, inaccessible area. Along the stream, as they returned to their camp, they saw the ruins of another abandoned town, built around a two-hundred-yard square, with corral areas nearby.[46]

The next day, Peck and Abert left the Río Puerco, following "a faint path that led off to the westward" in "the bed of a valley." They traveled about twenty-five miles west without finding water. When it grew dark, they had to camp and send a few men on in search of water. The next day, when they reached the nearby town of Moquino, they discovered that a raiding party of fifty Navajos had just crossed the Puerco Valley. They learned that the ruins near the river were called "Poblazon," but the Hispanic residents of Moquino could tell them nothing about the cornfield they had seen or the ruins that stood on the high bluff.[47]

The route that Peck and Abert followed had brought them to a part of Tamayame lands unknown to Merikaana. As they traveled along the river valley, they passed through areas that the Tamayame used for farming and herding in the summer. Tamayame who wanted to graze their sheep and cattle away from the pueblo would go "way back over there by . . . Mesa Prieta . . . and stay all summer there," tending crops of "corn, squash or melon" while their stock grazed.[48] When fall came, they would harvest their crops and return to the pueblo. Thus the field of corn and pumpkins where the soldiers grazed their mules and the empty shelter and corral probably belonged to Tamayame herdsmen. It would not have been unusual for a herdsman to have been away from his fields, attending to his stock elsewhere or even, at this time of year, at the Ranchiit'u helping with the corn harvest. The route the explorers followed that day could have taken them as far north as the location of the ancient Tamayame villages south of Siiku at Kene'ewa and Kwiiste Kene'ewa, villages built to shelter the Tamayame from the enemies who had attacked them at Kwiiste Puu Tamaya.[49] Merikaana's surveyors, however, knew neither the tradition nor the lives of the Tamayame, and they met no one who could answer their questions about this remote land.

Following the route that the Tamayame had taken long before them, Peck and Abert traveled on to Laguna and Acoma. Then they returned to the Río Grande, camping along the way on the Río Puerco, nine miles above its junction with the Río San José.[50] While the surveyors were in this area, Navajo raiders took fifty thousand sheep within twenty miles of Albuquerque.[51] In December, after exploring the lands to the south, Peck and Abert returned to Santa Fe along the familiar trail, traveling through Tamayame lands for the last time. They bought corn at Alameda, passed through Sandía, and camped near some "neat haciendas" at the north end of Bernalillo.[52]

Abert's report gave Merikaana's leaders their first glimpses of Tamaya, as well as a greater understanding of the region. Others soon added to Merikaana's knowledge of the Tamayame. In 1849 Lieutenant James H. Simpson led an expedition into Navajo country. Fifty-four pueblo auxiliaries and six "headmen" joined the expedition at Jémez in late August.[53] Among them were two leaders from Tamaya: Hosea Beale, chosen "captain to command all the Indians engaged in the expedition,"[54] and Salvadore, the war captain of Tamaya, named as "a leader of the Indian Militia."[55] Ten men, nearly a fifth of the pueblo troops, came from Tamaya: José Vigil, Salvadore Andrés, José de la Luc, José Romero, Armijo Navajo, García Juanico, Manuel Armijo, Manuel Rincón, Mañana Chávez, and Tapon.[56] Merikaana negotiated a treaty with the Navajo leaders, who agreed to return captives and stolen livestock. Like Kastera's officials before them, Merikaana's leaders recognized Tamaya and the other pueblos as valuable allies and complimented volunteers on "their gallantry and general good conduct." Two months later, however, those who had gone with Simpson were "complaining that they [had not yet been] paid for their services."[57]

The following year, another military leader, George Archibald McCall, inspected the defenses of New Mexico. Like earlier observers, he described the toll taken by Navajo raids, estimating that, in the past year and a half, Navajo raiders had taken more then 114,000 dollars worth of stock and killed about 20 people along the Río Grande. He reported that they used a trail that extended from Zuñi to the Río Abajo.[58] McCall recommended that the government continue to use pueblo auxiliaries, who had contributed significantly to earlier expeditions against the Navajos;[59] that troops be stationed along the trails used by the Navajos, rather than in the towns; and that storage depots be established throughout New Mexico, including one at Bernalillo, which was "central in the principal corn district."[60]

While Merikaana's soldiers explored the region and considered the problems of defending it, Merikaana's leaders began to install a government for the vast lands that became part of Merikaana with the signing of the Treaty of Guadalupe Hidalgo, which brought an end to the war with Mexico in 1848. Pueblo lands along the Río Grande, together with all of the lands west through modern Arizona, south to the border, and north into modern Utah and Colorado, became a part of the Territory of New Mexico. To rule this territory, Merikaana's president would confirm a governor, a delegate to Merikaana's Congress, and other officials. A territorial legislature and court system would be set up to provide local government, and a separate system would be established to have jurisdiction over the affairs of New Mexico's Indian peoples.

Under Spain and Mexico, a single system of government had jurisdiction over all of the residents of New Mexico, Indian and non-Indian alike. From time to time, an official had been appointed as Protector of the Indians to represent their interests in that system, and special laws and decrees had addressed the unique status, rights, and concerns of the Indian peoples, but the responsibility for carrying out those policies and implementing those decisions fell to the same governor, alcaldes, and other officials who had authority over Kastera's colonists.

Merikaana, however, had established a separate system to handle the affairs of Indians within its states and territories. Tribes who fought Merikaana, as well as individuals who remained "hostile" although their tribes had negotiated peace, became the responsibility of the War Department. A special agency known first as the Office, and later as the Bureau, of Indian Affairs was given responsibility for all matters involving peaceful Indians. Appointed representatives of this agency made up a chain that stretched from Merikaana's capital at Washington, D.C., to the remotest territories. Agents, sent to live among the various tribes, reported to a superintendent of Indian affairs in their territory, who answered in turn to the Washington office headed by the commissioner of Indian affairs and the secretary of the interior. These men were charged with carrying out the laws, policies, and orders of Merikaana's President and Congress, as well as the decisions of Merikaana's federal court system, the governing bodies with legal authority to determine Merikaana's relations with Indian peoples. Under Merikaana's law, the officials, courts, and legislatures of the individual states and territories had no jurisdiction over Indian peoples and lands.

By the time when agents were appointed for the new Territory of New Mexico, Merikaana had a formal policy toward Indians that had evolved during decades of westward expansion through Indian lands. The first goal of that policy was to send representatives to end any hostilities, negotiate treaties of peace with Indian nations, define the boundaries of Indian lands, and, if possible, to persuade the Indian peoples to exchange those lands for others more remote from Merikaana's settlements. The treaties they negotiated and the boundaries they defined would be submitted to Merikaana's Congress for ratification. The second goal of Merikaana's Indian policy was to educate the native peoples in Merikaana's ways, encourage them to become farmers, provide tools and teachers to train them, and protect them and their lands until they learned Merikaana's system. Like Kastera, Merikaana assumed that, having learned those ways, the native peoples would inevitably choose to adopt them.

When James S. Calhoun became the first Indian agent for New Mexico, his first task was to give his superiors an understanding of the many peoples who inhabited this vast new territory. From his reports and those of others who followed him, a consistent picture of the pueblos soon emerged.[61] New Mexico was the homeland of twenty pueblo groups with a total population of perhaps 10,000 people. Tamaya, with 399 people, was one of the smaller of these groups.[62] All of the pueblos were peaceful farming peoples,[63] and all refused to abandon their ancient traditions and ways of life.[64] Unlike the Navajos, Utes, Apaches, and Comanches, the pueblos posed no threat to Merikaana;[65] for many years they had been valuable allies[66] who honored their word. Merikaana's troops relied on them for supplies.[67] Hard-working, intelligent, and law-abiding,[68] they might well serve as a model for the other tribes.[69]

The reports of Merikaana's officials also showed, however, that the pueblos had problems that demanded Merikaana's attention. They had suffered heavily from Navajo raids.[70] Although they held unquestionable Spanish and Mexican grants for their lands, trespassers had begun to encroach on them. Their boundaries had not been surveyed, and some no longer possessed their original grant papers. As rumors spread that Merikaana would not protect pueblo lands, they grew uneasy. Some urgently needed additional lands to support their people.[71] Some had health problems.[72] The agents urged their superiors to send tools, blacksmithing equipment, additional agents, and teachers to establish schools in the pueblos.[73] Again and again the reports reminded Washington that these peaceful peoples, who had helped Merikaana in many ways, deserved Merikaana's assistance in protecting their land and their rights, and at least as much equipment and help as was being given to those who had fought Merikaana. As the years passed without any response from Merikaana, the officials reported increasing dissatisfaction among the pueblos.[74]

At first pueblo delegates came regularly to meet with Merikaana's officials. Within a week after Kearny took New Mexico in the name of Meri-kaana, "a deputation of Indian Pueblos" had gone to Santa Fe.[75] By 1852, pueblo delegates came to the city almost daily to speak with the superinten-dent of Indian affairs; to complain of trespass on their lands and the theft of their water; to discover the truth behind rumors about Merikaana's plans; to protest when raiders stole their livestock; to ask for permits to trade with distant tribes, and, returning from these trips, to bring information about these peoples to the office; and to discuss other important matters.[76]

For the Tamayame, of course, the most important of those matters was the question of Tamaya's lands. As early as 1848 some of the pueblo's documents had been recorded in Santa Fe; in 1852 Superintendent of Indian Affairs John Greiner made a clear copy of 31 documents, including the deeds to the Ranchiit'u purchases and records of the land disputes in the Angostura.[77] May 7, 1852, "the principal men of San Felipe" visited Superintendent Greiner to raise the old issue of the disputed lands. They told the superintendent that they were afraid that "the agent Mr. Baird would decide the claim against them," but Greiner reassured "them that Judge Baird would do them justice, and . . . was the proper person to investigate their claims."[78] Six days later, "Vicente and two others from Santa Ana" came to speak to the superinten-dent "about some animals and land," bringing with them "a letter from Genl Baird."[79] When Tamaya's delegation reached Santa Fe, the superintendent was not there, but the office "gave them all breakfast, dinner, and some of them supper and forage for their animals." Although they were not able to meet with the superintendent, one of them "had an interview with Col. Sumner," and the next morning, they "left . . . for home much pleas[ed]."[80] That September, another San Felipe delegation arrived in Santa Fe "with a complaint about some of their lands, which the Santa Ana Pueblos claim as theirs." Once again, the superintendent explained to them that he would not interfere in the matter and that they should speak to Judge Baird, the agent at Jémez.[81]

During this time, many Tamayame also made the trip to Santa Fe to request permits to trade with the Comanches. On June 22, the superinten-dent "gave Miguel Antonio Chacon and Juan Romero of the Pueblo of Santa Ana license to trade with the Comanches for two months."[82] A little more than a month later, two Tamayame traders went to Santa Fe "to report to this office, that they had got back from the trip to the Comanches," who sent word with them to ask Merikaana to attend a meeting of the Comanches with the Mescalero Apaches at Bosque Redondo.[83] On August 13, a Tamayame delegate came "to get a pass from this office to trade with the Comanches," not just for himself, but "to answer for twenty Indians from Santa Ana, and San Felipe pueblos." The delegate left with the pass and a message to carry to the Comanches from the Merikaana.[84] Twelve days later, another Tamayame was given a similar pass.[85]

Raiding and loss of livestock also brought the Tamayame and their neighbors to the superintendent's office. In May, a Navajo group complained that a group of Tamayame and a "Mexican" settler had attacked them, taking six animals.[86] Later that month another Navajo group arrived with a similar complaint.[87] In July, two Tamayame came "looking after stolen animals."[88] Although the office made note of these complaints, the superintendent generally told the delegates to see the agent nearest them, who would resolve the problem.

Not all who made the journey to Santa Fe found Merikaana's officials receptive to their concerns. Often pueblo delegates arrived only to learn that the superintendent was elsewhere, meeting with the hostile tribes. In early August 1852, six Tamayame and a delegation from Acoma came to Santa Fe to fulfill a promise they had made when they met with the superintendent at Acoma. Greiner, however, had gone to meet with the Apaches, and he had still not returned four days later, when several more Tamayame, accompanied by a group from Santa Clara and Santo Domingo, reached the capital. One of the staff in the office noted that the Tamayame had come "about some petty affairs," and he "put them all off" by telling them that Greiner "would not be back for two weeks."[89] The records of the superintendent's office indicate that Merikaana's officials often considered pueblo concerns insignificant, matters that the officials described as "trifling" problems or "no business of any consequence." Often the superintendent simply noted that a delegation had visited his office, but left no record in his journal of the concerns that had brought them there.[90]

Most of Merikaana's officials in New Mexico, however, did what they could to meet the pueblos' needs, but they could do very little because they lacked the money, time, and staff to resolve the problems, and the authority to effect any major change. During much of this period, a single agent was expected to serve all of the pueblos from the Río Grande to Hopi. The funds sent to New Mexico's Indian office were generally designated by Congress for specific tribes, and the agents had no authority to use these monies for other purposes, however urgent the needs. If the government in distant Washington, D.C., did not provide for the needs of New Mexico's pueblos, the agents could only appeal to their remote superiors for new policies and funds to address those needs. For many years, agent after agent wrote to Washington to explain that the pueblos needed and deserved Merikaana's help, but the reply was always the same: Congress had not authorized assistance, and no funds were available for the purpose.[91]

In explanation, Merikaana's officials in Washington reminded the agents in New Mexico that the government had limited funds and many urgent problems to resolve in the vast western territories: the unsettled boundary with Mexico had to be established; the hostile Indians who threatened Merikaana's settlers, miners, traders, and travelers must be controlled; roads, railroads, and stage routes were needed; the discovery of gold in California, the growing tension between northern and southern states, and the arguments of many other conflicting interests complicated the resolution of the territory's problems. Pleas for staff and funds came not only from Santa Fe, but from every agency under the office's jurisdiction.[92]

In distant Washington, D.C., it seemed clear to the officials who made Merikaana's policies and allocated the government's funds that the problems of the pueblos could wait. The agents themselves had said that the pueblos were "civilized," prosperous, and peaceful. Some officials argued that, if the pueblos could be considered citizens rather than Indians under the terms of the Treaty of Guadalupe Hidalgo, their problems—like those of any non-Indian citizens—could be resolved by New Mexico's legislature and courts. To the policy-makers, it seemed much more important to spend the limited federal funds to negotiate treaties with threatening tribes than to resolve the problems of those who were already peaceful. Their first concern was ending hostilities with the Navajo, Ute, Apache, and Comanche; with the tribes who caused damage to settlers along the Mexican border, for which Merikaana was legally obligated to compensate Mexico; and with the California tribes whose lands had been overrun by a hundred thousand gold-seekers.[93]

Thus, in Merikaana's first decades in New Mexico, the office of Indian affairs had little to offer the pueblos. Superintendent James Calhoun, who was also the governor of New Mexico, reported that he had signed treaties with some pueblos in 1851.[94] The next year, Congress approved a small sum that allowed a group from Tesuque to travel to Washington, D.C. and meet formally with Merikaana's leaders.[95] When pueblo delegates traveled to Santa Fe on official business, the superintendent sometimes offered them food and fodder for their animals.[96] Small sums were also set aside to buy tools and equipment for pueblo farmers,[97] but few of the tools actually reached them.[98] Even when the agency had tools to distribute to the pueblos, officials found that many pueblos, having heard that Merikaana intended to dispossess them, refused to accept the tools "lest it was intended to create a debt against them for which their lands would be taken."[99] In the years after Merikaana arrived, the pueblos had gone regularly to Santa Fe, hoping to meet with the officials of the new government. In 1851 and 1852, those officials reported that the pueblos had "besieged, almost, the superintendency." Among the visitors were delegates from Santa Ana, Zía, San Felipe, Santo Domingo, Cochití, and Sandía, who held a three-day council in Santa Fe in 1851, as well as six other pueblo delegations.[100] Superintendent Greiner explained that pueblos had come to see him almost every day except Easter Sunday in 1852.[101] Within a decade, however, the pueblos seem to have abandoned the quest for Merikaana's assistance, except in the most essential matters. By 1862, Superintendent Collins reported that the pueblos had "but little to do with the superintendency, except in the settlement of differences which arise between them and citizens who reside near their villages."[102]

For more than forty years, the Tamayame and their neighbors had supported Merikaana in many ways. They had offered food, supplies, and hospitality to traders, soldiers, and settlers. Pueblo volunteers had been valuable allies, marching with Merikaana's expeditions and providing information about hostile tribes. Although they feared that Merikaana planned to take their lands and grew increasingly dissatisfied with Merikaana's officials, who did little to help them, they had never taken up arms against Merikaana, even when Confederate soldiers marched into New Mexico to enlist their support against that government. For all of this time, they had watched as Merikaana's legal recognition and support went to tribes that had fought Merikaana from the start. Their initial contacts with government officials gave them few reasons to hope that Merikaana would protect their lands and their rights, but centuries of dealing with first Spanish and then Mexican officials had taught them that it was important to obtain the foreigners' papers, and that patience and persistence would be needed to do so.

At last that endurance was rewarded. In 1863, New Mexico's Superintendent, Michael Steck, traveled to Washington, D.C., to convince his superiors that Merikaana should formally recognize the pueblos, as Spain and Mexico had. With their approval, he ordered nineteen canes in Philadelphia, each tipped with silver and engraved with the date, the name of one of the pueblos, and the name of Merikaana's president, Abraham Lincoln. He also obtained land patents for some of the pueblos. Steck returned to New Mexico the following spring and arranged special ceremonies, held at the Peña Blanca agency in September and October 1864, to present Merikaana's canes of office to the pueblo governors.[103]

It seemed that Merikaana had at last recognized Tamaya for what it was:

the home of an ancient people, living in a land that had long been theirs, under a government long established. With that recognition, the time of informal contacts had ended, and Tamaya and Merikaana would meet as it was proper two governments should. When Tamaya's governor, holding the cane given to him as a token of his authority by Merikaana's president, spoke of the pueblo's lands and rights, Merikaana surely would listen. And it was urgent that Merikaana do so, for once again the coming of strangers had brought new threats to Tamaya.

EIGHT

Tamaya under Merikaana's Law

Only twenty years after Stephen Kearny marched into Santa Fe to claim New Mexico for Merikaana, as many as six thousand wagons a year made the journey from Merikaana to the Río Grande.[1] The travelers' journals were filled with descriptions of peaceful pueblo farmers planting, tending, and harvesting their crops in fields all along the river, and successful pueblo traders heading for the market in Santa Fe with pottery, "fruit, trout, and game from the mountains" to sell.[2] At Sandía and San Felipe, some visitors watched the people threshing their wheat, as the Tamayame did, in "a smooth piece of ground, surrounded by a circle of small trees, some seven feet apart, with strips of thong all around."[3] In the midst of this idyllic picture, however, observant visitors also saw the pueblo guards stationed in the fields to protect the crops from a host of threats: Navajo, Apache, and Comanche raiders, unchecked by Merikaana's presence; intruders who damaged the ditches that carried water to the fields; trespassers eager to claim pueblo land and water; and the travelers themselves, who often allowed stock to run loose through the fields. One writer, who observed the boys of San Felipe guarding the fields, explained that the pueblos had to keep "these watches over their crops . . . constantly . . . as they must not only protect the fields from intruders . . . but the acequias from incident."[4] New Mexico's first Indian agent reported that "numerous bands of thieving Indians, principally, Navajoes, Apaches, and Comanches, are straggling in every direction, busily employed in gathering their winter supplies, where they have not sown."[5] Amidst these dangers, the pueblos had remained law-abiding peoples. Between 1846 and 1866, not a single pueblo had been charged "for theft, or any kindred crime" in New Mexico.[6]

CHAPTER 8

Merikaana's new things gradually became part of the peoples' lives, as Kastera's had before them, but desire for new goods and new experiences did not obscure the people's respect for the ancient traditions. The pueblos attended plays performed in Spanish at a theater in Santa Fe, but they also gathered turquoise at the Cerillos mines, as their ancestors had done centuries before.[7] They sent delegations to speak with Merikaana's agents, but each pueblo retained its own leaders and its "own administration of justice," resolving its internal affairs "without any recourse to" Merikaana's "tribunals."[8] Many welcomed the efficient new farm tools Merikaana brought, but refused to accept them as a gift from Merikaana's agent for fear that taking them might compromise pueblo lands.

Passing through the region, Merikaana's travelers saw the pueblos clearly for what they were: ancient peoples, living in homelands long settled, under leaders and governments long established, recognized in more recent times by both Spain and Mexico. When Merikaana's government, however, turned its attention to the pueblos at last, it did not see the matter so clearly. Before Merikaana decided what to do about pueblo lands, its leaders wanted to know who, or what, the pueblos were.

Among the pueblos, who had just received canes of office from Merikaana's leaders, such a question would have seemed ridiculous. Had not Merikaana, like Kastera and Mexico before it, just recognized their government and their leaders? Centuries before Merikaana's recognition, the Hanu had been a sovereign people, guided by their leaders on their long journeys and within their homelands. For many generations, their government had passed from one group of leaders to the next. Those who met Merikaana still held the canes of office given to their ancestors by Kastera. Men still living could remember when Mexico had given the governors a second set of canes in recognition of their authority. Now Merikaana intended to impose its laws on the pueblos, as Spain and Mexico had done. But Merikaana's officials did not know what place the pueblos should have under these laws, which made a sharp distinction between people defined as "Indians" and people defined as "citizens."

Merikaana's understanding of Indian peoples, and the laws of the Trade and Intercourse Act of 1834, which defined Merikaana's relationship with them, resulted from contacts with peoples who were very different from the pueblos. The Indians Merikaana had dealt with had not, for the most part, been farming peoples living in large and permanent villages. Instead they had lived in bands and tribes, with economies based on hunting, gathering, and fishing throughout large territories, moving from area to area in a seasonal round that allowed them to use an area's resources effectively. They had no written titles to these lands, and neither their holdings nor their governments had been confirmed by European nations. Few spoke a European language or had lived under European laws. Most important, from Merikaana's point of view, many of them were hostile to Merikaana when the government established relations with them.[9]

Thus the first goal of Merikaana's policy was to negotiate with each tribe as quickly as possible, to draw up a treaty that would establish peace and ensure the safety of Merikaana's settlers, miners, and travelers. The tribe was asked to accept the authority of Merikaana's government in its relations with other peoples, to agree not to enter negotiations with other nations or to declare war without Merikaana's approval. Under the law, no nation was entitled to take lands claimed by native peoples without formally resolving the title to those lands. Thus each tribe was also asked to accept boundaries defined according to Merikaana's laws. In exchange for lands, water, and other rights the tribe relinquished, Merikaana would offer some compensation in the form of goods to be distributed to tribal members, unclaimed lands in another area, or the promise of services to be provided by agents, teachers, and other personnel.

It was accepted under Merikaana's law, however, that by signing such a treaty a native people did not relinquish its government or its authority over tribal affairs. A tribe that signed an agreement such as this acquired, in legal terms, the status of a "domestic dependent nation." Tribal members did not become citizens of Merikaana or of its states and territories. Just as local governments could not dictate to citizens of a foreign nation, they had no authority to enforce their laws on the members of an Indian tribe. Only Congress, the president and the federal courts—the three branches of government that represented Merikaana as a nation in its dealings with other nations—possessed the authority under Merikaana's law to deal with tribal groups.[10]

Over time Merikaana's law came to include a second definition of the status of Indian peoples, one that rested upon the assumption that they should, and eventually would, become citizens like their non-Indian neighbors, but that until they learned Merikaana's laws and ways of life, they were entitled to the protection of Merikaana's government. Under this definition, the government had the responsibility to act on their behalf as a trustee acted for a ward. For their protection, their property and funds would be held in trust by the government, and only those licensed by the government would be allowed to enter their lands. To prepare tribal peoples for their eventual role as citizens, Merikaana would provide them with teachers, agents, farmers, doctors, blacksmiths, and missionaries to teach them the new non-Indian language, beliefs, and ways.[11]

The pueblos, however, bore little resemblance to the tribes for whom these policies had been designed. They lived in large permanent villages, maintaining orchards, farms, livestock, and extensive irrigation systems. They had formal governments, with leaders who had authority to speak for the entire people in all matters that concerned them. Their experience with European systems of law and government dated back three hundred years, and their landholdings had been confirmed by Spain and Mexico in legal documents similar to those held by non-Indians. Many had worshipped in Christian churches for 150 years when Merikaana arrived in New Mexico. They had learned Kastera's language and had adopted many of Kastera's tools, types of clothing, and ways of doing things. Mexico's law had declared them to be citizens, although in practice the Mexican government had continued many Spanish policies and laws that recognized their status as Indians. All of these things made them appear, to many Americans, more qualified to be considered "citizens" under the law than any of the Indian peoples Merikaana had previously encountered.

At the same time, however, the pueblos differed in many essential ways from the non-Indian citizens among whom they lived. They had preserved their own ancient governments, traditions, and religions after three hundred years of contact with European civilization, and they clearly indicated their intention to continue to do so. Because each pueblo had originally held its land as a nation, long before any European power confirmed those landholdings, their status under Merikaana's law could never be the same as the status of an individual citizen who had acquired land in a country governed by European laws. Under the first aspect of Merikaana's Indian law, they could only be considered sovereign nations, who had, in relations with European powers, relinquished some of the external, but none of the internal, powers of sovereignty.

Nor was the pueblos' long familiarity with European ways sufficient reason, for many of Merikaana's officials, to conclude that they should no longer be considered Indians. It was true that they had adopted some of those ways, but most of the changes in their lives were only superficial. Although most could speak Spanish and their leaders had learned the intricacies of dealing with Kastera's officials, they still conducted their affairs in their native languages. Most still wore traditional clothing, sometimes adding a Mexican shawl or hat. They threshed their wheat with horses and occasionally used metal hoes, but many still planted with the digging sticks used by their ancestors. From the Spaniards they had learned to make adobe bricks, but they used them to build pueblos like those their ancestors had lived in. A church stood at the center of each pueblo, but few Anglo-European visitors would have recognized the familiar features of Christian services in the rituals observed there. After three centuries of contact with European peoples and their ways, the pueblos still treasured their ancient beliefs and ceremonies. And Merikaana's language, laws, and procedures were not Kastera's. Although some pueblo people had almost certainly begun to learn English, as their ancestors had mastered the Spanish language and the skills needed to obtain Kastera's papers to protect their lands and rights, it was hardly likely that, without any schools or teachers, in the short time Merikaana had been in New Mexico, they could have acquired a command of the skills to enter into complex legal transactions in this new language.

The question of the pueblos' legal status in Merikaana was far from academic, for the fate of the pueblos depended on the answer that Merikaana adopted. If Merikaana concluded that the pueblos were Indians under the law, they would receive the federal government's assistance and protection. Without permission from Merikaana's government, no pueblo would be able to sell, lease, trade, or give away its land and water, and no non-Indian would be allowed to enter pueblo lands. Merikaana's agents would have the obligation and the authority to protect them from trespassers who wanted those resources. The pueblos' own leaders and governments would be responsible for their internal affairs; as "Indian tribes" under the law, they would deal only with federal officials, not with those of the territory or its cities. They would be subject to no taxation. Merikaana would provide agents, teachers, and assistance to help them master the ways of this new culture, assistance that they could accept without fear of compromising their lands.

If, on the other hand, Merikaana concluded that the pueblos were citizens, they would have no relationship with Merikaana's government that acknowledged their special status as sovereign nations. Before Merikaana's law, their people would be simply individuals, like any others, with no special rights or constraints. Like non-Indian citizens, they would be able to vote, buy liquor, sell their lands, and conduct their business without any of the restraints imposed by the federal government on Indians. They would also be obligated to pay the same taxes, be subject to the same local laws, and appear before the same courts as their non-Indian neighbors. They would receive no federal support, no teachers, no agents, and no equipment or supplies. If their lands were threatened, they would have to hire their own lawyers and pursue justice in the local courts. If any pueblo individual wanted to sell his lands, he would have the right to do so, regardless of the wishes of the pueblo and its leaders. Whatever rights and possessions they could not defend in English under territorial laws before territorial judges, they would lose.

The debate over the pueblo's status began almost as soon as Merikaana claimed New Mexico and continued well into the next century. Although its outcome would determine their fate, the people of Tamaya and the other pueblos had little say in it. Instead, the question was argued in local legislatures by men for whom the pueblos could not vote, in courts where the pueblos were rarely represented, and in correspondence between men who had never seen New Mexico and knew its peoples only through what they read. Among the most vocal in this debate were those who, with the people of the pueblos, had the most to gain or lose from the decision: the non-Indian residents of New Mexico who had taken advantage of years of confusion to trespass upon, and then claim, pueblo lands and water rights.

These trespassers had prospered under Mexican rule, for Mexico had done little to protect pueblo lands. Now they, and others like them who eyed fertile pueblo fields and their supply of precious water, hoped to gain still more by convincing Merikaana that the pueblos should not be considered Indians. When local residents wrote the laws that would govern New Mexico Territory, they quickly exempted the pueblos from statutes applying to other Indians.[12] The man elected to represent New Mexico in Washington, D.C., soon tried to convince the commissioner of Indian affairs that the pueblos already had "many of the rights of citizenship," and were "quasi corporations" under New Mexico's law. As such, he said, they had the right to "appear in any court and sue and be sued by the name of their separate towns and villages." If Merikaana sent agents to take charge of them, the agents should only be able to offer them advice "whenever their causes or complaints are brought before the proper judicial tribunals." Like many other New Mexico residents, he also pointed out that the pueblos owned "the best land now under cultivation" in the territory.[13]

Meanwhile, Indian agents sent to New Mexico did not know exactly what responsibility they had to the pueblos. Although the federal government generally assumed that its agents had some duty to the pueblos, it provided little of the funding and none of the policies that would have enabled them to fulfill that responsibility, and no legal determination that would have quieted the insistence of local officials that the agents should have no jurisdiction in the pueblos. Many agents soon suspected that the local support for declaring that the people of the pueblos were citizens arose out of an interest in pueblo lands. James S. Calhoun, New Mexico's first Indian agent, explained that although each pueblo "had, from time immemorial, a separate and distinct political existence," in 1849 local "Prefects and Alcaldes" had tried to extend "some of the laws of this territory over these people—a matter they can not comprehend, and of which, they daily complain, and beg for relief." The fate of these people, he declared, "should invite the most searching consideration of the gravest, wisest, and purest men of our land."[14] He urged the government to set up agencies at all twenty pueblos, or at least provide an agent for each of eight pueblo districts.[15] Two years later, Calhoun was still asking his superiors for the "authority and means" to redress pueblo grievances.[16]

Others who followed Calhoun echoed his comments. Superintendent Meriwether explained that, although the pueblos held Spanish and Mexican land grants, none of those grants gave them title in fee simple, which would have allowed them to sell their lands like other citizens. He declared that the pueblos should not be considered citizens, in spite of the fact that local courts had already ruled that land in New Mexico could not qualify as "Indian territory," and he recommended that Congress pass an act to define pueblo status.[17] Not all of New Mexico's agents, however, were willing to state the case so bluntly. Some, like Agent Yost, simply pointed out the contradictions between territorial and federal law, and waited for their superiors to tell them what they should do.[18]

Through the 1850s, however, most of New Mexico's Indian agents argued that the pueblos should be considered Indians, and their superiors in Washington, D.C., tended to agree. In 1850, the commissioner of Indian affairs stated that, although the pueblos might be ready to hold citizenship in a few years, they should have agents in the interim.[19] Five years later, the commissioner asked Congress to repeal the New Mexico law that defined the pueblos as corporate entities that could sue and be sued in local courts. He explained that the pueblos had already suffered greatly from this law, because most suits were filed or encouraged by parties with an interest in pueblo lands. In the end, few but lawyers and "officers of the courts" benefitted from the law; he cited the example of cases pending between Acoma and Laguna, in which the legal fees would be "sufficient to cover all that the two pueblos are worth."[20] The U.S. House Election Committee confirmed a ruling that disallowed two hundred pueblo votes in a local election on the grounds that the pueblos did not have the right to vote.[21] Congress, however, did not act to define pueblo status, and Merikaana's policy remained confused. Agents were sent to the pueblos, just as they were sent to other tribes, but very little money was appropriated for them, and their authority was not clearly outlined.[22]

During the following decade, the confusion increased, as officials in Washington seemed to favor the position that they had no jurisdiction in the pueblos, while New Mexico's agents and superintendents pleaded that the pueblos needed and deserved Merikaana's protection. While Superintendent Steck was urging the government to recognize pueblo governments by presenting canes of office to the governors, the commissioner of Indian affairs told the local Indian agent that, because New Mexico was not "Indian territory," the agency had no authority to resolve pueblo conflicts.[23] The commissioner asked Congress to make "temporary appropriations for them," but he had concluded that existing laws placed the pueblos under territorial jurisdiction.[24] He suggested that perhaps the pueblos' special circumstances deserved a special government policy.[25] Two years later, Superintendent Norton urged Congress to treat the pueblos as it treated other Indian tribes, to prevent the sale of pueblo lands, and to invalidate any sales that had already been made. He recommended drawing up laws that would forbid the pueblos to buy or drink alcoholic beverages, and he argued that any lawsuits involving the pueblos should be heard in federal, not territorial, courts.[26] A special federal agent who visited New Mexico the same year, however, considered the pueblos so different from other Indians that he recommended that data about them be removed from the government's Indian statistics.[27]

Then, in 1867, New Mexico Chief Justice Slough ruled that the pueblos were not Indians under the definition of the Trade and Intercourse Act of 1834. The pueblo agents protested immediately, appealing to their superiors to protect the pueblos from the effects of the territorial court decision.[28] Agent John Ward explained that this ruling would ruin the pueblos, who welcomed the protection of Merikaana's government, but remained unwilling to abandon their traditional ways.[29] Noting that the federal district attorney had filed an appeal in the case before the U.S. Supreme Court, Agent W. F. M. Arny urged the government to protect the pueblos until the appeal was heard.[30] Superintendent Norton predicted that, as a result of Justice Slough's decision, the pueblos, who had already lost their best lands to trespass and sale, would lose still more unless the government altered its policy.[31] The commissioner of Indian affairs agreed, warning the secretary of the interior that the pueblos might be destroyed if Slough's ruling were allowed to stand.[32] The federal attorney general gave his support to District Attorney Elkins' plan to appeal the decisions of New Mexico's courts in this pueblo case and another, involving the Comanches, in which the court had held that the provisions of the Trade and Intercourse Act did not apply to any tribe in New Mexico.[33]

While the appeals were being heard, the potential consequences of New Mexico's position became ever more clear to those who had immediate responsibility for Merikaana's relations with the pueblos. Agent Ward explained that "the main and principal cause of most of the troubles . . . between the Mexican [Hispanic] Citizens and our Pueblo Indians results from the encroachments of the former, who will manage . . . to get some foothold within the grants of the latter." Ward pointed out that "the want of proper power and authority on the part of the officers of the Department" enabled these trespassers to take advantage of the pueblos.[34] Agents Ford and Cooper protested the injustice of Slough's ruling. The pueblos, Ford argued, were "*Indians* in every sense of the word, and until *all* tribal organizations are broken up, and Indian tribes no longer recognized as independent treaty-making powers, they are entitled to all the privileges and government protection accorded by law to the other tribes."[35] Agent Cole urged that the question of pueblo status be resolved,[36] and Agent Lewis warned that if the pueblos were declared citizens, they would be subject to trespass, fraud, and other outrages.[37]

Many of the agents explained that the pueblos would obtain no justice in the territorial courts, where they would be at the mercy of those who wanted their lands. It would be unjust, said Agent Ford, to allow these courts to determine the affairs of the pueblos:

> They know nothing of our laws or mode of procedure in our courts;
> and an action brought against a Mexican [Hispanic] by an Indian be-
> fore a Mexican [territorial] jury, would certainly be decided in favor
> of the defendant. These people have their own laws and form of gov-
> ernment. When any question arises among them it is decided by
> their own governor and head men, to the satisfaction of all parties.
> But when they are assailed from without, they can only look to the
> government, through their agent, for protection of their rights.[38]

Agent Lewis explained that the pueblos had no redress when non-Indians trespassed on their lands, for they would receive "no justice" in the local courts whose judges, elected by non-Indians, "almost invariably decide cases in favor of the Mexicans [Hispanics] and against the Indians, no matter how clear the evidence may be in favor of the latter." To "prevent such gross injustice," he advocated that Congress require that any suit involving a pueblo "only be brought before the United States district court." He concluded that the pueblos deserved "all the benefits derived by any tribe of

Indians," for "whatever may have been their position under Spanish rule, or however essentially different from their nomadic brethren their mode of living, they are Indians in every sense of the word." The pueblos could not vote for territorial officials,[39] and, as Superintendent Dudley pointed out, most had "in every instance . . . refused" to do so, even when candidates had tried to woo them, because they wanted to remain under government protection. Although Superintendent Dudley believed, "on general principles," that Indians should become citizens, he feared that the pueblos—because of their traditional ways, their limited knowledge of the law, and "the prejudice which exists against them on the part of the Mexicans [Hispanics]"—would suffer "if deprived of the care of an agent and the special protection of the Government."[40] When Agent Thomas received permission in 1876 to have the federal district attorney represent the pueblos, he was hopeful that this would help him to prevent trespass' and evict illegal settlers from pueblo lands.[41]

The pueblos had also made their position clear. Agent Cooper reported that "the Indians themselves ask that they may be tried for all offenses by United States authorities, and not by the alcaldes . . . . The Pueblo Indians do not want to be considered citizens." They recognized, as they told the agent, that they knew so little of Merikaana's laws and ways that they could be "easily imposed on." Cooper urged Congress to correct the problem by forbidding the sale of pueblo lands, declaring prior sales void, forcing non-Indians who claimed those lands to return them to the pueblos, and providing money for pueblo schools. The agent also reminded his superiors that if the pueblos had been "a warlike people, fighting against the government, they would receive presents of every kind," but because they remained peaceful and law-abiding, they had been "forgotten."[42] Agent Ford added that the question gave "rise to much uneasiness if not dissatisfaction among the Pueblos, and opens a way by which much injustice is done to them."[43] The commissioner of Indian affairs complained that "since the decision of Justice Slough . . . these very friendly and deserving people have been ill at ease; imposed upon and continually annoyed, they have not been permitted to pursue undisturbed their way of life according to ancient manners and customs, under their own governors and laws. . . ."[44]

While the case awaited decision in Merikaana's court, however, other federal officials suggested that ruling in the pueblos' favor would be costly for Merikaana. After visiting the pueblos in 1869, Special Inspector Colyer recommended that the pueblos be declared citizens and forced to pay taxes on their extensive crops, herds, and orchards.[45] Two years later, when Agent

Arny returned to the pueblos, he argued that non-Indian holdings within pueblo lands had such great value that Merikaana's government could not afford to expel non-Indian settlers and compensate them for their losses. Suggesting that the pueblos were willing to allow most of the intruders to remain, he recommended that Congress allow the pueblos to sell their lands and permit non-Indians to prove up homesteads within pueblo grants.[46]

In 1876, nine years after Justice Slough's ruling, Merikaana's Supreme Court brought an end to pueblo hopes by upholding New Mexico's claim that the provisions of the federal Trade and Intercourse Act of 1834 did not apply to the pueblos. Deciding the case *U.S. v. Joseph,* the court concluded that the pueblos could not be considered Indians under Merikaana's law.[47] Because none of the Indians within the boundaries of the United States when the Trade and Intercourse Act was passed had resembled the pueblos, the Office of Indian Affairs could not apply the provisions of the act to them. The court, however, addressed only half of the issue: it ruled that pueblos could not be considered Indians under the law, but it did not declare them to be citizens.[48]

Thus the Supreme Court decision, which was to define pueblo status under Merikaana's law for more than thirty-five years, placed the people of Tamaya and their neighbors in limbo. By ruling that they were not Indians, the court denied them the protection of the federal government and gave local courts and officials jurisdiction over them. By neglecting to define them as citizens, the ruling also deprived them of the right to vote for the local officials who would have authority over them, the right to hold local office themselves, and the opportunity to enjoy the other rights commonly held by citizens. The court left unanswered many questions that would continue to plague the pueblos and their agents. Could local governments, under this decision, legally tax the pueblos? What, if anything, did the law allow the federal government to do for the pueblos? Could pueblo governments, or pueblo individuals, sell pueblo lands? Would Merikaana's government be allowed to provide attorneys to represent the pueblos in local land cases? Were their agents entitled to offer them tools, funds, personnel, and services provided with funds appropriated for Indians? And how would Merikaana deal with the pueblos' land claims?

For Tamaya and the other pueblos, it was essential to obtain Merikaana's formal recognition for their land titles. Only then could they hope to control and evict trespassers, for without official papers the courts would not uphold their claims, and Merikaana's agents were virtually powerless to help them. The pressures on pueblo lands multiplied rapidly as the region's non-Indian population grew. By 1855, when Lieutenant Whipple surveyed a route for a railroad through the region, Santa Fe and Albuquerque together had more than 7,000 residents. Nearer to Tamaya stood the towns of Angostura, with 1,000 people; Algodones, with 1,500; and Bernalillo, with 504.[49] Many of the non-Indian residents hoped to take advantage of the transition in government and the debate over the pueblos' legal status to acquire valuable pueblo land and water.

In the treaty that ended the war with Mexico, Merikaana had agreed to honor all existing land grants and claims, both Indian and non-Indian. To gain Merikaana's recognition of their holdings, however, the peoples of New Mexico had, in effect, to prove that they truly held title to their claims. The first step was submitting their papers to New Mexico's surveyor general, who would examine the documents, check them against material in New Mexico's archives and against the records of adjacent claims, and, if necessary, obtain testimony from anyone who had information about the status of a claim. The boundaries would have to be defined, precisely measured, and marked according to Merikaana's system before any claim could be approved. When this procedure was complete, New Mexico's surveyor general would submit the papers to Merikaana's Congress, with a recommendation that the grant be confirmed or denied. If Congress approved, the landholder would be issued an official patent for the lands.[50]

The task of reviewing New Mexico's land claims was enormous and complex. Soon after the first surveyor general was appointed in 1854, more than 1,000 claims had been filed. The surveyor general was legally required "to ascertain the origin, nature, character, and extent of all claims to lands under the laws, usages, and customs of Spain and Mexico, and to report on all such claims as originated before the cession of the territory under the treaty of Guadalupe Hidalgo." The archives that contained the records of Spanish and Mexican grants in New Mexico, however, were in disarray. In the first years of American rule, some of the papers had been discarded by Americans who did not know what they were. Many people whose families had held land for generations no longer had the papers to prove their ownership, and scarcely any of the grants possessed boundaries that were clearly defined in Merikaana's terms. Most of Merikaana's officials spoke no Spanish, and few of the claimants had enough command of English to explain the complex legal history of their lands. As a result, the possibility for fraud and injustice was enormous, and unscrupulous individuals soon recognized that the process offered them the opportunity to acquire land or increase their holdings.[51]

Soon after the first surveyor general, William Pelham, took office, he began to study pueblo lands. He had a mandate to deal with all claims "precisely as Mexico would have done had sovereignty not changed." As soon "as the nature of the duty" would permit, he was to report to his superiors on the status of pueblo claims.[52] He noted in his annual report of September 1855 that "the grant to said pueblo of Santa Ana had been filed in his office, and by him examined and approved," but Tamaya did not appear in the report on the pueblos he submitted the following year[53] or the list of sixteen pueblos and eighteen non-Indians whose claims were submitted for congressional approval in 1858.[54]

Thus, when Superintendent Steck presented a cane of office to Tamaya's governor in 1864, the pueblo was not among those that received patents to their lands.[55] The same year, the pueblo agent stated that the Tamayame had not yet filed title papers for the pueblo's lands and, though the surveyor had requested funds six years earlier, Tamaya's grant had still not been surveyed.[56] Two years later, Tamaya, Zuñi, Acoma, and Laguna remained unsurveyed.[57]

When Merikaana's surveyor general at last presented Tamaya's claim to the original square for congressional review in 1867 and 1868, Tamaya no longer had the papers confirming the grant. Tamaya's Governor Antonio Esculla, "the legal custodian of the papers belonging to the pueblo," told Merikaana's officials that the pueblo had received a grant from the King of Spain, "the same as the other pueblos in the country," but the paper could no longer be found, "though it had been searched for diligently for a long time." Lieutenant Governor José Sarracino added that, as he understood it, Tamaya had once possessed a paper, but "as it was frequently necessary to produce it in settling questions or disputes, it at length got mislaid and has not since been found." Both men offered a description of the pueblo's lands. To the west, Tamaya shared a border with Zía; to the north, the boundary lay along the Borrego Spring; to the east, a stone marker near Venada Arroyo marked the edge of Tamayame land; and at the south, the line ran along Duran Hill. Three Santa Fe residents confirmed this testimony, agreeing that the pueblo was ancient, that the Tamayame had been in this land before the Spanish conquest, and that its location was as described. Simón Delgado reported that he had been at Santa Ana in 1833 or 1834, and that the county in which the pueblo stood had taken its name from Santa Ana. New Mexico Surveyor General John Clark stated that his office had examined, surveyed, and approved Tamaya's grant. The commissioner of the General Land Office argued that since eight other pueblos who no longer had their original grant papers had had their claims approved in 1858, Congress should confirm Tamaya's four-square-league grant, with the pueblo church as its center. After the first hearings, the House Committee on Private Land Claims reported:

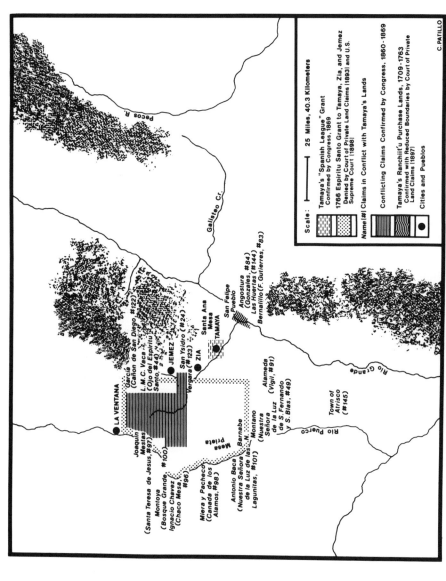

TAMAYA'S LANDS AND MERIKAANA'S LAWS

Scale: |————| 25 Miles, 40.3 Kilometers

Tamaya's "Spanish League" Grant
Confirmed by Congress, 1869

1766 Espíritu Santo Grant to Tamaya, Zia, and Jemez
Denied by Court of Private Land Claims (1893) and U.S.
Supreme Court (1886)

Name(#) Claims in Conflict with Tamaya's Lands

Conflicting Claims Confirmed by Congress, 1860–1869

Tamaya's Ranchíti'u Purchase Lands, 1709–1763
Confirmed with Reduced Boundaries by Court of Private
Land Claims (1897)

● Cities and Pueblos

C. PATILLO

LA VENTANA ●

García
(Cañon de San Diego #122)

L. M. C. Vaca
(Ojo del Espíritu
Santo, #44)

JEMEZ

San Ysidro (#24)

Vergara (#23)

ZIA ●

Santa Ana
Mesa

TAMAYA ■

San Felipe
Pueblo

Angostura
(Gonzales, #84)
Las Huertas, (#144)
Bernalillo(F. Gutierres), #83)

Joaquin
Mestas
(Santa Teresa de Jesus, #97)

Montoya
(Bosque Grande, #100)

Ignacio Chavez
(Chaco Mesa)

Mesa
Prieta

Miera y Pacheco
(Cañada de los
Alamos, #98)

Antonio Baca
(Nuestra Señora
de la Luz de las
Lagunitas, #101)

Barnabe
Montaño
(Nuestra
Señora
de la Luz
de S. Fernando
y S. Blas, #49)

Alameda
(Vigil, #91)

Town of
Atrisco
(#145)

Rio Puerco

Rio Grande

Pecos R.

Galisteo Cr.

On examination we find that many years ago the government of
Spain granted a certain tract of land to the pueblo of Santa Ana, in
the province of New Mexico; that said grant was in writing, and full
possession given of the lands granted in compliance with the laws,
usages, and customs of that nation; that such grant was recognized
by the republic of Mexico, and such possession was a continuous possession until the cession of said province of New Mexico.

On February 9, 1869, Congress approved a bill confirming Tamaya's first
grant.[58]

Confirmation of this grant, twenty-one years after Merikaana officially
came to New Mexico, offered some protection to the center of Tamayame
land. Two years later, however, in 1871, three non-Indian families still lived
on claims within the square grant.[59] And the rest of Tamayame lands still
had no protection at all under Merikaana's law. Once the pueblo's lands had
extended south to the area near Corrales and Alameda where Tamayame
farming villages had long stood, and west into the valley of the Río Puerco
south of Siiku, but the pueblo had not received Spanish or Mexican papers for
all of these lands. The pueblo held titles to the Ranchiit'u, which provided
essential farming lands for the pueblo, and to the Espiritu Santo grant, used
by Tamayame herdsmen, farmers, and hunters, but decades would pass before
Merikaana completed its review of these claims.

The confirmation process for the Espiritu Santo began in 1873, when New
Mexico's surveyor general submitted his report to Congress, more than eleven
decades after Kastera had granted this land to Tamaya, Jémez, and Zía. For
this claim, the pueblos had copies of all of the original documents. They had
submitted those papers, and translations had been made of the many testi-
monies, decrees, and reports that led up to the grant. To their documents, the
surveyor general added statements from two shepherds who lived in the
Cañon de Jémez, who said that the pueblos had "always pastured their stock
upon the tract," except in times "when the Navajo Indians were at war." The
shepherds also testified that for the last three or four years, a man named
Diego Baca had been living near the spring which gave the grant its name.
The two witnesses, however, did not know by what right Baca had settled
this land. The surveyor general concluded that the three pueblos had maintained possession of the grant since 1766 "without any objection . . . from
any adverse claimant." He was "of the opinion that the Indians show an
absolute grant and full possession under it, and Congress ought to confirm
the same." He explained that, although the documents had been translated

and the claim presented to his office in 1856, for "some reason," perhaps "some fear or disagreement among the Indians, it was withdrawn and not prosecuted." Had the claim been submitted, he had "no doubt these lands would have been confirmed when the others were."[60] Congress, however, took no action on the pueblos' claim to the Espíritu Santo.[61]

Three years later, Stephen McElroy completed a preliminary survey of the Espíritu Santo. The plat, survey, and field notes, dated October-November 1877, were approved by Surveyor General Atkinson. These documents described an area of 382,849 acres, with boundaries extending north from township 13 N to township 18 N and from Mesa Prieta and the Río Puerco on the west to the borders of Zía and Jémez on the east. The survey also showed, however, a host of claims conflicting with the pueblos' grant. Those claims, which included lands all around the periphery of the grant as well as a large portion in its center, in the valley of the Espíritu Santo, had been identified by name and marked by number: The Cañon de San Diego (no. 122), Joaquín Mestas (no. 97), Montoya (no. 100), Ignacio Chávez (no. 96), Cañada de los Alamos (no. 98), Antonio Baca (no. 101), Barnabe Montaño (no. 49), Vergara (no. 123), San Ysidro (no. 24), and in the valley and surrounding the spring, a smaller grant also called Espíritu Santo (no. 44). By the time when the survey was completed, Congress had already approved two of those non-Indian claims—the smaller Espíritu Santo and the San Ysidro grant. While the San Ysidro claim extended only a short distance into pueblo land, the non-Indian Espíritu Santo claim covered nearly one-third of the pueblos' grant, including the spring and the valley that had been one of the most significant parts of the original grant.[62] Louis María Cabeza de Vaca (or Baca) had filed his claim to this 125,875-acre section of the Espíritu Santo in 1856, declaring that he held the land under a grant dated 1813 or 1815. New Mexico's surveyor general approved Vaca's claim in 1860, and Merikaana's Congress confirmed it in March 1869, just a few months after Tamaya's square was confirmed (see map on page 156).[63]

Trespass on the Espíritu Santo had gone unchecked in the years since Merikaana's arrival. In 1855, José Leandro Perea of La Ventana ran 50,000 sheep on the pueblo grant during the winter; in the following ten years, joined by his nephew, Mariano Otero, he tripled the size of his herd. By 1870, the region's two major stockmen—Otero and Pedro Perea—had both established their headquarters in the Río Puerco lands and the Espíritu Santo. Farmers and would-be colonists moved into the region from Peña Blanca and La Jara in the hope of using the river to water their crops, and by the late 1880s, when Agent M. C. Williams made a special report on the Espíritu

Santo, "the greater part" of the pueblos' grant was "covered by other grants and claimed by other parties, some of them confirmed by Congress." The trespassers had claimed the best of the region's land and, according to Williams, "wherever there is water on said grant, it is occupied or claimed by citizens, some of them having grants as aforesaid." Speculators encouraged others to settle in the area around La Ventana, Casa Salazar, San Luis, and Cabezón. In 1890, fifty investors, most from England, established a settlement called Fruitvale within the Montano grant.[64] Because the territorial courts refused to evict anyone from a grant whose status had not been resolved, as many as forty settlers were using the pueblos' Ojo del Espiritu Santo lands. Some of the trespassers had been established there for many years[65] by 1888, when Merikaana's commissioner of Indian Affairs asked for, and received, a map showing the claims in conflict with the pueblo grant.[66]

By the late 1880s a new group of trespassers had joined stockmen, farmers, investors, and settlers on the Ojo del Espiritu Santo lands. The arrival of the railroad in New Mexico spurred a search for coal throughout the region. In 1874 local residents had testified that they knew of no "mines or minerals, or coal upon the land," but within sixteen years coal and other minerals had been discovered inside the pueblo grant, along the Río Puerco.[67] The 1890 census reported that "lately valuable mineral deposits have been discovered upon the grant, especially on the Rio Pero [sic] and near Salisaro." Prospectors had found "a 15-foot vein of lignite coal, also copper, gold and silver." The census-taker, Henry Poore, reported that the pueblos "threaten all comers to this valley who carry picks and shovels, though they show no inclination to mine themselves." The pueblos also complained "that immense flocks of sheep range on the land. Stock from the adjoining Mexican [Hispanic] village of San Ysidro frequently invades their corn and grain fields."[68]

Throughout this decade, complaints of trespass increased, but the pueblos had no recourse except to take their cases to the unreceptive territorial courts.[69] The Ojo del Espiritu Santo was essential to Tamaya, which was "well supplied with stock, most of which is herded on the large grant, used also by Zía and Jémez." Unfortunately, Merikaana offered little assistance to protect the pueblos' interests. Census-taker Poore, for example, suggested that the problem might be resolved by confirming the pueblos' right to use the original grant for pasture, but allowing non-Indians to mine within the grant's boundaries.[70]

Those staking claim to Tamaya's Espiritu Santo lands included two prominent New Mexico politicians, members of a "ring of lawyers, politicians and businessmen" who "managed to manipulate land grants throughout the territory."[71] Mariano S. Otero, a Bernalillo businessman and banker who had served as New Mexico's delegate to Congress in 1878,[72] was "accused of having an interest in the Ojo del Espiritu Santo and Bernalillo grants and six others" during the 1890 elections.[73] Two years later, Bernalillo County residents mounted a "feverish" but unsuccessful campaign against "the 'boss rule' exercised by Mariano S. Otero and his 'ring' of henchmen who had long governed the county."[74] Although Otero survived this election, he was able to maintain his claim to the Espiritu Santo for only a short time before he was outdone by "New Mexico's most successful land-grabber," Thomas B. Catron.[75] Catron, a lawyer who often took land-grant cases, had been so successful "that the land he acquired through legal fees or separate purchase gave him the reputation in 1883 of being one of the largest landowners in the nation."[76] At various times, Catron was accused of fraud, tax evasion, collaboration with the surveyors general in questionable land deals, and the use of undue influence, both alone and in collaboration with other New Mexico politicians, lawyers, and land speculators.[77] By 1893 his holdings included a two-thirds interest in "the 78,000 acres of the Espiritu Santo Grant";[78] three years later he claimed the entire "Espiritu Santo Grant of 113,141 acres."[79] And this was just a fraction of Catron's total holdings, which included interests in 75 grants and some 4 million acres for which he served as attorney or part owner, as well as 2 million acres that he owned outright.[80]

Tamaya was not alone in its complaints. After 40 years of American rule in New Mexico, the territory's land matters were in a state of chaos. In 3 decades, only 150 of more than 1,000 land claims had been reported to Congress, and Congress had acted on only 71. As critics had charged for years, this delay amounted "to a denial of justice." The arrival of increasing numbers of Anglo homesteaders, cattlemen, and railroad builders further complicated the matter. Fraud and speculation flourished, and lawyers, who often took their fees in shares of land or minerals, profited enormously. Something had to be done to settle New Mexico's land issues, and, in 1891, Congress created the Court of Private Land Claims to hear and resolve claims to lands in the region Merikaana had obtained from Mexico in 1848.[81]

When word reached Tamaya that the pueblo's claims to the Espiritu Santo and the Ranchiit'u, with all of the other unresolved claims, would be heard before this five-judge court, the Tamayame and their agent had many questions. In 1892, when the new court opened session in Santa Fe, Agent John Robertson reported that the trespassers had moved quickly to secure title to the lands they had acquired. The agent had discovered "that the boundaries of some of these filings cover lands which Pueblo Indians have claimed for many years." Some of the claimants were trying "to have the titles perfected by the Court in a very quiet manner," and Robertson had "only just learned" of their claims. What, he wanted to know, could he do to protect pueblo interests?[82] He needed information not only about government policy and pueblo status, but also about the specific claims and lands. Two days later, he asked that the surveyor general be required to furnish the pueblo agency with copies of plats and papers related to pueblo lands.[83]

Meanwhile, the people of Tamaya, Jémez, and Zía had their own questions. With the help of E. M. Fenton, the teacher at the Presbyterian School at Jémez, pueblo leaders wrote to the secretary of the interior. After reviewing the history of their Espiritu Santo grant, they explained that a lawyer, with their agent's approval, had offered to represent their claim in exchange for land and exclusive rights to mine coal on their grant. Before they made their decision on his offer, the pueblos wanted to know whether they would have to employ a lawyer and go to court to defend their claim. They asked Merikaana's official, if that were the case, to give them the name of a "good man" to represent them.[84]

Meanwhile, Merikaana's officials had begun reviewing the pueblos' legal status and trying to determine the answer to this question. In July 1891, almost a year earlier, the justice department in Washington, D.C., had ruled that trespassers on pueblo lands "may be ejected, or punished civilly by a suit for trespass, according to the laws regulating such matters in the Territories."[85] New Mexico's district attorney saw "no difficulty, under the laws quoted, in the way of the Pueblo Indian protecting his rights of property in the courts of this territory exactly as any other person may there protect like rights." He added that pueblos could "hire the best legal talent in the Territory . . . and I see no reason why the United States should aid" them. Since the pueblos owned some of the "best agricultural lands in New Mexico and as they pay no taxes," he thought that they could "well afford to pay for their private suits in our courts."[86] Merikaana's attorney general saw "no reason why the United States should appear in their behalf," and in April 1892 he ordered New Mexico's federal district attorney not to represent the pueblos.[87]

A month earlier, Agent Robertson had notified the teacher at the Jémez school that the pueblos would have to hire their own lawyer if they wanted one. He recommended that they accept the offer they had received, and he believed that it would be in their best interest to persuade the lawyer to accept land or coal leases instead of cash payment.[88] Then, in April 1892, the agent wrote directly to the governor of Jémez, explaining that the pueblos would have to employ their own lawyer. He urged them to do so without delay, to accept the offer made by Mr. George Hill Howard, and to notify the agency as soon as they had made their decision.[89]

So the Tamayame, with Zía and Jémez, hired the firm of Jeffries and Earle and Attorney George Hill Howard, the man recommended by their agent, to represent them in their suit for the Espiritu Santo lands. When the case was heard, Merikaana's district attorney did not simply refuse to represent Tamaya and the other pueblos; he actively questioned the validity of their grant. In short order, the Court denied the pueblos' claim August 18, 1893, ruling that "no evidence of actual possession had ever been presented." The decision held that even if the grant had been valid, it "would not convey title but was only a grazing permit."[90]

The following April, the pueblo agent received a letter from M. S. Otero of Albuquerque, who was interested in "the lands of the Santa Ana Indians lying on the Rio Grande and west of it." What he wanted to know was whether his "friends can file upon it as Public Domain." Agent Bullis, who claimed to have no data about the status of the land, referred Otero to the Santa Fe Land Office.[91] The following October, when the governor of Jémez wrote to ask the commissioner of Indian affairs about the pueblos' claim, Agent Bullis returned the letter without forwarding it to Washington, explaining that he could answer all of the governor's questions. The Court of Private Land Claims had denied the pueblos' claim to the Espiritu Santo lands, and Attorney George Hill Howard had appealed the case to the U.S. Supreme Court, which had as yet made no decision.[92]

While Tamaya, Zía, and Jémez waited for Merikaana's court to hear that appeal, the Tamayame, with Attorney Howard, filed their claim to the Ranchiit'u before the Court of Private Land Claims.[93] In November 1896, the case was postponed until the court's next term because Attorney Howard was ill.[94] The pueblo agent wrote to the attorney and, at the request of Tamaya's governor, sent the Tamayame a copy of one of the documents presented as evidence in the case.[95] In the suit, lawyer Thomas B. Catron, who claimed to own the Espiritu Santo lands, represented the people who claimed the Bernalillo and Angostura grants. In the presentation of the Angostura claim, Catron succeeded in introducing a new boundary for his clients—a boundary that extended the Angostura (Gallegos) grant south into the Ranchiit'u. The final decrees thus recorded that the northern boundary of the Ranchiit'u lay, not in the middle of the Angostura, as had been confirmed in earlier adjudications, but at a point more than half a mile south of Angostura, at a line of stones described as leading from the Rio Grande to a hill known as Loma Infernada. This was the site of the original south boundary, not the north boundary. Thus Jesus M. Castillo, Justiano Castillo, Mariano S. Otero, and Jose Leandro Perea gained title to lands within the Ranchiit'u. When this land was surveyed for the patent, one of the landholders, Justiano Castillo, who had claimed and been awarded a strip of land just north of this boundary, testified that he had seen "the stones placed" along this line. Even this direct statement of the recent origin of the markers, however, did not alter the court's findings.[96] In May 1897, the Court of Private Land Claims made its ruling. The court confirmed Tamaya's claim to the Ranchiit'u, but redefined its boundaries substantially and reserved the rights to gold, silver, and quicksilver within the grant to the United States.[97] Although the Court's decision "purported to confirm all of the purchases made by Santa Ana beginning in 1709," the lands awarded to Santa Ana amounted to only a fraction of the original landholdings. The combined area of the Ranchiit'u purchases was "some 87,000 acres"; the area confirmed by the Court amounted to "only 4,945.24 acres," mainly a part of the lands purchased from Quiteria Contreras. The ruling excluded "virtually all of the lands west of that tract, and north on the west side of the river to the Salida de Angostura and the Arroyo Cuerbo . . . without explanation." On a sketch map prepared for the court hearings, the Río Puerco, which formed the western boundary of two of the tracts, was drawn just west of the junction of the Río Jémez and the Río Grande. Other difficulties with the boundaries emerged in the following years. In 1899 Surveyor General Quimby Vance asked a special examiner to look into conflicting boundaries established by the 1898 Angostura survey and the 1859 Clements survey of San Felipe Pueblo, which showed conflicts with the boundaries established for the Ranchiit'u, Angostura, and Santa Rosa de Cubero grants. Although these surveys showed overlapping claims, and there were serious questions about the way the Clements survey had been made, the government did nothing to resolve the inconsistencies before issuing patents with the boundaries recommended by the Court of Private Land Claims.[98] Meanwhile, in 1898, the U.S. Supreme Court upheld the lower court's decision on the Espiritu Santo lands, ruling that Tamaya, Zía, and Jémez had not documented their claim to the grant.[99]

Three hundred years after Tamaya's representative had listened at Santo Domingo while Oñate performed the ceremony by which Kastera claimed their lands, Merikaana had decided the last of Tamaya's land claims. In those centuries, Tamaya's lands had been reduced in turn by the governments of Spain, Mexico, and the United States, until, in 1898, Tamaya held title, under Merikaana's law, only to the square grant around the pueblo and a fragment of the Ranchiit'u. The Tamayame had received Merikaana's papers for the square in 1883, and by 1909 they would hold patents to the part of the Ranchiit'u that Merikaana had approved.[100] The pueblo still faced legal challenges to the lands and water rights Merikaana had confirmed,[101] and it seemed that the Espiritu Santo and a large part of the Ranchiit'u had been lost, but for the time, the people of Tamaya had pursued their land claims as far as Merikaana's laws would allow.

No sooner had the pueblo's lands been confirmed by Congress than they were threatened again. While Tamaya pursued the pueblo's claims in Merikaana's courts, another scheme had been taking shape. As soon as the courts ruled that the pueblos were not Indians, some New Mexicans had begun to argue that pueblo lands should be subject to taxes, like the lands of non-Indian citizens. If the pueblos could not pay the taxes, they would have to forfeit those lands, just as any individual delinquent in his tax payments had to.[102] Many, like New Mexico Governor Ross, argued that the pueblos received the benefits of territorial government, but bore none of the "burdens." As citizens—and owners of some of the territory's most valuable properties—it was only fair that the pueblos pay their share of the taxes.[103] Others suggested that having to pay taxes would force the pueblos to cultivate—or sell—more lands and to use more modern agricultural methods, which would, in turn, make them more "civilized."[104]

By the mid-1880s the pueblos had learned of this threat, and a pueblo delegation, including Tamaya's representative, had visited Washington, D.C., to explain the problem to Merikaana's leaders. Fearing that the agent's questions might lead to the imposition of taxes, many pueblos refused to provide any information about their numbers or the lands and livestock they owned.[105]

Some of New Mexico's residents also expressed concern about this new strategy. Sister Blandina Segale, a nun assigned to the Sisters of Charity schools in Albuquerque and Santa Fe, recalled in her journal that she had been visited by "a prominent lawyer from New Albuquerque, who is to represent Bernalillo County at the next session of the territorial legislative assembly." After mentioning Isleta's fine cattle, he asked if she did not think the pueblo should be taxed. Sister Blandina, who did not think so, replied that the government might as well "tax the atmosphere they breathed" and reminded the lawyer that when American troops had entered New Mexico and "the officers were entirely without funds," the pueblo of Isleta had provided them with eighteen thousand dollars, which the government had not repaid for twelve years. "And these," she concluded indignantly, "are the Indians the lawyer wished to tax!"[106]

Merikaana's commissioner of Indian affairs also opposed the scheme, realizing that if it succeeded the pueblos would be forced to sell their lands and deprived of their land base. Reminding the secretary of the interior that the government had always treated the pueblos as Indians, he urged that Congress pass measures to protect them and asked territorial officials to refrain from taxing the pueblos until Congress could consider the matter.[107]

New Mexico's officials, however, had no intention of waiting until Congress could stop their scheme. In 1899, only one year after Tamaya's claims were settled, the officials of Bernalillo County, in which Tamaya and Ranchiit'u were located, listed the pueblos "in the published delinquent tax list for 1898 and prior years." The notice warned that if the taxes were not paid by the end of the year, the tax collector would apply "to the district court of Bernalillo County" for a judgement and orders of sale. Federal officials moved quickly to protect the pueblos, ordering the special pueblo attorney "to present every reasonable defense against the proposed tax sale." Once again the commissioner of Indian Affairs recommended passing federal legislation "to exempt them from taxation," explaining that "payment by the Pueblos of these taxes, even for one year, would be to them a very serious matter and unexpected burden, since they have never before been compelled to pay taxes upon their lands."[108]

Early the next year, the case was heard before Judge Crumpacker of the Bernalillo district court, who ruled that pueblo property was not taxable because he believed the issue should be carried to New Mexico's Supreme Court.[109] In the January 1902 term of that court, the territory brought suit "against all of the Pueblo Indians in the county of Bernalillo." The pueblo attorney presented a series of reasons why the pueblos should not be subject to taxation: they had never been declared citizens, they could not alienate their lands, and they had not enjoyed the benefits of citizenship, such as voting.[110] In spite of those arguments, the territorial court ruled against the pueblos in early 1904.[111]

The Santa Fe *New Mexican* estimated that each Indian in the pueblos might be liable for as much as a thousand dollars in tax payments.[112] The pueblos reacted swiftly, just as they had long ago responded to Kastera's threats. In April, sixty-four delegates, representing every pueblo except Zuñi and Jémez, met in Santa Fe. Among them were the "governors, assistant governors, and minor officers and principal merchants" of the pueblos. Meeting at the Indian Industrial School, they drafted a statement of protest to be sent to the president, Congress, and the Interior Department, reminding Merikaana that "they were the original owners of the lands, that their ancestors owned it before the advent of the Spaniards in New Mexico" and "before the organization of the Mexican government." Through interpreters Pablo Abeita of Isleta, Ulysses Grant Paisano of Laguna, and Harvey Townsend of San Felipe, the pueblo leaders exchanged greetings and heard Pueblo Attorney Abbott and Superintendent Crandall explain the status of the case.[113] In addition to the petition drafted at this meeting, Abbot, Crandall, and the Pueblo governors also wrote to the commissioner of Indian affairs to ask that pueblo lands be exempted from taxation and to inquire what else might be done to safeguard their lands.[114] Each of the pueblos contributed to pay the court costs related to the case; Tamaya received a bill for $2.50 for its share in 1907.[115]

Merikaana's Congress responded quickly. In the 1905 session, Congress passed a law stating "the lands now held by the various villages or pueblos of Pueblo Indians, or by individual members thereof, within Pueblo reservations or lands, in the Territory of New Mexico, and all personal property furnished said Indians by the United States, or used in cultivating said lands, and any cattle or sheep now possessed or that may hereafter be acquired by said Indians shall be free and exempt from taxation of any sort whatsoever, including taxes heretofore levied, if any, until Congress shall otherwise provide."[116]

While the case moved through Merikaana's courts, the Bureau of Indian Affairs reviewed several options to protect pueblo lands should the Supreme Court rule against the pueblos. Officials considered basing a defense on the enabling act drawn up when New Mexico became a state, which removed the pueblos from state jurisdiction by including a clause that defined pueblo lands as part of Indian territory.[117] Such a defense, however, did not seem likely to protect pueblo lands if the courts ruled against them. In 1912, concerned by a New Mexico ruling in a case involving the sale of liquor to a pueblo Indian, the agency called a meeting of all the pueblos at Santa Fe to suggest other solutions. First, Superintendent Lonergan reviewed the problem, pointing out that the state taxed grazing land at fifty cents an acre; in addition, New Mexico had road taxes (three cents), school taxes (twelve mills), and a state tax (five mills). New Mexico law allowed county officials to seize lands and sell them for nonpayment of taxes. Lonergan and the pueblo attorney recommended that the pueblos send a delegation to Washington, D.C., to explain their problems in person. They also suggested that pueblos might consider deeding their land to the federal government for a time if the Supreme Court ruled against them. They assured the pueblos that this course of action would protect their claims, allow them continued use of their lands and resources, and be carried out with the help of officers "who in most cases would be Indians chosen by" the pueblos themselves to see that no one trespassed on the lands. Among those who listened silently to this proposal was Tamaya's delegate, Juan Venancio.[118]

In the end, the pueblos did not have to consider that option, for Merikaana's Supreme Court decided the matter in their favor. Reviewing the *Sandoval* case in 1913, the court ruled that Congress could enact laws for the pueblos just as it did for other Indian tribes, and that pueblo lands had rightfully been included in the definition of "Indian country" in New Mexico's enabling act. The *Joseph* decision, which had created such harm by providing support for the claim that the pueblos were not Indians, was overturned.[119] After sixty-five years of confusion, Merikaana had finally recognized its responsibility to protect the pueblos.

That ruling came in time to prevent the sale of the pueblo lands to pay New Mexico's taxes, but for Tamaya and many of the pueblos, it came decades too late to protect land and water taken by trespassers, land speculators, and neighboring ranchers. Three years after the ruling, Thomas B. Catron received a patent to the lands of the Espiritu Santo,[120] where for decades the agent had been unable or unwilling to prevent stock from trespassing on Tamaya's land.[121] Irrigation companies had been allowed to divert Tamaya's water,[122] and the boundaries of the Ranchiit'u had been reduced. The damage that had been done during those years could not be undone simply by a court ruling.

NINE

Merikaana Moves toward Tamaya

As the months passed, the people of Tamaya still followed a cycle of activities as familiar as the outline of the dark volcanic mesa above the pueblo. Each year they would gather at Tamaya for the ceremonies brought into this world so many centuries ago at Kashe K'atreti. Even Merikaana was becoming a familiar part of this pattern, as Kastera had in decades past become a part of the life of Tamaya. But signs of change, like the ruts left in the ancient mesa by the wheels of Merikaana's stagecoaches, had begun to leave their marks on the pueblo.

In late February or early March, as spring came to the Río Grande and the Río Jémez, the Tamayame would make the familiar journey from Tamaya, with its "plains of wind-swept sands, dotted by stunted cedars," to the rich Río Grande fields of the Ranchiit'u. This journey, however, was no longer a daily event, for when spring arrived in the last decades of the nineteenth century, all of the Tamayame moved to "two small villages" near the fields, taking with them their "furniture, cooking utensils, mural ornaments, as well as the eagles, dogs, and livestock necessary to farming." Only the cats and two men (a guard and a messenger chosen by the governor) would remain at Tamaya through the summer to watch the two-story buildings, the cedar corrals, the guest house, and the church with a bell that bore "the date of 1710." Alone in the pueblo, the two men would spend the summer working at tasks like making thread from "cow tendon" while they watched over Tamaya.[1]

The rest of the Tamayame would tend the fields, the irrigation ditches, the stock, and the "orchards of peach, apple, and plum trees and small vineyards" planted around the two villages in the Ranchiit'u. While the farmers tended the long narrow plots of corn and the fields of wheat, melons, and chilies, the herdsmen would care for the pueblo's livestock, which had increased to 600 horses and more than 2,000 cattle, as well as "30 yoke of work oxen and 150 burros." Some watched the cattle grazing on the mesa, while others moved their stock to summer pastures in the "large grant, used also by Zía and Jémez," or took sheep and goats east, toward Placitas, to graze. In late summer, the Tamayame would harvest their corn crop, "one of the finest to be seen on the Rio Grande," gather and thresh their wheat, and carry the crops back to Tamaya to be stored for winter. Traveling from Tamaya to Ranchiit'u in late summer 1890, the census-taker "passed 8 wagons, drawn by 4 and 6 oxen, carrying half a ton of grain each." In the fall, when the harvest had been stored, the people would gather up their belongings to leave the Ranchiit'u villages and return to the old pueblo for the winter.[2]

Still the dry years could bring disaster to a pueblo, or the rivers, sweeping over their banks in a wet year, could wash away crops and homes.[3] The diseases carried north by Kastera might reappear and spread rapidly through the region. Merikaana's officials, like Kastera's, brought vaccine to cut the toll taken by smallpox, but the threat of measles, diphtheria, and other diseases remained.[4] And always the pueblo had to be on guard against those who would steal its land and water, with a watchfulness learned in centuries of contact with Kastera and Merikaana. Pueblo governors traveled to Santa Fe "to pay their respects to [Merikaana's] new governor" as their ancestors had visited his Spanish predecessors nearly two hundred years earlier, carrying their canes of office. Miguel Otero, who served as governor of New Mexico from 1897 to 1906, recalled in his memoirs that "many of them had black ebony canes with silver heads, all engraved. These canes were presented to them by President Abraham Lincoln, and were used in each pueblo as a sign of authority, and passed from one governor to another."[5] With that authority, each governor acquired the responsibility of caring for Tamaya's papers and speaking for the pueblo in protest against those who trespassed on the pueblo's land, stole the pueblo's water, violated the people's rights, and threatened Tamaya's very existence. It was a responsibility that grew ever heavier, for Merikaana was moving west with numbers and plans unlike any before seen in this ancient land.

To Merikaana, New Mexico seemed isolated and undeveloped. The first officials sent to this remote land filled their letters with complaints: the mails were slow and irregular; the territory had few roads, and many of those, like the trail from Tamaya to Bernalillo, were often "almost obliterated by the shifting of the surface;"[6] goods were scarce and therefore expensive. One of the first of Merikaana's agents complained that "the necessities of life, such as we have been accustomed to in the States, and the delicacies and luxuries which we require, must all be brought from the United States."[7] Another told his superiors that, given the conditions in New Mexico, it would take two men at least two months to visit all the pueblos under his charge.[8]

Because Merikaana's miners, settlers, officials, and travelers would not tolerate what they regarded as deprivation for long, Merikaana had begun to study the best routes for additional roads and trails even before the region became a part of the United States.[9] For centuries a single main road, leading down the Río Grande to Mexico, had served Kastera, but Merikaana would need new roads connecting New Mexico with the center of Merikaana's government in the East, and with the West, where gold fields and fertile farmlands had already drawn thousands of emigrants. Merikaana's travelers demanded that these roads be made safe, so Merikaana soon sent soldiers to guard the trails, control the hostile Indians nearby, and build forts through-out the remote regions of New Mexico that were home to Navajos, Apaches, and other hostile tribes. At first, the soldiers used old trails, like the one that ran up the Río Jémez, past Tamaya, to Zuñi and the Navajo country,[10] but within a short time the soldiers began to build wagon roads following the old trails, so that wagonloads of food and supplies could be sent to the forts. Then Merikaana installed lines for a military telegraph, to allow contact between the central officials and the soldiers in isolated areas.[11]

Settlers, traders, and travelers, as well as soldiers, continued to demand more and better roads and means of transportation. When a new road was built from Santa Fe to the Río Abajo in 1866, replacing "the old road to Algodones," the Santa Fe *New Mexican* proudly announced that this route would be "of incalculable benefit to the county of Santa Ana, which had hitherto been without the advantges [*sic*] of a main road traversing it."[12] Mail delivery to the Río Abajo "increased to three trips per week so as to make regular connections with the eastern mail."[13] Nine years later, when one of the deliveries was lost "crossing an arroyo near the Galisteo creek," it in-cluded a sack of mail for Bernalillo as well as a sack of way mail.[14] A stage line followed this southern route through Bernalillo and on to El Paso.[15]

At the same time, the old trail north past Tamaya and through the Espiritu Santo became a thoroughfare that carried traffic to Fort Wingate and Arizona. To serve this traffic, the town of Cabezón was founded in 1872 on the site of a Spanish grant, dating from 1767, that bordered Tamaya's Espiritu Santo lands along the Río Puerco. By 1875, the Star Line Mail and Transpor-

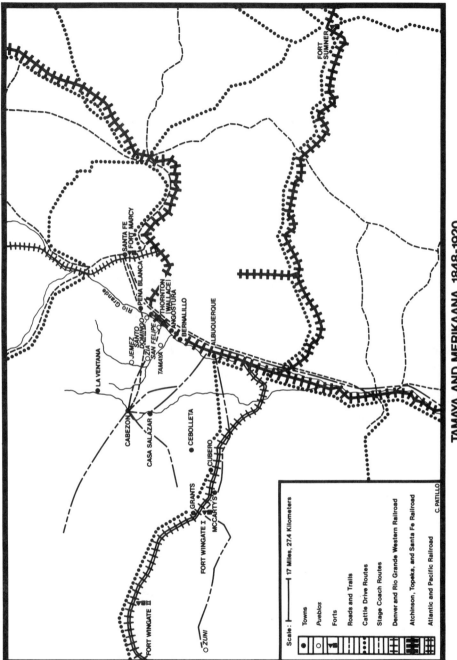

TAMAYA AND MERIKAANA, 1848-1920

Scale: |——| 17 Miles, 27.4 Kilometers

● Towns

○ Pueblos

⚑ Forts

|||||||||| Roads and Trails

••••• Cattle Drive Routes

||•||•|| Stage Coach Routes

Denver and Rio Grande Western Railroad

Atchinson, Topeka, and Santa Fe Railroad

Atlantic and Pacific Railroad

C. PATILLO

FORT SUMNER

SANTA FE
FORT MARCY

PEÑA BLANCA

THORNTON
WALLACE
ANGOSTURA

JEMEZ
SANTO
DOMINGO
SAN FELIPE

BERNALILLO

ALBUQUERQUE

LA VENTANA

TAMAYA

CABEZON

CASA SALAZAR

● CEBOLLETA

CUBERO

GRANTS

FORT WINGATE I

McCARTYS

FORT WINGATE II

○ ZUNI

Rio Grande

tation Company ran a regular stage along this route, with small coaches that began at Santa Fe, went to Peña Blanca, and then (probably following the old trail across the Santa Ana Mesa) passed through San Ysidro, crossed the Espiritu Santo to Cabezón, and traveled on to Fort Wingate and Arizona. As traffic increased, the town of Cabezón grew rapidly: by 1880, when Surveyor Henry Allen Tice passed through the town, it had "a small general store kept by a very intelligent Mexican [Hispanic], who served the traffic on the roadway and the neighboring Pueblo Indians." By the end of the decade, seven other traders had opened saloons or stores, stocking a variety of goods that included calico, candy, cookies, perfume, tobacco, and fancy metal buttons as well as tools, fabric, and staples like coffee, sugar, and flour. These goods attracted both Navajos and pueblos, who brought weaving, jewelry, and sheep to trade. Through this trade, many of the storekeepers soon acquired large herds of sheep. One had sixteen thousand sheep and two thousand cattle; another, a herd of ten thousand sheep. By 1891 the townspeople had enough sheep to fill "seventeen wagons . . . drawn by 67 horses" with wool for market in Albuquerque, and a new road had been built to connect Cabezón with Bernalillo and Albuquerque to the south.[16]

This development touched Tamaya in many ways. It brought Merikaana's traders and settlers to Tamaya's borders, carried travelers through Tamayame lands, and even brought the residents of Cabezón to Tamaya itself for fiestas. The traders' goods drew the area's residents, as well as neighboring peoples like the Navajo, to the towns. As the traders prospered and their herds increased, the pressure on pasturelands around—and often within—Tamaya's Espiritu Santo grazing lands increased.[17]

These trails, stage lines, and mail routes, however, represented only a fraction of the vast network of transportation that Merikaana planned for the region. For decades, businessmen and leaders in Merikaana had dreamed of a vast system of railways and telegraph lines that would link the entire continent. In 1880, that system reached Tamaya. The Atchison, Topeka, and Santa Fe Railroad laid its tracks and telegraph lines down the Río Grande, through the Ranchiit'u, to Albuquerque, and soon new roads, small spur railroads, and stage lines connected outlying towns with the railroad.[18]

Twenty years after the arrival of the railroad, Tamaya was no longer an unknown, isolated pueblo far from the main routes of travel. The railroad encouraged passengers to visit the pueblos along its route, and guidebooks were soon published to offer Merikaana's travelers information about the region. One recommended that "a day's delay at Albuquerque enables the traveler to visit four interesting pueblos—Santa Ana, Sandía, Zía, and Jémez—

in a day's stage ride between Jémez and Albuquerque."[19] Another told travelers that Tamaya was "about eight miles off the line on the stage from Albuquerque to Jémez Springs." Visitors could also reach the pueblo "by private conveyance in six hours from Albuquerque." The stage left three times a week, beginning the nine-hour trip at 5:00 a.m. on Tuesdays, Thursdays, and Saturdays, for a round-trip fare of twelve dollars. A "fairly good road" also ran from the railroad town of Thornton, just south of Santo Domingo, across the Santa Ana Mesa and north to Jémez. With his flatboat, Narcisco Zamora ferried wagons across the river at Bernalillo.[20]

In addition to the travelers passing through the region, the railroad carried settlers, miners, traders, businessmen, and speculators who came to stay. The non-Indian population of New Mexico had grown slowly since Merikaana's arrival, rising from 60,000 to more than 80,000 between 1850 and 1860,[21] and increasing by 10,000 during the next decade.[22] When the railroad reached Tamaya, New Mexico's non-Indians numbered 119,000; that population grew to 195,000 in the next 10 years[23] and reached 327,301 by 1910.[24] The region south of Santa Fe and the towns near the railroad boomed: Albuquerque, which had scarcely more than 2,000 residents when the railroad came, counted 5 times that many by the end of the decade.[25] In the same period, Bernalillo became a town of 2,000 with its own newspaper.[26] From 1880 to 1890, property values in the region increased almost sixfold.[27]

The development of industry paralleled the growth in population. Soon New Mexico's leaders proudly reported that miners were prospecting in the mountains throughout the territory. When coal—needed by the railroad— was discovered in the Espíritu Santo lands along the Río Puerco in 1890, the Tamayame soon had to defend their lands against a flood of eager miners.[28] Others prospected north of Tamaya in the Jémez and Nacimiento mountains.[29] An old Spanish mine was reopened near Las Huertas, southeast of the Ranchiit'u in an area where old Tamayame villages had stood and Tamayame herdsmen still grazed their stock. Miners found both gold and coal in the Ortiz Mountains near Paak'u.[30]

The railroad also brought growth to the cattle industry, as Texas stockmen drove great herds north to New Mexico's mines, forts, and railroad towns. Soon regular cattle drives brought stock from El Paso to Albuquerque and then west through the Río Puerco Valley to Arizona. Cattle trails also ran to Fort Sumner, Roswell, Las Vegas, and Santa Fe.[31] New Mexico's stockmen also prospered. Bernalillo County alone had 475,000 sheep and 41,700 cattle in 1883.[32] In the decade after the railroad reached Tamaya, cattle herds increased nearly fivefold, from 347,000 to 1,630,000 head,[33] and the terri-

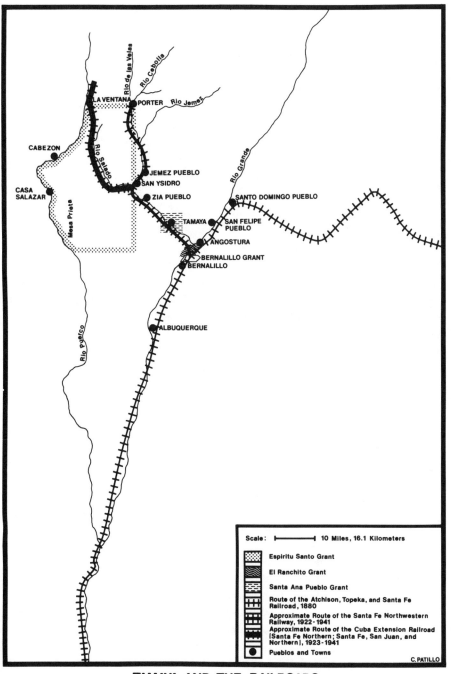

TAMAYA AND THE RAILROADS

Scale: |————————| 10 Miles, 16.1 Kilometers

Espiritu Santo Grant

El Ranchito Grant

Santa Ana Pueblo Grant

Route of the Atchison, Topeka, and Santa Fe Railroad, 1880

Approximate Route of the Santa Fe Northwestern Railway, 1922-1941

Approximate Route of the Cuba Extension Railroad (Santa Fe Northern; Santa Fe, San Juan, and Northern), 1923-1941

Pueblos and Towns

C. PATILLO

tory's sheep increased to 5 million head.[34] By 1900, the upper Río Grande carried 533,000 animal units.[35]

For many of New Mexico's most recent arrivals, even this growth was not enough. The territory established a Bureau of Immigration, which provided information about the region and its history and encouraged travelers and immigrants to come to New Mexico; its president boasted that "every train goes into the Territory full . . . . The towns are growing fast, and the mining districts are filling up rapidly." New Mexicans also organized territorial fairs to attract visitors and showcase their cities, businesses, products, and activities. Many, like the Albuquerque fair in 1881, had printed programs, allowing local businessmen to promote the region's benefits and advertise their own services. Photographer W. Henry Brown, for example, proclaimed that "tourists, pleasure-seekers, and business men will find ready means of easy access to this hitherto almost inaccessible country; and will find much of interest"; he also reminded his readers that they could see a sampling of the items of interest by purchasing his eight series of scenic views of the pueblos, ancient ruins, and towns along the railroad route. Some New Mexicans encouraged travelers and immigrants to come to their territory in the belief that a growing population would benefit the region generally; others had more specific interests. The Atlantic and Pacific Railroad, which held grants in western New Mexico, urged immigrants to travel west and buy its land. Various Christian organizations and their supporters invited religious groups to send missionaries and churchmen to work among the Indians. Local leaders hoped to attract a larger non-Indian population so that the territory might achieve statehood. Residents encouraged tradesmen and artisans to bring desirable merchandise and skills to New Mexico. Almost all of these boosters promised travelers and immigrants that opportunities abounded, land and water were ample, and newcomers would be welcomed.[36]

Not all of New Mexico's peoples, however, wanted to see Merikaana's trains bring ever more travelers and immigrants to the region. If new settlers symbolized prosperity and growth for the territory's most recent arrivals, for the pueblos the trainloads of immigrants, and the railroad itself, promised new threats to pueblo land and water.

Roads, railroads, telegraph lines, and irrigation companies sought rights-of-way through pueblo land and usually obtained them over the pueblos' objections. At Tamaya, leaders notified their agent that they did not want a route on their land years before the railroad arrived.[37] When the railroad reached the Río Grande, none of the pueblos welcomed it. Anthropologist Adolph Bandelier reported "considerable disturbance about the new railroad" at Santo Domingo soon after the tracks were laid. Pueblo leaders were not satisfied with the reassurances of the priest at Peña Blanca, who promised that he would "secure compensation for any damage done."[38] Seeing their protests ignored, some of the pueblos began to express their opposition in other ways: the year after the tracks were laid, telegraph officials began to complain that pueblo Indians regularly damaged the telegraph wires and insulators between Bernalillo and Wallace (Thornton), south of Santo Domingo. One of the railroad officials reported that "This trouble has always occurred since our road & wires have been done there & efforts have been made to stop it without success. It is now becoming a serious matter & some steps should be taken at once to remedy it."[39]

Throughout these decades, trespassers posed an almost constant problem at Tamaya. Miners, stockmen, and ranchers near the borders of the Espiritu Santo and the Ranchiit'u frequently crossed the borders into Tamayame land, and many even tried to obtain title to it. The agent warned trespassers in 1867.[40] In 1877 Bernalillo resident José Perea filed suit against Tamaya before a local justice of the peace, charging the pueblo with trespassing on his claim,[41] although the land in question, as the pueblo officers testified, was a plot that Tamaya had purchased from Spaniards in 1739.[42] Two years after Perea filed suit, Tamaya's governor complained that his stock crossed Tamaya's lands daily.[43] The same year, the pueblo agent warned that "the railroad is rapidly approaching the Rio Grande, and as immigration flows into this country, the land of the Pueblos will become more and more valuable, and correspondingly difficult to keep free of trespassers and designing men."[44] The following year, Tamaya's leaders protested against "the robberies committed on the pueblos of Santa Ana and of Cia." Their cattle were stolen, and they complained that when "they catch the thieves, these fire upon them." Their agent did not "assist them," so they planned to meet with other pueblos and "have their grievances placed before Congress."[45] When Tamaya complained of stock trespass again in 1882, the pueblo agent in Santa Fe advised Tamaya's governor, Pedro Yunague, to take the pueblo's complaints to the local justice of the peace.[46] Three years later, Agent Sánchez reported that non-Indians had already taken the best pueblo farming and grazing lands.[47] Tamaya's neighbors at San Felipe and Santo Domingo had begun to use force against trespassers and to withhold water from settlers near their lands.[48] In 1887, the agent reported railroad damage at Santa Ana.[49]

In 1890, when Special Agent Henry Poore took the census, he found that "not a single pueblo . . . from Taos to Isleta" had "preserved its grant as confirmed by the Congress of 1858 and with patent signed by the hand of

Abraham Lincoln in 1863." At one pueblo after another, leaders assured Poore that they had sold none of their grant lands—and then took him to see the houses of "squatters who were either owners or lessees and whose presence among them was variously explained." The squatters remained, "in the face of many appeals to the Indian agent or others having a show of authority in the government." Pueblo land was particularly desirable, as Poore explained, because "the location of the pueblos has in most cases been selected with great judgement by the Indians." The census taker reported that because "every foot of land in the territory available for agriculture has long since been taken, all immigration hangs upon the borders of these pueblo reservations."[50]

Tamaya, the census taker found, was no exception. The lands of the Espiritu Santo had long attracted stockmen, and the discovery of coal, copper, gold, and silver on the grant in 1890 brought an influx of miners. To protect their lands, Poore reported, "the Indians threaten all comers to the valley who carry picks and shovels." Livestock from the nearby town of San Ysidro "frequently" invaded pueblo "corn and grain fields."[51] The towns of Cabezón, San Luis, Guadalupe, Casa Salazar (or Salisaro), and San Ysidro had grown up along the mail routes and near the mineral discoveries in the Espiritu Santo.[52] The Ranchiit'u was also threatened. The census report stated: "The grant of the ranches touches the town of Bernalillo on the south. Nine years ago the first Mexican [Hispanic] house was built upon this land; there are now 11, inclosing 85 acres."[53]

The complaints continued through the last decade of the nineteenth century. By the late 1890s, as many as forty people lived on or used Tamaya's lands in the Espiritu Santo; some had been there for years.[54] Pueblo agents posted warnings that those who cut pueblo timber would be subject to fines and imprisonment.[55] In response to inquiries, they stated that the Indian office did not "sanction the sale or leasing" of pueblo lands.[56] In 1894 Agent Bullis ordered numerous trespassers off of the pueblo's land. Ramedio Trujillo and others who had planned to build on Tamaya's land were told to leave in March.[57] Three months later, Juan Gurule received notice to remove the fencing he had put up on the pueblo's land.[58] That September the agent sent a letter ordering Metro Montoya of Bernalillo and six other stockmen to remove their fences and livestock from Tamaya's land.[59] In 1898, another new agent, N. S. Walpole, posted notices warning of punishment for all trespassers, including those who cut timber or grazed their stock on Tamaya's land.[60]

A major dispute began in the 1890s, when the Albuquerque Land and Irrigation Company sought a right-of-way to place a ditch across Tamayame land. The pueblo opposed the company's request "because at certain seasons of the year the Rio Grande has not sufficient water to supply the ditches of these pueblos and of the company at the same time and the Indians fear that as the headworks of the proposed canal are above the head of their ditches it will cause a scarcity of water in their ditches."[61] Since the pueblo wanted nothing to do with the proposed ditch, the company went to court, seeking an order that would condemn Tamaya's land for the right-of-way. In early February 1898, Tamaya's governor received word that the new Indian agent, Lieutenant Charles Cooper, would investigate the pueblo's complaints. A month later, Cooper advised the Tamayame to attend a hearing on the case, which also involved San Felipe and Sandía. The agent also asked Pedro Perea of Bernalillo to go to the hearing and "do what you can for them."[62] In February 1899 Walpole sent welcome news to Tamaya's governor: "The Court has refused to appoint the Commissioners to condemn land for the ditch of the Albuquerque Land and Irrigation Company. The Company cannot condemn your land at present."[63] In July the agent explained that a ten-dollar legal fee the pueblo had not paid would cover the cost of an appeal in the ditch case, not their lawyer's fees.[64] By August, when Walpole filed his annual report, the case had "been decided in the court in favor of the company." The ruling allowed the company to invoke the right of eminent domain to take the land for the ditch, but it also offered some protection for Tamaya's water rights, by forbidding the company from taking any water "the Indians at present have." The agent also noted that "a question as to a survey under the confirmation of their grant is pending before the land court."[65] That November Walpole reminded Tamaya's governor that the company had received permission to begin building the ditch. The only legal question still unresolved was what Tamaya would be paid for the right-of-way. The pueblo's attorney, George Hill Howard, had advised Tamaya not to appeal, believing that a jury would probably reduce the amount of the settlement.[66]

The courts, Merikaana's agent, and their lawyer considered the matter settled, but the Tamayame refused to accept a decision that would compromise their land and water rights. Three days after Walpole's letter was sent, the Tamayame announced that they would send two delegates, Higinio García and Jesús Moya, to appeal the matter directly to Merikaana's president. They drafted a petition explaining that the proposed ditch would "take up a large and best portion of our lands" against the pueblo's wishes. The petition, signed by all of Tamaya's officers and principals, read, in part:

> We therefore have proposed to ourselves to send a petition to you,
> Mr. President, for the protection of our rights which it seems are not

taken in proper consideration by those who are charged to protect us, as we have made on . . . [several] occasions complaints to them against such parties attempting to intrude upon our . . . [property] and have only received for an answer to accept all the money which said Company would offer us. This we absolutely and unanimously refuse to accept. For we do not want any money nor that said Company should trespass in any way on our lands but that our rights be duly respected.[67]

No record of President McKinley's answer remains, but the following year a member of the Board of Indian Commissioners described the arrival of a delegation from an unnamed pueblo during the winter of 1899–1900.

A delegation of the Indians had come all the way from New Mexico, at their own expense, to personally plead with the President for the protection of their water rights. Immediately after their arrival at the railroad station they proceeded to the White House to visit the Great Father, who was so engrossed with important matters of state that he could give them but little attention, and advised the delegation to call at the Indian Office. This they did, and related . . . how they had paid their respects to William, and that he did not ask them to stop with him, but that if he had called to see them in their Western home, they would have asked him to remain with them during the time of his sojourn there; and now, feeling they could ask no one to entertain them, they desired work, so that they might earn sufficient to meet their expenses while in the city.

The Indian office made "provision for the comfort of the delegation while in the city,"[68] offering them the hospitality that Merikaana's president had not volunteered. In late December, the General Land Office sent the commissioner of Indian affairs a map of Tamaya's land for the pueblo delegates.[69] If Merikaana's leaders also made an attempt to protect the pueblo's land and water rights, the report did not mention it. Meanwhile, while the delegates were still in Washington, the agent notified the pueblo that their appeal, scheduled for a hearing before the Supreme Court in January 1900, would be dropped if they did not pay the court fees.[70]

By that February, the pueblos whose lands the ditch would cross had lost patience. Meeting at San Felipe, they wrote another petition, signed by Governor José Manuel Enrique and the leaders of Tamaya as well as the governors and leaders of San Felipe, Santo Domingo, Sandía, and Isleta. The Albuquerque Land and Irrigation Company had made a new survey that would place the ditch in the middle of Tamaya's best fields. They argued that, if the company had "a right to make" the ditch, as they had been told, then the least their agent could do was to "tell the company not to work through this new survey," which would do the greatest possible injury to Tamaya. Once again they reminded the agent that the people of the pueblos "do not give their consent nor will ever receive payment for it, as they do not want it built. . . ." And, they concluded, if their agent did not act for them, they would do what they could to protect themselves:

> The pueblos now call to you as our Agent to protect us, that if the canal Co. begins to work on their new survey that the work shall not be done even if it costs the lives of all the Indians of the Pueblos named below.[71]

Their agent's first response was to warn the ditch company of their intentions and to notify Tamaya's officers that if they interfered with the construction, the company could legally defend itself with force, and any pueblo people involved would be arrested.[72] After sending those letters, Agent Walpole did ask the Albuquerque Land and Irrigation Company to make repairs where they had damaged Indian lands, including the place where their canal crossed one of Tamaya's ditches.[73] When he sent a copy of that letter to the pueblos, he included a note in which he claimed that the company had not changed its survey since 1898 and promised that the pueblos would retain their water rights, since "if there is a scarcity of water and any ditch must run dry it will be the company's." Once again he told the pueblos that

> It can do you no possible good to refuse to take this money, as they receive the right of way from the court as soon as they pay the money to the court and your refusal to take the money will not prevent the building of the canal any more than the refusal of the Pueblo of Santo Domingo to take the money paid by the railroad some years ago prevented the building and operating of the railroad.[74]

Meanwhile, the Tamayame had taken their message directly to the company, stating simply: "This is to let you know that we in the name of all our comrades from this Pueblo, together with the Sandías and others . . . will under no circumstances permit you to come through our respective lands. If you do so, you will have to suffer the consequences. I the bearer of this Note, Jesus Moya, as Chief of war of this Pueblo, will do all it is in my power against you."[75]

The pueblos also warned the company's workers that they would not allow the ditch to be completed. Led by their *mayordomo*, Maserio Trujillo, the Tamayame told the company's "engineer and director" that Tamaya would not allow them to "place any flume across its . . . ditch . . . [or] to construct its . . . ditch along its right-of-way across the lands of the Pueblo," because the ditch would take "so much of the cultivated lands" that it would do the pueblo great harm. After giving this warning, the Tamayame "caused the . . . cut to be filled up with dirt taken from the banks of the ditch."[76]

The following day, 3 March 1900, lawyers for the Albuquerque Land and Irrigation Company requested an order from the district court to prevent the pueblos from interfering with the ditch. The lawyers declared that earlier, at San Felipe, the pueblos had "attempted to and did interfere by force and threats," keeping the company from running its survey. To prevent similar trouble on Tamaya's lands, they asked the court to issue an injunction restraining the pueblos from interfering "in any manner by threats, violence or otherwise" with the construction, with the company's workers, or with the completed ditch.[77] Within two days, the court issued the order.[78]

That, however, did not stop the pueblos from a final attempt to prevent the construction of the ditch. Soon after the court issued its restraining order, Bernalillo County Sheriff Thomas Hubbell arrested ten Tamayame for interfering with the construction. March 20, their agent told Judge Crumpacker that he believed the Tamayame would agree not to interfere with the ditch if the matter were fully explained to them. He also explained that it was "important for their families that they be released as soon as they become convinced that they must obey the orders as it is crop season."[79] Two days later, Agent Walpole asked Sheriff Hubbell how many Tamayame he had arrested and how long he intended to hold them.[80] March 24, in reply to a letter from Ambrosio Tenorio, Tamaya's cacique, the agent said that all of the Tamayame prisoners who had promised to obey the court order had been released from jail. Only Jesús Moya, Tamaya's captain of war, remained in prison—and the agent stated that he would be kept there "until he will agree to obey the orders of the Court."[81] In a letter to the commissioner of Indian affairs written the same day, Walpole explained that Moya was "being held until he becomes more calm." The agent told his superior that "Everything possible was done to prevent the Indians getting into this trouble, but I believe that the lesson has been a wholesome one."[82]

By early April, the Tamayame had made their decision. A "delegation of Santa Ana Indians" visited Agent Walpole to say "that they were thoroughly convinced that it was necessary to obey the orders of the Court and the laws of the Territory" and that they had decided to "remove Jesus Moya from his position as Spanish Interpreter in the Pueblo." As a result of this visit, Walpole asked "that Jesus Moya be brought into Court and given an opportunity to state whether or not he will in future be amenable to . . . [word illegible] law and, in case he so promises, that he be released from custody."[83]

By October, Tamaya's last appeal against the Albuquerque Land and Irrigation Company had been decided. The court refused to grant an injunction to halt construction of the ditch, but the ruling did guarantee the pueblo's prior rights to water.[84]

While Tamaya went to court to defend its lands and water rights from trespass, confiscation, and taxation, new trespassers followed old onto the pueblo's land. In 1900, and again in 1904, agents warned trespassers that they could not enter Tamaya's lands or cut wood on them.[85] In 1909 the Tamayame at last received a patent for the Ranchiit'u lands,[86] but before a year had elapsed the pueblo's superintendent had informed the special pueblo attorney, Francis C. Wilson, that the dispute between Tamaya and Bernalillo over the boundaries of the Ranchiit'u should be investigated.[87] Juan Venancio filed an affidavit describing the pueblo's use of the Santa Ana Ditch and the irrigation in the Ranchiit'u.[88] Two years later Venancio, then the lieutenant governor of Tamaya, wrote a letter to Washington explaining the problems created by trespass on the grant. Tamaya's agent, who believed that "the Indians have a very just cause for complaint" and considered the situation "grave," had "spent two days trying to adjust matters" in a dispute that involved "ownership to the tract of vega or pasture land approximating three or four hundred acres." In a letter to the commissioner of Indian affairs, he summarized Tamaya's difficulties and recommended a survey and a suit to quiet title to the land in question:

The Santa Ana Indians are very good, industrious people and probably have lost several thousand acres of land from their grant by trespassers on other portions of it not complained of at present. This loss, occurred some years ago . . . ten years' residence upon the land is sufficient to acquire title to it under the New Mexico statutes, and if something is not done immediately the ten year limit of the statutes will have run against some of the land and Mr. Wilson will be powerless to regain it for the Indians. This seems inexcusable when the fact is known that money for this purpose was available and that if a suit had been commenced title to some of this land could have been saved and a loss to the Indians that may amount to $1000 or more have been prevented by the expenditure of $100 or $200 . . . . In order to avoid further difficulties Mr. Wilson should be given money to cover the initial expense so that suit may be commenced immediately and sufficient funds placed to my credit for a survey of the grant.

He added that the Tamayame had "complained . . . many times since the matter was taken up with the Office."[89] The Indian office, which had considered adding some lands to the pueblo's holdings, possibly setting "aside for the use of the San Felipe, Isleta and Santa Ana Pueblos certain tracts within the Manzano National Forest," had "abandoned" that idea by this time,[90] but the department did authorize some funds to survey Tamaya's disputed lands. In September 1912 the surveyor reported that he had "surveyed the farming lands . . . South of the So Bdy line of the Santa Ana and they seem to be very much pleased." He had also surveyed the "cultivated lands" on the west boundary at the pueblo's request, finding "most all the old stones."[91] The following year, the superintendent reported that "considerable surveying work" had been done; he asked for money to finish the surveys and to begin a suit to quiet title to the disputed lands.[92] In June 1913, Pueblo Attorney Francis Wilson filed a suit in district court against those who claimed lands within the Ranchiit'u.[93] The dispute focused on a seventeen-acre tract that extended from the northwest corner of the Bernalillo grant. The claimants offered two separate arguments. One group held that their claims were valid because they had lived on the land for more than twenty years.[94] The second argued that the land in question lay within the Bernalillo Grant, not the Ranchiit'u, and that Tamaya therefore had no title to it.[95] On behalf of the Tamayame, the pueblo attorney denied all of these claims.[96]

While trespass continued in the Ranchiit'u, Merikaana ratified the trespass that had occurred in the Espiritu Santo, awarding a patent for a large portion of the lands to Thomas B. Catron in 1916.[97] The pueblos' remaining grazing lands were threatened by non-pueblo livestock owners established all around the edges of the Espiritu Santo, by the new roads being developed in the region, and by the damage that resulted from overgrazing and timber cutting in the adjacent lands. Since 1900 new roads had been built running north from Albuquerque past Corrales and north toward Zía, then heading west to San Ysidro and splitting into three routes that crossed the Espiritu Santo to Casa Salazar, Cabezón, and La Ventana. Wagons loaded with freight, stages carrying passengers and mail, and stockmen driving their herds all passed over these routes. Drought, which had been widespread in New Mexico from 1871 to 1880, continued well into the twentieth century along the Río Puerco.[98] This drought, combined with periodic floods and pressures from the growing number of animals using the land, led to gullying and erosion.[99] Heavy timber-cutting along the river increased the flood damage. Residents of Cabezón and nearby Navajos ran increasing numbers of stock on the range. As these pressures increased, weeds and ring grass began to replace the native perennial grasses along the Rio Puerco.[100] As a former pueblo herdsman later explained, the Tamayame had always taken care to move their stock regularly to prevent damage to the land. They allowed the grass to "rest a week at a time" so that when the rains returned the plants would be renewed. While cows could be herded in an area for as much as a month, horses and sheep had to be moved more frequently so that they would not tear the grass down to the ground or pull it out with their teeth.[101] They had protected their pastures by this method, so that the grass would return year after year, but they could not protect them from the damage caused by neighbors and trespassers oblivious to the needs of the land.

The rapid growth of Merikaana's towns, the building of transportation routes, and the development of mining, timber-cutting, and livestock industries had, as the pueblos feared, brought disaster to their lands. Their land and water rights were constantly threatened. If a pueblo defended itself against one threat, the land-hungry settlers would soon adopt a new scheme to justify the theft of pueblo land and water.

During the last decades of the nineteenth century and the first of the twentieth, land and water were not the only pueblo rights under siege. As Kastera had done years before, Merikaana decided, during this time, that the pueblos' way of life must change. When Merikaana arrived in New Mexico, hostile tribes there and elsewhere still threatened trails, ranches, mines, and settlements. Merikaana's first priority, in New Mexico and the other western territories, was to bring an end to this threat. Three decades later, by force and by treaty, they had largely achieved that goal.[102] As the likelihood of Indian hostility declined, the emphasis of Merikaana's policy began to shift. Where once Indian agents had hoped primarily to maintain peace, they began to dream of transforming Indians into self-sufficient, English-speaking, Christian farmers who would dress, live, work, and worship as their non-

Indian neighbors did. Traditional Indian leaders would lose their influence, tribal structures would disappear, and Indian lands would be divided so that each Indian could own—and sell—his own plot of land. Some agents believed that this change was inevitable; some, that Merikaana would have to provide assistance to help Indian peoples make the transition; others, that force would be required to make the people give up their traditional ways.[103]

The changing goals of Merikaana's policy were reflected along the Río Grande. When the first soldiers and agents arrived, they praised the pueblos as models of the progress that all tribes could be expected to achieve. The pueblos were, the agents reported, a peaceful, "civilized," and prosperous group who needed, it seemed to Merikaana, only to learn English, obtain modern tools and equipment, and receive patents for their lands before they would be ready to take their place beside non-Indians in Merikaana's society.[104]

By the 1870s, however, some agents had begun to see the pueblos differently. It was true that the pueblos were, for the most part, successful farmers, but many farmed as their ancestors had, using digging sticks to plant their fields and horses to thresh their grain. Most pueblos did attend services in the Catholic churches, but to the largely Protestant agents and missionaries, the fiestas held in those churches seemed almost as "pagan" and "superstitious" as the native traditions, beliefs, leaders, and ceremonies that the pueblos still honored. Agents accused the pueblos of "clinging to" these "superstitions." In addition, after decades of trespass, the "peaceful" and "law-abiding" pueblos had begun to defend themselves with force when necessary. They had not made the great and rapid "progress" toward assimilation that the first of Merikaana's officials had anticipated. Gradually the tone of the agents' reports changed. Where once Merikaana's officials had praised the pueblos as intelligent, law-abiding, and "civilized" peoples, they soon condemned them as "backward," "superstitious," and "unsanitary" peoples who had not achieved nearly enough "progress" given the advantages they had enjoyed.[105]

To those who decided Merikaana's Indian policy, the answer seemed clear: the pueblos needed schools and teachers to show them how to live as their non-Indian neighbors did. With this assistance, they would soon speak English. Farmers would master the technology that Merikaana had developed on the Great Plains. Missionaries would teach the pueblos the beliefs of Protestant Christians. Agency employees would show the women how to make clothes like those Merikaana wore, to cook meals similar to those Merikaana consumed, and, with the agency's help, to transform their homes into replicas of Merikaana's own. Men would learn how to obtain jobs and to labor for wages; the railroad camps might offer employment and the trains could carry unemployed men far from the pueblo to find work. Nearly every pueblo agent from the 1860s to 1915 drafted a proposal to create or improve schools for the pueblos.[106]

A few missionaries, like Baptist Samuel Gorman, also tried to establish special schools for the pueblos in this period. Most expected the pueblos to welcome them, but, like Gorman, found the pueblos wary of Merikaana's religions. At Laguna, traditional leaders told Gorman that "if they become educated they fear their people will forsake their ancient customs, to which they cannot consent." Both Catholic priests and traditional pueblo leaders opposed the establishment of government and mission schools.[107]

In 1864 only 40 of the more than 7,000 pueblo people could read and write,[108] and most of the literate were "far advanced in years." The agent believed that "It could not be otherwise. Not a single place properly entitled to the name of school is to be found among the pueblos, nor a teacher of any capacity whatever."[109] When Merikaana's government at last decided to set up schools for the pueblos in 1870, William Arny was chosen as a special agent to establish this educational system.[110]

During the next year, when Arny visited the pueblos to discuss the proposed schools, he found that all of the pueblos were "very anxious for schools . . . . They say they are poor but will furnish land and give aid in building houses for schools and dwellings for teachers, but are not able to pay competent teachers, and they are grateful to the Government for the appropriation made for this purpose." At Tamaya, where he found that only one of the 373 residents could read and write, he hired "Josefa Muniz, at $40 per month, as teacher at this pueblo."[111]

Although Arny hired Spanish-speaking teachers and at first bought books in Spanish as well as English for the pueblos, he believed that the pueblos should be taught only in English. By the end of 1872, he had convinced officials to fire all teachers who could not speak Merikaana's language.[112] The following year, only five of the government schools remained open; all of those that had employed Hispanic teachers, including the one at Tamaya, were closed.[113] Two years after the schools had opened, fewer than one in a hundred pueblo people had learned to read English.[114]

Throughout the 1870s, the pueblo schools struggled to obtain both funding and competent teachers. The pueblo agents complained that they did not have the money to hire good teachers. Some suggested that using bilingual teachers would both improve the schools and allow the pueblos themselves to be trained as teachers. The prevailing policy, however, held that the children would be best educated if they were removed from the pueblos. Agents explained that when pueblo children attended local day schools, parents took them from class to herd stock and to work in the fields. Children spoke "their native language . . . out of school hours," attended traditional ceremonies, and learned to respect pueblo leaders. If the children were sent to distant boarding schools, they would be removed "from their home influences and distractions" and better able to learn what Merikaana's leaders called "everything pertaining to civilized life." In this way they would be prepared to return to their homes and "introduce . . . new ideas" to their elders.[115]

When the government opened the first off-reservation boarding school for Indians from all tribes in Carlisle, Pennsylvania, in 1879, pueblo children were among the first to enroll.[116] In 1881, a year after the first pueblo students were sent to Carlisle, a delegation of six pueblo men went to inspect the school. Their agent, who accompanied them on the journey, reported that the pueblo delegates were "highly gratified by the improvement in the appearance of their children."[117]

Although Merikaana's agents praised the pueblo schools and reported enthusiastically about the students' progress, school attendance figures suggested that the pueblos were less than satisfied with their performance. Of some 2,000 school-age pueblo children, only 134 attended any school in 1881: 18 had been sent to Carlisle; an average of 38 went to the Albuquerque boarding school; and others were enrolled in day schools at Jémez, Laguna, and Zuñi.[118] Two years later, an agent complained that as many as 1,500 pueblo children did not attend any school.[119]

At a loss to explain such reluctance, the agents complained that the pueblos were "stubborn" and "conservative." Pueblo parents, however, could have offered other explanations. They had observed what happened to their children at the schools, and what happened when they returned to their homes. Carlisle, like many of Merikaana's Indian schools, was patterned after military schools. These schools enforced a rigid discipline, forbidding students to speak their native languages and punishing them if they showed any sign of the traditional ways and beliefs that their teachers condemned. Because many educators believed that Indian children could not learn academic subjects, the schools offered little more than basic English and vocational training. Boys learned trades such as carpentry, farming, wagon-making, harness-making, tailoring, painting and baking, while girls were taught to keep house as the women of Merikaana did. Students spent a great deal of their time performing manual tasks related to the care and operation of the school, including the sewing, laundry, cooking, and maintenance of the school and grounds. After spending years in these strict schools, far from their families and their peoples, the children were sent home, only to discover that the experience had isolated them. Few could use their training to obtain jobs on or near their tribal lands. Because they had been taught to reject their people's traditional ways, beliefs, and language, many returned only to discover that an enormous gap had been created between them and their families. Torn between the dimly remembered life from which they had been uprooted in childhood and the "progressive" life that the school teachers had promised them, most soon discarded the clothing they had worn home from the schools, as well as many of the ideas and values these schools had tried to teach them. For students and parents alike, however, it was a trying experience.[120] And not all students returned from the distant schools. In the 1886–1887 school year, 5 of the 128 Pueblo students at Carlisle died.[121] When pueblo parents saw what Merikaana offered their children, many who had once been eager to have schools began to oppose them.

Despite the agents' preference for boarding schools and English-speaking instructors, many new pueblo schools in New Mexico soon competed for pueblo pupils. Those who ran these schools typically argued that Merikaana should maintain "neighborhood schools" and local boarding schools, rather than sending children to distant schools that would create "a wide gulf between parent and child." Some, like one superintendent of the Albuquerque school, suggested locating the boarding schools "within easy reach of their homes, so that parents may often visit their children" and children would be able to "spend each year a long vacation at their homes." The distant boarding schools might be converted to teacher training schools for older Indian students better prepared to move far from their homes.[122]

Through the 1880s, a variety of local schools competed for pueblo students. In 1881 the Presbyterian Church established an Indian boarding school in Albuquerque.[123] The following year, the Laguna day school had copies of *McGuffey's Reader* printed in the Keres language.[124] In 1885 Catholics applied for contracts to run six pueblo day schools. Church leaders argued that the pueblos wanted Catholic schools and Spanish-speaking teachers, supporting their claims with statements from the governors of ten pueblos.[125] The University of New Mexico operated a contract school for Indians in Santa Fe. Isleta, Jémez, Laguna, Santa Clara, and Zuñi had day schools.[126] The Sisters of Loretto ran a school in Bernalillo.[127]

In 1887, when the government took over the Albuquerque boarding school, the new superintendent visited some pueblos to recruit students. He found that, after seven years' experience with Merikaana's schools, "opposition to the schools of the most violent and obstinate kind had taken root" at several pueblos, where the agent was unable to convince pueblo leaders "by the arts of persuasion, reason, or tact." The people seemed "suspicious of everything and everybody." When they explained to him that "they had been so often deceived that they could not put faith in the promises we made them" he concluded, "Much of this state of things, I am forced to believe, is due to the questionable, not to say reprehensible, devices that have been for years systematically resorted to to secure children." As the superintendent began to prove that he intended to keep his promises, more children went to Albuquerque. Among them were ten Tamayame students, the first of the pueblo's children to appear in the school records, who were enrolled in 1887.[128] Three years later, eleven of the pueblo's seventy-nine children went to Albuquerque, but the other sixty-eight did not attend any school.[129]

The Albuquerque boarding school, like many others, still suffered from inadequacies that even its superintendent admitted. The school had trouble finding and keeping enough qualified teachers, and it needed better buildings, more equipment, libraries, and other facilities. Each year, many of the students were children who had never before attended any school. Epidemics often spread through the school. During the first year that Tamayame children attended the school, one child died of measles, another, of typhoid, and in 1890, three students died.[130]

Although the teachers agreed that pueblo children were "very much interested in acquiring knowledge from books,"[131] and the schools engaged in a "brisk competition for pupils," many classrooms remained unfilled. In 1887 the Albuquerque boarding school, the two government day schools, seven contract schools run by the Catholics, and four schools operated by the Presbyterian Board of Missions in New Mexico enrolled a total of 680 pueblo pupils; another 100 attended Carlisle. The schools all engaged in "a brisk competition for pupils." In 1890 the Albuquerque school's third superintendent in three years was ready to use force instead of persuasion to recruit students. He suggested that "a Pueblo agent, armed with authority to compel the Indians to send their children to school, and a man who would display the proper degree of firmness, could fill all the Indian schools in a short time."[132]

Agents elsewhere had used similar tactics to force Indian parents to send their children to Merikaana's schools. Some agencies withheld the food and supply rations guaranteed to a tribe by treaty, distributing badly needed rations only when the agent decided that the tribes had sent enough children to the schools. Other officials punished parents who did not enroll their children. Some children were simply kidnapped and taken to the schools by force. New Mexico's Indian agents, however, soon learned that they could not use these schemes to make pueblo children attend school. Because the pueblos were neither citizens nor Indians under Merikaana's law, neither the federal statutes governing Indian education nor state laws that required compulsory school attendance could be applied to them. In addition, New Mexico's agents had little to give or withhold that could be used to intimidate the pueblos. Most pueblos had signed no treaties with Merikaana. They received no rations and needed none, except in times of disaster. All that Merikaana's agents had to withhold was their advice and the few tools that the government sent for the pueblos, things the pueblos could easily afford to reject. For many years, they had refused Merikaana's tools and equipment to avoid compromising their land titles in any way.[133]

Pueblo governments, with centuries of experience dealing with the agencies of other governments, soon developed a sophisticated arsenal of tactics to keep their children out of the schools. When the agent threatened to withhold government services from Santo Domingo unless the children attended the Santa Fe school, the pueblo governor appealed to the Catholic church to protect his people's rights.[134] Isleta parents presented a list of grievances against the school: children were required to attend in the summer, when they were needed in the fields; those who spoke their native languages or Spanish instead of English would be whipped; and parents who tried to visit had been "beaten up." When the school failed to resolve these issues after three years, Isleta parents went to court and obtained writs of habeas corpus to force the school to release their children.[135] Some pueblos, like Zía, requested day schools so that their children would not have to leave home.[136] From time to time, pueblo complaints against the schools appeared as charges of brutality in local newspapers.[137] Many pueblos refused to give, sell, or lease any land or buildings to the government for school use.[138] As Pueblo opposition to the schools increased in the 1890s, parents refused to send their children to distant boarding schools, and enrollment in all of the schools dwindled.[139] Some pueblos did not allow any of their children to enroll, while others sent a few children (usually boys who had already attended one of Merikaana's schools), so that the other pueblo children would be spared.[140]

Throughout the decade, few Tamayame children attended school. Some were sent to the Albuquerque government school, and others may have gone to the Bernalillo boarding school operated by the Sisters of Loretto, but the majority were not enrolled in any of Merikaana's schools. In 1892, only seven of the pueblo's fifty-four school-age children attended any boarding school. The following year, the agent asked Tamaya's governor to send at least ten children to the Albuquerque Indian School, promising that the children would be allowed to visit their homes during the year[141] and that pueblos who enrolled their children would receive a generous issue of supplies from the agency.[142] Two years later, the superintendent of the Bernalillo County School District asked permission to open a school at Santa Ana for as many as forty students, with José Martín Gutiérrez as the teacher, but the pueblo agent recommended against approving the contract.[143]

Not until 1899 did Tamaya have its own school. Agent Walpole, like many agents before him, requested a government school for the pueblo in 1898, noting that the Tamayame wanted a school and offered to furnish buildings for it. The agent proposed to operate the school at Ranchiit'u seven months out of the year; during December, January, and February, the teacher would move to the old pueblo with the Tamayame and instruct the adults in Merikaana's ways.[144] By August 1899 the school had been approved, and the agent asked Tamaya's governor to see that the schoolrooms were ready for the students and the teacher by September.[145] Meanwhile Walpole ordered a catalog of kindergarten materials and a desk for the new teacher, James Hovey.[146]

Eighteen Tamayame children attended the school in its first year, but within two years the average attendance had fallen to sixteen. Sometime during 1901 the school seems to have closed; in 1902 the agent reported that it had been "started up again under a new teacher," Ethel E. Gregg. That year, attendance rose to thirty-two children, and the Tamayame began to construct a larger building for the school. Classes ran through the summer, so that students could take their vacation during the winter, "when the Indians go to the old pueblo to engage in the annual religious dances." The following year, however, attendance had fallen to eighteen, and by 1905 only thirteen Tamayame children attended. When the parents of these children agreed to send the students to Albuquerque, Tamaya's first school closed.[147] Meanwhile, Tamaya's governor had signed an agreement allowing the Catholic church to build a chapel and school at Ranchiit'u.[148] Nearly fifteen years would pass, however, before Merikaana opened another school for the Tamayame.

Years of low school attendance had convinced Merikaana's officials that the pueblos would not readily exchange their ways and their beliefs for Merikaana's. They might readily trade "the old two-wheeled cart" for a "Studebaker wagon," but Merikaana's officials were learning, as Kastera's had long before, that "the practical point is that the Pueblo Indian is still unchanged in his old ideas and customs, and stubbornly intent upon maintaining them." Many, like Superintendent Dorchester, complained that the pueblos "still hold to the ceremonies of the former religion. Though in some of the Pueblos these ceremonies are observed more secretly, yet in others they are observed as openly as ever." Merikaana's officials were beginning to understand, with frustration, that "ofttimes, when these pueblos express a desire for a school in their villages, what we mean by education has not once been in their minds." Quoting another official, Dorchester summarized what the problem was in Merikaana's eyes: the pueblos, "having so long possessed all knowledge," had "steadily" resisted Merikaana's "efforts to show them their ignorance."[149]

Convinced of their own wisdom, Merikaana's officials were at a loss to understand this stubborn resistance, but they recognized that the attitude had its roots in the traditional ways maintained by pueblo elders. Slowly the officials began to suspect that schools alone might not be enough to bring about the kind of transformation they desired. Like Kastera's friars before them, they concluded that it would be necessary to outlaw the old customs and destroy the influence of traditional leaders. Without their influence, surely Merikaana could bring "progress" to the pueblos. With that goal, Merikaana's agents set about prohibiting anything that seemed to have any connection with the old ways.

One of the first targets of this policy was contact between the pueblos and other, less "progressive," Indian peoples. From the first, Merikaana had tried to control these contacts, by requiring pueblo traders to obtain passes to visit the Comanches and other tribes. The trade continued, however, until the end of the nineteenth century. As late as 1880 a group of men from Tamaya, Santo Domingo, and Sandía met at Santo Domingo to make preparations for a trading trip. Tamaya's delegate carried a "common piece of wood in his hand, [with] as many cuts in it as there were young men to go from his pueblo." Fourteen Tamayame would make the trip—Lorenzo Calabaza, Pedro Pino, Salvador Barranco, Miguel Silva, Miguel Tomás, Cruz Abiel, Antonio Mintiego, Manuel Armijo, Manuel Agustín, Pedro Yanahua, Pedro Montoya, Domingo Montoya, Juan de Dios de Chorra, and José Antonio Loreto. They planned to leave soon after the September meeting; it would take them "a month to get to the Comanche, and one month also to return." When the pueblos arrived, a council would be held to exchange presents and, speaking in signs, to establish the rules for the trading. If the Comanches had many hides and other goods to offer, the trading might be completed in only two days. Then the pueblos would return, reaching Tamaya in time for the winter ceremonies. When the pueblos requested permission for a similar trips to trade with the Comanches in Oklahoma Territory eighteen years later, however, Merikaana's agents repeatedly refused their requests.[150]

CHAPTER 9

By the 1880s, Merikaana's agents had begun their attack on pueblo traditions. In 1883, Agent Sánchez, who reported to his superiors that he lectured pueblos regularly about their "barbarous" customs, ordered the pueblos to move their graveyards away from the villages.[151] By the end of the decade, Merikaana's agents had begun a more drastic course of action, targeting not only individual customs but also the sovereign rights of pueblo governments. In the 1890s, agents attempted to depose pueblo governors and replace them with men of their own choosing at Acoma, Laguna, and other pueblos.[152] Then, in a 1903 ruling, New Mexico's territorial court outlawed the traditional government at Isleta.[153] Pueblo governors were told that "all old customs which are opposed to morality and progress and improvement will have to be given up,"[154] and it was clear that Merikaana's officials would use every means they could devise to achieve that goal.

Tamaya and the other pueblos, however, had no intention of abandoning their ways of life. They had welcomed Merikaana, and at first they had been eager to learn the new language and acquire the skills to use the new and useful tools that Merikaana brought. Many had asked for schools that would teach their children to read and write in this new language. They had offered Merikaana hospitality, assistance, and trade, and some had taken jobs in Merikaana's towns, ranches, and industries. For centuries they had learned the ways and languages of newcomers in their lands, making desirable elements of the new cultures a part of their own way of life. Merikaana's wagons might replace the wheeled carts that Kastera's blacksmith had taught them to make, and Merikaana's finely woven cloth might be incorporated in pueblo clothing. Pueblo leaders would master the new language and procedures that they needed to conduct the pueblo's business with Merikaana's officials. Accepting these necessary or desirable changes, however, would not alter the fact that they were the Hanu.

Again and again, Merikaana's agents told them that they must give up their ancient way and accept what Merikaana called "progress." The things these men praised and desired, however, had brought little good to Tamaya. The crowded trains were filled with men who would take pueblo lands, and the thriving towns soon demanded pueblo water. The mail might come regularly and frequently, but it contained little welcome news for the people of the pueblos. Instead it brought letters ordering them to give up their way of life, accept the loss of their land and water, or send their children to distant schools where those who survived would be taught to abandon their languages, their way of life, and their cherished beliefs and traditions. Messages from Merikaana's lawyers passed rapidly over the telegraph wires, but they had done little to protect—and much to damage—the lands through which the wires ran. Trains and stage coaches might carry pueblo leaders to distant Washington to meet with Merikaana's president, but too often the same trains brought the leaders back without the protection and recognition they had traveled so far to seek. Merikaana's tools were efficient, but better tools would be of little use to farmers who no longer had water for their crops and herdsmen who had no pastures for their livestock. The wages from Merikaana's jobs were welcome in an economy that depended increasingly on cash payments rather than exchange of goods and necessary in a system where agents regularly reminded the pueblos that Merikaana's courts would not hear their cases until they paid the required fees. No amount of money, however, could buy back the lands taken by speculators or the life of a child who would not return from a distant school. To abandon what they had learned long ago at Kashe K'atreti for the most desirable of Merikaana's new things would have been foolish; to make the exchange, as Merikaana's agents seemed to expect that they should, for things that brought them only harm was incomprehensible.

Photograph of a Tamayame man at a waterhole, taken to support Santa Ana's grazing lease applications in 1937–38. Courtesy of the National Archives (RG 75, BIA, UP-12681-37-301).

Corn, the first major crop of the Hanu, c. 1938. Courtesy of the National Archives (RG 75, BIA, UP-38155-37-031).

Tamayame man using a horse-drawn binder, c. 1938. Courtesy of the National Archives (RG 75, BIA, UP-13416-36-03).

The pueblo's thresher probably bought in the 1930s with Pueblo Lands Board funds. Courtesy of the National Archives (RG 75, BIA, UP-13416-36-031).

Unidentified group in front of ovens and buildings at Tamaya, c. 1935. Photograph by T. Harmon Parkhurst, courtesy of the Museum of New Mexico (neg. no. 4884).

Unidentified group at Tamaya, c. 1935. Photograph by T. Harmon Parkhurst, courtesy of the Museum of New Mexico (neg. no. 4883).

Domingo Montoya, c. 1936. Photograph by T. Harmon Parkhurst, courtesy of the Museum of New Mexico (neg. no. 3769).

Lupe Sanchez, c. 1935. Photograph by T. Harmon Parkhurst, courtesy of the Museum of New Mexico (neg. no. 12747).

Tamayame man drumming for tourists at Coronado Monument, 1948. Courtesy of the New Mexico State Records Center and Archives.

TEN

Tamaya's Lands, Merikaana's Rulings

Each spring, as the seedlings emerged along the Río Grande, the farmers watched with apprehension. As always, there was the fear that the rains would not come, that another dry year would bring hardship to the pueblo. That familiar danger, however, was less urgent than the new threat created by intruders who prowled the borders of pueblo lands. More dangerous than any of those who had stolen pueblo harvests in the past, these men would not be satisfied with carrying off the year's crops or raiding the storerooms. What they wanted was the land itself, and the streams that watered it. As a man would labor to save his crops and fields from the rising water, the pueblos worked desperately to hold off the flood of trespassers that swept toward their fields. Too often, however, they had even less success than a single man might have against a raging river. Daily the pressure increased, while the fragile barriers that protected pueblo lands weakened.

By the early twentieth century, only a few decades after Merikaana's government had recognized the authority of the pueblo governors, Merikaana's citizens clamored for pueblo lands. Although many pueblos had received papers extending Merikaana's protection to part of their lands, the problem of trespass had not been resolved, and it grew rapidly as the railroads delivered ever more settlers in search of farmlands. By 1902 one of Merikaana's officials reported that New Mexico's "desirable public land" was nearly gone, but the "demand for agricultural land" continued to increase. He predicted "that the pressure on these Indians will be greater than in the past." What little help the agents had given the pueblos seemed only to have made pueblo lands more desirable to outsiders. Some pueblos had received "much-needed aid" in bringing water to their fields; irrigation, however, made the fields "remarkably productive" and thus "very valuable."[1]

Having taken pueblo lands by force or fraud, the trespassers set about acquiring documents that would grant them legal title to their acquisitions. According to New Mexico law, a man might establish legal claim to a piece of land by occupying it for ten years. The superintendent of the Santa Fe school reported that many hoped to use that law to defraud the pueblos.[2] When the pueblos sought justice in New Mexico's courts and legislature, they found no remedy, for, as the pueblo attorney noted, many of the judges and legislators were themselves "claiming rights adversely to the Indians."[3]

During the first two decades of the twentieth century, the federal government took some steps to protect the pueblos from the most urgent threats. Congress passed a law exempting pueblo lands and property from taxation. Funds were appropriated to hire a lawyer for the pueblos and to survey and mark the boundaries of pueblo grants.[4] In 1912 a surveyor reported that he had finished marking Tamaya's south and west boundaries,[5] and that the Tamayame were pleased with his work. The following year, after more surveys, Pueblo Attorney Francis Wilson brought suit "to quiet title of Indians to the Santa Ana grant"; to complete this work, he noted, three hundred dollars would be required.[6] Naming thirty-two claimants, he asked the court to declare that these men and any other trespassers had "no estate or right whatever" in the Ranchiit'u.[7] Inspectors from Washington, D.C., visited the pueblos and made reports on their needs,[8] and a second pueblo agency was established so that officials could serve the pueblos more effectively. Tamaya fell within the jurisdiction of the Albuquerque office of the Southern Pueblo District.[9]

Through these years, pueblo leaders continued to work for the protection of their lands. During this time, Tamaya's governor negotiated an agreement with the Atchison, Topeka, and Santa Fe Railroad for a private railroad crossing for the pueblo.[10] None of these actions, however, could resolve the crucial underlying problems created by a policy that had allowed trespass on pueblo lands to continue for decades.

By 1920, when the U.S. House of Representatives Subcommittee on Indian Affairs came to investigate the situation in the pueblos, the extent of the resulting land problems shocked officials. At Tesuque alone, the committee found "some 2,000 disputes" involving pueblo lands. Many of the non-Indian claims, which had existed for years,[11] involved squatters who had "located on Indian lands" and claimed "title or the right to remain thereon." Between such "encroachments" and "adverse decisions of the courts," much pueblo land had been lost. The secretary of the interior explained that "notwithstanding the appointment of special attorneys for the Indians, but little seems to have been accomplished in removing the transgressors and quieting title to their lands."[12]

The afternoon of 17 May 1920, the subcommittee visited Tamaya. The pueblo, subcommittee members learned, was concerned not only about the ever-present threat of trespass, but also about the actions—and inactions—of Merikaana's government and the New Mexico legislature. The federal government had condemned Tamayame land for a school site and compensated the pueblo, but the land sat vacant since no funds were available to build the school. Plans had also been made for a new federal highway from Albuquerque to Jémez, which would cut fifteen miles from the fifty-three-mile journey by crossing pueblo lands. Trespass continued to plague the pueblo, which had no money to build its own roads and bridges or mark the boundaries of its lands. Leo Crane, superintendent of the pueblo agency, told the visitors that "eighty percent of the trouble from the outside would cease if pueblo lands were fenced." The Tamayame had volunteered to provide "all the posts and all the labor free" if the government would supply the wire to fence their lands, and the superintendent urged the government to provide this assistance. He also reminded the representatives that the pueblos' greatest need was not federal funds but "a firm, consistent, square-deal policy." It was "a mystery," he said, "that one-half of the pueblos are not on the warpath and the other half in jail. They have been the most patient people to be imagined after half a century of exploitation." They had heard that the government planned to file suits "to remove the squatters" and "to settle the rights of the Indians to the use of water from irrigation ditches" taken by the settlers, and they hoped that this would be done at last. Their superintendent added his hope "that proposed legislation now before Congress will not operate to turn these people over to those who wish to exploit them in the future, after having robbed them in the past."[13] The legislation under consideration, however, included a bill that would place the pueblos under state jurisdiction and divide pueblo lands into allotments held by individuals—a procedure that had already reduced the landholdings of tribes across the country.

Officials like Superintendent Crane, who actively supported pueblo interests, might help a pueblo defend its lands, but pueblo leaders were not willing to leave their fate in the hands of outsiders. Throughout these troubled decades, the pueblos met and took action on their own. United by common danger, as they had been in 1680 when they joined together to expel Kastera, they worked as a group to protect their lands and rights from further encroachment. In 1904, when New Mexico tried to tax the pueblos of Bernalillo County, sixty-four delegates from seventeen pueblos met to draft a resolution asking Congress to protect their lands. Their protest succeeded, and legislation soon prohibited the taxation of pueblo property.[14] In April 1920 the southern pueblos gathered at Tamaya to oppose the legislation designed to place them under state jurisdiction and open their lands to individual allotment. Led by Tamaya's governor, Manuel Pena, and nine other pueblo governors, the participants sent a long telegram to the Indian Office in Washington, D.C., explaining that because they were surrounded by individuals "largely opposed to" their "best interests" and because state residents had blocked "the enactment of such laws as are necessary to Indian government," they needed the protection of the federal government "to continue to exist." The pueblos concluded that it was "urgently necessary to send a delegation to Washington, accompanied by our agent, to present our views."[15] They met frequently in the following weeks and months to consider their strategy and to choose those who would represent them; Jesús Baca of Jémez was selected to speak for the people of Tamaya, Zía, and Jémez. By December, when a government stockman from Algodones attended one of the pueblo meetings, the delegates were ready to leave for Washington.[16] The agency superintendent recommended that Jesús Baca and the others "should be in Washington the first week of January 1921" and that the "delegation should not be delayed," even though the pueblos would be installing new officers at that time. He also advised them that they would need to raise at least three hundred dollars for each delegate: one hundred dollars each way for fares and meals on the train, and another hundred to pay their expenses during "several weeks" in the city.[17]

The same year, Merikaana at last began the official process of resolving the status of pueblo lands. The federal government appointed a special attorney with instructions "to investigate thoroughly all Pueblo titles, including the original grants, surveys, history of individual holdings, [and] disputes concerning water rights," and then "to make a comprehensive report upon which can be based a request for legislation . . . which will give justice to the Indians or the settlers."[18] By the end of the year, the special attorney had filed a report that outlined the extent of this mammoth task. He argued that the bills then being considered were "quite liable to act to the prejudice of the Indian" and that parts of the legislation were "clearly anti-Indian." He found that trespass on pueblo lands had, for many years, been "the rule rather than the exception" and that the pueblos had obtained no justice from local courts and juries. Volumes of Spanish, Mexican, and American laws and court decisions had legal impact on the situation, and the many disputes over land, water, and legal jurisdiction were so complex that the special attorney concluded the existing systems would be inadequate to resolve them. Thus he recommended the creation of a special "forum" to hear and resolve pueblo land matters.[19]

New Mexicans who claimed pueblo lands also wanted the issues to be resolved, but in a way that would guarantee them title to the lands they had taken. They urged that local courts, long favorable to their interests, be given jurisdiction to settle the land matters. In April 1922 New Mexico Senator Holm Bursum introduced a bill designed to protect those non-Indian interests. The bill provided that any persons or corporations that had occupied lands within pueblo grants for a least ten years before June 20, 1910, "shall be entitled to a decree in their favor . . . for the whole of the land so claimed." Under this legislation, state courts were to be given jurisdiction over any pueblo land separated from the grants. Where claimants could prove that they had occupied pueblo lands for ten or more years, the district court would survey the claims, determine the value of the land at the date of the decree, and award the pueblos tracts of public land "as nearly adjacent to the said pueblo as possible, equal in area and value or equal in value" to the original grant land. If no such lands were available—and it was virtually certain that none would be, since New Mexico's well-watered farmlands and good grazing lands had been taken long ago—a cash payment for the value of the claims would be made to the secretary of the interior, to be spent for the "best advantage and interest" of the pueblo. The bill allowed the pueblos only the irrigation water they actually used at that time; if they needed more, they would have to obtain it under New Mexico's general water laws rather than claiming their aboriginal right to it. The bill even allowed non-Indians to acquire title to pueblo lands without presenting any title deeds or proving that they had used the land for ten years, simply by demonstrating that they had settled a plot "in good faith" and making a payment for it.[20]

Incredibly, this legislation gained the support of the officials charged with protecting the Indians—the secretary of the interior and the commissioner of Indian affairs. Before the pueblos had even heard of the Bursum Bill, the United States Senate had passed it. As news of the bill's contents spread, however, the voices of opposition began to be heard. In September 1922, the Santa Fe *New Mexican* printed a complete copy of the bill, with the commentary that "enough has been said about 'relief' for the non-Indian settlers on Indian land. It is time to keep an eye on the other side of the question." After struggling "through the maze of legal phraseology in this bill," the writer concluded that it looked "like the same old squeeze." He reminded readers that Santa Fe had a vital interest in legislation related to the pueblos: the city hoped to become the center of a movement "to re-energize the creative arts of the Pueblos," but the pueblos could not "develop their ancient arts and crafts for the delight and education of the world [without] . . . enough to eat . . . , the compact lands to which they are justly entitled and which are vital to their life, and . . . the irrigation water necessary to farm their lands."[21] Within a short time, many Santa Feans had "taken up the protest against the passage of the bill in its present form." Not just in Santa Fe, but across the nation, pueblo supporters argued against legislation that would "cripple some of the Indian pueblo communities and . . . destroy others."[22]

Meanwhile the pueblos had learned of the threat, met to consider what to do, and prepared an appeal to the people of Merikaana, which was printed in the November 6 issue of the *New Mexican:*

> United in action for the first time since they arose and drove out the Spaniards in 1680, nearly one hundred delegates, traveling afoot and on horseback, and including eight governors, representing the eight thousand Pueblo Indians in nineteen Pueblos in New Mexico, assembled at the Pueblo of Santo Domingo on Sunday, adopted a memorial to the American people "for fair play and justice and the preservation of our pueblo life." . . . Alleging that they have not been consulted, that official explanations have been refused, that the bill will destroy them as a people, that it will make them to go into courts to settle tribal matters they have always adjusted among themselves, and that the government to which they look for protection in their rights has deserted them, they say in conclusion, "The bill will destroy our common life, and rob us of everything we hold dear; our lands, our customs and our traditions. Are the American people willing to see this happen?"[23]

The Santa Fe newspaper continued to provide information about the pueblos in the following weeks, reminding its readers that the government had "by inaction allowed . . . squatters to occupy large areas of their grants by encroaching continually thereon until the Indians have but one or two acres of cultivated land left, per capita, an insufficient amount for maintenance." Trespassers had been allowed to "remain unmolested and to encroach more and more from year to year." Again and again the pueblos had "expressed dissatisfaction with the appointment of the tribal attorney whose duty it is to look after their land interests. . . . ." They had complained that they were not "consulted in the selection of their legal advisor" and that they wanted to "be certain he would be a man who would be free from all influences which might be antagonistic to their interests."[24] As word of the pueblos' appeal and understanding of their grievances spread, people throughout the country began to take an interest in the matter.

Criticizing these outsiders for "interfering" in local matters, the bill's supporters angrily tried to deny the evidence they had produced. The Albuquerque *Morning Journal* claimed that the proposed bill would not "'rob' the Indians of a single acre of land which they have occupied during the last twenty-two years."[25] New Mexican R. E. Twitchell, who had helped to draft earlier versions of the bill, traveled to Washington, D.C., to defend the legislation.[26] The Washington *Herald* described the controversy as a "propaganda war," and another paper in the city called the opponents of the bill "hot air merchants and poison gas distributors."[27] E. B. Merritt, the assistant commissioner of Indian affairs, told Congress that the government had already spent huge sums on the pueblos, and that the pueblos had done nothing for America in return. Like many of the opposition's claims, this was an outright lie, as Leo Crane, the superintendent of the pueblo agency, explained in later years when he published a history of the pueblos. "With the utmost departmental composure," Crane recalled, "Merritt introduced, as evidence of government charity to the Pueblo Indians, thousands upon thousands of dollars expended . . . on the . . . Navajo, Jicarilla Apache, . . . and . . . Mescalero Apache Indians," money that had been squandered on "bridges that a Pueblo Indian proper would never likely see, much less cross," and dollars spent on other things no pueblo would ever use. The fact was, as Crane explained, that only scant funds had ever been set aside for the pueblos. Eleven of the Río Grande pueblos, Tamaya among them, had received an average of only slightly more than three hundred dollars a year for irrigation— "about enough to build footbridges over their community ditches." Contrary to Merritt's charge, the pueblos had in fact served Merikaana's government generously. And even had they done nothing for Merikaana, they held land titles under Merikaana's law. Did the assistant commissioner mean to say, Crane asked, that legal rights were valid only "in proportion to the amount of taxes paid or services rendered by the claimant to the United States? Is the United States a government that, before yielding to justice, must be tipped like a waiter?"[28]

Concerned men and women, from all parts of the country, joined the opposition to the Bursum Bill. Some provided information to disprove the statements of the bill's supporters, generating widespread publicity about the intent and likely effects of the legislation. Others made sure that the pueblos received current information about the progress of bill and that they understood the legal complexities of proposed changes. Many volunteered to help pueblo groups organize their opposition to the bill.[29]

With this support, the pueblo appeal for justice from Merikaana was heard at last. The Bursum Bill was defeated, Congress authorized the resolution of New Mexico's land disputes, and the Pueblo Lands Board Act, approved June 7, 1924, established procedures for examining claims to pueblo lands and safeguarding pueblo interests.[30]

Claimants who had "color of title"—those who had bought or received pueblo lands in good faith and held valid deeds to them—would have to show that they had occupied the lands since January 6, 1902, and had paid all of the land taxes. Claimants without "color of title" would have to prove that they, or their ancestors, had occupied the lands continuously since March 16, 1889. A three-member board would investigate all of the claims presented at each pueblo and make a full report. A non-Indian claim to pueblo lands could be upheld only if all three board members agreed that it was valid. When the board identified valid claims, it would then determine whether the government might have recovered the land or water rights for the pueblo "by seasonable prosecution," and if the government had failed to protect the pueblo's land and water, the pueblo would be paid for its loss. After studying each valid non-Indian claim, the board would also decide whether it would be in the pueblo's interest to remove the claimants by buying the lands. If so, the secretary of the interior would ask Congress to pass legislation authorizing the purchase of the land and appropriating funds for any necessary surveys and for the original court proceedings. When the board had completed its work, the United States attorney general would file suit to quiet the pueblo's title to all of the lands confirmed to it.[31]

To prevent similar problems from arising in the future, the Pueblo Lands Act clearly stated that no one could use New Mexico laws to obtain title to pueblo lands; that no transfer of pueblo land would be valid without the approval of the secretary of the interior; and that when Congress awarded monetary compensation to the pueblos for lost lands, the money could be used only for "the purchase of lands and water rights to replace those which have been lost to said pueblo or to said Indians, or for purchase or construction of reservoirs, irrigation works, or the making of permanent improvements upon, or for the benefit of, the lands held by said pueblo or said Indians."[32]

The three board members selected were Robert Walker, a New York lawyer who would represent Merikaana's president; Herbert J. Hagerman, who would act for the secretary of the interior; and C. H. Jennings, who would represent the United States attorney general.[33] Within a year, the board had decided on its policies and procedures, and had set up an office in Santa Fe.[34] Meanwhile, three thousand claims had been filed on behalf of nearly twelve thousand individuals who believed they had some right to pueblo lands.[35]

By September 1925, the Pueblo Lands Board had filed its first reports, on the pueblos of Tesuque, Jémez, and Nambé. Hagerman explained that the board had examined all of the claims at these pueblos, made the necessary surveys, and met with all of the claimants to explain the law to them. Each claimant had submitted a formal petition, which was translated if necessary. The board then held hearings on each claim; at the hearings, a special pueblo attorney and a lawyer "retained by the American Indian Defense Association" represented the pueblo.[36]

A year later, officials established a new pueblo council to serve as the official voice of the pueblos. In the years of opposition to the Bursum Bill, many pueblo groups had been formed, some with the assistance of non-Indian organizations and supporters such as John Collier of the Indian Defense Association. These councils, however, had no official status; the new U.S. Pueblo Indian Council (later known as the All Pueblo Council) was to be the pueblos' official link to Merikaana's government.[37] Lands Board Member H. J. Hagerman chaired the first three-day session, held at the Indian School in Santa Fe in November 1926. Participants included Tamaya's governor Hilario Sánchez and alternate Porfirio Montoya, leaders from the other pueblos, Pueblo Lands Board members, agency officials, the special pueblo attorney, a representative of the American Indian Defense Association, and two interpreters. Hagerman declared that the pueblos might meet as often as they wished and with whomever they wished, but this new council would be their official link with Merikaana's officials, who would attend its meetings and carry the pueblos' messages to Washington, D.C. By establishing this council, Hagerman explained, the "government of the United States" was "again recognizing the governors of the pueblos as official authorities . . . ," just as Spanish rulers and President Lincoln had done in the past by presenting the governors with canes of office "as the badges of" their "authority."[38]

The following year, the Pueblo Lands Board came to Tamaya. Claimants were notified that hearings would be held in Albuquerque April 18 through April 21, 1927. Board members quickly confirmed the land in Tamaya's square grant, for none of the outsiders reported on the grant in the past filed a claim to the lands they had occupied. The only non-Indian holding within the square was a right-of-way that Tamaya had granted to the Santa Fe Northwestern Railway the previous year. Through this agreement, signed in March of 1926, the railroad obtained permission to use a 100- to 200-foot strip running from the southeast corner of the grant west to the Jémez River and north along the river through pueblo lands. In exchange, the pueblo received $297 in compensation and the promise that the right-of-way would revert to pueblo ownership when the railroad no longer needed the strip.[39]

The situation in Tamaya's Ranchiit'u lands was more complicated. Non-Indians filed claims to twenty-seven parcels of land within the grant. An error made by the Court of Private Land Claims had included nearly thirty acres of the original Ranchiit'u lands in the Bernalillo or Felipe Gutiérrez Grant. The most recent surveys showed an area of nearly seven hundred acres in the Angostura region—part of the old Santa Ana-San Felipe conflict—as lying within the San Felipe grant, although this land had been part of Tamaya's Ranchiit'u purchase. Various parties claimed rights in the three irrigation ditches (Santa Ana, Bernalillo, and Bosque) that ran through the Ranchiit'u.[40] On the last day of the hearings, Governor Otero gathered up pueblo documents from the box in which they were stored and presented the Tamaya's claims to the Pueblo Lands Board.[41]

For the next four weeks, the board members studied piles of deeds, tax records, and documents. They met with the claimants, the Tamayame, and other individuals who knew the history of the area's lands. By May 16, Hagerman had prepared a list of recommendations outlining his conclusions. He believed that the Santa Ana-San Felipe conflict area "has all along been cultivated and irrigated by the Santa Anas and not the San Felipes." Even San Felipe's governor had told the Board that "the land is and has for a long time been conceded to the Santa Ana Indians by the San Felipe Indians," and that the Tamayame had been using said land "ever since the Ranchito tract was acquired by the Santa Anas, that is, over a hundred years." Because Tamaya had no written evidence of its title to these lands and he believed that San Felipe did, however, Hagerman recommended against confirming Santa Ana's right to this land. Finding "no controversy and apparently no shortage of water for the Santa Ana Indians within the Ranchiit'u," he ruled that the pueblo used only the Santa Ana Ditch and that the other two ditches had rights-of-way through the Ranchiit'u. He confirmed Tamaya's ownership and use of a 29.97-acre tract within the Bernalillo grant, but he argued that non-Indians possessed clear title to the lands in the southern part of the

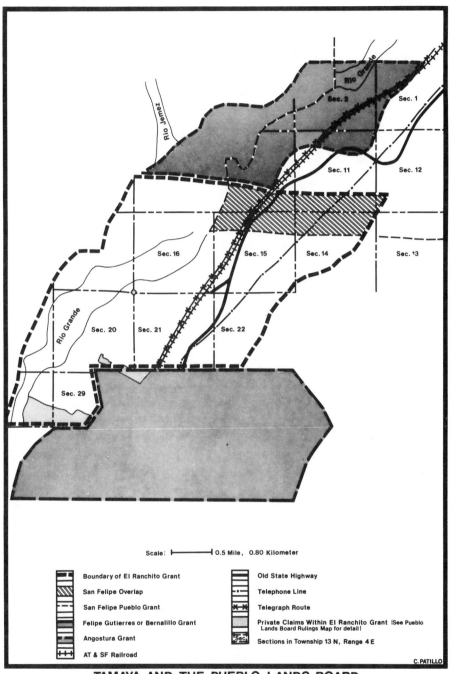

Sec. 2

Sec. 1

Rio Grande

Rio Jemez

Sec. 11

Sec. 12

Sec. 16

Sec. 15

Sec. 14

Sec. 13

Rio Grande

Sec. 20

Sec. 21

Sec. 22

Sec. 29

Scale: ├────────┤ 0.5 Mile, 0.80 Kilometer

Boundary of El Ranchito Grant		Old State Highway
San Felipe Overlap		Telephone Line
San Felipe Pueblo Grant		Telegraph Route
Felipe Gutierres or Bernalillo Grant		Private Claims Within El Ranchito Grant (See Pueblo Lands Board Rulings Map for detail)
Angostura Grant		Sections in Township 13 N, Range 4 E
AT & SF Railroad		

C. PATILLO

TAMAYA AND THE PUEBLO LANDS BOARD
Redrawn from Exhibits A and B, Pueblo Lands Board, "Report on Title to
Lands Purchased by Pueblo Indians," 19 July 1927

Ranchiit'u. He also concluded that non-Indians had used these lands since the eighteenth century and that the Tamayame had not thought "that they had any claim to that until the Lands Board operations commenced." Since this land had been lost before Merikaana's arrival, he recommended that the pueblo not be paid for it. He recommended that the government buy only one of the claims—that of Sostenes Jaramillo—for the pueblo, but he expected that "Collier and his group" would probably "contest the finding of no damages."[42]

In July the board presented its final report on Santa Ana lands. It upheld Santa Ana's title to five claims within the Ranchiit'u (see map on page 215), which were, however, burdened with rights-of-way for the Santa Fe Northwestern Railway; the Atchison, Topeka, and Santa Fe Railway; the Western Union Telegraph Line; the Postal Telegraph Line; and the Mountain States Telephone and Telegraph Line. The board also confirmed Tamaya's ownership of a 29.69-acre tract within the Bernalillo Grant.[43] The remaining twenty-one claimants to Ranchiit'u lands had, the board concluded, valid claims to approximately 96 acres in the southern part of the Ranchiit'u (see map on page 215). The western section of the disputed area was pasture; the eastern part, above the Bosque ditch, was farmland "in a comparatively high state of cultivation, in vineyards, orchards, gardens, and other valuable crops." Contrary to Hagerman's recommendations, the board ruled that all of this land "could have been recovered for said Indians by the United States." They proposed a compensation payment of $5,035, approximately $2,000 less than the appraised value of the claims. Tamaya would receive $60 per acre for nearly 41 acres of cultivated land and an acre of vineyard; half that amount for nearly 27 acres of uncultivated land and 23 acres of meadowland; and $10 per acre for 5.4 acres of *ciénega*. Arguing "that there would be no benefit to the Indians in anywise in removing any of such non-Indian claimants" since these lands were all a mile or more from the Ranchiit'u villages, the board concluded that the government should not buy back any of these lands for the pueblo. The members decided against ruling on the Santa Ana–San Felipe overlap until they had examined the San Felipe claims.[44]

With those findings, the board wound up its work at Santa Ana and moved on. By November 1927, the pueblo attorney had filed suit to quiet Tamaya's title to the land,[45] and by January 1928, the board had returned the papers presented by individual claimants, the Catholic church, and the railroad and telegraph companies.[46] In May 1929, the district court overturned the board's ruling on the Sostenes Jaramillo claim, holding that Sostenes Jaramillo did have a valid claim to 6.35 acres in the Ranchiit'u, which had

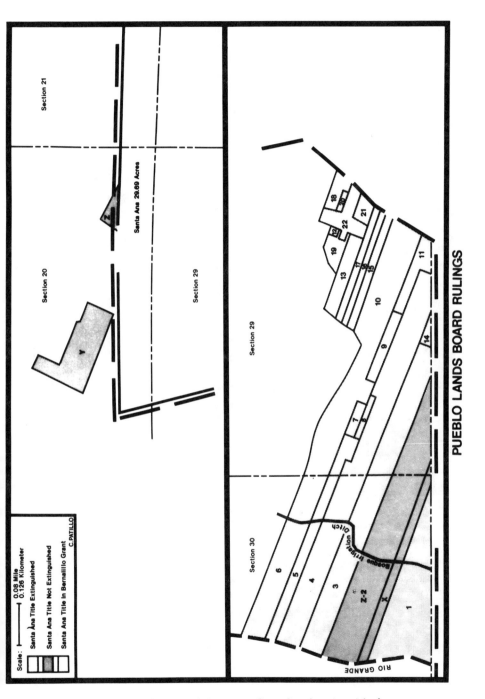

PUEBLO LANDS BOARD RULINGS

See pages 275–76 for identification of claims confirmed and extinguished.

been appraised at more than $900. The pueblo attorney accepted this ruling, and the Pueblo Lands Board amended its report accordingly, recommending that Congress increase Tamaya's award by the amount needed to buy the tract.[47] The government made new surveys showing the boundaries established by the board, and a survey party helped to fence Tamaya's land.[48]

These rulings had given Tamaya secure title to an important part of the pueblo's lands, but the Lands Board had not resolved claims to the lands in the Angostura disputed with San Felipe or to the Ojo del Espiritu Santo Grant the pueblo shared with Zía and Jémez. When the U.S. Pueblo Council met at Santa Fe in November 1927, pueblo representatives—governor Emiliano Otero and alternate Porfirio Montoya of Tamaya, and Jesús Baca of Jémez—raised the issue of the Espiritu Santo lands, asking "if the contract made by the Government of Spain and the United States is still in effect." The pueblo attorney replied that he could "only state what I have stated to you before," that the Court of Private Land Claims and the Supreme Court had denied the pueblos' claim. Assistant Commissioner of Indian Affairs E.B. Merritt added that the courts' decision was final and the officials had no power to reverse it. Tamaya's governor replied that he understood what the officials had said about the Espiritu Santo, but the pueblo also wondered whether "a little strip of land" between the Ranchiit'u and the pueblo grant, which would be "a benefit and good for the people," might be bought for them. Merritt promised to "look into the land matter," but told the governor that Indian reservations could not be enlarged without a special act of Congress.[49]

Four years after its initial report on Santa Ana, at Tamaya's request, the Pueblo Lands Board held a meeting "at the school house on the Santa Ana Pueblo Grant . . . in connection with a conflict between the Santa Ana and San Felipe Grants of about 695 acres." Among those present were the three lands board members, the pueblo attorney, agency personnel, and "about fifty Indians," including Tamaya's Governor Otero, San Felipe's Governor Valencia, and four unnamed men from San Felipe. Governor Otero explained that Tamaya had "had this land in possession for many years, and also the patent, or the purchase." Tamaya had cultivated almost all of this land and irrigated much of the portion east of the railroad; with the exception of one parcel near the river and another near the hills that could not be irrigated, it was "very good land." No one else, to the knowledge of the governor and the elders, had cultivated it or made a claim to it during their lifetimes. Even the governor of San Felipe agreed that he did not "know anything about it" and neither he nor the other San Felipe delegates knew of any San Felipe who had "occupied and used any part of the land in conflict." Still, Governor Valencia made clear, the San Felipes hadn't "come down here to make any decision, they only came down here to listen and they will have another meeting and then they will decide whether they own the land or not." After hearing the statements of both pueblos, board members asked the Tamayame who cultivated these lands to show the area to them.[50]

Four months later, in June 1931, the board made its report on the overlap, which had been investigated "at the urgent request of the Indians of Santa Ana Pueblo." The board members, who had apparently seen few of the historic documents involving the disputed lands, were still confused about the area's history. They gave no indication that they were aware of the problems created by the changing course of the Río Grande, the interpretation of the Clements Survey that had altered the boundaries of San Felipe in the nineteenth century, or the rulings of the Court of Private Land Claims that had created a new boundary for the Angostura Grant. Unfamiliar with the history of Tamaya's eighteenth-century Ranchiit'u purchases, they considered title to the lands established by San Felipe's 1689 pueblo grant, a document later proved to be a forgery. That left the board with a dilemma it could not resolve. Although San Felipe seemed to have title to the land, the board concluded that it did not "appear from the evidence that the Indians of San Felipe have ever, in the memory of any living Indian, been in actual possession of this tract of land. On the contrary, it does appear that this area in conflict was included in the land purchased by the Santa Ana Indians, known as the Ranchitos tract, which was patented to the Santa Ana Pueblo in 1909." Tamaya had not been "disturbed in possession" of these lands, but the board recommended that "this controversy should be settled once and for all and their legal as well as equitable title hereto determined."[51]

Board members, however, concluded that they could not implement that recommendation, for they had authority to resolve only disputes between Indians and non-Indians, not claims that involved two pueblos. Since they had "been begged again and again, not only by the Indians of Santa Ana but by the Superintendent of the Southern Pueblos, to either pass upon it ourselves or to make some recommendation which will enable the matter to be settled in the courts," they suggested that a "friendly suit" between the pueblos might resolve the matter.[52] After reviewing the report, the U.S. attorney general saw "no reason why the suggested suit should not be instituted." He recommended that each pueblo hire its own attorney, but he asked board member Hagerman to discuss the matter with the pueblo attorney before a decision was made.[53] Hagerman suggested to the pueblo attorney that the New Mexico Association on Indian Affairs might be able to provide funds for such a suit.[54]

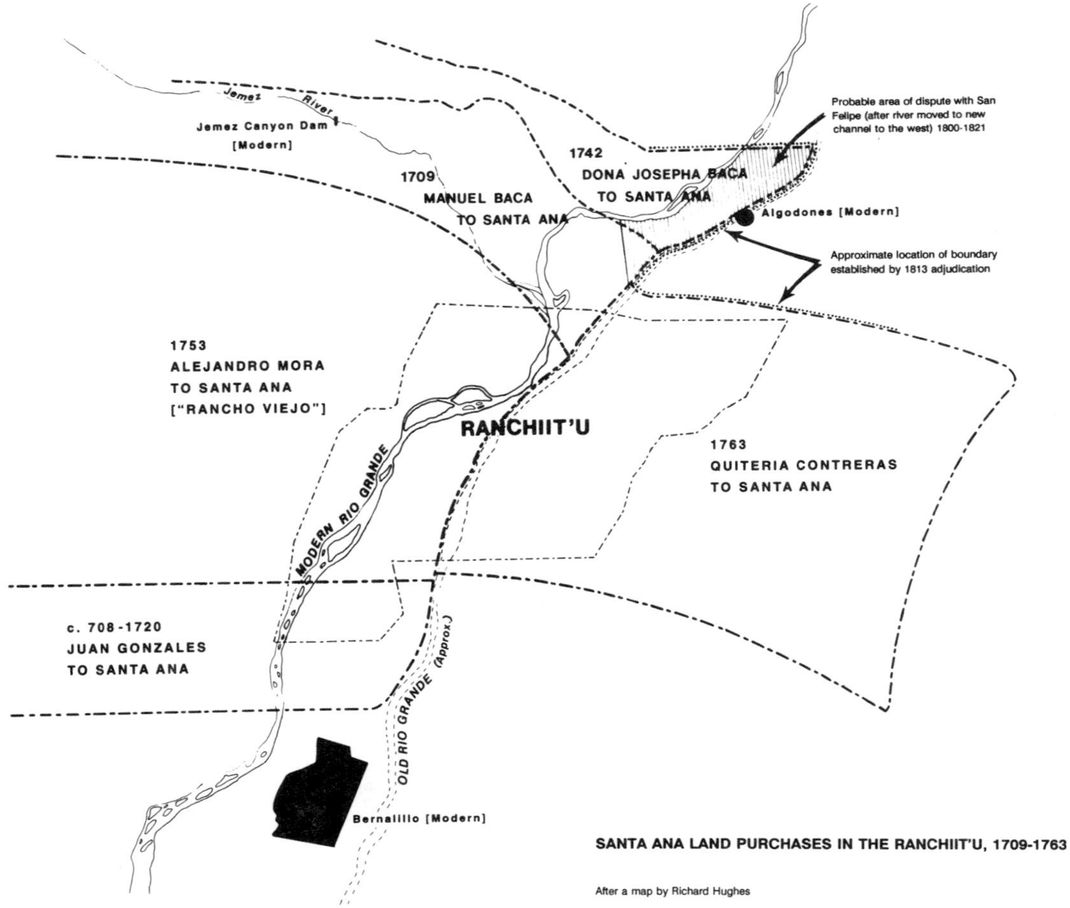

Probable area of dispute with San Felipe (after river moved to new channel to the west) 1800-1821

Approximate location of boundary established by 1813 adjudication

Algodones [Modern]

1742
DONA JOSEPHA BACA
TO SANTA ANA

1763
QUITERIA CONTRERAS
TO SANTA ANA

MANUEL BACA
TO SANTA ANA

1709
RANCHIIT'U

Jemez River

Jemez Canyon Dam
[Modern]

OLD RIO GRANDE (approx.)

Bernalillo [Modern]

MODERN RIO GRANDE

1753
ALEJANDRO MORA
TO SANTA ANA
["RANCHO VIEJO"]

c. 708-1720
JUAN GONZALES
TO SANTA ANA

SANTA ANA LAND PURCHASES IN THE RANCHIIT'U, 1709-1763

After a map by Richard Hughes

By the following year, however, officials had begun to reconsider this solution. Special Attorney Fraser raised a series of practical and legal objections to the suit. He had searched for the old Spanish documents, but many were missing. He had also tried to arrange an agreement between the pueblos, but found that there was "no use attempting to procure the consent of San Felipe to a declaration of ownership by Santa Ana . . . because . . . [San Felipe], when approached on the subject, merely states that if the conflict area lies within its Grant, it continues to claim it." If a suit were to be brought, the government would be in an "impossible situation," forced to violate the interests of at least one of the pueblos it had the obligation to represent: "the United States as guardian for one ward . . . [would be] suing another ward of which it was also guardian." If the suit were heard in the federal courts, which had jurisdiction over other pueblo land cases, the government would have to sue as the plaintiff; if one pueblo sued the other in state court, federal attorneys would have to appear for both sides. Fraser worried that, under New Mexico law, "no matter how strong the equitable rights of the Santa Anas may be, the result of the contemplated suit might be a dismissal or even a decree in favor of the San Felipes on the ground of priority of title." He concluded that "the whole situation is extremely difficult and confused . . . I will continue to work on it but, up to the present, although recognizing what seems to be the clear and predominant equity of Santa Ana, I do not see just how that equity can be enforced in court."[55] He found "no legal remedy" for Tamaya unless San Felipe would voluntarily give a quit-claim deed to the lands, an action that he believed San Felipe would reject. For these reasons, he decided that "while it is unsatisfactory to leave the just claim of Santa Ana without legal protection, yet no actual harm is done so long as the possession of the pueblo remains undisturbed." He recommended letting the matter rest,[56] and the commissioner of Indian affairs agreed, for he was afraid that a "friendly suit" to settle the matter might "end in bitter hostility and animosities between people who otherwise would and should be more kindly disposed toward each other." For the time being, the government would do nothing, "in the hope that it will ultimately be disposed of by a friendly agreement between the two pueblos."[57]

Thus, by 1932, the work that the Pueblo Lands Board had begun five years earlier at Tamaya was complete. Congress authorized payment of $8,897 dollars to the pueblo, an award which included the original payment recommended by the Pueblo Lands Board, additional funds to allow the purchase of the Jaramillo claim, and money set aside by the Chavez Bill to allow the pueblos to buy back land and water and to improve their lands. Non-Indians received $946 compensation for the claims they relinquished. After the award, the governor and council of Tamaya met with Superintendent Towers to discuss their plans. The agency had already spent $1,302 for fencing, posts, and wire for the pueblo. The Tamayame hoped to buy back two plots: "a small area between the highway bridge across the Rio Grande and the south line of the lands awarded them within their grant" and "the one claim within their grant located near their village and that part of two claims [held by Jacobo Perea] extending into their grant from the north." The pueblo, however, had no plans to purchase the other claims in the southern part of the Ranchiit'u.[58] It seemed to the superintendent that it might still be possible to reach a "friendly agreement" with San Felipe to secure Santa Ana's rights to the lands in the overlap.[59]

Thus Tamaya formally presented its claims to Merikaana a second time. The Pueblo Lands Board, like the Court of Private Claims before it, had upheld the Tamayame's rights to their central lands, restoring some of the land taken by trespassers. In compensation for lands declared lost, the pueblo had received a small sum that would help the Tamayame fence and protect their remaining lands and perhaps buy back some of what had been taken. The pueblo's deeds and papers had been returned and were once again stored safely under the governor's care. Merikaana's officials had affirmed their recognition of pueblo authority, and many of Merikaana's citizens had demonstrated their support for the pueblos. Once again the people of Tamaya had joined with their neighbors to save their lands and their way of life from the gravest of threats.

Yet these were only partial victories, not the full justice that the pueblos had sought. Merikaana had protected only a fraction of Tamaya's land, and the courts had done little to redress nearly a century of wrongs. The three pueblos were simply told that the Espiritu Santo was lost, and nothing could be done about it. Although Merikaana's officials had recognized Tamaya's right to the farmlands in the Angostura, the pueblo still had no legal protection for these lands. A large part of the Ranchiit'u had been confirmed to non-Indian claimants, and Merikaana saw no reason to buy back this land for Tamaya. For decades trespassers had enjoyed the benefits of Tamaya's land and water, and now they reaped the rewards of Merikaana's negligence.

The pueblos had learned that, while Merikaana's papers, like Kastera's, could be essential to claiming their rights under Merikaana's law, deeds and titles would do nothing to protect their rights from those willing to disregard the law. A pueblo might hold the deeds, but if a man cut their timber, drove his stock across their land, or used their water, the pueblo's papers would not undo the damage. If a railroad wanted to run its tracks, a telegraph company its lines, or an irrigation company its ditches across Tamaya's lands, the papers would not prevent them from having their way. In time the law itself might recognize acts of trespass as a basis for awarding rights to the very individuals who had violated the law and disregarded the pueblo's rights initially. For the time, Tamaya had done what it could to protect its lands through Merikaana's legal procedures, but no Tamayame would have called the result justice. Merikaana considered the matter resolved, but Tamaya would not be satisfied until the pueblo's rights and lands were restored.

ELEVEN

Tamaya Yesterday and Today

The young corn rose toward the sky and the bushy cotton plants spread in the fields as they had for centuries.[1] Each year the seasons passed and the people gathered for ceremonies held since the Hanu came into this upper world. The dry years came still to parch the fields, and the rivers now and again swept over their banks, threatening the fields and homes of the Río Grande peoples. Passing by, a traveler might hear the sound of drums and ancient songs. Each year the potters went to the hills to gather clay, the farmers carried the harvest back from the fields to the pueblo, and hunters returned with game for the winter. These ancient, familiar activities, however, took place in a world far different from the Río Grande that Coronado had marched into or the pueblos Stephen Kearny had seen.

Tamaya's farmers still planted their crops each spring, but they guided mechanical plows through fields where their fathers had dug the earth with sharp oak sticks. The grain, once gathered by hand and threshed by horses, would be harvested with binding and threshing machines. When the threshers had finished their work, they would load the grain, not in oxcarts lined with hide, but in pick-up trucks, automobiles, or horse-drawn wagons for the trip back to the pueblo. On the shelves where the harvest was stored for the winter, jars of fruit, vegetables, and meat canned by pueblo women stood beside the dried meats, chilies, and baskets of corn.[2]

And the harvest was no longer carried back to the old pueblo beneath the mesa, for, about 1935, the Tamayame had decided to make their homes in the Ranchiit'u year round. Still they would return each year to the old pueblo for the ceremonies, but they would dwell in two villages near their fields.[3]

CHAPTER 11

Often now the Tamayame journeyed far from their homes. They went, not on short trips like the two-month journeys that had taken their ancestors to the land of the Comanches to trade for hides and buffalo, but to find work that would keep them in the fields of Colorado and California or in distant cities and factories for many months. In the summers, some of the men lived in camps, not to patrol as their grandfathers had for Navajo and Apache raiders, but to take jobs building roads and bridges, fighting fires, and digging wells in programs set up by Merikaana's government. Once again, Merikaana's government called for the pueblos' assistance in times of conflict, and once again the governors of Tamaya and the other pueblos offered their support. During the Second World War, Tamayame served in the armed forces and in the civilian defense, the governor himself traveled to Santa Fe to deliver money collected at Tamaya for war bonds, and the pueblo offered food to the hungry people of Europe and China. Throughout these years, Tamaya's governors went, as many had gone before them, to speak with Merikaana's leaders in distant cities, but automobiles, trains, and airplanes rather than horses and coaches carried them on their errands. Still the people waited anxiously for word of their success, but now the news reached the pueblo almost immediately, by telegraph or telephone.[4]

Tamaya's children grew up in this new world. Like all of the generations before them, they learned the pueblo's ways from their elders, but they would also attend Merikaana's schools. Some of their parents recalled the long unhappy journeys to distant boarding schools where teachers told them that they must abandon the ways of their people, where they had been whipped if they were caught speaking the language of the Hanu or talking of the things their elders had taught them. These children, however, would come home regularly, with accounts of teachers who encouraged them to speak their own languages, study their own culture, and learn the arts and crafts of their people as well as Merikaana's new skills. From the 1920s on, nearly all of the pueblo's children would be enrolled in one of Merikaana's schools: the day school at Tamaya, St. Catherine's, the Bernalillo school run by the Sisters of Loretto, the Albuquerque and Santa Fe Indian schools, and, in later years, the Bernalillo public schools.[5]

Again in these years, the pueblo's governors would take out the ragged papers given to them with their grants and protest the decision that had taken the Espiritu Santo lands from them. For those who held Tamaya's canes in the mid-twentieth century, the task of defending the pueblo's land and water would be a heavy one. Farmers and herdsmen watched the skies and the streams anxiously, for water, always important in this dry land, became crucial as Merikaana's cities and ranches grew. During these hard years, the Tamayame dwindled until only slightly more than two hundred people remained. Hardly a family had not been touched by disease, as epidemics of smallpox, measles, tuberculosis, and influenza swept through the pueblo. Most adults could remember when Tamaya had been twice as large, and the oldest men and women could recall when the pueblo had been larger still. For a time it seemed that the Tamayame might not survive: by the 1930s, one outsider described the pueblo as a "tiny, disappearing village."[6]

Change had always been a part of the upper world, but the changes had never come so quickly. Men and women born at the end of the last century could recall the time when farmers had used canoes to travel to the fields. They told their children how the people had trained burros to lie still in the canoes and described how they had used "wooden plows with one handle which they made from the branches of cottonwood trees." They could remember farming east of the Ranchiit'u ditch, as far as Algodones, as well as the time when the Río Grande had shifted in the Ranchiit'u. They recounted the arrival of the railroad in their childhood, explaining how they had placed cornmeal on the track so that this strange "spirit" could eat, until they discovered that the train was only a "moving house" that carried people from place to place. As boys, some men had led oxen in the fields, while others had taken the pueblo stock to graze, herding the animals south toward Corrales, west in the Espiritu Santo, and east to Placitas. All could tell of the winters, when they had returned to the old pueblo.[7]

The changes had come so rapidly that these things were unfamiliar to their children. The boys who hid from the trains would watch their sons and daughters, wearing stylish modern clothing or crisp uniforms like those worn by their non-Indian neighbors, board trains that would carry them to distant schools, jobs, and battlefields. Children whose parents had used hard oak sticks to plant corn grew up using wooden plows; as adults, they would meet to decide what price the pueblo should pay for mechanical combines, threshers, and harvesters. Women whose mothers and grandmothers had made the bowls and pots used in nearby Spanish villages would trade their own pottery for food during years when crops were destroyed by grasshoppers and drought. As they grew older, they would encounter tourists willing to pay cash for their pottery and museums eager to display it, not for the long service it would give, but for its decoration.[8]

This generation would grow up in a world where Tamaya was no longer a remote, isolated place of little interest to outsiders. The Bursum Bill had drawn national attention to the pueblos, and long after the bill had been defeated, the story and the ways of these ancient peoples would fascinate non-Indians throughout the nation and even in remote European lands. As a result, children whose parents had been whipped for talking about their traditions in school were suddenly encouraged to speak of their people's ways. In 1934 pueblo school children began a painting project using the traditional natural colors. Teachers asked pueblo parents to help find the clays and earth substances to make "the rich reds, browns, and white colors" that "had long been used by native women for painting designs on their pottery." To ensure that all of the students would have access to as many colors as possible, each school gathered materials and exchanged them with the others. Both teachers and students learned that making paint from earth and clay was "a long and tedious process." First the materials had to be ground, pounded, sifted, and soaked; then the paint was skimmed and dried; finally water and glue had to be added to these dried colors before they could be used. In spite of this time-consuming process, the children were eager to use traditional paints instead of the "commercial colors formerly provided," and in the spring they proudly exhibited their paintings in Albuquerque.[9]

Paintings by Tamayame children were among the seventeen chosen from this display to represent America in an international exhibit, sponsored by the College Art Association, that toured the country the following year. The pueblo children's work "received favorable comment and created much interest in Indian arts in general." Later the same year, pueblo students at the Santa Fe school designed posters for an exhibit of American Indian art that traveled to Paris. The next year, Vincent Armijo, a student at Tamaya's day school, exhibited his painting "Driving Horses Home" in a display at New York's Rockefeller Center. Children at the Albuquerque Indian School presented a puppet show on land use and conservation; they made the puppets, designed posters, and wrote the script, as well as related essays and editorials. By the end of the 1936–37 school year, the children at the Santa Fe school had exhibited their art in more than thirty shows across the country and published their work in several magazines, including one in London.[10]

Pueblo arts were in demand for exhibitions throughout the country. In 1938, the "carpentry, silversmithing, and carving departments" in the schools worked with "the craftsmen in the pueblos" to build a model room for the Gallup Indian Ceremonial. Pueblo exhibits were displayed at the San Francisco Exposition and in Washington, D.C. By the following year, the New Mexico fair had a special building to display Indian arts. Among its exhibits was a miniature pueblo, constructed by school children, with a tiny irrigation system to water fields of real alfalfa and wheat sprouts. The model showed a pueblo during a fiesta, complete with tourists "bargaining for pottery" and "visiting Navajos" with their "covered wagons." With the help of San Felipe's governor, students completed traditional paintings for the model.[11]

Children were not the only Tamayame artists who began to receive recognition from Merikaana during these years. A visitor to Tamaya in 1933 could go to "a little curio shop," which sold pueblo pottery, paintings on buckskin, watercolors, and drums like the two "painted a sky blue, with white rain clouds around each end" that one woman purchased there.[12] Tamayame men had learned silversmithing from the Navajos in the 1890s, and José Rey León, who "learned the craft from a Navajo in the San Ysidro region," had taught "several of the younger men of the village." By the 1940s, Tamaya had four active silversmiths who did most of their work in the winter, after the crops had been harvested. José Rey León sold his silver in "the nearby towns."[13] Like other Indian silversmiths, these men found that the high demand for Indian silver produced many "cheap imitations." To protect pueblo artists from these inexpensive and often shoddy duplicates, the government established an Indian Arts and Crafts Board and designed a trademark that enabled prospective buyers to distinguish genuine Indian arts.[14]

Although Tamaya's painters and silversmiths found their work in great demand in the 1930s, few outsiders were initially interested in the work of Tamaya's potters, whose bold and vivid designs were not in fashion. One visitor even claimed that Tamaya's pottery was poor because the clay was "not suitable." By the following decade, however, appreciation of and interest in this pottery had begun to increase. For many years, Eudora Montoya was the only potter working at Tamaya; later Crescenciana Peña and her daughter, Lolita, also made pots that were sold in Sunday markets and at the Coronado State Monument. Other Tamayame artists and craftspersons also found their work in demand at the Coronado Monument: among them were Don Lujan, Old Man Joe García, and Valencio García, all of whom did weaving and woodcarving; María Lujan, who did embroidery and made dolls; and Porfirio Montoya, who made paintings and woodcarvings and did straw inlay work. In 1948 a group of Tamayame artists displayed their work at the Chicago Railroad Fair, with such great success that the man in charge of the Coronado Monument had soon made plans to send them on another similar trip.[15]

The sale of traditional arts played an important role in Tamaya's changing economy. For hundreds of years, the Tamayame, like most of their New Mexico neighbors, had relied on a system of barter, exchanging their goods directly for whatever they needed. In this way, they had acquired the lands of the Ranchiit'u in exchange for livestock, pottery, blankets, and other goods. In the harshest years, the women of the pueblo had traded pottery for food; in more abundant times, they supplied the residents of nearby towns with pottery in exchange for other desirable goods. When Merikaana's traders first reached New Mexico, they learned that most purchases were made in this way. By the early twentieth century, however, a cash economy had replaced the barter system, and cash transactions had become a necessary part of the peoples' lives. Cash was required to process a claim in Merikaana's courts, to purchase seeds and tools, to buy and maintain the wagons and trucks that transported the pueblo harvest from field to storehouse, to obtain tools and materials to repair the irrigation ditches, and to buy gas to operate the community tractor.

The sale of pueblo arts thus became an important source of cash income. The pueblos could also borrow cash from a reimbursable fund set up by the government to enable Indians to purchase seed, farm machinery, and irrigation improvements; they would repay the fund by selling part of their crops. With the encouragement of Merikaana's officials, many pueblo people soon took jobs for wages, often working for the railroads or in the Colorado beet fields. Pueblo children learned trades at Merikaana's schools, which then placed them in summer jobs with non-Indian families in Albuquerque and Santa Fe. By 1930 the government had set up a placement center in Albuquerque to find off-reservation jobs for adult Indians.[16] Pueblos who joined Merikaana's armed forces during World War I returned home with salaries, pensions, and eligibility for veterans' loan programs.

By the 1930s, the names of Tamayame workers appeared frequently in the records of the area's cash economy. One Tamayame filed suit against a non-Indian who owed him three hundred dollars; another requested federal funds to build a windmill near his home and then used his veteran's compensation certificate as collateral for a loan to improve his farm.[17] During the Great Depression, many Tamayame participated in New Deal employment and public works projects and in the special Indian work projects established by the Bureau of Indian Affairs under John Collier, including programs sponsored by the Civilian Conservation Corps (CCC), the Works Progress Administration (WPA), and the Soil Conservation Service (SCS). Tamayame working for the CCC programs served on fire crews in the region and helped to protect the pueblo from floods. At the end of the decade, Tamaya was approved for participation in a WPA project to translate documents related to pueblo lands; participants reported to the project in January 1940. The SCS sponsored projects to control erosion by putting up fences and windbreaks. By 1941, almost all of the Tamayame (224 persons, in 56 households) relied on one or more of these programs for income.[18]

The compensation awards also brought cash to the pueblos, who used this money, with the encouragement of the agency, to improve their farmlands and equipment. Like farmers across the country, they recognized that new machinery would enable them to farm more efficiently and produce larger crops. When Merikaana first came to Tamaya, farmers who used walking plows, hand sickles, and hand-threshing had to spend fifty to sixty hours to cultivate one acre, producing only twenty bushels of wheat. With the gang plows, binders, threshing machines, and horses and wagons available in 1890, the same task required only eight hours. With a tractor, disk, harrow, combine, and truck, a farmer in 1930 could cut his labor to three or four hours.[19] At Tamaya, where the population had fallen to its lowest level ever and many of the men were forced to seek jobs away from the pueblo, such labor-saving machinery was welcome. In 1935, when Governor Hilario Sanchez requested permission to buy a "badly needed" community binder, the Tamayame had only a "hand reap hook" to harvest their crops.[20] In the following years, the Tamayame used their compensation funds to buy and repair a community tractor and to buy gas and oil, seed, fertilizer, and insecticide. In 1949, they cashed three savings bonds to buy a new combine and built a community warehouse to store their grain and machinery. Reimbursable funds made it possible for some Tamayame to buy wheat, alfalfa, and bean seeds, better cattle, and wagons.[21] Others added to their income by joining AAA farm and range programs.[22]

Through the late 1930s, farming provided most of Tamaya's income, although pueblo wage-earners outnumbered pueblo farmers by the middle of the decade. In 1936, the pueblo's 60 farmers raised more than $13,000 worth of crops, an increase over the previous year. They harvested 6,200 bushels of corn and 3,250 bushels of wheat, which had become a more important crop at Tamaya after the turn of the century. Farmers also raised melons, beans, and chilies, and grew alfalfa for fodder. The pueblo's orchards produced 100 bushels of apples and 4,000 bushels of grapes. Under Merikaana's law, however, the Tamayame could no longer make wine as their ancestors had. The pueblo owned cattle, horses, swine, and chicken valued at more than $6,000, but stock sales produced only $700 in income. Seventy-four Tamayame worked for wages, earning a total of more than $3,000 for the year.[23]

Beginning in the 1940s, the Tamayame had another source of income: the fees paid by outsiders to lease pueblo lands. Leases and permits were granted to firms hoping to mine bentonite, sand, clay, gravel, pumicite, and volcanic ash, and an oil company applied for a permit to make surveys. The pueblo agency leased the Taylor place as headquarters for a range-rider. One firm obtained permission to post billboards. By the 1960s, Tamaya had begun to lease some of its farming and grazing lands.[24]

The years from 1930 to 1950 were a time of hardship for the Tamayame, in spite of the new sources of income. Throughout the Southwest, drought and depression reduced livestock prices drastically and made increasing demands on the region's limited irrigation water. Farmlands suffered from floods and silting. Tamaya's livestock industry, which had once provided half of the pueblo's income, dwindled.[25]

The Taylor Grazing Act of 1934, which was designed to control the use of rangeland in the West, brought a new threat to Tamayame stockmen. The act provided that no one could graze livestock on public lands without a permit. First priority in obtaining permits and leases was to be given to those who had used the lands during the past four years, those who had water rights in the area, and those who owned nearby property. Until the law was amended in 1936 to extend the period of use, few of the Tamayame and their Indian neighbors could qualify for leases.[26]

Among the lands open for grazing applications was the Espiritu Santo region granted to Tamaya, Zía, and Jémez by Kastera. At a meeting of the All-Pueblo Council in 1936, the Tamayame appealed to Commissioner of Indian Affairs John Collier to restore their grant, which they had been told was "public land and not in line for purchase." They declared their "earnest determination to provide the future generation with a solid foundation to stand on as we find ourselves in the bewildering wilderness of modern civilization." To achieve that goal, they needed a "way of livelihood." All three pueblos had an "immediate and pressing need" for more grazing land, and the Espiritu Santo lands were "rightfully" theirs "through early Spanish treaty." Their "ancestors" had "made some developments, such as water holes," on the Espiritu Santo. The next day, Collier replied: the Espiritu Santo was public land and could not be withdrawn from the grazing program, but he would file grazing-lease applications for the three pueblos.[27]

A few days later, Tamaya submitted its formal application for Taylor grazing lands. By October that request—and every other pueblo application—had been denied. The Tamayame voiced their protests at a hearing and resubmitted the pueblo's application in January 1938. In March, they filed new applications in the names of individual Tamayame stockmen rather than that of the pueblo. In early April, the board turned down all of their applications, on the grounds that the lands they had applied for were needed to fill the requests of non-Indian applicants and to create a stock driveway. In May the Tamayame appealed again, requesting federal rangeland for 690 cattle. This time they received permission to graze 450 head. With the assistance of their attorney, they filed yet another appeal, asking for permits to use the rest of the rangeland and urging the board to remove the stock driveway bordering their lands. As their lawyer pointed out, Tamaya was legally entitled to lease these lands: the pueblo owned the base lands and water to qualify, had made prior use of the area, and could provide photographs of the potholes and water sources that they had used in townships 13, 15, and 15 north, ranges 3 and 4 east. After hearing this evidence, one of the grazing board officials believed that the matter might be settled without a formal hearing.[28] Apparently, however, the problems were not resolved, for Tamaya received a notice in February 1939 that pueblo stockmen had violated the lease by allowing their cattle to graze outside the allotted land.[29]

During the decades that followed, the Tamayame regularly applied for grazing permits. In 1941, they were granted a one-year permit to graze on the Santa Ana allotment and the Jémez community allotment. Two years later, they received a temporary permit to use state land, as well as permission to lease the area between the Río Grande and the pueblo. In 1944, they were given a ten-year permit to graze on federal land in the Santa Ana and Bernalillo allotments, as well as a temporary permit for state land. They renewed a five-year lease on state lands in 1949 and again in 1954, at a rate of three cents per acre. With the annual grazing fee sent to the Bureau of Land Management in 1957, the pueblo included a note that they were paying the fee in spite of previous droughts. Throughout the 1960s Tamaya regularly renewed the leases for these grazing lands (see map on page 232).[30]

Decades of drought, flooding, erosion, and overgrazing had caused severe damage to the rangeland throughout the region. In 1937 a range examiner reported that of all Tamaya's lands, only the mesa itself remained relatively intact. Elsewhere there was severe erosion; "extensive sand dune areas" had formed along the Jémez River; ring grass and snakeweed had replaced the native grasses in much of the pasture land; and silting had ruined crops and clogged one of the pueblo's two wells, leaving only a single well to provide domestic water. The old pueblo still had "corrals for domestic livestock," and most of the Ranchiit'u had been fenced, but the inspector found no other "existing range improvements." He recommended fencing the entire grant; installing cattle guards, corrals, and wells; developing range water; and establishing a range management plan to restore the land and the grasses so that the pueblo could "develop a stable and economic livestock industry." The inspector could find "no accurate figures" on "the actual number of stock in

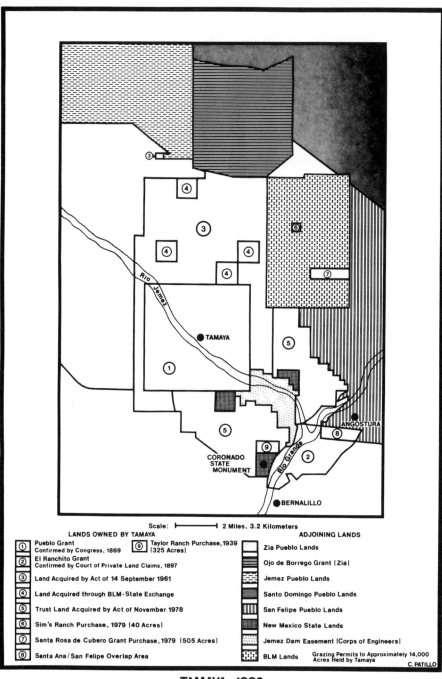

Scale: |—————| 2 Miles, 3.2 Kilometers

LANDS OWNED BY TAMAYA   **ADJOINING LANDS**

①	Pueblo Grant Confirmed by Congress, 1869	⑨	Taylor Ranch Purchase, 1939 (325 Acres)		Zia Pueblo Lands
②	El Ranchito Grant Confirmed by Court of Private Land Claims, 1897				Ojo de Borrego Grant (Zia)
③	Land Acquired by Act of 14 September 1961				Jemez Pueblo Lands
④	Land Acquired through BLM-State Exchange				Santo Domingo Pueblo Lands
⑤	Trust Land Acquired by Act of November 1978				San Felipe Pueblo Lands
⑥	Sim's Ranch Purchase, 1979 (40 Acres)				New Mexico State Lands
⑦	Santa Rosa de Cubero Grant Purchase, 1979 (505 Acres)				Jemez Dam Easement (Corps of Engineers)
⑧	Santa Ana/San Felipe Overlap Area				BLM Lands — Grazing Permits to Approximately 14,000 Acres Held by Tamaya

C. PATILLO

TAMAYA, 1982

trespass on pueblo lands." In its current condition, he declared, Tamaya's rangeland could support only "39 head of cattle or horses on a yearlong basis," or 117 head moved from pasture to pasture during the year and given additional feed during the winter. The grassland east of the railroad tracks would support an additional 15 horses. The report concluded that this plan might require "a reduction in the numbers of stock owned at present."[31] In fact, since the Tamayame owned 634 cattle and several hundred horses, his plan would have allowed them to keep less than sixteen percent of their stock at best.[32] Fortunately a Forest Service report, released in the same year, explained that since the range examiner's plan had not considered the pueblo's grazing leases, a new plan would have to be submitted when the lease question was settled. The forester also reported that the Tamayame had made a stock census and that they used their hay, alfalfa, and grain as supplemental feed. He agreed with the range examiner that the pueblo should build fences and drift fences and develop the water on the range. In subsequent years, the pueblo made plans to develop additional range water, and by 1950 Tamaya, Zía, and Jémez had submitted a joint range-management plan of their own.[33]

Throughout these decades, Tamaya leased any available grazing lands to support pueblo livestock and relieve the pressure on the grant lands, but the Tamayame never gave up the hope of recovering the Espiritu Santo. Again and again they asked agency officials if they could buy back this land that Kastera had granted them. They brought out their deeds and papers and explained once again what they had told Merikaana for many years: these lands had been given them in the place of the children that Kastera had taken from them. Repeatedly, however, the officials denied their request. In 1936 they were told that they could not use money appropriated by the Wheeler-Howard or Indian Reorganization Act to purchase the Espiritu Santo grant, but they might use these funds to buy the Perea, Taylor, and Wade lands within the Ranchiit'u. Two years later, Tamaya sent a petition to the secretary of the interior. Having been told that they must remove seven hundred sheep from the rangeland, they had immediate need for grazing lands. Why, they asked, could they not use the Espiritu Santo for grazing as their ancestors had? In January 1938, by executive order, the Bureau of Indian Affairs gained jurisdiction over the smaller Espiritu Santo grant that had been part of the original grant to Tamaya, Zía, and Jémez. Non-Indian stockmen in the region, however, protested immediately, and by summer the BIA had signed a memorandum agreeing to give the Espiritu Santo lands to the Department of Agriculture and the Soil Conservation Service in exchange for the Sedillo grant. As part of that agreement, Jémez, Zía, and Laguna were granted grazing privileges in the Espiritu Santo, but Tamaya received nothing.[34] From 1949 to 1951, the elders of Tamaya, Zía, and Jémez gave information about the pueblos' use of the grant to their attorneys, who were preparing a case to be presented to the Indian Claims Commission, a special court created by Congress to hear Indian claims and award compensation for lands and resources wrongfully taken. Nearly twenty-five years later, the three pueblos would receive a monetary award from the Claims Commission for the Espiritu Santo lands, but the lands themselves would not be returned.[35]

Slowly, however, Tamaya began to rebuild its landholdings in other areas. In the 1930s, the BIA used funds from the Submarginal Land Purchase Program to acquire land for Indians. The first acquisition under this program in New Mexico was the Zía-Santa Ana Purchase Project, an area of forty-seven thousand acres. In 1934 non-Indian claimants were paid and Tamaya regained control over the claims within the Ranchiit'u extinguished by the Pueblo Lands Board. Using compensation money and funds from the Wheeler-Howard Act, the pueblo began to buy back additional lands in the Ranchiit'u whenever the grantholders were willing to sell. In 1937 Tamaya made an offer for private claim 20, parcel 1, then owned by David and Carolina García; probate delayed the sale, which was completed three years later. In 1950 the Tamayame also bought the Taylor Ranch, an area of more than three hundred acres. They also discussed Mariano Montoya's offer to sell five acres (private claims 8 and 15), and considered buying the Archibal property. Tamaya also proposed an exchange of land along a stock driveway. By acts of Congress in 1961 and 1978, the pueblo obtained trust lands north of the square, extending to the Borrego Grant, and the land between the square and the Río Grande. Early the following year, the pueblo was able to purchase the area known as Simms Ranch, approximately 14,000 acres of pastureland north of the old pueblo on the mesa, lying between the trust lands awarded to Santa Ana in 1978 and the lands of San Felipe pueblo. The Simms Ranch lands included 545 acres of private holdings, 1,288 acres of state land under lease, and 12,160 acres of federal land under lease from the Bureau of Land Management. After buying the ranch, the pueblo began working for legislation that would transfer the federally owned land to the pueblo in trust, but, although the BLM supports the proposal, Congress has not yet approved it. In 1979 Tamaya was also able to purchase the Santa Rosa de Cubero Grant.[36]

In the following decade, Santa Ana acquired two tracts of land that have provided the basis for substantial economic development: the Duke Parcel and the Coronado Monument Exchange. Both acquisitions involved complex legal issues that originated in the 1940s. The Duke parcel, patented to Eva

Wade Duke in the 1930s, lay just south of the Taylor Ranch. Santa Ana controlled the only access to it—the Jémez Canyon Dam Road, which had been built in the 1950s on a right-of-way previously granted to Santa Ana for a BIA truck trail that provided access to the Taylor Ranch. When the heirs to the Duke lands tried to develop the property in the 1970s, Santa Ana opposed their plans, which included a trailer park in the southern section owned by Sunnyland Development and the mining of sand and gravel in the northern segment owned by local politician H. E. Leonard. The pueblo refused to grant access on Tamaya's right-of-way, preventing the developments. Leonard protested to the state's congressional delegation; his protests led to a series of meetings that included representatives of the pueblo, the Bureau of Indian Affairs, the Corps of Engineers, Senator Pete Domenici and Congressman Manuel Lujan. The group worked out an agreement that allowed the pueblo to obtain a loan, to be paid back from the development of the sand and gravel resources, from the Bureau of Indian Affairs to buy the Leonard property. The land was to be held in trust for the pueblo by the United States. In September 1981 the transaction was completed. The following year, Tamaya purchased a 140-acre parcel at the south end of the tract from First American Title Company, which had acquired the property from Sunnyland Development. In the following years, the pueblo bought the two remaining tracts in the Duke Parcel: a ten-acre plot that include "the old Duke residence, a large southwestern style structure built of 'terrones,' adobe-like bricks actually cut from the ground," and a 47-acre parcel "that included a large residence that had been built by Harold Brooks of Albuquerque." The pueblo has since acquired several small tracts "south of the Duke parcel along Highway 44."[37]

As the developers began to submit proposals for the Duke property, Santa Ana's attorneys discovered that a portion of the Coronado State Monument— a state park with a visitor center, campground, and other facilities at the site of a large pueblo ruin on the west bank of the Río Grande just north of Highway 44—had in fact been built within Tamaya's Ranchiit'u lands. In the 1930s, the United States had deeded a large tract of land containing pueblo ruins to the University of New Mexico. While excavating a pueblo now known as the Kuaua Ruin, the university discovered that the ruin extended onto Tamaya's land and made a proposal to exchange a ten-acre strip of university land in the area for the lands within the Ranchiit'u that contained the ruin. The Bureau of Indian Affairs accepted this proposal, and Congress authorized the exchange in 1940, but for some reason, the deed of exchange was never signed. Meanwhile the university went ahead with its excavation; later the State Parks Department took over the administration of the site and constructed the visitor center. When Santa Ana discovered this situation—nearly fifty years after the original excavation—the federal government, at the pueblo's request, sued the state and the university in federal district court for trespass. The court ruled that "the United States could not sue the State on behalf of an Indian tribe," but the ruling was overturned by the 10th Circuit Court of Appeals, which upheld "the Government's sovereign interest in asserting Indian land rights, and reinstated the action." The parties then negotiated a settlement, through which Tamaya acquired a parcel of nearly 120 acres, north and west of the Coronado Monument, in exchange for title to approximately 24 acres in the State Park. In 1986, Congress confirmed this agreement.[38]

The pueblo quickly moved to develop these newly acquired lands. In 1982 they established a sand and gravel operation on the northern portion of the Duke Parcel. Although this development was not "entirely successful" and the pueblo decided to withdraw from active operation of the enterprise, the sand and gravel remained a "valuable asset" for the pueblo, and these initial efforts eventually led to the development of sand and gravel resources elsewhere on Tamayame lands. In subsequent years, Tamaya also developed the old Brooks residence as a community center; established a "high quality mobile home park" on the Brooks parcel; and leased the old Duke home to an Albuquerque restaurant owner for a fine restaurant, the Prairie Star, which has become very successful. On the remaining Duke lands and the adjacent parcel acquired in the Coronado Monument exchange, the pueblo constructed a 27-hole championship golf course, which it now owns outright. An office complex and other facilities are being constructed on the lands south of the Duke Parcel on Highway 44.[39]

While the pueblo acquired new lands, pueblo officials continued their efforts to protect the lands they had purchased two-hundred years earlier. Disputes over land in the Angostura region continued throughout the 1940s and 1950s, and both Tamaya and San Felipe asked officials to search for information about the disputed lands. The Tamayame also met to gather information about the claim. Those who had herded stock in the grant described the boundaries as they knew them, and those who had presented evidence to the Pueblo Lands Board and other officials recalled the history of the dispute. They reviewed the mass of documents that had accumulated in nearly two hundred years, as well as more recent complications, such as the state highway right-of-way granted through the disputed area, which gave compensation to the heirs of those who had acquired Santa Ana's land from San Felipes.[40] At last, in the case of *Pueblo of Santa Ana v. Alfredo Baca and*

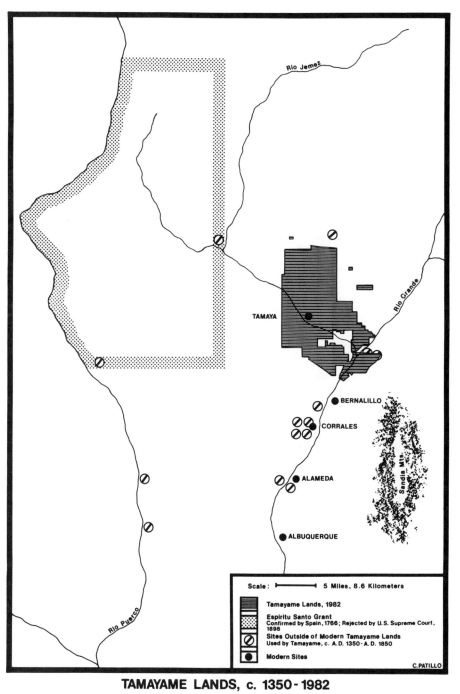

TAMAYAME LANDS, c. 1350 - 1982

Mary Lou Baca, the federal district court ruled that "the Pueblo of Santa Ana has had good and indefeasible title in fee simple to the lands in the overlap area . . . since 1763," that the adjudication of the matter in 1813 had "conclusively determined this dispute in favor of Santa Ana," and that the pueblo would have established its title to these lands through continuous use, dating at least from the 1930s, even if it had not held deeds to the land. That decision was affirmed three years later, in 1988, by the Tenth Circuit Court of Appeals.[41]

While the Tamayame presented their complaints to Merikaana's officials and courts, outsiders continued to seek pueblo lands. The development that accompanied statehood in New Mexico generated numerous applications for right-of-way through Tamaya's lands. In the late 1920s, the pueblo granted right-of-way to the short-lived Santa Fe Northwestern Railroad, which ran up the Jémez River through the pueblo grant. The following year the New Mexico Power Company asked for a fifty-year right-of-way across the Ranchiit'u. In 1933 the pueblo complained that the Atchison, Topeka, and Santa Fe Railroad lines had damaged a flood-control dike and caused erosion, and the railroad superintendent proposed a plan to repair the dike. In later years, Tamaya granted passageways to the state highway, a stock driveway, the Albuquerque Gas and Electric Company, the Texas-New Mexico Pipeline, and the Atrisco Feeder Canal, as well as approving an easement for the Jémez Dam.[42]

As the years passed, governor after governor protested trespasses on Tamaya's lands. In 1936 the governor told the pueblo agency that the Ranchiit'u boundary would have to be fenced to control stock from Bernalillo, which was causing serious problems. Markers on the west boundary of the Ranchiit'u had been moved, and would-be homesteaders began to erect fences on the Tamayame's land. For three years, fishermen had driven over the pueblo's pastureland and set fires within the grant. Some trespassers dumped trash on the Ranchiit'u, while others cut the pueblo's timber and hauled the wood away. The pueblo asked that their crooked and dangerous access road, which ran through Charles Brown's land, be straightened, but Brown would not agree. The pueblo also asked that a twenty-foot road, which ran from the highway to a pumping station, be closed. In 1946, Tamaya complained that a non-Indian had destroyed the pueblo's fence along the riverside road, and then tried to charge the pueblo for the damage when Tamayame stock entered his land. Zía sheepmen crossed the southwestern corner of the Borrego Grant onto Tamaya's land. Frank Bond, a sheepholder with headquarters in Bernalillo and on the Espiritu Santo, also allowed his sheep to trespass on the pueblo's land. There were several disagreements over who bore the responsibility to fence land between non-Indian property and the pueblo. Eventually the pueblo reached agreements with Zía and Bernalillo to set up range lines and to decide the use of wells.[43]

As New Mexico's population grew and the demand for water in the arid region increased, Tamaya's water became as attractive to outsiders as its land had been to earlier trespassers. Local farmers and ranchers, fearing that they would not have enough water to keep their stock and crops alive in dry years, began to ask the government to build dams to store water, provide irrigation, and control flooding. Merikaana's agents had begun to study pueblo water use and to develop projects to improve irrigation, domestic water supplies, and range water, under a program that obligated the Indians, in time, to repay the government for these improvements.[44]

In 1908 Merikaana's Supreme Court heard the case of *Winters v. U.S.,* which defined the principles of Indian water rights under Merikaana's law. With water, as with land, Indian rights differed from non-Indian rights. Indians, as the original holders of these natural resources, had prior and paramount rights to all of the water they needed in the present or in the future. Those rights did not depend on state or local laws, on whether a tribe had signed a treaty, or on whether a tribe had made use of all of the water to which it was entitled. In times of shortage, Indian rights had to be honored before the claims of other users, and agreements signed to create dams or to apportion water could not reduce Indian water without the Indians' consent. The justices also held that the government, as trustee for Indian tribes, was responsible for protecting those rights.[45]

By the 1920s, the pueblos' neighbors had begun to test those rights. In March 1920, the residents of Bernalillo sought to divert water from a branch of Tamaya's ditch into the Bernalillo Community Ditch. Although they told the irrigation office that their plan would not interfere with Tamaya's water use, the irrigation officer was suspicious and quickly wrote to ask the pueblo attorney what he should do to protect the pueblo's interests. The lawyer recommended that he draw up a written agreement of the terms of joint use, making sure that the Bernalillo Ditch users acknowledged Tamaya's rights and that the document clearly stated that the pueblo's water rights did not fall under state jurisdiction. In April, the ditch company signed an agreement drawn up under these terms.[46]

The question of pueblo water rights became a major issue in 1926, when New Mexico drew up plans for a conservancy district that would have charge of water matters along the Río Grande. As the proposal was first drafted, nearly all of the pueblos opposed it, but by early 1928 a revised version of the proposed legislation had won pueblo approval. In a series of meetings, the pueblos authorized John Collier, of the American Indian Defense Association, to act as their representative in Washington and convey their approval of the proposal, which provided that if the district did work on pueblo lands, the pueblos would be liable for no more than $67.50 an acre, and they would have at least forty years to pay off the debt. In Congress, however, the terms of the bill were changed. One early version increased the amount of debt that the pueblos might incur by half a million dollars, included provisions that could have forced a pueblo to begin repayment as soon as the work was completed, and defined the six pueblos within the district—Tamaya, Cochití, Santo Domingo, San Felipe, Sandía, and Isleta—as a single unit. That meant that each pueblo might have to pay for work done at the others instead of being liable only for its own improvements. A pueblo like Tamaya, with less land eligible for the programs, might end up paying nearly twice its share.[47]

John Collier brought this bad news to the pueblos at a meeting held at Santo Domingo in March 1928. He explained that he had appealed to the Senate Committee on Indian Affairs, and in the end, the bill had been revised to allow the Indians to use as much as four thousand acres of improved land while paying only operation and maintenance charges. But the revised bill also permitted a higher debt than the pueblos had agreed to, and under its provisions any rent or lease money the pueblos obtained for the land might have to be used to repay the debt. Collier had persuaded a famous lawyer, Louis Marshall, to represent the pueblos without charge if the matter went to court, but officials hoped that the problem might be settled without legal action. By the end of the year, the secretary of the interior had approved an agreement under which the new Middle Río Grande Conservancy District promised to provide conservation, irrigation, drainage, and flood control for Tamaya and the other pueblos.[48]

Throughout the 1930s, those who held the pueblo's canes of office had the added responsibility of negotiating complex legal agreements involving the pueblo's water. In 1930 the pueblo refused to sign a contract that included the Bernalillo Community Ditch Company, explaining that Tamaya "had never been successful in co-operative work with the people of Bernalillo" and that they feared that if they signed the agreement, they would have continual "controversy" and "difficulties in getting the work done." Officials responsible for the pueblos tended to agree.[49] The following year, Tamaya signed an agreement with the New Mexico State Highway Commission, which promised to remove silt, maintain a ditch on the Ranchiit'u, and pay the pueblo three hundred dollars. The pueblo also agreed to permit the conservancy district to build and maintain a headgate at the intake of the canal that served the Ranchiit'u, and to allow construction of a new drain and levee to the north and a wasteway ditch to run between the Bernalillo, Desagua, and Bosque ditches.[50] District officials refused to maintain Tamaya's old ditch system without payment, but they provided water to the pueblo without charge, as they had promised to do. In 1934 and 1935, the district paid Tamaya $4,672 for a right-of-way to build a new ditch across the Ranchiit'u. The Tamayame had agreed to allow non-Indians to use their water for fifty cents an acre, but by September 1936, Tamaya's lieutenant governor had warned the non-Indians that if they did not pay, the pueblo would no longer supply them with water. An agreement reached the following year with the district, however, established terms for non-Indian water use, and the Tamaya received payments through the end of the decade.[51] During this time, the government established the National Resource Committee to approve water projects and the Río Grande Advisory Committee to coordinate the plans for the Río Grande region. The pueblo agency prepared a ten-year plan to conduct soil surveys, improve irrigation, and develop range and domestic water, and a CCC well-rig was moved to Tamaya to develop range water.[52]

The age-old water problem that reappeared in early 1941, however, could not be resolved by ten-year plans, committees, or negotiations. By late May rivers throughout the region had risen dangerously. Swollen by heavy rains and the melting snow pack from the mountains, the rivers soon endangered pueblo homes and farms, including those in the Ranchiit'u. With a hundred inches of snow still in the mountains, Tamaya faced the threat of disastrous floods. A month after the floods had subsided, *Indians at Work* told the story, with photographs of Porfirio Montoya riding watch along the pueblo dike and other Tamayame working to strengthen the dike and move a truck that had slipped off the levee. Bridges, dams, and phone lines had washed out. By late May, it seemed certain that the dike at Ranchiit'u, where the Jémez River emptied into the Río Grande, would fail, flooding both Ranchiit'u and Bernalillo. Many Tamayame moved "without fuss or confusion or protests" to the pueblo's day school and the Albuquerque boarding school, where the government had set up kitchens and beds for those who had to leave their homes. During the flood, measles and pneumonia spread among the people, and Tamaya's day school also became an emergency hospital. By May 22, the river was "chocolate colored," with five-foot waves that broke against the banks, pulling the sand out. Exhausted men from Tamaya and the neighboring towns and pueblos worked day and night, stopping only for a quick meal of food canned at Tamaya and some "nice, good, thick coffee." After working for hours in the cold rain, they were "wet to the skin and shivering" in spite of the raincoats provided by the government, but they still "laughed and joked." When at last the river began to subside, the dike remained standing, thanks to the "heroism" of the workers.[53]

As the people of Ranchiit'u returned to their homes to repair the flood's damages, government agencies began to consider ways to prevent another such flood. Soon after the water receded, Congress passed the Flood Control Act of 18 August 1941, under which the Army Corps of Engineers began developing a plan to survey the Río Grande region and study the possibility of building dams. As news of this plan spread, letters from all parts of the country poured into the offices of the commissioner of Indian affairs, the newspapers, and the officials responsible for the plan; remembering the Bursum Bill, many individuals wrote to protest that the new project might threaten pueblo lands, and the national media focused attention on the issue. A delegation representing five pueblos traveled to Washington to express concern. To quiet the opposition, Commissioner Collier explained that the bill permitted only exploration, not dam building. Surveying, studying flooding and silt buildup, and drilling test holes were not likely to harm pueblo lands, but the pueblos would be paid for any damage that occurred. Collier argued that such a study was urgently needed, for the range, the watershed, the farmlands, and the homesites near the river were in terrible condition. Without surveys and testing, pueblo land titles could not be resolved and the government could not determine how to prevent damage to pueblo lands from silting and floods.[54]

When the All-Pueblo Council met in April 1943, the pueblos were divided over the question. Opponents of the bill spoke all morning; then agency personnel argued for the potential advantages of the project. Before the delegates reached a conclusion, Tamaya's governor spoke. They had heard many who opposed the bill in the name of the pueblos, he said, but Tamaya was also a pueblo, and Tamaya's concerns had not been mentioned. He reminded the other delegates that "if the river had gone up two or three inches more in 1941 Santa Ana would have lost all their crops and all of the lower village." The Tamayame were concerned that if nothing were done they would be left "completely unprotected against such floods." They did not know whether building dams was the answer, but they did not want to see the proposal dismissed without "a full consideration of the case." The council's final resolution reflected the concerns of all the delegates: the pueblos declared their opposition to this bill, to the construction of dams at San Felipe and Otowi, and to the preparation of plans for their lands in which they were not consulted, but they also expressly stated that they did not oppose flood-control measures.[55]

Over their opposition, however, the Corps of Engineers had begun its survey by October. Although the commissioner of Indian affairs reassured San Felipe's governor that no dams were planned, the first survey led to others, and soon the agencies proposed a five-year intensive study of sedimentation in the Middle Río Grande Valley. A bill to provide flood protection and construct a floodway in the Ranchiit'u just north of the day school was drawn up.[56] Meanwhile pueblo complaints about the conservancy district increased. The pueblos asked Congress to extend the period of time they had been given to pay operation and maintenance fees, charging that the district had not lived up to the promises made in 1928 and that many of them had lost crops as a result. Some pueblos had not received the water they were guaranteed; others had had their supply cut off. The district had not met its obligation to repair and maintain the ditches. Tamaya's ditch boss, Unelio Menchego, described the shortages that had occurred at Tamaya, and Porfirio Montoya listed the unkept promises that the district had made to the pueblos at earlier meetings. The Tamayame still had no flood control, and silting remained a serious problem. While these promises remained unmet, new proposals continued to be drafted. The Atomic Energy Commission prepared a plan to divert water from the Jémez watershed, over the opposition of the pueblos along the Río Jémez, who feared that their water rights might be compromised and their farming threatened by the project. When disputes over pueblo rights to stored water arose, the pueblos worked to secure their entitlement to water impounded in El Vado reservoir. As plans to place a dam near the mouth of the Jémez River went forward, Tamaya's governor was asked to allow engineers to drill on the pueblo's land.[57] The Flood Control Act of 1948 authorized the Army Corps of Engineers to construct a dam and reservoir on the Jémez River to control flooding and sediment flow in the Río Grande. The corps drew up plans for a dam within Tamayame land, "just downstream from the old pueblo," and asked the pueblo to grant it the rights and easements required to construct the dam. Its proposal included provisions for a levee to protect Tamaya from flooding if the reservoir were filled to its design level; a one-lane bridge across the Río Jémez to provide access to Tamaya when the reservoir was full; construction of various improvements, including a well, a windmill, a water-storage tank, and a stock-watering tank for the pueblo; and $3,000 compensation for the pueblo. Tamaya gave its approval in February 1952, and the dam was constructed.[58]

For nearly 30 years, no permanent reservoir existed at the Jémez Dam;

water was stored behind the dam only temporarily, when it was necessary to control river flows to prevent flooding. Then, in the early 1980s, the Corps created a small permanent reservoir behind the dam. Santa Ana, which had acquired the federal lands on which the dam was built, as well as lands surrounding the reservoir, began to consider the possibility of developing recreational facilities on the shore of the reservoir. Meanwhile, engineers revised their estimates of the maximum potential flood at the headwaters of the Río Jémez. In 1986 the Corps of Engineers increased the dam's height without making provision to protect the pueblo in the event of such a flood; as a result, were such a flood to happen now, the water would flow over the levee originally constructed to protect Tamaya, and damage, or possibly even destroy, the old pueblo.[59]

Waiting for the young men of the pueblo to return safely from distant camps, working to rescue homes and crops from rising floodwaters, and protecting the lands of Tamaya in the twentieth century all evoked memories of past journeys, past floods, and past dangers, but they also required new skills and new ways of understanding. Once, when the pueblo needed new rooms, the men gathered timber in the mountains to erect the walls, the women prepared and applied plaster, and in a short time a family had a new home or the pueblo had new storage rooms ready for the harvest. In the 1960s and 1970s, when the Tamayame needed new housing, pueblo leaders had to negotiate contracts with federal agencies like the Bureau of Indian Affairs and the Department of Housing and Urban Development. Parents passed the traditions of the Tamayame on to their children, as the elders of the pueblo always had, but they also worked with the Bernalillo County School system to determine the school curriculum. To provide health care and community services for the Tamayame, pueblo leaders participated in programs sponsored by agencies such as the Public Health Service and Community Action programs. Shortages of employment and income, in an economy that requires cash payment in exchange for goods and services, have become a problem as serious as drought to a farming people; the search for answers to this problem has led the pueblo into complex arrangements to develop Tamayame land and resources in ways that will provide jobs and income for the people while preserving the pueblo's resources. To survive in this complex world, Tamaya must understand both the old and the new, the ancient traditions and the intricacies of modern legal systems and technologies.

In the centuries that have passed since the Hanu entered this upper world, change has always been a part of the people's lives, but perhaps never before have the changes been so many, so rapid, and so great as in the past decades.

Tamaya Yesterday and Today

The Tamayame, who had watched their seedlings grow in every settlement since the first at Kashe K'atreti, lived through a time when the pueblo planted no crops at all. Sons and daughters of those who had led horses into the threshing ground would take jobs far from Tamaya, assembling aircraft that could carry the people farther in hours than their ancestors journeyed in all the years they spent searching for their homeland. And that homeland, once a haven with abundant land and water for the Tamayame, now stands within a crowded world, kept safe only by the people's ability to master the legal complexities that protect their homes and rights. The people of Tamaya have learned that a few words on a piece of paper may bring greater dangers than the harshest winter or the most severe flood, and that the threat may come more rapidly than the swiftest raiders once swept down upon the fields, with no warning.

Yet through these dangers, as through the dangers of the past, the Tamayame have survived. Still the ceremonies are held, and still the leaders guide the people in accordance with the instructions they received when they entered this upper world. Today's journeys may cover greater distances than the paths the Hanu followed to Paak'u, Tamaya Kuwasaya, Kwiiste Puu Tamaya, K'enewa, and Kwiiste K'enewa before settling along the Río Jémez, but the Tamayame still return to the homeland they chose on that first journey. Their lands and their lives are far different from those their ancestors knew, but the traditions remain alive, just as ancient designs reappear in new forms on recent pottery. Through fire and flood, through disease and drought, and even through the vast changes of the twentieth century, the pueblo's foundations have stood firm. Again and again the people have had to rebuild the walls, but Tamaya still stands below the dark mesa in the land that the Hanu were told of many years ago.

APPENDIX ONE

Tracing the History of the Tamayame before Tamaya

Evidence of ancient life fills the Southwest. Beside the bones of long-extinct mammoths lie stone points made by the men who hunted them. The ashes of ancient fires lie in hearths that have been cold for centuries. Seed corn, never used by those who stored it so carefully, remains sealed in tightly woven baskets. Pieces of pottery abide beneath fallen roof beams and crumbling walls. Dams and ditches still stand, though the farmers who built them have not tended their crops for six hundred years or more. Traces of the ancient ones lie all about, in caves, on cliffs and mesas, and buried within the earth.

Among the peoples who left these traces in the lands we know as the Southwest were the ancestors of the Tamayame. But which of the ancient ones were they? Where did they come from? When did they arrive, and what did they find when they entered this land? What journeys did they make before they reached their homeland? In which of the ruined settlements did they once live? How and when did they come to Tamaya? And what was their life like in those early years?

To begin to answer such questions, scholars must examine many kinds of evidence. The things left by ancient peoples, the land itself, and the records of later centuries all hold clues to the distant past. The languages, traditions, and lifeways of modern peoples may help to explain their ancestry. But all of this evidence is like a tangle of faded threads. It is easy to see that these snarled threads must once have been part of a large and intricate tapestry, but it is not easy to tell what the fabric once looked like or how it was woven or where each thread belonged. To begin to restore that tapestry, experts must weave together information from many sources.

Oral tradition, which provides the basis for the account in the first chapter of this book, is one of the most valuable sources. For centuries, the stories that make up the tradition have been passed from one generation to the next. These stories, still told today, are the people's own record of their history, the only source that speaks directly about the past. The stories explain how the people came into this world and recall what they found in it: the homes they built, the peoples they met, the times of danger or disaster. Together the stories of the oral tradition record not just what the people did, but how they saw—and see—their own origins and history. The tradition records a part of the people's past that no other source can, for it alone reveals their beliefs and values, their hopes, interests, concerns, and fears.

Yet there are also aspects of the past that the tradition can not, or does not, record, and others that the stories preserve only in part. It may be difficult, or even impossible, to identify the exact time or place spoken of in a story, for the ancient ones did not measure the land in miles, acres, or degrees of latitude; date events according to the Julian calendar; or identify places by the English or Spanish names they bear today. And it is not only the names and the languages that have changed since the stories were first told. The land itself is no longer the same: rivers run in different courses, hills have been worn by erosion, trees grow where ancient farmers tended open fields. Like the ancient landmarks, the stories too may have changed as time passed. For hundreds of years, each storyteller has retold the tales in his own words, speaking in the greatest detail of what he knew best or believed most important. Each family and each generation has heard, and told, the stories in its own way.

Thus details of great interest to a modern scholar may be missing from the oral accounts, for these stories were never meant to be records in the way that reports, census figures, or maps document more recent events. The tradition explains how the people came into this world, but it does not give the date when their journeys began. A story may recall how the people first learned to farm, but the tradition is not likely to identify the species of corn that they raised a thousand years ago or the size of the fields in which it was grown. The story may mention that there were potters among the ancient ones, but it probably will not describe the exact designs a potter used six hundred years ago, or just where she dug her clays, or what substances she used to make her glazes. To restore these parts of the tapestry, scholars must turn to other sources, including the objects of the past, which lie in ruins throughout the Southwest.

Ancient towns and tools may evoke an image of the past for anyone, but to specialists they can reveal much more. From the size, shape, and placement of rooms in an ancient pueblo, scholars can calculate how many people once lived in the town. The type of masonry used to construct the buildings may help to identify the builders, and the condition of the ruins may suggest what happened to the residents. Pottery styles can help experts reconstruct a people's movements and contacts. In rock formations and layers of earth, scientists can read a history of the land itself, discovering clues that indicate when an arroyo was cut or a river altered its course. Changes in tree-ring patterns may point to times of change in weather and rainfall. Fragments of pollen may reveal the numbers and kinds of plants that grew in the region, while small pieces of animal bone show what animals lived there. From these fragments, a scholar can determine not only what resources the people relied on, but how they cooked their meals and how the craftsmen used the raw materials to make clothing, tools, and other goods. An object's position in the surrounding layers of earth, the styles of pottery present at a site, the tree-rings in a building's posts and beams, or the amount of carbon 14 that remains in anything once alive can all help to date the things made and used by ancient peoples. Almost any object, from the smallest seed to the most imposing pueblo, offers a wealth of information about the people who used it.

All of these things, however, also pose riddles that no object can answer. Experts can tell when a stone tool was made and where the stone was quarried; they can measure and weigh the tool, and analyze its style; they can determine whether it was burned or broken or worn from long use. But these dates and measurements and descriptions do not directly identify the people who made it, or explain how it was made or why it was abandoned. On these matters, the objects are silent, and the oral tradition rarely speaks, perhaps because neither the people who told the stories nor those who listened to them would have needed an explanation of the things they themselves made and used.

So scholars must look elsewhere, to the ways of modern peoples and the records of more recent times. Because a people's ways are not unchanging, neither their present lives nor their recent past can provide definite answers about the ways of their distant ancestors, but they can suggest a direction of inquiry. A nineteenth-century description will not reveal how a tool was used in the tenth century, but it may show how it could have been used. Evidence that the weavers in a sixteenth-century pueblo were male does not establish the gender of earlier weavers, but if documents show that men have woven the people's cloth for four centuries, scholars will have reason to suspect that men, and not women, wove the cloth among the people's remote ancestors. Watching an irrigation crew in 1980 or reading an account of dam building in 1880 will not tell a scholar how the people built their ditches in 1480, but it may help researchers understand why ancient dams have been found in some locations and not others, or determine where to look for evidence of old dams, or guess how a mysterious object could have been used to bring water to ancient fields.

Clues to a people's past can also be found in the very language they speak, for language changes constantly, in ways that reflect the history and movements of the people who speak it. In any language, new words, forms, and structures continually replace old ones. As long as the people who speak that language remain together, the same changes affect everyone's speech, but if some of the speakers are separated from the others, each group's speech will change in slightly different ways. At first, all of the people will be able to understand each other with no difficulty, but the longer the groups remain apart and the greater the distance between them, the more different their speech will become, until at last each speaks its own dialect. As time passes, each dialect will continue to change; after thousands of years, the people who speak one will no longer be able to understand those who speak the others. Because this change happens so slowly, these peoples may not even remember the time when their ancestors shared a common language, and an outsider might not recognize that the two languages were once linked, but a specialist may guess the relationship and trace the connections far into the past to learn when, and even where, the split began.

Thus traces of the past are preserved in many ways: the things an ancient people made and used, the lands where they lived, and the languages spoken by their descendants may all yield information about them. Essential parts of a people's history will have been preserved in their own stories and perhaps even in the tales of other peoples they encountered. Yet, using all of this evidence, even the best scholars cannot restore the entire tapestry to its original condition. The more threads they find and follow into the past, the more certain the outlines of the tapestry will seem, but large sections may be lost forever. Details may be restored with great accuracy, yet it may be impossible to determine where they once fit in the whole. New evidence, continually being discovered, may demonstrate that long-held theories cannot be correct. The reconstruction is particularly difficult in a region like the Southwest, which has long been the home of many peoples with similar ways of life. For centuries these peoples have exchanged goods and ideas, traveled throughout the region, made and abandoned settlements, and lived in close contact with one another. Each has left behind traces of its journeys, its settlements, its farms and ditches, and the many things the people made, used, and traded. Evidence is everywhere, and what has been discovered and studied represents only a fraction of what once existed. Fitting all of this information into even the broadest outline of the region's past is a difficult and uncertain task; trying to reconstruct the history of any one people within this massive tapestry is still more challenging.

Scholars began by trying to sketch the broad outlines of the region's earliest history. How, they asked, did human beings come to the Southwest, and when did they arrive? Slowly, they developed a theory: the first people to reach the Americas were Asiatics who traveled over a broad land bridge in the Bering Strait. They could have crossed that bridge more than thirty thousand years ago, but without doubt, they had reached North America twelve thousand years ago. Gradually these peoples moved south through passages between the great ice masses that covered much of the continent at that time.[1] At least eleven thousand years ago, and perhaps earlier, some of them reached the Southwest, where mammoths and long-horned bison still roamed.

These first Southwesterners were a hunting people, for the stone points of their weapons have been found in the remains of the mammoths and other large animals. Within two thousand years of the hunters' arrival, however, the large animals were extinct, replaced by species of bison, deer, and antelope still known today. The hunting peoples learned to rely on these smaller animals, and when the game began to move generally north and east toward the Plains, the first Southwesterners seem to have followed.[2]

By about 6000 B.C., signs of a new way of life had appeared in northwestern New Mexico. This way of life, which anthropologists call the Archaic Culture Stage, was to become common throughout the Southwest and in many parts of North America.

Tracing the History of the Tamayame

All of the Archaic peoples relied on plants and small game rather than large animals, and they traveled in a seasonal pattern that allowed them to use an area's resources efficiently. Throughout the year, the people moved from one camp to another, timing their journeys so that they would arrive at each location at the best time to harvest the plants and animals native to that region. They soon learned to make many kinds of tools to gather and prepare these resources, tools that could be easily carried from camp to camp or left behind and replaced in the new camp. Instead of making fragile pottery for cooking, carrying water, and storing food and supplies, for example, they wove baskets, which were durable and easy to carry. This way of life would not support great numbers of people in large permanent homes; the Archaic peoples typically traveled and camped in small groups.[4]

The first traces of Archaic peoples in northwestern New Mexico appeared between 6000 and 5500 B.C. Their arrival seems to mark an abrupt change in lifeways, and for that reason scholars believe that they were not related to the hunting peoples who preceded them. Probably they moved into the region from the west, settling in lands left vacant when the first hunters followed the game eastward. For the next six thousand years, the Archaic way of life was to dominate the region.[5]

The Archaic peoples of the Southwest, whose way of life has been called the Oshara Tradition, shared many of the traits of Archaic peoples across the continent. Their ways changed slowly, but not drastically, during their six-thousand year history. Like all Archaic peoples, they lived in small camps that allowed them to use the region's resources effectively. Even in the beginning, however, the Oshara seem to have depended somewhat less on the seasonal round than many Archaic peoples, and as time passed their camps became larger and more permanent, and they made more tools and more kinds of tools. Their numbers increased steadily after 4800 B.C. Winter settlements of as many as fifty people appeared soon after 1800 B.C., and in the period from 800 B.C. to A.D. 1, these larger camps became more common.[6]

Then the Oshara peoples were caught up in a wave of change that swept through the region, bringing new ways and ideas north from distant Mesoamerica. In the period from A.D. 1 to A.D. 450, these new influences reached the Mogollon and Hohokam peoples of the Southwest and, through them, the Oshara. The mingling of old and new traditions was to produce a new way of life in the Southwest, that of the Anasazi, but before A.D. 450, the lives of the Oshara peoples were little changed. The first, and most significant, manifestation of change was the increasing importance of cultivated crops. Farming itself was not new to the Southwest, where Archaic peoples had grown maize as early as 2000 B.C., but never before had horticulture been central to the people's lives. Although some of the Oshara had raised corn, they maintained a way of life based on the necessities of the seasonal gathering of natural resources.[7]

By A.D. 450, which marks the beginning of the Basketmaker III period, however, the new emphasis on farming had begun to transform the people's lives. Instead of setting up camps in areas close to natural resources, they began to live in places well suited to farming. As their crops yielded a reliable supply of food in one place, they

APPENDIX 1

built more permanent villages—clusters of underground dwellings, or pithouses. Each village had one or more special rooms, often above ground, set aside for storage. Some had larger pithouses that may have been used for meetings or ceremonies. A more settled life allowed the people to make and use fragile items, like pottery, that would not have survived the regular journeys of the hunting and gathering peoples.

As the years passed, the Basketmaker peoples began to raise turkeys and to plant beans in addition to maize and squash. Their crops and domesticated animals, combined with the harvest of natural resources, gave them a still larger and more dependable food supply, which in turn allowed them to build larger villages. In only three hundred years, this new way of life essentially replaced the old pattern of seasonal movement.[8]

In the following centuries, the Anasazi way of life developed and spread throughout the Southwest. During the Pueblo I period (A.D. 750 to A.D. 900) some Anasazi groups still lived in small pithouse villages, but others began to build larger towns, with masonry dwellings that had rooms above ground for living as well as for storage. Some had special underground rooms, or kivas, for meetings and ceremonies. The people grew cotton and began to use true looms to weave it. Throughout Anasazi lands, pottery was replacing basketry for most household uses, and the numbers and kinds of pots multiplied rapidly.[9]

After this period of development, the Anasazi expanded rapidly. At the beginning of the Pueblo II period (about A.D. 900), the Anasazi were clustered in the Four Corners region. Within two hundred years, their territory extended south into central New Mexico and east beyond the Río Grande.[10] Many of the new towns had the large, multi-storied buildings that would come to be known as pueblos. Some of these structures were built of masonry and had as many as a hundred rooms. Dams and ditches brought water to the farmers' fields. Chaco Canyon alone had more than a dozen large, thriving pueblos linked to hundreds of smaller towns by a network of roads. Trade brought copper bells and tropical birds from Mexico, and shells from the Pacific Coast, to these villages. Throughout the region, prosperous and secure Anasazi towns flourished.[11]

Then, suddenly, the towns were abandoned, the carefully irrigated fields deserted, the kivas empty, the plazas silent. By A.D. 1300, virtually all of the great Anasazi pueblos were empty ruins.[12]

What had happened to the Anasazi? Scholars proposed a range of explanations: perhaps hostile invaders forced the Anasazi out of their homes; perhaps the towns warred with one another; perhaps disease swept through the region; perhaps drought or erosion or a change in climate brought ruin to the farmers. As scholars examined the ruins, they found evidence of events like these, but little to suggest that any one of these explanations could account for the disappearance of the Anasazi. Some new peoples did arrive in the Southwest about this time, but they did not come in great numbers, and it would have been very difficult for small migrating groups to dislodge the Anasazi from numerous and secure towns. Nor did the evidence suggest

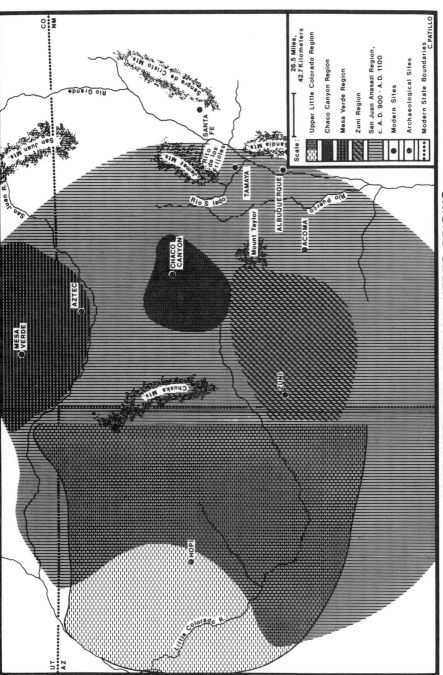

SOUTHWEST REGIONS AND KERES ORIGINS

that large-scale warfare or disastrous epidemics had brought an end to the Anasazi. These were dry years in the Southwest, but the worst periods of drought did not begin until some time after most of the Anasazi disappeared. Some areas were eroded, but these skilled farmers could have moved their fields elsewhere, and even if crops had failed completely, the region still had abundant natural resources.[13]

No one of these factors alone seemed adequate to explain the disappearance of the Anasazi, but scholars began to suggest that, in combination, such events could have accounted for their decline. Their very success may have made them vulnerable: hundreds of years of steady population growth may have strained the region's resources. If raiders then appeared and the residents of smaller outlying towns fled to the larger centers for security, those towns would have needed to harvest more food to support the refugees, as well as their own growing populations. A slight drought, a change in rainfall patterns, or the loss of fields to erosion or sedimentation could, under those circumstances, have brought disaster. In a village already suffering from crowding and food shortages, even a slight increase in disease would have been deadly. As threat added to threat, the Anasazi may have decided that, to survive and maintain their way of life, they had to find new lands with richer soil and more water, a climate better suited to farming, and protection from enemy raiders.[14]

Where they had gone was, for many years, a question as perplexing as why they had left. As scholars studied more of the region's sites, however, a pattern emerged: at the same time that the Anasazi towns were being abandoned, the population in other parts of the Southwest increased dramatically. Through the twelfth and thirteenth centuries, many new people settled in the Río Grande, Río Puerco, and Little Colorado River regions.[15] The pueblo peoples who now occupy these lands resemble the Anasazi in many ways, and both the disappearance of the Anasazi and the origins of the modern pueblos could be explained by the theory that the Anasazi had not vanished, but moved south to rebuild their villages. All of the evidence seemed to suggest that at least some of the pueblo peoples were descendants of the Anasazi.[16] Thus the threads of pueblo history were woven into those of the Anasazi to form continuous strands extending far into the past, to the time of the Oshara peoples.

That theory, however, still left one major gap in the tapestry of the Southwest. What had happened between the thirteenth century, when the Anasazi moved south, and the sixteenth, when Spaniards found more than sixty pueblos along the Río Grande? That three-hundred-year period must have been a time of great change—but what sort of change? And how were those events related to the histories of the pueblos we know today?

Language provided the first clues to locate the Tamayame in that great puzzle. Today, as when the Spaniards arrived in 1540, the native languages of the Pueblo Southwest can be divided into four major groups. In the west are two unrelated languages: Zuñi, which has not been linked to any other language, and Hopi, which belongs to the Uto-Aztecan family. Three Tanoan languages—Tewa, Tiwa, and Towa—are spoken along the Río Grande. The fourth language group, the Keres, appears in both regions, among the peoples of Acoma and Laguna in the west, and at the eastern pueblos of Santo Domingo, San Felipe, Cochití, Zía, and Tamaya.[17] All seven Keres pueblos speak dialects so similar that the peoples cannot have been separated from one another much longer than six hundred years. Some dialects, like those of Santa Ana and Zía, are so like one another that those who speak them must have remained together even longer.[18] The evidence of language thus suggests that the Keres speakers were still very close to one another when the Anasazi were moving south and the pueblo region was being settled, and that the history of the Tamayame in this time of change must be intertwined with the histories of the other Keres-speaking peoples.

In 1540 the Spaniards recognized the Queres, or Keres, peoples as a distinct group. In the four hundred years following Coronado's arrival, however, few scholars tried to trace the ancient history of the Eastern or Río Grande Keres. Those who first attempted the task focused on settlements near the modern pueblos, sites from which the Keres might have moved to their modern homes. In the late nineteenth and early twentieth centuries, scholars linked the Keres peoples with a cluster of sites in the Pajarito Plateau-Frijoles River region. Adolph Bandelier, Edgar Hewett, and others described these ruins, which were identified in the peoples' oral traditions as the homes of their ancestors.[19] Three decades later, Hewett and Edward Curtis discussed these sites in more detail. The two scholars agreed that many of the sites had been occupied by successive groups of Keres peoples, the last of whom were the ancestors of the Cochití. Hewett argued that the Cochití had left the sites by A.D. 1500, and both men suggested that other Keres speakers, possibly the ancestors of Zía and Santa Ana, had moved south earlier.[20]

These suggestions provoked little debate, but there was less agreement about the larger questions of Keres movement. Where had the Keres peoples come from? How and when did the Eastern Keres reach the Frijoles area? What routes did they follow when they moved on? And had they settled in other places as well, before their journeys brought them to their modern lands? Linguist Edward Sapir argued that the Keres language could be linked with the Hokan-Siouan languages of the Plains.[21] If that assumption were true, the Keres, and perhaps other pueblo peoples as well, could have come from the east, where those languages were spoken.[22] Other scholars suggested that Keres speakers could have come from the Little Colorado River region to the west.[23] Noting that pottery made in the Keres lands looked much like that made earlier at Mesa Verde, H. P. Mera raised still another possibility: perhaps the Keres were related to the Mesa Verde Anasazi.[24] Even in 1940, however, there was little evidence to prove or disprove any of these theories. Exactly four hundred years after the Spaniards arrived, Elsie Clews Parsons appealed to "all students of the Southwest." No one, she pointed out, had yet addressed two questions central to the region's early history: "Where were the present tribes at the close of the thirteenth century, and then what did they do?" Yet another decade was to pass before scholars attempted to answer those crucial questions.[25]

By that time, the experts had begun to discard some of the earlier suggestions. Linguists found no reason to link the Keres with the Hokan-Siouan language group.[26] Physically and culturally, the modern pueblos resembled the earlier peoples of the Southwest, so there was no need to look to the east for their ancestry.[27] Nothing suggested that the Keres could have come from the south, and it was unlikely that the all of the ancestors of the numerous Río Grande peoples could be traced to the sparse population that had settled the region before A.D. 1300.[28] Thus the search narrowed to the two most probable areas of origin: the west and the north.

In three articles published in 1949 and 1950, Erik Reed outlined a theory that placed the ancestors of the Keres in the west. A variety of new things, he pointed out, had appeared in the Río Grande region between A.D. 1300 and A.D. 1380. The most striking of these was a red pottery decorated with glaze, totally unlike the black-on-white pottery common in the east. At the same time, rectangular kivas, unusual cradleboards, and a new type of stone axe also appeared in the east. All of these things, though new to the eastern region, had been made earlier in the west. Reed believed that people from the upper Little Colorado River had moved first to the Zuñi-Acoma region and then to the Río Grande. Assuming that these people spoke a Keres language would explain how the Tanoan-speaking peoples along the Río Grande had been split into two groups, as well as accounting for the likenesses and differences between the societies of the eastern and western Keres groups.[29]

Other scholars had taken note of these similarities and traits, but they did not all support Reed's theory. Florence Hawley and others argued that Keres origins lay elsewhere, perhaps in the Chaco Canyon area.[30] Although Fred Wendorf agreed that Keres ancestry might be traced to parts of the Chaco region and the Acoma-Río Puerco area to the west, he did not believe that a fourteenth-century migration had brought them to the Río Grande. He argued that, to account for all of the Keres peoples on the Río Grande, such a migration would have to have involved large numbers of people, who would have settled either in large sites or in many smaller ones. If Reed's theories were accurate, archaeologists could have expected to find such sites, each containing the red glazed ware, the axes, and the other traits, but not even one site like this had been identified. Therefore, Wendorf argued, the theory of a large migration did not fit the evidence. He considered it more likely that some of the peoples who already lived in the Río Grande region had learned to make the pottery, perhaps from a small group of westerners, and he concluded that if the Keres had come from the west in a large group, they must have reached the Río Grande about A.D. 900, long before the glazed pottery appeared.[31]

In 1955 Wendorf and Reed reconsidered these questions.[32] All of the Río Grande peoples, they pointed out, had had many contacts with one another and with their neighbors to the east, west, and south. Ideas, goods, and styles had passed readily from one group to another, but such interchange did not require large migrations from one region to another. A people already in the Río Grande area could have obtained the pottery in trade or learned the technique from a small group of

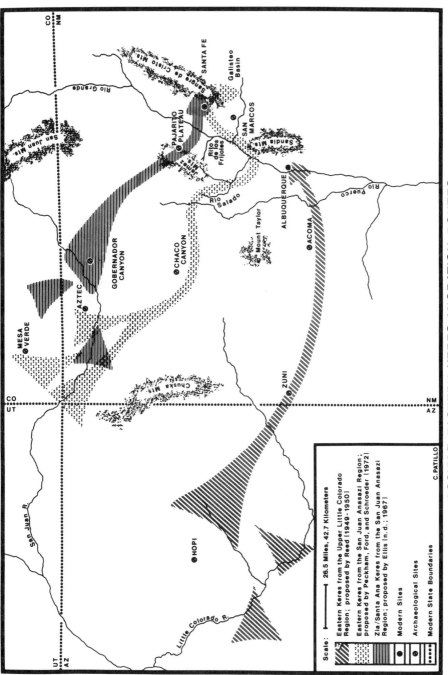

POSSIBLE EASTERN KERES MIGRATION ROUTES

Scale: |———| 26.5 Miles, 42.7 Kilometers

Eastern Keres from the Upper Little Colorado Region; proposed by Reed (1949-1950)

Eastern Keres from the San Juan Anasazi Region; proposed by Peckham, Ford, and Schroeder (1972)

Zia/Santa Ana Keres from the San Juan Anasazi Region; proposed by Ellis (n.d.: 1967)

● Modern Sites

◉ Archaeological Sites

•••••• Modern State Boundaries

C. PATILLO

westerners. Perhaps only the style, and not the people who practiced it, had traveled east.

But if the Keres had not come from the west, where had they come from? Wendorf and Reed returned to the suggestion made earlier by H. P. Mera, who had hinted at a link between the pottery of Mesa Verde and the Río Grande Keres. By A.D. 1300, when the Anasazi had abandoned their Four Corners homeland, a pottery much like the San Juan Anasazi black-on-white ware had begun to appear along the Río Grande and in the Galisteo Basin. The evidence showed that large groups of people had arrived in those regions at the same time. Perhaps, Wendorf and Reed proposed, the newcomers were Keres-speaking peoples who came from the San Juan Anasazi region, bringing their traditional pottery with them. Because the Keres languages had no traceable connection with any other language, the Keres-speaking peoples must have had a long history as a distinct group, a history similar to that of the San Juan Anasazi. This theory accounted for all of the evidence better than any previous explanation had.[33] Thus scholars at last accepted the idea that the Río Grande Keres had probably come from the north, just as the peoples' own traditions said.

Working from this theory, others have begun to trace the routes of the Keres journeys. Albert Schroeder, Richard Ford, and Stewart Peckham have proposed a general outline of pueblo movements that includes the Keres.[34] The three agree that the Keres moved south from a homeland in the San Juan region that included the Aztec, Mesa Verde, and Chaco areas. Ford and Peckham believe that the middle Río Puerco area may also have been a part of this homeland. Schroeder suggests that the Keres traveled from Chaco Canyon to the Puerco region about A.D. 1150, and he and Ford agree that the eastern Keres moved east from the Puerco, reaching the Salado River Valley below the Jémez River by A.D. 1300, and then following the Río Grande to the Frijoles Canyon area. By the fourteenth century, the Keres had settled in the Galisteo Basin. Later they returned to the Río Grande, where the Spaniards found them in the sixteenth century. Peckham proposes a somewhat different route and timetable: he believes that the Keres, moving south from Mesa Verde, reached the San Juan Basin in the twelfth century and the Río Grande in the thirteenth.

Within this broad pattern, however, there must have been many smaller journeys, for by A.D. 1300 the Keres people had split into four groups. From the first group came the modern dialects of the Western Keres (Acoma and Laguna); from the second, that of Cochití; from the third, that of San Felipe and Santo Domingo; and from the fourth, that of Zía and Santa Ana. Perhaps each of the four groups set out separately from Mesa Verde or another San Juan homeland,[35] and the seven modern Keres peoples began to emerge as distinct groups during the journey south.

It is in this period, then, that the first traces should appear of the Tamayame as a separate people. Anthropologist Florence Hawley Ellis has sketched their movements by combining the evidence of archaeology with the clues provided by language and the oral tradition. Keres ancestry, she suggests, runs through the San Juan Anasazi to the local Archaic tradition. According to her reconstruction, the ancestors of Zía and

Santa Ana moved south from the San Juan country together in the thirteenth century, passing through Gobernador Canyon. The Zía people settled on the Pajarito Plateau; the Tamayame may have remained with them or moved on to settle near the site of modern Santa Fe. Later in the thirteenth century, the Tamayame moved into the Galisteo Basin without their Zía relatives, and by the end of the century, the separation was complete.[36]

From the Galisteo Basin, Ellis believes, the Tamayame traveled to the Río Grande, reaching the river in the Angostura region near modern Bernalillo. There, according to one version of the oral tradition, the Tamayame split into two groups, with one group moving south to settle at Paak'u (Paako, LA 162).[37] A second version of the oral tradition suggests that the Tamayame may have traveled to Paak'u as a group. Ellis believes that some of the Tamayame settled at Paak'u and established farming villages along the Río Grande through the fourteenth century, while a second group made a long journey to the west.[38]

As Ellis reconstructs the journey, the Tamayame traveled north from the Río Grande, settling for a time near the villages of the Kitichina Zía in the Borrego Grant area. The Zía people and the Tamayame then moved together to the banks of the Río Puerco, where the Zía built a settlement on the east bank, and the Tamayame, one on the west. Later, the Tamayame left this village, following the Río Puerco south to Acoma, where they settled for a short time. Then they moved on, traveling south again. Somewhere near modern Socorro, they crossed to the east bank of the Río Grande and turned north.[39]

They rejoined their kin at Paak'u, but Ellis believes that they did not remain there long. By A.D. 1425 the Tamayame had returned to the Río Grande valley, where they built settlements along the river from the Angostura to the region of modern Albuquerque and Corrales. Except in the Angostura, Tamayame villages generally stood on the west side of the river, often facing Tiwa towns on the east bank.[40]

But where were the Tamayame a hundred years later, when the Spaniards reached the Río Grande? Ellis notes that six of the Tamayame settlements along the river (Coffman, SDA, Gonzales or LA 280, LA 1844, Angostura Mill, and Puaray II) were still occupied between A.D. 1450 and A.D. 1650.[41] Only one of these Tamayame towns (LA 1844) seems to have been abandoned before the eighteenth century.[42] About A.D. 1515 Keres peoples established another village on the southeast corner of Santa Ana Mesa (LA 2049).[43] Of Tamaya itself at this time, the records say nothing. Thus it would seem, from the evidence of pottery and the oral tradition, that the Tamayame were living in villages along the Río Grande (and perhaps elsewhere as well) in early September 1540, when the first of Coronado's men reached the region.

These Spaniards described the Río Grande region as the Tiguex Province, the home of the Tiwa people. They also reported that seven Keres villages, including Zía, which they visited, lay beyond the Tiguex lands. Although they recognized the difference between Tiwa and Keres languages, they did not distinguish any of the

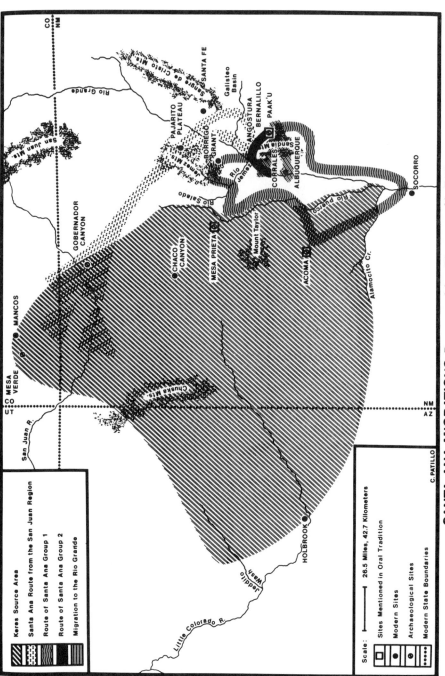

SANTA ANA MIGRATIONS Proposed by Florence H. Ellis

Keres Source Area

Santa Ana Route from the San Juan Region

Route of Santa Ana Group 1

Route of Santa Ana Group 2

Migration to the Rio Grande

Scale: ⊢————⊣ 26.5 Miles, 42.7 Kilometers

□ Sites Mentioned in Oral Tradition

● Modern Sites

◉ Archaeological Sites

⋯⋯ Modern State Boundaries

C. PATILLO

villages along the Río Grande as Keres towns. And of the Tamayame, whether in the Tiguex province or the Keres lands beyond, they say nothing.[45]

In the chronicles of the Spanish conquest, that omission is of little consequence. The explorers recorded a tale in which pueblos were of interest only insofar as they demonstrated an ability to meet Spanish needs or threaten Spanish interests. For those who received the expedition's reports, the native peoples would be little more than a curiosity, each as alien, intriguing, or open to conversion as the next. Thus the expedition's records tell first of the optimistic search for gold and silver, fabled kingdoms, and souls to be saved, and later of a desperate scramble to find enough food and clothing to keep the struggling army through the winter. It mattered little to Coronado's hungry men whether the pueblo that gave them food spoke a Tiwa language or a Keres one; to those who read in their reports that this province had no treasures, it would matter even less.

For the history of Tamaya, however, what the records omit is critical. Where the people were during the fall and winter of 1540 could have made a great difference in their experience, for the pueblos nearest to Coronado's camps bore the heaviest burden. By March 1541, the Spaniards had occupied one pueblo, besieged and burned two others, and killed several hundred pueblo people. The storerooms of the nearest pueblos had been emptied to feed and clothe the Spaniards, and ten pueblos in addition to those burned by the soldiers had been abandoned. As the Spaniards exhausted the region's supplies, they visited more distant pueblos to demand food, clothing, and tribute, but in the villages more remote from the Río Grande, the soldiers, if they appeared at all, were only occasional visitors, not a constant and deadly presence.[46] None of the available evidence, however, reveals where the Tamayame spent these harsh winters. The stories explain that the Tamayame settled along the Río Grande for a time, but they do not indicate when the people abandoned these villages. The archaeological record suggests that both eastern Keres peoples and Tiwa-speaking peoples built villages along the Río Grande, and that the Tamayame could have used at least six sites in the region during the mid-sixteenth century. Archaeologists have found several distinct sequences of pottery in the villages along the Río Grande. One typically occurs in pueblos known to belong to the Tiwa; a second appears in settlements that Florence Hawley Ellis links with the Keres and the Tamayame. This sequence includes early fragments of black-on-white ware, much like the Anasazi pottery of the Mesa Verde region, and several kinds of glaze-painted pottery, dating from the fourteenth to the sixteenth century, found in association with remnants of Puname Polychrome, made by Zía and Santa Ana in the seventeenth and eighteenth centuries, and Santa Ana and Ranchitos polychrome, made by Santa Ana in the nineteenth and twentieth centuries.[47] It is, however, difficult if not impossible to tell from a five-hundred-year-old shard who made the ancient pot and how that pot reached the location where it was found. And even if it could be shown without doubt that this was the work of Tamayame potters and that their kinsmen lived in these settlements, the fragments would not reveal whether the

Tamayame were present at these sites during the critical times between December 1540 and March 1541.

Thus the question can be answered in several ways, but it cannot be answered with any certainty. First there is the possibility that the Tamayame were not anywhere near Coronado's Tiguex Province along the Río Grande in 1540. They could have been living in the seven Keres villages beyond Tiguex, or in some other remote location, such as the pueblo on Black Mesa. Perhaps Tamaya already stood at its modern site. The assumption that the Tamayame were not living along the Río Grande, however, leaves several unanswered problems. This theory would force scholars to reinterpret, or even discard, the evidence of archaeology. And it does not explain why the Spaniards encountered no Tamayame in the Keres region. In the sixteenth century, the pueblo's population seems to have been many times larger than it is today, perhaps, as Ellis suggests, even as large as seven thousand.[48] If several thousand people had been living in a single pueblo near the Río Jémez, the Spaniards who visited Zía and mentioned the Keres towns would almost certainly have noticed it or heard of it. Searching desperately for food and clothing, they would not have been likely to miss or ignore a town of such size.

The opposite assumption—that the Tamayame were living along the Río Grande in 1540—however, likewise creates serious difficulties for scholars. Why did the Spaniards, who scrupulously recorded the languages spoken at each pueblo they visited, not leave any account of hearing Keres spoken near their camps? Perhaps the Spaniards overlooked the Keres settlements, or perhaps they simply chose not to mention the presence of the Tamayame for some other reason. If they saw Tamayame individuals along the river, they may have assumed that these people belonged to the neighboring Tiwa pueblos. But why, if the Tamayame suffered great losses in those winters, did no account of this first meeting with Europeans survive in Tamaya's oral tradition? It may be that the tradition once told of these events, and that the stories have simply been lost in the centuries that have passed since that time. It could be that, unlike the other peoples in this region, the Tamayame did not bear the brunt of the expedition's force. All of these difficulties, however, weigh heavily against the possibility that large Tamayame groups were living in pueblos beside the Río Grande when the soldiers set up their camps there.

There is yet another possibility. Both the tradition and the historic record tell of Tamayame farmers who raised crops at a distance from their settlements. Until they moved permanently to the Ranchiit'u in the twentieth century, the Tamayame did not live year-round in these farming villages. For more than two hundred years, they traveled from Tamaya to the Río Grande throughout the spring and summer, some-times returning daily to the pueblo, sometimes camping near the fields. As soon as the harvest had been gathered, however, all of the people returned to Tamaya, sometimes leaving a few guards to watch the fields until it was time to prepare for the new year's planting. If something like this was their practice in the sixteenth century as well, most of the Tamayame would probably have left the Río Grande

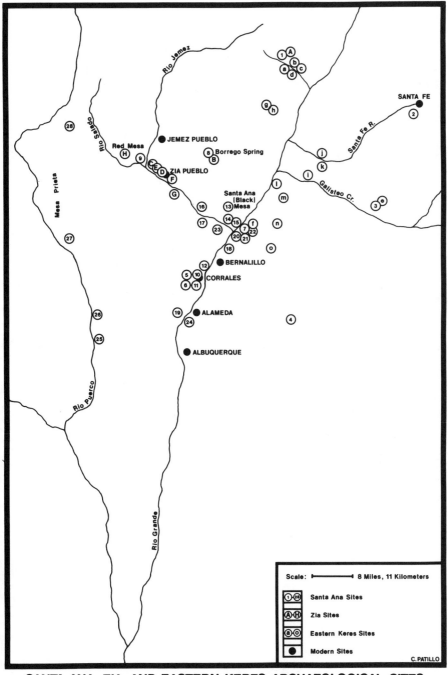

SANTA ANA, ZIA, AND EASTERN KERES ARCHAEOLOGICAL SITES, c. A.D. 1200-A.D. 1850

See pages 265–66 for site identification.

fields before the Spaniards arrived, for winter had already begun to set in when the advance party reached the region, and the main group did not appear until late December. If the Río Grande Tamayame were not living near the Spanish camp in the winter of 1540, they would have been unlikely to return to their fields in the spring, knowing that the Spaniards had destroyed two pueblos and killed several hundred people in the immediate area. Like their Tiwa neighbors, they would probably not have reoccupied the region as long as the soldiers remained. This theory still does not explain why the Spaniards failed to encounter the people of Tamaya in their journeys through Keres lands, but it fits the evidence better than the other two assumptions.

Where were the people of Tamaya in 1540, and what happened to them at this turning point in their history? Of that part of the tapestry, little remains. Soon after that time, the history of the Tamayame before Tamaya comes to an end. In 1598 the people of Tamaya appear by name in a historical document for the first time.[49] That record does not reveal where they were living or whether they had settled at the modern site of Tamaya, but it does mark a new period for those who tell the history of the Tamayame. From that time on, the people's past may be traced in the written record as well as in the stories of the oral tradition, the ruins of the Southwest, the elements of language, and the broken pottery that could have been left behind by the Tamayame on their long journey.

No.	Site	Dates of Occupation	Identified by
	Santa Ana, Zía, and Eastern Keres Archaeological Sites c. A.D. 1200–A.D. 1850 shown on the map on page 263		
	Santa Ana Sites		
1	Frijoles Canyon	c. A.D. 1200–A.D. 1359	Hewett, Ellis
2	Santa Fe Region	c. A.D. 1200–A.D. 1359	Ellis
3	Galisteo Basin Region	c. A.D. 1200–A.D. 1359	Ellis, Ortiz
4	Paak'u (Paa-ko, LA 162)	c. A.D. 1200–A.D. 1425	Lambert, Ellis
5	Coffman Site	c. A.D. 1200–A.D. 1850	Ellis
6	SDA Academy Site	c. A.D. 1200–A.D. 1850	Ellis
7	Angostura Mill Site	c. A.D. 1200–A.D. 1850	Ellis
8	Borrego Spring Site	c. A.D. 1200–A.D. 1359	Ellis
9	Kwiiste P̶u̶u̶ Tamaya (Tamayama)	c. A.D. 1350–A.D. 1450	Ellis
10	Gonzales (LA 288)	c. A.D. 1350–A.D. 1850	Ellis
11	LA 1844	c. A.D. 1350–A.D. 1650	Ellis
12	Buraikana (Puaray II, LA 728)	c. A.D. 1350–A.D. 1850	Ellis
13	Black Mesa Site	c. A.D. 1450–A.D. 1850	Bandelier
14	LA 2049	c. A.D. 1515–A.D. 1850	Ellis
15	East Point	c. A.D. 1600–A.D. 1850	Ellis
16	Tamaya	c. A.D. 1700–present	Ellis
17	"Santa Ana"	c. A.D. 1602–A.D. 1700	Enrico Martínez Map
18	Ranchiit'u (El Ranchito)	c. A.D. 1709–present	Ellis
19	Black Site II	c. A.D. 1600–A.D. 1850	Ellis
20	Railroad Tamaya	c. A.D. 1600–A.D. 1850	Ellis
21	Fisher #47	c. A.D. 1600–A.D. 1850	Ellis
22	Fisher #22	c. A.D. 1600–A.D. 1850	Ellis
23	Arroyo Site (2 miles west of dam)	c. A.D. 1600–A.D. 1850	Ellis
24	Whipple Site	c. A.D. 1750–A.D. 1850	Ellis
25	P2-5 Site	c. A.D. 1750–A.D. 1850	Ellis
26	P3-BSW Site	c. A.D. 1750–A.D. 1850	Ellis
27	Base of Mesa Prieta	c. A.D. 1750–A.D. 1850	Ellis
28	Espiritu Santo Grant	granted A.D. 1766	Brayer

(continued)

APPENDIX 1

Santa Ana, Zía, and Eastern Keres Archaeological Sites
(*continued*)

No.	Site	Dates of Occupation	Identified by
	Some Zía Sites		
A	Frijoles Canyon	c. A.D. 1200–A.D. 1450	Hewett, Ellis, Mera
B	Kitichina Zía Villages	c. A.D. 1200–A.D. 1450	Ellis
C	LA 241	c. A.D. 1350–A.D. 1700	Mera
D	Zía Pueblo (LA 28)	c. A.D. 1350–present	Ellis, Mera
E	Punamesh (LA 392)	c. A.D. 1350–A.D. 1450	Ellis, Mera
F	Kawasaiya Zía (LA 377)	c. A.D. 1350–A.D. 1450	Ellis, Mera
G	Fish House (LA 374)	c. A.D. 1300–A.D. 1700	Ellis, Mera
H	Red Mesa Refuge (LA 2048)	c. A.D. 1680–A.D. 1694	Ellis, Mera
	Some Eastern Keres Sites		
a	LA 216	c. A.D. 1350–A.D. 1450	Mera
b	LA 82	c. A.D. 1350–A.D. 1700	Mera
c	LA 217	c. A.D. 1350–A.D. 1650	Mera
d	LA 78	c. A.D. 1350–A.D. 1450	Mera
e	San Marcos Pueblo	c. A.D. 1350–A.D. 1700	Mera
f	Angostura (LA 931)	c. A.D. 1350–A.D. 1450	Mera
g	LA 35	c. A.D. 1350–A.D. 1650	Mera
h	LA 79	c. A.D. 1350–A.D. 1450	Mera
i	LA 182	c. A.D. 1350–A.D. 1650	Mera
j	LA 5	c. A.D. 1350–A.D. 1490	Mera
k	LA 7	c. A.D. 1350–A.D. 1515	Mera
l	LA 412	c. A.D. 1350–A.D. 1650	Mera
m	LA 278	c. A.D. 1350–A.D. 1515	Mera
n	LA 240	c. A.D. 1350–A.D. 1650	Mera
o	LA 442–47	c. A.D. 1350–A.D. 1700	Mera

APPENDIX
TWO

Map Sources

The maps included here have been compiled from a wide variety of sources, including some not readily available to the reader. Most of those that show Tamaya's lands in detail rely on unpublished archival documents. Those that illustrate Spanish exploration and settlement, by contrast, have benefitted from many published maps and accounts of Spanish-pueblo contacts, which have been redrawn to focus on the relation of geography, routes, and historic events to the history of Tamaya. Below, by category and period, we acknowledge our debts to the many previous cartographers, historians, anthropologists, and archaeologists, too numerous to cite on the individual maps, whose works we have drawn on. These works are cited here in short form; full bibliographical data can be found in the notes to the corresponding chapters.

The Tamayame before Tamaya

Prehistory and Archaeology in Chapter 1 and Appendix A

The maps included in Chapter 1 (pages 2 and 4) have been drawn to illustrate the Tamayame's own accounts of their origins, their journeys, and their early settlements; those included in Appendix 1 (pages 253, 257, 260, and 263) show the routes, sites, and areas identified by anthropologists and archaeologists as pertinent to Santa Ana history. These two sets of maps do not always agree; discrepancies between them are discussed in the appendix and its notes, and in the notes to Chapter 1.

The sites named and the routes shown in the maps in Chapter 1 are those identified by Tamayame oral tradition; the published sources cited below have in some cases been used to locate these sites, but the locations were subsequently verified by knowledgeable pueblo officials. Many of the tapes in the Santa Ana Oral History Project collection discuss these sites and routes in detail; among the most helpful in preparing these maps were a series of interviews with Porfirio Montoya,

APPENDIX 2

Floyd Montoya, Thomas Leubben, and Donna Pino recorded in tape nos. 2 (16 January 1980), 3 (21 January 1980), 4 (21 January 1980), 8 (4 February 1980), 12 (11 February 1980), 13 (n.d.), 15 (10 March 1980), and 16 (25 March 1980). Floyd Montoya developed rough maps from the traditional accounts and, after consultation with Donna Pino, revised the spelling of site names to correspond with the standard Keres system developed at the Bilingual Department of the University of Albuquerque. The rough maps were revised by Greg Wight, corrected by Floyd Montoya, reviewed with pueblo officials, and redrawn by Catherine Patillo.

The oral tradition includes accounts of others who settled in the region, and archaeology confirms that many sites in the area were occupied, or being settled, about the time when the Tamayame reached Paak'u. Those referred to in Tamayame accounts are shown in the map on page 4, with locations and dates drawn from H. P. Mera, *Population Changes in the Rio Grande Glaze-Paint Area;* Linda S. Cordell, ed., *Tijeras Canyon: Analyses of the Past;* and Marjorie F. Lambert, *Paa-ko, Archaeological Chronicle of an Indian Village in North-Central New Mexico.* Unnamed sites are identified by the number assigned to them by the Laboratory of Anthropology (LA). The map on page 6 illustrates the journey of the Tamayame to the west as told in the oral tradition; the map on page 9 shows their settlements and farming areas along the Rio Grande during this period.

The maps in Appendix 1 chronicle the development of scholarly interest in, and theories about, the origins of the modern pueblo peoples. The map on page 253, "Southwest Regions and Keres Origins," relies on Jesse D. Jennings' work on the extent of the Anasazi cultures at various periods, illustrated in *Ancient Native Americans, Prehistory of North America,* and *Prehistory of Utah and the Eastern Great Basin,* and on the work of John C. McGregor, who maps the early peoples of the Upper Little Colorado and Zuñi regions in *Southwestern Archaeology.* An earlier source, C. V. Kidder, *An Introduction to the Study of Southwestern Archaeology,* also locates these culture areas and Anasazi regions.

The map on page 257 illustrates three major migration routes that scholars have suggested were followed by Eastern Keres peoples, including the ancestors of Santa Ana. The first was outlined by Erik K. Reed in a series of articles published in 1949 and 1950: "East-Central Arizona Archaeology in Relation to the Western Pueblos"; "The Significance of Skull Deformation in the Southwest"; and "Sources of Upper Rio Grande Pueblo Culture and Population." With Fred Wendorf, Reed proposed a revised version of this hypothesis in "An Alternative Reconstruction of Northern Rio Grande History" (1955). The second route follows the theories outlined by Richard I. Ford, Albert H. Schroeder, and Stewart L. Peckham in *New Perspectives on the Pueblos,* ed. Alfonso Ortiz. The third route, which focuses on the Zía / Santa Ana migration, was proposed by Florence Hawley Ellis in a published article, "Where Did the Pueblo People Come From?" and an unpublished manuscript, "Anthropological Findings Supporting the Land Claims of the Pueblos of Zia, Santa Ana, and Jemez."

The map on page 260 focuses on the theories developed by Ellis, the only anthropologist who has published material devoted specifically to the origins, migrations, and settlements of the Tamayame. Her studies, which have included examination of both the archaeological evidence and the oral tradition, have led her to propose a route similar, but not identical, to the one described in Chapter 1.

The final map in the appendix, shown on page 263, recapitulates the sites that various archaeologists and anthropologists have attributed to Santa Ana, Zía, and the Eastern Keres peoples generally. These attributions have largely been based on the pottery sequences found in the sites, a form of correlation between peoples and artifacts that many scholars now consider tenuous at best. The record of these sites, however, serves several purposes in this history: it documents the pattern of settlement in the region near Tamaya before the arrival of the Spaniards, and it illustrates the development of theories proposed to explain Santa Ana's prehistory. The individual site numbers, proposed dates of occupation, and scholarly sources listed in the accompanying table have been identified in H. P. Mera, *Population Changes in the Río Grande Glaze-Paint Area;* F. H. Ellis, "Anthropological Findings Supporting the Land Claims of the Pueblos of Zia, Santa Ana, and Jemez"; Edgar L. Hewett, *Pajarito Plateau and Its Ancient Peoples;* Adolph Bandelier, *Final Report of the Investigations among the Indians of the Southwestern United States Carried on Mainly in the Years from 1880 to 1885;* Richard I. Ford, Albert H. Schroeder, and Stewart L. Peckham, *New Perspectives on the Pueblos,* ed. Alfonso Ortiz; and Marjorie F. Lambert, *Paa-ko.* The site labeled "Santa Ana," no. 17, is shown on the Enrico Martínez Map of 1602, which appears on the endpapers of George P. Hammond and Agapito Rey, *The Rediscovery of New Mexico, 1580–1594.*

Tamaya and Kastera

The Spanish and Mexican Periods, Chapters 2 though 6

Many scholars have attempted to determine and illustrate the routes taken by the various Spanish explorations in the area now known as New Mexico; clarifications of the often vague accounts recorded in Spanish journals and interpretations of possible routes are widely available in published sources. The maps included here are intended only to provide a general orientation for the reader who may be unfamiliar with the sites and routes mentioned in the text, and to place those locations in the context of Santa Ana history. In areas that might have been occupied or used by the Tamayame, the routes have been checked against the accounts in the explorers' journals; the reader will find a discussion of the implications of possible routes in the text and the notes. Key archaeological sites attributed to Santa Ana and Keres peoples have been marked as reference points on many of the maps; these locations have been identified in Chapter 1 and Appendix 1, relying on the sources cited above. It must be remembered, however, that the dates assigned to these sites typically cover much longer time spans than the incidents discussed in the text, and that, in the absence of other records, there can be no certainty that a particular site was in use, or that it was occupied by Tamayame, when a given expedition passed through the region.

The map on page 15 shows the general areas explored by the Coronado expedition of 1540–1542, the first Spaniards to travel through the region. The map includes both the party's main route through pueblo lands and the forays of smaller exploring parties who traveled into Keres lands near the Río Grande, into the Galisteo Basin, and further east onto the Plains. Since neither the explorers' routes nor the location of Tamaya and the Tamayame at this time can be identified with any precision, this map offers, at best, only an indication of where Tamayame might have met the men of Kastera. The routes shown here generally follow the descriptions in George F. Hammond and Agapito Rey, *Narratives of the Coronado Expedition, 1540–1542.* They also draw on the discussions and maps in Myra Ellen Jenkins and Albert H. Schroeder, *A Brief History of New Mexico;* Herbert Eugene Bolton, *Coronado on the Turquoise Trail: Knight of Pueblo and Plains,* and *Spanish Explorations in the Southwest, 1543–1706;* John Francis Bannon, ed., *Bolton and the Spanish Borderlands;* and Lynn I. Perrigo, *The American Southwest: Its Peoples and Cultures.* Here and throughout, two sources have provided general references: Warren A. Beck and Ynez Haase, *Historical Atlas of New Mexico;* and T. M. Pearce, ed., *New Mexico Place Names.*

The map on page 29 depicts the routes of late sixteenth-century Spanish explorers in the region, omitting the routes of the Bonilla-Humaña and Morlete parties, which cannot be traced with any accuracy. The journals of all of these expeditions can be found in two volumes edited by George P. Hammond and Agapito Rey: *The Rediscovery of New Mexico* and *Don Juan de Oñate.*

Maps on pages 62 and 67 document the Spaniards' retreat during the Pueblo Revolt of 1680 and subsequent Spanish attempts to reconquer the region. They draw on the journals of these events found in Charles Wilson Hackett, *Revolt of the Pueblo Indians of New Mexico and Otermín's Attempted Reconquest, 1680–1682,* and José Manuel Espinosa, *The First Expedition of Diego de Vargas into New Mexico, 1692.* The punitive forays of Reneros de Posada and Petriz de Cruzate are described in Hubert Howe Bancroft, *History of Arizona and New Mexico, 1530–1888; The Mercurio Volante of Don Carlos de Sigüenza y Góngora;* Clive D. Hallenbeck, *Land of the Conquistadores;* Ralph Emerson Twitchell, *The Leading Facts of New Mexico History;* Jack D. Forbes, *Apache, Navajo and Spaniard;* Florence H. Ellis, "Anthropological Evidence Supporting the Land Claims of the Pueblos of Zia, Santa Ana, and Jemez"; and Interview with Porfirio Montoya et al., Santa Ana Oral History Project, Tape no. 8.

Three maps (on pages 100, 105, and 108) focus on the movements of the pueblos and the surrounding non-pueblo Indians throughout the Spanish and Mexican periods. These maps reflect both the movement of tribal groups and the impact of Kastera's presence on all of the peoples of the region, including pueblo movements and non-pueblo raids on Hispanic and pueblo settlements. The location of pueblo sites relies on the work of Edward H. Spicer, *Cycles of Conquest;* D. W. Meinig, *Southwest: Three Peoples in Geographical Change, 1600–1700;* Albert H. Schroeder,

Map Sources

"Pueblos Abandoned in Historic Times" and "Shifting for Survival in the Spanish Southwest"; and Edward P. Dozier, *The Pueblo Indians of North America*. In keeping with the Tamayame oral tradition and the research of Florence H. Ellis, however, some sites generally attributed to non-Keres groups (Paak'u and the villages along the west bank of the Río Grande south of Bernalillo) have been designated in these maps as Eastern Keres areas during the appropriate periods. Information about non-pueblo Indian movements and raids has been drawn primarily from three works by Alfred B. Thomas (*After Coronado; Forgotten Frontiers;* and *The Plains Indians and New Mexico, 1751–1778*); in the chapter notes, the reader will find additional references to the many sources that deal with the histories and movements of particular tribes in the adjacent regions.

The map on page 82 attempts to provide an overview of Tamayame landholdings in 1766, after the pueblo had completed its major purchases in the Ranchiit'u, and the three pueblos of Santa Ana, Zía, and Jémez had received the joint grant to the Espiritu Santo lands. These maps, however, do not accurately reflect the boundaries of the pueblo's lands as they would have been recognized by the Spanish government, because the maps have been drawn from nineteenth-century survey maps prepared by agents of the United States government. These maps have been used as a base for two reasons: they are the earliest surviving maps that show precise boundaries for Tamaya's lands, and the American government relied on them when it reviewed the pueblo's land claims. Confusions in the documentation of pueblo land claims and the survey of New Mexico's lands were legion, and errors in the government's maps and surveys resulted in significant reductions of Santa Ana's landholdings.

To date, no contemporary description of Tamaya's "Spanish league" precise enough to document the boundaries of the original square grant surrounding the pueblo has been found. The earliest extant records that indicate the grant's boundaries are those gathered in the nineteenth century when the grant was presented to the U.S. Congress for confirmation.

Spanish deeds for the Ranchiit'u lands have survived, but few of these records provide enough information to allow an uncontested depiction of all of the eighteenth-century boundaries of each of the parcels that made up the purchase. To complicate the matter further, most of these deeds locate boundaries in relation to landmarks that have long since disappeared or changed: the houses, fences, and outbuildings of adjacent settlers; the location of large or distinctive trees; or the banks of the Río Grande, which is known to have altered its course frequently in the intervening years. Further research may pinpoint the locations of some of these essential reference points, but it will come too late to affect the incidents described in this text. It is clear, however, that during the process of confirmation by the Court of Private Land Claims, the boundaries of the Ranchiit'u purchases were substantially reduced; the land that was confirmed is essentially the area of a single purchase—the lands acquired from Quiteria Contreras. The western boundary, which according to the original deeds extended to the Río Puerco or the "Ceja" of that river, was reduced dramatically, and boundaries in the Angostura region were shifted south. Inaccuracies in the Clement Survey created an overlapping area patented to both Santa Ana and San Felipe, in spite of records that documented Santa Ana's historic ownership of the lands.

The map on page 218, based on a map provided by Richard Hughes, focuses more closely on the Ranchiit'u purchase areas adjoining the Río Grande, where shifts in the course of the river, probably about 1739, led to a series of disputes that persisted through the following two centuries. This map also shows the probable line of the boundary established by adjudication in 1813.

The Espiritu Santo holdings shown in the map on page 82 suffer from similar confusions, compounded by imprecise language in the original grant and an error in the initial U.S. survey. Spanish documents record that the three pueblos requested an area bounded on the east by "the said pueblos, and on the west the Caja del Rio Puerco, and on the north a place called, 'la Bentana,' which is where some Apaches and Navajos live, and on the south the lands of the neighboring settlers of the Rio Puerco." After inspecting the area, the local alcalde reported that no objections had been made to these boundaries and recommended that the grant be made as the pueblos had requested. The act of grant, however, established the eastern boundary at the "pueblo of Zía." (See H. Pierce to Dr. Aberle, 28 September 1943, SPA, and the notes to Chapter 5). New Mexico's Surveyor General apparently recognized this discrepancy in 1874, when he wrote that "from the language of the granting decree of Gov. Cachupin it is evident that he intended to extend the boundaries of the pueblo lands so as to include the grant now under examination." Three years, later, however, the official survey ran the east boundary along a straight line on the western edge of the Zía Grant in townships 13–18 N., range 2 E., a line that is not contiguous with the edge of Tamaya's square grant as approved by the U.S. Congress.

Thus the map on page 82, and subsequent maps that provide these boundaries for reference, should be understood to represent only the approximate location of Tamaya's Spanish grants and purchases, as those landholdings were depicted in the following nineteenth-century surveys: "Plat of the Indian Pueblo of Santa Ana Surveyed by US Deputy Surveyors Sawyer and McBroom, August 1876," StA 221, encl. in letter from Harry M. Atkinson, US Surveyor General, 30 December 1876, Map. no. 1628, RG 75, BIA, NA; "Plat of the Zía, Santa Ana, and Jémez Grant Surveyed by Stephen C. McElroy, US Deputy Surveyor, October-November 1877," StA 225, RG 75, BIA, NA; and "Map Showing Exterior Boundaries of Santa Ana Pueblo or El Ranchito Grant in T13N, R4E, NMPM," StA 307, SPA. Additional discussions of problems with these surveys and boundaries will be found in the chapter notes.

Tamaya and Merikaana

The American Period

The map on page 172 superimposes the evidence of Merikaana's arrival in the region—trading and exploring routes, military forts, towns, and cities—on a map showing general pueblo locations in the nineteenth century. This map relies on four published sources: Max L. Moorehead, *New Mexico's Royal Road*, which shows the Chihuahua Trail, traveled by the first Americans in the region; Jenkins and Schroeder, *A Brief History of New Mexico*, which includes maps of the forts, stage lines, counties, and trails of nineteenth-century New Mexico; George A. Dorsey, *Indians of the Southwest*, which includes a map of the region in 1903 and discusses turn-of-the-century railroad and stage routes; and Jack D. Rittenhouse, *Cabezon*, which shows the early trails in and around Tamaya's Espiritu Santo lands. In addition, this map relies on a series of manuscript maps from various archives, which have been copied and included in the Santa Ana Tribal Archive: StA 219, "Sketch Map Prepared by Calhoun in 1849 Suggesting Localities of Indian Agencies," CA 255(1), RG 75, BIA, NA; StA 220, James S. Simpson and Edward M. Kern, "Map of the Abert Expeditions, 1849," LCMD; StA 211, Jno. G. Parke, "Territory of New Mexico, 1851," Map 8904, RG 75, BIA, NA; StA 218, "Territory and Military Department of New Mexico, 1859," LCMD; StA 222, revised version of StA 218, corrected to 1867; H. D. Rogers and A. Keith Johnston, "Territory of New Mexico, c. 1860," LCMD; StA 226, "Native Races of the Pacific States, New Mexican Group, c. 1870," LCMD; StA 200, "Rand, McNally & Company's New Railway Guide Map of the Territories and the Pacific Coast," 1 June 1876, LCMD; StA 212, "Rand, McNally & Company's New Mexico," 1882, LCMD; and "11th Census, 1890, Map Showing Locations of the Pueblos in New Mexico," LCMD.

Maps on pages 156, 213, and 215 document the American government's formal review of Tamaya's landholdings. The map on page 156, drawn from the official surveys listed above for the map on page 82, shows the Court of Private Land Claims rulings related to Tamayame Lands. The map on page 213 shows land claims reviewed by the Pueblo Lands Board; the following map documents the board's rulings. Both maps are based on the following manuscript sources: StA 307, which shows the boundaries of the Ranchiit'u, the conflicting claims within those boundaries, and the Pueblo Lands Board determinations; "Supplemental Plat showing Private Claims in Section 20, Pueblo of Santa Ana or El Ranchito Grant," as approved 31 May 1920 and amended 7 April 1931 and 15 February 1932 to show the court rulings in the Sostones Jaramillo case; "Supplemental Plat Showing Private Claims in Section 29, Pueblo of Santa Ana or El Ranchito Grant," filed 4 August 1932; and "Plat Showing Private Claims in Section 30, Pueblo of Santa Ana, or El Ranchito, Grant," as amended and filed 4 August 1932.

The map on page 175 illustrates the railroads that ran through Tamayame land. It has drawn on two published sources: David F. Myrick, *New Mexico's Railroads*, which includes a general map of railroad routes; and Robert G. Athearn, *Rebel of the Rockies*, which includes maps of the Española-Antonito branch of the Denver & Rio Grande Railway (later the D&RGW) routes through pueblo land. These routes are shown in more detail in manuscript maps in the Santa Ana Tribal Archive: StA 307; StA 310, "Section 29," c. 1930, SPA, which shows the El Ranchito–Bernalillo boundary with

APPENDIX THREE

Private Claims in the Ranchiit'u
(shown on the map on page 215)

Santa Ana Title Extinguished by Pueblo Lands Board

Parcel	Claimant	Area
1) P.C. 19, p. 1	Charles F. Brown	(10.9 acres)
2) See Z-2, below		
3) P.C. 16, p. 1	Juan H. Griego	(16.5 acres)
4) P.C. 13, p. 1	Emiliano Gallegos	(20.4 acres)
5) P.C. 14, p. 1	Atilano Gallegos	(4.1 acres)
6) P.C. 8, p. 1	Mrs. Rosa Montoya	(26.6 acres)
7) P.C. 13, p. 1	Mrs. Rosa Montoya	(9.2 acres)
8) P.C. 12, p. 1	Mrs. Rosa Montoya	(8.7 acres)
9) P.C. 11, p. 1	F. E. Fairchild	(1.5 acres)
10) P.C. 10, p. 1	Mrs. Pedro Montoya (Vitalia Montoya)	(0.9 acres)
11) P.C. 9, p. 1	Mrs. Emma Brown	(1.04 acres)
12) P.C. 4, p. 1	Diego Gutiérrez	(0.12 acres)
13) P.C. 4, p. 2	Diego Gutiérrez	(2.6 acres)
14) P.C. 4, p. 3	Diego Gutiérrez	(0.3 acres)
15) P.C. 7, p. 1	Mrs. Rosa Montoya	(2.2 acres)
16) P.C. 6, p. 1	Felipe and José Lujan	(1.5 acres)
17) P.C. 6, p. 1	Adolfo Perea	(1.5 acres)
18) P.C. 1, p. 1	Victoriano Leyba	(1.0 acres)
19) P.C. 1, p. 2	Victoriano Leyba	(1.4 acres)
20) P.C. 2, p. 1	Abel Gallegos	(0.16 acres)
21) P.C. 2, p. 2	Abel Gallegos	(0.9 acres)
22) P.C. 3, p. 1	Abel Gallegos et al.	(2.467 acres)

APPENDIX 3

Santa Ana Title Confirmed by Pueblo Lands Board

Parcel	Claimant	Area
X) P.C. 18, p. 1	Charles F. Brown	(3.5 acres)
Y) P.C. 20, p. 1*	Sostenes Jaramillo	(6.4 acres)
Z) P.C. 21, p. 1	Catholic Church	(0.84 acres)
Z-1) P.C. 21, p. 2	Catholic Church (Chapel)	(0.83 acres)
Z-2) P.C. 17, p. 1	Virginia Perea Carlota P. Otero Barbara Perea Yrisarri	(18.6 acres)

*Reversed by U.S. district court, 1930.

APPENDIX FOUR

Missionaries at Tamaya, 1700–1821

Compiled from Fray Angelico Chávez, *Archives of the Archdiocese of Santa Fe, 1678–1900* (Washington, D.C.: Academy of American Franciscan History, 1957), pp. 25, 241–62.

Fray Francisco Alvarez	May 1700–July 1701
Fray Agustín de Colina	February 1701–July 1703
Fray Juan de Garaycoechea	December 1703–September 1704
Fray Salvador López	June 1705–May 1709
Fray Pedro Montaño	July 1710–June 1711
Fray José Antonio Torres	September 1711
Fray Antonio Miranda*	1712–25 March 1714
Fray Pedro Montaño*	25 March 1714–13 January 1718
Fray Juan George del Pino*	13 January 1718–7 August 1718
Fray Domingo de Araos*	7 August 1718–10 March 1719
Fray Lucas de Arévalo*	10 March 1719–13 July 1719
Fray Domingo de Araos*	13 July 1719–19 January 1721
Fray Lucas de Arévalo*	19 January 1721–14 November 1721
Fray Juan Antonio de Celis*	17 November 1721–14 October 1722
Fray Domingo de Araos,*	
Fray Juan Antonio de Celis*	14 October 1721–19 December 1723
Fray Domingo de Araos	May 1726–November 1729
Fray Diego Arias de Espinosa de Los Monteros	September 1731–August 1733
Fray Juan George del Pino	January 1733
Fray Antonio Gabaldón*	July 1734, September 1734–January 1735
Fray Diego Arias de Espinosa*	September 1734

Fray Pedro Montaño	10 January 1735–30 October 1735
Fray Carlos José Delgado	30 October 1735–September 1736
Fray Pedro Diaz de Aguilar	April 1737
Fray Cayetano de Otero	July–November 1737
Fray Pedro Antonio Esquer	February 1739
Fray Juan Antonio Sánchez	April, June 1739
Fray Francisco Bruno de la Peña	May–August 1740
Fray Manuel Gonzales Maqueda	September 1740–June 1741
Fray Pedro Montaño,	
Fray Pedro Antonio Esquer	1743–1744
Fray Miguel Gómez Cayuela	September 1745
Fray Juan Sanz de Lezaun	June 1750–April 1752
Fray Francisco Dávila	1752
Fray Francisco Guzmán	March 1765–September 1767
Fray Estanislao Mariano de Marulanda	August 1768–17 June [?]
Fray José Gabriel de la Quintana	September–November 1768
Fray Ramón Salas	November 1770–March 1774
Fray Silvestre Vélez de Escalante	January 1777
Fray José de Burgos	February 1777
Fray José Mariano Rosete y Peralta	May 1777–December 1778
Fray José de la Prada	February 1779–April 1783
Fray Francisco Martín Bueno	November 1782–March 1783
Fray José Vílchez	May 1783–July 1791
Fray Mariano Zaldívar	June 1790–April 1792
Fray José Ignacio Sánchez	April 1792–February 1793
Fray José Pedro Rubí de Celis	April–May 1795
Fray Diego Martínez y Arellano	May 1795–February 1798
Fray Isidro Cadelo	June 1798
Fray Antonio Barreras	March 1799–July 1800
Fray José Pedro Rubí de Celis	August 1800–June 1801 August 1801
Fray Jácome Gonzalez	October 1802–May 1803
Fray José Benito Pereyro	May 1803
Fray José Pedro Rubí de Celis	July 1803–April 1804
Fray Mariano José Sánchez Vergara	May 1804–January 1809
Fray José Pedro Rubí de Celis	January 1809–June 1810
Fray Gerónimo Riega	August 1810–March 1811
Fray Juan Caballero Toril	April 1811–May 1814
Fray Gerónimo Riega	May 1814–September 1820
Fray Isidoro Barcenilla	March–April 1815
Fray Manuel Martínez	October 1820–July 1821

* Nonresident missionaries

APPENDIX
FIVE

Superintendents of Indian Affairs, New Mexico, 1851–1874

1851	Governor James S. Calhoun
1852	Governor Lane
1853	Governor David Meriwether
1857–May 1863	James L. Collins
September 1863	Michael Steck
1866	Felipe Delgado
1866–1867	A. B. Norton
1868	L. E. Webb; Captain H. M. Davis, Acting Superintendent
1869	J. M. Gallegos, Major William Clinton
1870	Major William Clinton
1871	Nathaniel Pope
1873	L. Edwin Dudley
30 June 1874	Superintendency discontinued

APPENDIX
SIX

Pueblo Indian Agents Responsible
for Santa Ana, 1849–1931

James S. Calhoun	1849–1850
New Mexico Agents:	1851–1852
Richard H. Weightman	
Abram R. Wooley	
John Greiner	
Edward H. Wingfield	
E. A. Graves	1853–?
A. G. Mayers	1856
Samuel M. Yost	1857–?
—Archuleta	1859
Silas F. Kendrick	1860–?
William Frederick Milton Arny	1862–?
John Ward	1864–1866
Toribio Romero	1866
John Ward, W. F. M. Arny	1867
John Ward	1868
First Lieutenant George E. Ford	1869
First Lieutenant Charles L. Cooper	1870
W. F. M. Arny	1871–1872
Jno. Orme Cole	7 August 1872–1 July 1873
Edwin C. Lewis	1 July 1873–1874
Ben. M. Thomas	1875–1883
Pedro Sánchez	1884–1885
Dolores Romero	1885–13 Sept. 1886
M. C. Williams	13 Sept. 1886–?
W. P. McClure	6 August 1889–16 December 1889

Pueblo Indian Agents

Special Agent Frank D. Lewis	16 December 1889–6 March 1890
José Segura	6 March 1890–1891
John W. Robertson	1891–1893
John L. Bullis, Acting Agent	1893–1896
Chas. E. Nordstrom, Captain, 10th Cavalry	April 1897–1898
Chas. L. Cooper, Captain	1898
Nimrod S. Walpole	1 July 1898–1901
John B. Harper, Irrigation Superintendent	1901–1902
Ralph B. Collins, Superintendent, Albuquerque Indian School	1902
James K. Allen, Superintendent, Albuquerque Indian School	20 June 1902–1906
Burton B. Custer	1906–?
P. T. Lonergan	1913–?

Southern Pueblo Agency, created 1 September 1919

Leo Crane	1920
H. P. Marble	1923
C. E. Faris	1 April 1924
R. F. McCormick	1926
Lem A. Towers	1929–1931

APPENDIX
SEVEN

Tamaya's Officers

1682	El Pupiste or El Cupiste
1694	Bartolomé de Ojeda [?]
1706	Don Felipe
1763	Christoval, Governor
	Matheo, War Chief
	Agustin, Lieutenant of the Cacique
	Ambrosio, Lieutenant
	Joseph, Lieutenant
	Miguel, Sacristan
	Antonio, Sacristan
	Lorenzo, Captain
	Julio, Captain
	Christoval, Interpreter
	Pedro, Chief Fiscal
	Alonso, Fiscal
	Thomas, Fiscal
	Alonso, Cook
	Domingo, Cook
1813	Eusebio (or Eusevio) Mairo, Governor
1819	Juan Jose El Cuate, Governor
1868	Antonio Esculla, Governor
	José Sarracino, Lieutenant Governor
1877	Pedro Pino, Governor
1882	Pedro Yunague, Governor
1898	Jesús María Antonio Moya, Governor

Tamaya's Officers

1899   Ambrisio Tenorio, "Chief"
       Pedro Yollanagua (or Llonagua), Governor
1900   José Manuel Enrique, Governor
       José León, Lieutenant Governor
       Jesús Moya, War Captain
1907   Bautista García, Governor
1912   Juan Venancio, Lieutenant Governor
1917   José García, Lieutenant Governor
1924   Daniel Otero, Governor
1925   Hilario Sánchez, Governor
       Santiago Tenorio, Lieutenant Governor
       Felipe Ortiz, Captain
       Victoriano Montoya, Assistant Captain
       Emiliano Raton, Major Domo
       Garvinio Lujan, Assistant Major Domo
1926   Emeliano Otero, Governor
       José Rey León, Lieutenant Governor
       Crusito Ambrosio, War Captain
       José Porfirio Montoya, Lieutenant War Captain
       José Bobe Montoya, Ditch Boss
       Ventura Sánchez, Lieutenant Ditch Boss
       José Martino, Fiscal
       Perfilio [?] Montoya, Lieutenant Fiscal
1927   Emeliano Otero, Governor
       José Rey León, Lieutenant Governor
1928   Emeliano Otero, Governor
       José Rey León, Lieutenant Governor
1929   Hilario Sánchez, Governor
       Valentino Montoya, Lieutenant Governor
1930   Hilario Sánchez, Governor
       Valentino Montoya, Lieutenant Governor
1931   Daniel Otero, Governor
       Porfirio Montoya, Lieutenant Governor
1932   Daniel Otero, Governor
       Porfirio Montoya, Lieutenant Governor
1933   Hilario Sánchez, Governor
       Eligio Montoya, Lieutenant Governor
1934   Emeliano Otero, Governor
       José Bobe Pino, Lieutenant Governor
1935   Hilario Sánchez, Governor
       Leo Pena, Lieutenant Governor

1936   José Bobe Pino, Governor
Manuel Gonzales, Lieutenant Governor
1937   Leo Pena, Governor
Fabianio López. Lieutenant Governor
1938   Porfirio Montoya, Governor
Longinio Otero, Lieutenant Governor
1939   Santiago Tenorio, Governor
Eligio Montoya, Lieutenant Governor
1940   Manuel Gonzales, Governor
José Rey León, Lieutenant Governor
1941   Eligio Montoya, Governor
Christo García, Lieutenant Governor
1942   José Rey León, Governor
Hilario Otero, Lieutenant Governor
1943   Jesús Manuel, Governor
Hilario Otero, Governor
Leo Pena, Lieutenant Governor
1944   Hilario Otero, Governor
Pamifilo Montoya, Lieutenant Governor
1945   Louise Pena, Governor
Fabiano López, Lieutenant Governor
1946   Manuel Gonzales, Governor
Unelio Menchego, Ditch Boss
Fidel López, Lieutenant Governor
1947   Valentino Montoya, Governor
José García, Lieutenant Governor
1948   José Rey León, Governor
Porfirio Montoya, Lieutenant Governor
1949   Eligio Montoya, Governor
Santiago Armijo, Lieutenant Governor
1950   Longinio (Lojenio) Otero, Governor
Unelio Menchego, Lieutenant Governor
1951   Leo Pena, Governor
Fedelino Sánchez, Lieutenant Governor
1952   Fidel López, Governor
Christo García, Lieutenant Governor
1953   José Rey León, Governor
Santiago Armijo, Lieutenant Governor
1954   Unelio Menchego, Governor
Albert Montoya, Lieutenant Governor
1955   Fedelino Sánchez, Governor
Tony Menchego, Lieutenant Governor

1956   José Bobe Pino, Governor
       Christo García, Lieutenant Governor
1957   José Bobe Pino, Governor
       Christo García, Lieutenant Governor
1958   Santiago Armijo, Governor
       Santiago Barela, Lieutenant Governor
1959   Albert Montoya, Governor
       Miguel Armijo, Lieutenant Governor
1960   Joe Y. García, Governor
       Leo Pena, Lieutenant Governor
1961   Miguel Armijo, Governor
       Joe García, Governor
       Leo Pena, Lieutenant Governor
1962   José Rey León, Governor
       Santiago Armijo, Lieutenant Governor
1963   Porfirio Montoya, Governor
       Christo García, Lieutenant Governor
1964   Santiago Armijo, Governor
       Vicente Armijo, Lieutenant Governor
1965   Miguel Armijo, Governor
       Clyde León, Lieutenant Governor
1966   Porfirio Montoya, Governor
       Vicente Armijo, Lieutenant Governor
1967   Miguel Armijo, Governor
       Christo García, Lieutenant Governor
1968   Vicente Armijo, Lieutenant Governor
       Porfirio Montoya, Lieutenant Governor
1969   Clyde León, Governor
       Lawrence Montoya, Lieutenant Governor
1970   Vicente Armijo, Governor
       Sam Armijo, Lieutenant Governor
1971   Lawrence Montoya, Governor
       Leo Pena, Lieutenant Governor
1972   Vicente Armijo, Governor
       W. H. Gallegos, Lieutenant Governor
1973   Miguel Armijo, Governor
       Eligio Montoya, Lieutenant Governor
1974   Clyde León, Governor
       Lawrence Montoya, Lieutenant Governor
1975   Sam S. Armijo, Governor
       Leonard Armijo, Lieutenant Governor

1976   Elesio Raton, Governor
      Wilfred Tenario, Lieutenant Governor

1977   Clyde León, Governor
      Lawrence Montoya, Lieutenant Governor

1978   William H. Gallegos, Governor
      Augustine García, Lieutenant Governor

1979   Sam Armijo, Governor
      Ray P. Montoya, Lieutenant Governor

1980   Lawrence Montoya, Governor
      Louis Armijo, Lieutenant Governor

1981   Lawrence Montoya, Governor
      Louis Armijo, Lieutenant Governor

1982   Clyde León, Governor
      Roy Montoya, Lieutenant Governor

1983   Elijio Montoya, Governor
      Andres León, Lieutenant Governor

1984   Clyde C. León, Governor
      Lawrence A. Montoya, Lieutenant Governor

1985   Eliseo Raton, Sr., Governor
      Anthony Montoya, Lieutenant Governor

1986   Lawrence Montoya, Governor
      Ernest J. Lujan, Lieutenant Governor

1987   Andres León, Governor
      Arthur Menchego, Lieutenant Governor

1988   Eligio Montoya, Jr., Governor
      Leonard Armijo, Lieutenant Governor

1989   Clyde León, Governor
      Andrew A. Gallegos, Lieutenant Governor

1990   Clyde León, Governor
      Andrew A. Gallegos, Lieutenant Governor

1991   Lawrence Montoya, Sr., Governor
      Ivan Menchego, Lieutenant Governor

1992   William Henry Gallegos, Sr., Governor
      Bruce Sanchez, Lieutenant Governor

1993   Eliseo Raton, Sr., Governor
      Bennett Armijo, Lieutenant Governor

1994   Andrew A. Gallegos, Governor
      George M. Montoya, Lieutenant Governor

Notes

Abbreviations Used in the Notes

Archives

AB	Archives Branch
BAE	Bureau of American Ethnology
BIA	Bureau of Indian Affairs
FRCD	Federal Records Center, Denver, Colorado
LCMD	Library of Congress Map Division, Alexandria, Virginia
MAI, HF	Museum of the American Indian, Heye Foundation, New York, New York
MNM	Museum of New Mexico, Santa Fe, New Mexico
NA	National Archives, Washington, D.C.
NMSRCA	New Mexico State Records Center and Archives, Santa Fe, New Mexico
RG 75	Record Group 75, the Records of the Bureau of Indian Affairs
SINAA	Smithsonian Institution National Anthropological Archives, Washington, D.C.
SPA	Bureau of Indian Affairs, Southern Pueblo Agency, Albuquerque, New Mexico

Archival Collections and Files

ASBP	Alice Scoville Barry Papers
CCF	Central Classified Files
CF	Central Files

Abbreviations

CPLC	Court of Private Land Claims
df	Decimal Files
JSC	Jules Seligman Collection, University of New Mexico, Albuquerque, New Mexico
LR	Letters Received
LS	Letters Sent
MLS	Miscellaneous Letters Sent
P	Pueblo(s)
P&AA	Pueblo and Abiquiu Agency
P&JA	Pueblo and Jicarilla Agency
RF	Reference Files
SANM	Spanish Archives of New Mexico
SF	Santa Fe
SP	Southern Pueblo(s)
SPA	Southern Pueblo Agency
SP&A	Southern Pueblo and Acoma
UP	United Pueblo(s)
UPA	United Pueblo Agency

Published Government Documents

AD	Accompanying Document
AP	Accompanying Paper
ARCIA [year]	*Annual Report of the Commissioner of Indian Affairs for the year . . .*
ARSI [year]	*Annual Report of the Secretary of the Interior for the year . . .*
Cong.	Congress
GPO	Government Printing Office
HED	House Executive Document
HMD	House Miscellaneous Document
H. Rept.	House Report
ID ed.	Interior Department Edition (of the *Annual Report of the Commissioner of Indian Affairs*)
RBIC	*Report of the Board of Indian Commissioners*
SED	Senate Executive Document
sess.	session

Correspondence and Bureau of Indian Affairs Records

A(.)	Acting
ACIA	Acting Commissioner of Indian Affairs
A.Asst.	Acting Assistant

Abbreviations

A. Asst. Adj. Gen.	Acting Assistant Adjutant General
AIA	Acting Indian Agent
ACGLO	Acting Commissioner of the General Land Office
ASI	Acting Secretary of the Interior
AA	Abiquiu Agency
AC	Agency Clerk
AFR	Annual Forestry Report
Agt.	Agent
AIS	Albuquerque Indian School
Albq.	Albuquerque
Alltg. Agt.	Allotting Agent
Am.Leg.	American Legion
ARCIA [year]	Annual Report of the Commissioner of Indian Affairs for the year . . . [unpublished form]
AT&SFRR	Atchison, Topeka, and Santa Fe Railroad
ARIEW	Annual Report of the Indian Extension Worker
BCIM	Bureau of Catholic Indian Missions
BIA	Bureau [or Office] of Indian Affairs
BIC	Board of Indian Commissioners
CGLO	Commissioner of the General Land Office
CIA	Commissioner of Indian Affairs
CPLC	Court of Public Land Claims
DLALU	Division of Land Acquisition and Land Utilization
DS	Day School(s)
eo	ex officio
IA	Indian Agent
IRA	Indian Reorganization Act
IS	Indian School
AIS	Albuquerque Indian School
BIS	Bernalillo Indian School
CIS	Carlisle Indian School
LIS	Laguna Indian School
RIS	Ramona Indian School
SFIS	Santa Fe Indian School
MRGP	Middle Río Grande Pueblos
MRGCD	Middle Río Grande Conservancy District
NMS	New Mexico Superintendency
NMSIA	Superintendent of Indian Affairs for New Mexico
NPA	Northern Pueblo Agency
PA	Pueblo Agency
P&AA	Pueblo and Abiquiu Agency
P&JA	Pueblo and Jicarilla Agency

Abbreviations

PC - , p. -	Private Claim [number], parcel [number]
PDS	Pueblo Day School(s)
PIA	Pueblo Indian Agent
PLB	Pueblo Lands Board
PWA	Public Works Administration
RBIC	Report of the Board of Indian Commissioners [unpublished form]
RGCC	Río Grande Compact Commission
SA	Secretary of Agriculture
SCS	Soil Conservation Service
SD	State Department
SFNWRR	Santa Fe Northwestern Railroad
SG	Surveyor General
SI	Secretary of the Interior
SIA	Superintendent of Indian Affairs
SIS	Superintendent of Indian Schools
SLPS-RA	State Land Planning Specialist—Resettlement Administration
SPA	Southern Pueblo Agency
SP&JA	Southern Pueblo and Jicarilla Agency
Sp.IA	Special Indian Agent
Sp.IC	Special Indian Commissioner
ST	Secretary of the Treasury
StA	Santa Ana
Stat. at Lg.	Statutes at Large
Surv. Cond.	Survey of Conditions of the Indians of the United States, Hearings Before a Subcommittee on Indian Affairs
TC-BIA	Technical Cooperation—Bureau of Indian Affairs
TD	Treasury Department
WD	War Department
WUTC	Western Union Telegraph Company

Chapter 1

1. The account of Tamaya's early history presented here is based on oral tradition. For documentation the authors have drawn on a series of interviews taped in both English and Keres. Porfirio Montoya discussed that history in great detail in a series of tapes made from 16 January to 25 March 1980 (Tape nos. 2, 3, 4, 8, 12, 13, 15, and 16), Santa Ana Pueblo Oral History Project. In addition, information about early history is included in a general discussion (Tape nos. 6 and 7) between Porfirio Montoya, Elijio Montoya, Louis Armijo, Lawrence Montoya, Clyde León, Alfonso García, Albert Montoya, Vicente Armijo, Roy Montoya, Andy León, and Floyd

Montoya with the tribal lawyers, 25 January 1980, and an interview with Christo García, 4 February 1980 (Tape No. 9), Santa Ana Pueblo Oral History Project. Other Tamayame, named in individual notes below, provided information about aspects of the pueblo's later history. Finally, to ensure accuracy, knowledgeable pueblo members reviewed the drafts of this text.

Few scholars have directed their attention to the prehistory of Tamaya; their contributions are acknowledged specifically in the notes below. For a general discussion of the scientific and technical evidence pertaining to Tamaya's early history, the theories proposed to account for it, and the problems in its reconstruction see Appendix 1. Although scholars were once very skeptical of the oral tradition, today most would agree that the evidence confirms the historical accuracy of the traditions of the Tamayame and other Keres peoples, whose own accounts place their origin north and west of their present locations.

2. Michael A. Glassow, *Prehistoric Agricultural Development in the Northern Southwest: A Study in Changing Patterns of Land Use,* Ballena Press Anthropological Papers, no. 16 (Socorro, NM: Ballena Press, 1980), pp. 45–54, describes the irrigation techniques used in the prehistoric Southwest. For additional discussion of pueblo agriculture and water use, see Kirk Bryan, "Pre-Columbian Agriculture in the Southwest, as Conditioned by Periods of Alluviation," *Annals of the Association of American Geographers* 31, no. 4 (December 1941):219–42; D. Bruce Dickson, "Settlement Pattern Stability and Change in the Middle Northern Rio Grande Region, New Mexico: A Test of Some Hypotheses," *American Antiquity* 40, no. 2 (April 1975): 159–72; Guy R. Stewart, "Conservation in Pueblo Agriculture," *Scientific Monthly* 51, nos. 3 and 4 (1940): 201–20, 329–40; Guy R. Stewart and Maurice Donnelly, "Soil and Water Economy in the Pueblo Southwest," *Scientific Monthly* 56, nos. 1 and 2 (1943):31–44, 134–44; and R. Gwinn Vivian, "An Inquiry into Prehistoric Social Organization in Chaco Canyon, New Mexico," in *Reconstructing Prehistoric Pueblo Societies,* ed. William A. Longacre (Albuquerque: University of New Mexico Press, 1970), pp. 69–78, for additional discussion of pueblo agriculture and water use.

3. Marjorie F. Lambert, *Paa-ko, Archaeological Chronicle of an Indian Village in North Central New Mexico,* monograph 19, 1–5 (Santa Fe: School of American Research, 1954), p. 9. Lambert's "Paa-ko" is here designated "Paak'u." According to the evidence of pottery, Paak'u was occupied twice: once during the period from approximately A.D. 1300 to A.D. 1425, and again from approximately A.D. 1525 to A.D. 1626 or later. The later occupation was Tanoan, and Lambert suggests that the early one was also primarily Tanoan. She believes that some Keres people may have been there during the first period, and suggests that they could have introduced the red-glazed pottery from the west about A.D. 1325, following the route proposed by Erik Reed (see Appendix 1). Florence Hawley Ellis, on the other hand, believes that archaeological evidence from Paak'u confirms the Tamayame tradition. In "Anthropological Evidence Supporting the Land Claim of the Pueblos of Zia, Santa Ana, and Jemez," manuscript, University of New Mexico, Library of Anthropology, Department of

Anthropology, n.d., p. 14, Ellis states that "there is no evidence that the early occupation was Tanoan."

4. Lambert, *Paa-ko*, pp. 4–5; Linda S. Cordell, "Late Anasazi Farming and Hunting Strategies: One Example of a Problem in Congruence," *American Antiquity* 42, no. 3 (July 1977): 455–58.

5. Lambert, *Paa-ko*, pp. 3–5.

6. Ibid., p. 4; Anna O. Shepard, *Rio Grande Glaze-Paint Ware: A Study Illustrating the Place of Ceramic Technological Analysis in Archaeological Research*, Contributions to American Anthropology and History, vol. 7, no. 39 (Washington, D.C.: Carnegie Institution, 1942), p. 188, notes areas where lead was found.

7. Lambert, *Paa-ko*, pp. 3–5; Willis H. Bell and Edward F. Castetter, *The Utilization of Yucca, Sotol, and Beargrass by the Aborigines in the American Southwest*, University of New Mexico Bulletin, Biological Series, vol. 5, no. 5, Ethnological Studies in the American Southwest, no. 7 (Albuquerque: University of New Mexico Press, 1941), pp. 7–9.

8. Lambert, *Paa-ko*, pp. 145–57.

9. Ibid., pp. 39–86.

10. Ibid., pp. 48, 86–87, 110, 157–60, 179–80; in "Late Anasazi Farming and Hunting Strategies," Cordell describes the fourteenth-century settlements at San Antonito and Tijeras Pueblo, just south of Paak'u.

11. The account of the route used here differs slightly from versions cited by Ellis in "Anthropological Evidence Supporting the Land Claim," pp. 9–10, 13–14. According to that account, the split occurred somewhere in the Río Grande region, not at Paak'u. After the split, according to Ellis, some of the Tamayame traveled north to the Borrego Grant area, some remained at the Angostura Mill site, and some went south to Paak'u. In a more recent article, Ellis mentions both versions of the tradition. See Florence Hawley Ellis, "Where Did the Pueblo People Come From?" *El Palacio* 74, no. 3 (Autumn 1967): 41. To see the major differences between Ellis's version and the traditional account of the route presented here, compare the maps in Chapter 1 with those in Appendix 1.

12. Just when the Navajo reached this area is the subject of considerable scholarly debate. Ellis, in "Anthropological Evidence Supporting the Land Claim," p. 11, points to the theory that the first Navajo-Apaches arrived in the thirteenth and early fourteenth centuries and began to raid the Pueblos during this time; William D. Lipe, "The Southwest," in *Ancient Native Americans*, ed, Jesse D. Jennings (San Francisco: W. H. Freeman and Co., 1978), pp. 377–89, agrees that small groups of Athapascan-speaking people probably entered the region between A.D. 1100 and A.D. 1400, but after the Anasazi centers had been abandoned. Some scholars argue that the Navajo arrived later, about A.D. 1725. Others have recently suggested that the Navajo might have come much earlier, even as early as the ninth century. See Peter Iverson, *The Navajos: A Critical Bibliography*, Newberry Library Center for the History of the American Indian, Bibliographical Series (Bloomington and London:

Indiana University Press, 1976), pp. 12–14, for a list of sources that consider the question.

13. Paguate is a satellite settlement of Laguna. Since the Laguna also speak a Keres Language, and recent scholarship suggests that they may have occupied this area much earlier than once proposed, it is difficult to establish whether the name had its origin in the words of the Tamayame travelers. The name "Kwisti" or "Questi" for the Paguate site is mentioned in the Laguna account of the migration; see Bertha P. Dutton and Miriam A. Marmon, *The Laguna Calendar,* University of New Mexico Bulletin, Anthropological Series, vol. 1, no. 2, (Albuquerque: University of New Mexico Press, 1936), p. 21. For this portion of the journey, Ellis again describes a slightly different route. She does not mention that Paguate area, but suggests that the Tamayame followed the Río Puerco south toward Acoma. See Ellis, "Anthropological Evidence Supporting the Land Claim," p. 13.

14. Ellis, "Anthropological Evidence Supporting the Land Claim," p. 13.

15. Lambert, *Paa-ko,* pp. 9–22, 37.

16. Cordell, "Late Anasazi Farming and Hunting Strategies," p. 456; Lambert, *Paa-ko,* pp. 3–4.

17. Ellis, "Anthropological Evidence Supporting the Land Claim," pp. 13–16, summarizes the traditional account of the Tamayame's first journey through the Río Grande region and lists the sites occupied there during this period. She identifies these sites as Keres / Santa Ana primarily on the basis of a pottery sequence that differs significantly from that in neighboring Tiwa sites; she also mentions the Tamayame oral traditions that tell how the people settled along the Río Grande. For further discussion of these pottery types, the occupation of Río Grande Keres sites, and the traditional attribution of this area to the Tiwa, see Appendix 1.

18. Ellis, "Anthropological Evidence Supporting the Land Claim," pp. 15–16.

19. Ibid,. p. 13; Lambert, *Paa-ko,* p. 9.

20. Just how the Tamayame moved from Kwiiste Haa Tamaya to the modern site of Tamaya has not been established. Archaeology suggests that the people of Tamaya occupied a number of sites on the west bank of the Río Jémez, north of its junction with the Río Grande. Bandelier and others have identified a site on the Black Mesa that was probably occupied by the Tamayame during the early Spanish period. H. P. Mera, *Population Changes in the Rio Grande Glaze-Paint Area,* Archaeological Survey, Technical Series Bulletin no. 9, (Santa Fe: Laboratory of Anthropology, 1940), pp. 26–27 and Maps of Keres Division, periods 4 and 5, identifies a site on a mesa north of the junction of the Río Grande and the Jémez known as Laboratory of Anthropology (hereafter cited as LA) 2049. He notes that some Santa Ana people stated that the Tamayame had occupied this site in the late seventeenth century. Ellis, "Anthropological Evidence Supporting the Land Claim," p. 16, believes, on the evidence of pottery samples, that this site was settled by the Tamayame about A.D. 1515. When Tamaya was established in its present location is also unclear. The accounts of Coronado and other early Spanish explorers mention the presence of

Keres-speaking peoples in the region, but do not provide enough detail to identify any of the Santa Ana sites. The first specific mention of Tamaya, found in the records of the Oñate expedition of 1598, probably referred to a site on the Black Mesa described by Bandelier as halfway between Santa Ana and San Felipe. See Adolph Bandelier, *Final Report of Investigations Among the Indians of the Southwestern United States Carried on Mainly in the Years from 1880 to 1885*, Archaeological Institute of America Papers, American Series, no. 4, (Cambridge: John Wilson and Son, University Press, 1892) pt. 2, pp. 193–94. It is possible that the modern site of the pueblo was not occupied until a century or more after the Oñate expedition, and that even then not all of the Tamayame were living there (see Chapter 2).

Chapter 2

1. "Report of Fray Marcos de Niza, August 26, 1539," in *Narratives of the Coronado Expedition, 1540–1542*, ed. George P. Hammond and Agapito Rey (Albuquerque: University of New Mexico Press, 1940), p. 79 and passim.

2. "Muster Roll of the Expedition, Compostela, February 22, 1540," in Hammond and Rey, *Narratives*, pp. 87–109; "Introduction," in ibid., pp. 7–8; Herbert Eugene Bolton, *Coronado on the Turquoise Trail: Knight of the Pueblos and Plains* (1949: reprint, Albuquerque: University of New Mexico Press, 1964), pp. 68–69.

3. "Introduction," in Hammond and Rey, *Narratives*, pp. 9–12.

4. Ibid., p. 15.

5. "Castañeda's History of the Expedition," in Hammond and Rey, *Narratives*, pp. 254–55; "Jaramillo's Narrative," in Hammond and Rey, *Narratives*, p. 300.

6. "Introduction," in Hammond and Rey, *Narratives*, pp. 15–17.

7. "Traslado de las Nuevas: Transcript of the Information and News They Furnished Concerning the Finding of a City, Which They Named Cíbola, Located in the New Land," in Hammond and Rey, *Narratives*, p. 181.

8. "Introduction," in Hammond and Rey, *Narratives*, pp. 17–18.

9. "Letter of Coronado to Mendoza, August 3, 1540," Hammond and Rey, *Narratives*, pp. 173–74.

10. "Coronado's Testimony Concerning the Expedition," Hammond and Rey, *Narratives*, pp. 324–25.

11. Ibid.; "Castañeda's History," in Hammond and Rey, *Narratives*, p. 217.

12. "Castañeda's History," in Hammond and Rey, *Narratives*, p. 218; Bolton, *Coronado*, pp. 182–83.

13. Bolton, *Coronado*, pp. 184–85; "Discovery of Tiguex by Alvarado and Padilla," in Hammond and Rey, *Narratives*, p. 183. The latter report, often attributed to Alvarado, might have been written by Padilla; see ibid., p. 329, n. 14.

14. "Discovery of Tiguex," in Hammond and Rey, *Narratives*, p. 183.

15. "Castañeda's History," in Hammond and Rey, *Narratives*, p. 219.

16. "Coronado's Testimony," in Hammond and Rey, *Narratives*, p. 326; "Testi-

mony of López de Cárdenas," in Hammond and Rey, *Narratives*, p. 347; Bolton, *Coronado*, p. 193.

17. Bolton, *Coronado*, pp. 179–92.

18. "Castañeda's History," in Hammond and Rey, *Narratives*, pp. 220–21.

19. Ibid., pp. 223, 254–55; "Coronado's Testimony," in Hammond and Rey, *Narratives*, pp. 328–29; "Jaramillo's Narrative," in Hammond and Rey, *Narratives*, p. 300.

20. "Castañeda's History," in Hammond and Rey, *Narratives*, pp. 254–55; "Jaramillo's Narrative," in Hammond and Rey, *Narratives*, p. 300.

21. "Coronado's Testimony," in Hammond and Rey, *Narratives*, pp. 329–30.

22. "Castañeda's History," in Hammond and Rey, *Narratives*, p. 224.

23. "Testimony of López de Cárdenas," in Hammond and Rey, *Narratives*, p. 351.

24. Ibid., pp. 348–49, 351–52; "Castañeda's History," in Hammond and Rey, *Narratives*, pp. 224–25; Jack D. Forbes, *Apache, Navajo, and Spaniard* (Norman: University of Oklahoma Press, 1960), pp. 7–8, argues that knowledge of the Spaniards was widespread among the Indians between Sonora and New Mexico by 1539 because of slave raids and the activities of Nuño de Guzmán. Forbes suggests that as a result, the Indians had already developed a "basic antagonism" toward the Spaniards, and that "this prejudice may well have extended to New Mexico." He also suggests that the Zuñi recruited "aid from neighboring peoples" when the Spaniards approached Hawíkuh.

25. "Discovery of Tiguex," in Hammond and Rey, *Narratives*, p. 183.

26. "Testimony of López de Cárdenas," in Hammond and Rey, *Narratives*, p. 348.

27. "Castañeda's History," in Hammond and Rey, *Narratives*, pp. 226–27; "Coronado's Testimony," in Hammond and Rey, *Narratives*, p. 333; "Testimony of López de Cárdenas," Hammond and Rey, *Narratives*, p. 353. Scholars differ about the number of casualties at Arenal. Hammond and Rey, *Narratives*, p. 227, n. 5, suggest that Castañeda's figures were "exaggerated" and that the total number of prisoners was about eighty. Both Forbes, *Apache, Navajo, and Spaniard*, p. 13, and Edward H. Spicer, *Cycles of Conquest: The Impact of Spain, Mexico, and the United States on the Indians of the Southwest, 1533–1960* (Tucson: University of Arizona Press, 1962), p. 155. place the total at "hundreds." Bolton, *Coronado*, describes the events, pp. 201–13, and reports, p. 230, that Cardeñas was "charged with burning only thirty Indians" at Arenal; he argues that altogether "eighty or more" were killed and several hundred captured.

28. "Castañeda's History," in Hammond and Rey, *Narratives*, p. 227; "Testimony of López de Cárdenas," in Hammond and Rey, *Narratives*, p. 358.

29. "Castañeda's History," in Hammond and Rey, *Narratives*, pp. 228–29; "Coronado's Testimony," in Hammond and Rey, *Narratives*, pp. 333–34; Bolton, *Coronado*, pp. 216–30.

30. "Castañeda's History," in Hammond and Rey, *Narratives*, p. 233; "Coronado's Testimony," in Hammond and Rey, *Narratives*, p. 330.

31. "Castañada's History," in Hammond and Rey, *Narratives*, pp. 233–34.

32. "Coronado's Testimony," in Hammond and Rey, *Narratives*, pp. 329–30; Bolton, *Coronado*, p. 225.

33. "Castañeda's History," in Hammond and Rey, *Narratives*, p. 233.

34. Ibid.

35. Ibid., pp. 234–35, 240–41, 244.

36. Ibid., pp. 244–45.

37. Ibid., p. 241.

38. Ibid., p. 265.

39. "Relation del Suceso: Relation of the Events of the Expedition that Francisco Vázquez Made to the Discovery of Cíbola," in Hammond and Rey, *Narratives*, p. 294.

40. "Castañeda's History," in Hammond and Rey, *Narratives*, p. 265.

41. Ibid., pp. 266–71; Bolton, *Coronado*, pp. 317–54.

42. Florence Hawley Ellis, "Anthropological Evidence Supporting the Land Claim of the Pueblos of Zia, Santa Ana, and Jemez," manuscript, University of New Mexico, n.d., pp. 13–16, argues that between A.D. 1450 and A.D. 1650 Santa Ana occupied six sites along the Río Grande and within the boundaries of the Tiguex, or Tiwa, Province. She lists Coffman, SDA, Gonzales (LA 280), and LA 1844, all in the Corrales region, and Puaray II (LA 728) and Angostura Mill, to the north near Bernalillo, as Santa Ana sites. She adds, pp. 45–46, that the "Spanish identification of all this area as the Tiguex province, with the implication that its inhabitants were of the Tiwa tribe, obviously is incorrect, for the Tiwas are known to have" made a different kind of pottery than that found in these sites.

43. Ellis, in ibid., p. 16, notes that the site on the southeastern corner of Santa Ana Mesa (LA 2049) was built about A.D. 1515. Adolph J. Bandelier, *Final Report of Investigations among the Indians of the Southwestern Unites States Carried on Mainly in the Years from 1880 to 1885*, Archaeological Institute of America Papers, American series no. 4, pt. 2 (Cambridge: John Wilson and Son, University Press, 1892) pp. 193–94, described the site on Black Mesa, noting that the ruins were on "a considerable elevation" midway between Santa Ana and San Felipe. Scholars have not established the date when Tamaya itself was founded. The village described by Oñate in 1598 as Tamy or Tamaya could have been located either at the modern site or at the Black Mesa site. Ellis, in "Anthropological Evidence Supporting the Land Claim," p. 23, speculates that Santa Ana people moved to the main pueblo site in the seventeenth century as a result of Spanish pressure and that, during this period, "LA 2049 and perhaps a number of small pueblos probably lost their inhabitants" to Tamaya itself, but the Corrales sites and Puaray II were still occupied.

Chapter 3

1. The records of the Oñate expedition provide the most detailed primary accounts of pueblo life during this period. See "Investigation of Conditions in New Mexico,

1601," in *Don Juan de Oñate: Colonizer of New Mexico, 1595–1628,* ed. George P. Hammond and Agapito Rey (Albuquerque: University of New Mexico Press, 1953), pp. 623–69; "Report of the People Who Remained in New Mexico, 1601," in Hammond and Rey, *Oñate,* pp. 710–39; and "Inquiry Concerning the New Provinces in the North, 1602," in Hammond and Rey, *Oñate,* pp. 836–77. Three articles by Albert H. Schroeder discuss the location of the pueblos, Navajos, Apaches, and Caddoan Teyas in the sixteenth century and the trade and relations between pueblo and non-pueblo groups during this period. See Schroeder, "Shifting for Survival in the Spanish Southwest," in *New Spain's Far Northern Frontier: Essays on Spain in the American West, 1540–1821,* ed. David J. Weber (Albuquerque: University of New Mexico Press, 1979), pp. 239–42; idem, "Navajo and Apache Relationships West of the Rio Grande," *El Palacio* 70 (Autumn 1963): 5–7; and idem, "Rio Grande Ethnohistory," in *New Perspectives on the Pueblos,* ed. Alfonso Ortiz (Albuquerque: University of New Mexico Press, 1972), pp. 49–50.

2. Schroeder, "Rio Grande Ethnohistory," p. 44; James Schoenwetter and Alfred E. Dittert, Jr., "An Ecological Interpretation of Anasazi Settlement Patterns," in *Anthropological Archaeology in the Americas,* ed. B. J. Meggars (Washington D.C.: Anthropological Society of Washington, 1968), p. 58. Information about climatic change is drawn from tree-ring studies and from the records of Spanish explorers who visited the region in the late sixteenth century. Where Coronado had found well-watered lands with abundant crops, later explorers reported recurring drought, poor harvest, and crops destroyed by frost.

3. "Introduction," in *The Rediscovery of New Mexico, 1580–1594: The Explorations of Chamuscado, Espejo, Castaño de Sosa, Morlete, and Leyva de Bonilla and Humaña,* ed. George P. Hammond and Agapito Rey (Albuquerque: University of New Mexico Press, 1966), pp. 6–8.

4. Ibid., p. 8; "Gallegos' Relation of the Chamuscado-Rodríguez Expedition," in Hammond and Rey, *Rediscovery,* pp. 67–68; "Testimony of Hernando Gallegos, May 16, 1582," in Hammond and Rey, *Rediscovery,* p. 134.

5. "Gallegos' Relation," in Hammond and Rey, *Rediscovery,* p. 72.

6. Ibid., p. 76.

7. Ibid., p. 79.

8. Ibid., pp. 85–86.

9. Ibid., p. 85.

10. Ibid., p. 83.

11. Ibid., p. 85.

12. Ibid., p. 86.

13. "Testimony of Hernando Gallegos," in Hammond and Rey, *Rediscovery,* p. 135; "Testimony of Pedro de Bustamante, May 16, 1582," in Hammond and Rey, *Rediscovery,* p. 130.

14. "Pedrosa's List of Pueblos," in Hammond and Rey, *Rediscovery,* pp. 117–18; Albert H. Schroeder, "Pueblos Abandoned in Historic Times," in *Southwest,* ed.

Alfonso Ortiz, vol. 9 of *Handbook of North American Indians,* ed. William C. Sturtevant (Washington, D.C.: Smithsonian Institution, 1979), pp. 244–45.

15. "Testimony of Pedro de Bustamante," in Hammond and Rey, *Rediscovery,* p. 130; "Testimony of Hernando Gallegos," in Hammond and Rey, *Rediscovery,* p. 135.

16. "Introduction," in Hammond and Rey, *Rediscovery,* pp. 12–13; "Gallegos' Relation," in Hammond and Rey, *Rediscovery,* pp. 86–93.

17. "Gallegos' Relation," in Hammond and Rey, *Rediscovery,* p. 94.

18. Ibid., p. 95.

19. Ibid., p. 99.

20. "Fathers López and Rodríguez Remain at Puaray, February 13, 1582," in Hammond and Rey, *Rediscovery,* p. 125.

21. "Gallegos' Relation," in Hammond and Rey, *Rediscovery,* pp. 108–10; "Testimony of Hernando Gallegos," in Hammond and Rey, *Rediscovery,* p. 137.

22. "Testimony of Hernando Gallegos," in Hammond and Rey, *Rediscovery,* p. 138; "Testimony of Pedro de Bustamante," in Hammond and Rey, *Rediscovery,* p. 143.

23. "Brief and True Account of the Discovery of New Mexico by Nine Men Who Set Out from Santa Bárbara in the Company of Three Franciscan Friars," in Hammond and Rey, *Rediscovery,* p. 143.

24. "Testimony of Hernando Barrado, October 12, 1582," in Hammond and Rey, *Rediscovery,* p. 140.

25. "Introduction," in Hammond and Rey, *Rediscovery,* pp. 15–19; "Report of Antonio de Espejo," in Hammond and Rey, *Rediscovery,* pp. 213–14.

26. "Introduction," in Hammond and Rey, *Rediscovery,* pp. 22–23; "Diego Pérez de Luxán's Account of the Espejo Expedition into New Mexico, 1582," in Hammond and Rey, *Rediscovery,* pp. 174–77.

27. "Diego Pérez de Luxán's Account," in Hammond and Rey, *Rediscovery,* p. 177.

28. Ibid., p. 178.

29. "Report of Antonio de Espejo," in Hammond and Rey, *Rediscovery,* p. 221.

30. "Diego Pérez de Luxán's Account," in Hammond and Rey, *Rediscovery,* p. 178.

31. Ibid., p. 179.

32. "Report of Antonio de Espejo," in Hammond and Rey, *Rediscovery,* p. 223.

33. "Diego Pérez de Luxán's Account," in Hammond and Rey, *Rediscovery,* p. 179.

34. Ibid., p. 180.

35. "Report of Antonio de Espejo," in Hammond and Rey, *Rediscovery,* p. 223.

36. Ibid., pp. 225–26; "Diego Pérez de Luxán's Account," in Hammond and Rey, *Rediscovery,* pp. 198–99.

37. "Diego Pérez de Luxán's Account," in Hammond and Rey, *Rediscovery,* p. 199.

38. Ibid., p. 203.

39. Ibid., p. 204.

40. Ibid., p. 223.

41. Ibid., pp. 205–12; "Report of Antonio de Espejo," in Hammond and Rey, *Rediscovery,* p. 229.

42. "Report of Antonio de Espejo," in Hammond and Rey, *Rediscovery*, pp. 230–31.

43. "Introduction," in Hammond and Rey, *Rediscovery*, pp. 28–50.

44. Albert H. Schroeder and Dan S. Matson, *A Colony on the Move: Gaspar Castaño de Sosa's Journal, 1590–1591* (Santa Fe: School of American Research, 1965), pp. 11–12.

45. Ibid., pp. 14–15, 140–41; "Castaño de Sosa's 'Memoria,'" in Hammond and Rey, *Rediscovery*, pp. 285–86. Schroeder and Matson believe these four pueblos were at Cochití; Dorothy Hull, "Castaño de Sosa's Expedition to New Mexico in 1590," ed. Charles Wilson Hackett, *Old Santa Fe* 3, no. 12 (October 1916): 327, suggests that they were in the area of Santo Domingo.

46. "Castaño de Sosa's 'Memoria,'" in Hammond and Rey, *Rediscovery*, p. 290.

47. Ibid., pp. 291–92.

48. Ibid., p. 293.

49. Ibid., p. 294.

50. "Instructions to Captain Juan Morlete for an Expedition to New Mexico in Pursuit of Gaspar Castaño de Sosa and His Companions," in Hammond and Rey, *Rediscovery*, pp. 298–300; "Don Luis Velasco to the King, February 23, 1591," in Hammond and Rey, *Rediscovery*, pp. 301–2.

51. "Fragment of a Letter from Juan Morlete to Viceroy Don Luis de Velasco, July 25, 1591," in Hammond and Rey, *Rediscovery*, p. 303.

52. "Introduction," in Hammond and Rey, *Rediscovery*, pp. 48–50; "Account Given by an Indian of the Flight of Leyva and Humaña from New Mexico," in Hammond and Rey, *Rediscovery*, pp. 323–26.

53. "Inspection Made by Juan de Frías Salazar of the Expedition, September 1597 to February 1598," in Hammond and Rey, *Oñate*, pp. 221–23.

54. "Act of Taking Possession of New Mexico, April 30, 1598," in Hammond and Rey, *Oñate*, p. 330.

55. Ibid., p. 335.

56. "Record of Marches by the Army, New Spain to New Mexico, 1596–98," in Hammond and Rey, *Oñate*, p. 319.

57. "An Act of Obedience and Vassalage by the Indians of Santo Domingo, July 7, 1598," in Hammond and Rey, *Oñate*, pp. 337–39.

58. Schroeder, "Pueblos Abandoned in Historic Times," identifies the pueblos by language group. See also F. W. Hodge, "Pueblo Names in the Oñate Documents," in Hammond and Rey, *Oñate*, pp. 363–75.

59. "An Act of Obedience and Vassalage," in Hammond and Rey, *Oñate*, pp. 337–41.

60. Hammond and Rey, in *Oñate*, pp. 342–63, also include the acts of obedience at San Juan Bautista, Acolocu, Cueloze, Acoma, Zuñi, and Mohoqui.

61. "Introduction," in Hammond and Rey, *Oñate*, p. 17.

62. "Act of Obedience and Vassalage by the Indians of San Juan Bautista, September 9, 1598," in Hammond and Rey, *Oñate*, p. 346.

63. Ibid., p. 347.

64. "Introduction," Hammond and Rey, *Oñate*, pp. 18–19.

65. "Letter from Alonso Sanchez, Treasurer of New Mexico, to Rodrigo Rio de Losa, Knight of Santiago, February 28, 1599," in Hammond and Rey, *Oñate*, p. 425.

66. "Trial of the Indians of the Pueblo of Acoma for Having Wantonly Killed the Maese de Campo, Don Juan de Zaldívar, Two Captains, Eight Soldiers, and Two Servants, and for Other Offenses, December 1598 to February 1599," in Hammond and Rey, *Oñate*, pp. 456–64, 477–78.

67. "Introduction," in Hammond and Rey, *Oñate*, p. 29; "Proceedings of the Lieutenant Governor of New Mexico with Regard to Breaking Camp, September 7, 1601," in Hammond and Rey, *Oñate*, pp. 627–89.

68. Ibid., p. 684.

69. "Investigation Made by Don Francisco de Valverde by Order of the Viceroy, Count of Monterrey, Regarding Conditions in New Mexico, July 1601," in Hammond and Rey, *Oñate*, pp. 628, 637, 648, 663.

70. Ibid., p. 657; "Captain Luis Gasco de Velasco to the Viceroy on Conditions in New Mexico, March 22, 1601," in Hammond and Rey, *Oñate*, p. 610.

71. "Fray Juan de Escalona to the Viceroy, October 1, 1601," in Hammond and Rey, *Oñate*, p. 696.

72. "Investigation Made by Don Francisco de Valverde," in Hammond and Rey, *Oñate*, p. 657.

73. "True Report Drawn from the Letters, Statements, and Papers which Governor Don Juan de Oñate Enclosed with His Letter of March 22, 1601, Addressed to His Brothers and Relatives," in Hammond and Rey, *Oñate*, p. 619.

74. "Report of the Loyal Colonists Who Remained in New Mexico, October 2, 1601," in Hammond and Rey, *Oñate*, pp. 706, 709, 711–12, 716, 720, 724, 727–28, 734; "Official Inquiry Made by the Factor, Don Francisco de Valverde, by Order of the Count of Monterrey Concerning the New Discovery Undertaken by Governor Don Juan de Oñate toward the North Beyond the Provinces of New Mexico, April 1602," in Hammond and Rey, *Oñate*, pp. 850, 861.

75. "Captain Luis Gasco de Velasco to the Viceroy," in Hammond and Rey, *Oñate*, p. 610.

76. "Investigation Made by Don Francisco de Valverde," in Hammond and Rey, *Oñate*, pp. 654, 667.

77. "Proceedings of the Lieutenant Governor of New Mexico with Regard to Breaking Camp, September 7, 1601," in Hammond and Rey, *Oñate*, pp. 675–76.

78. "Captain Luis Gasco de Velasco to the Viceroy," in Hammond and Rey, *Oñate*, pp. 613–14.

79. "Proceedings of the Lieutenant Governor of New Mexico," in Hammond and Rey, *Oñate*, pp. 675–76.

80. Ibid.; "Captain Luis Gasco de Velasco to the Viceroy," in Hammond and Rey, *Oñate*, p. 610.

81. "Fray Juan de Escalona to the Viceroy," in Hammond and Rey, *Oñate,* p. 693.

82. "Captain Luis Gasco de Velasco to the Viceroy," in Hammond and Rey, *Oñate,* p. 615.

83. "Proceedings of the Lieutenant Governor of New Mexico," in Hammond and Rey, *Oñate,* pp. 675–76.

84. "Discussions and Proposal of the Points Referred to his Majesty Concerning the Various Discoveries of New Mexico," in Hammond and Rey, *Oñate,* p. 911.

85. "Don Alonso de Oñate to the King," in Hammond and Rey, *Oñate,* pp. 969–70.

86. "Discussions and Proposal of the Points Referred to His Majesty," in Hammond and Rey, *Oñate,* p. 912.

87. "The Marquis of Montesclaros to the King, March 31, 1605," in Hammond and Rey, *Oñate,* pp. 1001–2.

88. "Resignation of Don Juan de Oñate as Governor of New Mexico, August 24, 1607," in Hammond and Rey, *Oñate,* pp. 1042–45.

89. "Oñate Resignation Accepted, February 27, 1608," in Hammond and Rey, *Oñate,* pp. 1048–49; "Don Luis Velasco to the King, December 17, 1608," in Hammond and Rey, *Oñate,* pp. 1067–68; "Viceroy Velasco to the King, February 3, 1609," in Hammond and Rey, *Oñate,* p. 1080.

90. "New Mexico to be Maintained: Decree Regarding What Fathers Fray Lázaro Ximénez and Fray Ysidro Ordóñez Have Been Ordered to Take to New Mexico, January 29, 1609," in Hammond and Rey, *Oñate,* 1076–77; "The King to the Viceroy, 1609," in Hammond and Rey, *Oñate,* pp. 1078–79.

91. Florence Hawley Ellis, "Anthropological Evidence Supporting the Land Claims of the Pueblos of Zia, Santa Ana, and Jemez," manuscript, University of New Mexico, n.d., pp. 15–16.

92. Ibid., p. 16; H. P. Mera, *Population Changes in the Rio Grande Glaze-Paint Area,* Archaeological Survey Technical Series Bulletin, no. 9. (Santa Fe: Laboratory of Anthropology, 1940), pp. 26–27.

93. Ellis, "Anthropological Evidence Supporting the Land Claim," p. 16.

94. Adolph J. Bandelier, *Final Report of Investigations among the Indians of the Southwestern United States Carried on Mainly in the Years from 1880 to 1885,* Archaeological Institute of America Papers, American Series, no. 4, pt. 2 (Cambridge: John Wilson and Son, University Press, 1892), pp. 193–94.

95. Schroeder, "Pueblos Abandoned in Historic Times," pp. 244–45; "Gallegos' Relation," in Hammond and Rey, *Rediscovery,* p. 105 and note 12.

96. Ellis, "Anthropological Evidence Supporting the Land Claim," p. 16.

97. "Diego Pérez de Luxán's Account," in Hammond and Rey, *Rediscovery,* p. 204, n. 119–23.

98. Ibid.; Schroeder, "Pueblos Abandoned in Historic Times," pp. 244–45.

99. "Diego Pérez de Luxán's Account," in Hammond and Rey, *Rediscovery,* p. 204, n. 119–23.

100. Ibid.; Ellis, "Anthropological Evidence Supporting the Land Claims," p. 19,

suggests that La Milpa Llana was Santo Domingo; Schroeder, "Pueblos Abandoned in Historic Times," pp. 244–45, identifies Tipoliti as Gipuy (LA 182); the "Enrico Martinez Map of 1602," Hammond and Rey, *Rediscovery,* endpapers, frontispiece, and errata sheet, places the pueblo of "Tepotin," which Schroeder believes was the same as "Tipolti," in the region of Santo Domingo.

101. "Report of Antonio de Espejo," in Hammond and Rey, *Rediscovery,* p. 223.

102. "An Act of Obedience and Vassalage by the Indians of Santo Domingo," in Hammond and Rey, *Oñate,* p. 337; Schroeder, "Pueblos Abandoned in Historic Times," p. 245.

103. "An Act of Obedience and Vassalage by the Indians of San Juan Bautista," in Hammond and Rey, *Oñate,* p. 346; Schroeder, "Pueblos Abandoned in Historic Times," p. 245; Ellis, "Anthropological Evidence Supporting the Land Claims," p. 21, suggests that the towns listed after Tamaya were smaller Santa Ana settlements.

104. "Record of the Marches by the Army," in Hammond and Rey, *Oñate,* p. 321.

105. "Enrico Martínez Map of 1602," in Hammond and Rey, *Rediscovery,* end-papers, frontispiece, and errata sheet; also printed in Herbert Eugene Bolton, *Spanish Exploration in the Southwest, 1542–1706* (New York: Charles Scribner's Sons, 1916), following p. 212.

106. "The Fiscal's Opinion on New Mexico, May 14, 1602," in Hammond and Rey, *Oñate,* p. 897.

Chapter 4

1. Albert H. Schroeder, "Rio Grande Ethnohistory," in *New Perspectives,* ed. Alfonso Ortiz (Albuquerque: University of New Mexico Press, 1972), pp. 51–56; Erik K. Reed, "Transition to History in the Pueblo Southwest," *American Anthropologist* 56, no. 4., pt. 1 (August 1954): 594–95; Edward H. Spicer, "Spanish-Indian Acculturation in the Southwest," *American Anthropologist* 56, no. 4., pt. 1 (August 1954): 667–68, 670; Nancy Fox, *Pueblo Weaving and Textile Arts,* Museum of New Mexico Press Guidebooks, no. 3 (Santa Fe: Museum of New Mexico Press, 1978), p. 83.

2. "New Mexico to Be Reinforced, March 5, 1609," in *Don Juan de Oñate: Colonizer of New Mexico, 1595–1628,* ed. George P. Hammond and Agapito Rey (Albuquerque: University of New Mexico Press, 1953), pp. 1082–83; "Appointment of Don Pedro de Peralta as Governor of New Mexico, March 30, 1609," in Hammond and Rey, *Oñate,* pp. 1084–86.

3. "Instructions to Don Pedro de Peralta, Who Has Been Appointed Governor and Captain General of the Provinces of New Mexico in Place of Don Juan de Oñate, Who Has Resigned the Said Offices, March 30, 1609," in Hammond and Rey, *Oñate,* pp. 1087–91; the passages quoted are from p. 1090.

4. Ward Alan Minge, "Outline for History of Santa Ana Pueblo During Spanish and Mexican Periods," manuscript, December 1980, Santa Ana Tribal Archive, pp. 16–18; France V. Scholes, *Church and State in New Mexico, 1610–1650* (n. p.:

Historical Society of New Mexico, 1950), cited in Minge, "Outline"; Marc Simmons, *Spanish Government in New Mexico* (Albuquerque: University of New Mexico Press, 1968), pp. 66–67, 81, 112, 188–89.

5. Frederick Webb Hodge, George P. Hammond, and Agapito Rey, eds., *Fray Alonso de Benavides' Revised Memorial of 1634* (Albuquerque: University of New Mexico Press, 1945), p. 2; Cyprian J. Lynch, "Introduction," *Benavides' Memorial of 1630*, trans. Peter P. Forrestal, Documentary Series, vol. 2 (Washington, D.C.: Academy of Franciscan History, 1954), p. xx; Edward H. Spicer, *Cycles of Conquest: The Impact of Spain, Mexico, and the United States on the Indians of the Southwest, 1533–1960* (Tucson: University of Arizona Press, 1962), p. 293.

6. Spicer, *Cycles of Conquest,* pp. 288–93.

7. Scholes, *Church and State,* pp. 151, 154–55; Lansing B. Bloom, "Instructions to Eulate," *New Mexico Historical Review* 3 (1928): 357–80, and 5 (1928): 288–98. For a discussion of the problems that led to these decrees, see also Warren A. Beck, *New Mexico: A History of Four Centuries* (Norman: University of Oklahoma Press, 1962), pp. 64–69, and Clive D. Hallenbeck, *Land of the Conquistadores* (Caldwell, Idaho: Caxton Printers, 1950), pp. 88–100.

8. Bloom, "Instructions to Eulate," pp. 357–80, 288–98; Scholes, *Church and State,* pp. 151, 154–55; Spicer, *Cycles of Conquest,* p. 302.

9. Ibid.

10. Beck, *New Mexico,* pp. 62–63; Hallenbeck, *Land of the Conquistadores,* pp. 186–91; France V. Scholes, "The Supply Service of the New Mexico Missions in the Seventeenth Century," *New Mexico Historical Review* 5, nos. 1, 2, and 4 (1930): 94.

11. Scholes, "Supply Service," pp. 100–105; for a sample listing of the supplies sent with one caravan, see "Supplies for Benavides and Companions Going to New Mexico, 1624–1626," in Hodge et al., *Benavides' Revised Memorial,* pp. 109–24.

12. "Supplies for Benavides," in Hodge et al., *Benavides,* pp. 109–24.

13. Ibid.

14. "New Mexico to Be Maintained," in Hammond and Rey, *Oñate,* p. 1076.

15. Lynch, "Introduction," in Forrestal, *Benavides' Memorial of 1630,* p. 24 and n. 50; Hallenbeck, *Land of the Conquistadores,* pp. 103–6; Marc Simmons, "Settlement Patterns and Village Plans in Colonial New Mexico," in *New Spain's Far Northern Frontier: Essays on Spain in the American West, 1540–1821,* ed. David J. Weber (Albuquerque: University of New Mexico Press, 1979), pp. 58–59, 65.

16. *Relaciones by Zarate Salmeron,* Alicia Ronstadt Milich, trans. (Albuquerque: Horn and Wallace Publishers, 1966), pp. 13–14, 26; Hodge et al., *Benavides' Revised Memorial,* p. 263, n. 77, states that Bandelier said that Tamaya was a visita of Zía "in 1614, circa 1641, 1663, and 1782 . . . . It is not certain that a separate convent was ever established there, its usual status being that of a *visita* of Sia."

17. "The Queres Nation," in Forrestal, *Benavides' Memorial of 1630,* pp. 20–21; the version quoted here is from the revised edition of 1634 in Hodge et al., *Benavides' Revised Memorial,* p. 65.

18. Hodge et al., *Benavides' Revised Memorial,* pp. 258–63, n. 77.

19. Interview with Porfirio Montoya, Donna Pino, Floyd Montoya, and Tom Leubben, February 4, 1980, Santa Ana Pueblo Oral History Project, tape no. 8, p. 8.

20. Scholes, *Church and State;* Beck, *New Mexico,* pp. 64–74; Hallenbeck, *Land of the Conquistadores,* pp. 103–42; Spicer, *Cycles of Conquest,* pp. 158–61; Jack D. Forbes, *Apache, Navaho, and Spaniard* (Norman: University of Oklahoma Press, 1960), pp. 113–76.

21. Forbes, *Apache, Navaho, and Spaniard,* pp. 113–76.

22. Scholes, cited in Minge, "Outline," p. 22.

23. Marc Simmons, *New Mexico: A Bicentennial History* (New York: W. W. Norton and Co., 1977) p. 65; Schroeder, "Rio Grande Ethnohistory," p. 54.

24. Spicer, *Cycles of Conquest,* p. 161.

25. Ibid., p. 162; Simmons, *New Mexico,* p. 65.

26. Schroeder, "Rio Grande Ethnohistory," p. 55; Forbes, *Apache, Navaho and Spaniard,* p. 139; Spicer, *Cycles of Conquest,* p. 169.

27. Spicer, *Cycles of Conquest,* p. 169; Florence Hawley Ellis, "Anthropological Evidence Supporting the Land Claim of the Pueblos of Zía, Santa Ana, and Jémez," manuscript, University of New Mexico, n.d., pp. 55–56.

28. Beck, *New Mexico,* p. 74; Hallenbeck, *Land of the Conquistadores,* pp. 138–42; Charles Wilson Hackett, *Revolt of the Pueblo Indians of New Mexico and Otermín's Attempted Reconquest, 1680–1682,* pt. I, trans. Charmion Clair Shelby (Albuquerque: University of New Mexico Press, 1942), pp. lv–lvi.

29. Hackett, *Revolt of the Pueblo Indians,* pt. I, p. xlviii.

30. Ibid., pp. xxiv–xxviii.

31. "Opinion of Luis Granillo, Place Opposite El Socorro, August 26, 1680," in Hackett, *Revolt of the Pueblo Indians,* pt. I, p. 80.

32. "Auto of Alonso Garcia, La Isleta, August 14, 1680," in Hackett, *Revolt of the Pueblo Indians,* pt. I, p. 68.

33. "Opinion of Luis Granillo, in Hackett, *Revolt of the Pueblo Indians,* pt. I, p. 80.

34. "Notification and Arrest," in Hackett, *Revolt of the Pueblo Indians,* pt. I, p. 63.

35. "Opinion of Luis Granillo," in Hackett, *Revolt of the Pueblo Indians,* pt. I, p. 80.

36. "Auto of Alonso Garcia," in Hackett, *Revolt of the Pueblo Indians,* pt. I, p. 66.

37. Ibid., pp. 66–67; "Opinion of Luis Granillo," in Hackett, *Revolt of the Pueblo Indians,* pt. I, p. 81.

38. "Opinion of Luis Granillo," in Hackett, *Revolt of the Pueblo Indians,* pt. I, p. 81.

39. "Notification and Arrest," in Hackett, *Revolt of the Pueblo Indians,* pt. I, p. 64.

40. "Opinion of Luis Granillo," in Hackett, *Revolt of the Pueblo Indians,* pt. I, p. 81.

41. "Letter of the Governor and Captain-General, Don Antonio de Otermín, from New Mexico [to Fray Francisco de Ayeta], in which He Gives Him a Full Account of What Has Happened to Him Since the Day the Indians Surrounded Him," in Hackett, *Revolt of the Pueblo Indians,* pt. I, pp. 100–101.

42. Ibid., pp. 100–105; "Letter of the Very Reverend Father Custodian, Fray

Francisco de Ayeta [to the Most Excellent Señor Viceroy, El Paso, September 11, 1680]," in Hackett, *Revolt of the Pueblo Indians,* pt. 1, pp. 106–8; "List and Memorial of the Religious Whom the Indians of New Mexico Have Killed [1680]," in Hackett, *Revolt of the Pueblo Indians,* pt. 1, pp. 108–11; "Auto [of Antonio de Otermín, Fray Cristóbal, September 13, 1680]," in Hackett, *Revolt of the Pueblo Indians,* pt. 1, pp. 112–14.

43. "Auto of the Marching and Halting Places [August 24–26, 1680]," in Hackett, *Revolt of the Pueblo Indians,* pt.1, pp. 22–23; "[Continuation of Otermín's March, 26 August, 1680]," in Hackett, *Revolt of the Pueblo Indians,* pt. 1, p. 27; "[Opinion of the Cabildo of Santa Fe. La Salineta, October 3, 1680]," in Hackett, *Revolt of the Pueblo Indians,* pt. 1, p. 178.

44. "Auto of the Marching and Halting Places," in Hackett, *Revolt of the Pueblo Indians,* pt. 1, p. 23.

45. "[Opinion of the Cabildo of Santa Fe]," in Hackett, *Revolt of the Pueblo Indians,* pt. 1, p. 178.

46. Ibid.; "Auto of the Marching and Halting Places," in Hackett, *Revolt of the Pueblo Indians,* pt. 1, pp. 22–23; "[Continuation of Otermín's March]," in Hackett, *Revolt of the Pueblo Indians,* pt. 1, p. 27.

47. "[Opinion of the Cabildo of Santa Fe]," in Hackett, *Revolt of the Pueblo Indians,* pt. 1, p. 178.

48. "Declaration of One of the Rebellious Christian Indians Who Was Captured on the Road, [Place of El Alamillo, 6 September, 1680]," in Hackett, *Revolt of the Pueblo Indians,* pt. 1, p. 61.

49. "Declaration of Pedro Garcia, an Indian of the Tagno Nation, a Native of Las Salinas, [Near the Estancia of Cristóbal de Anaya, 25 August, 1680]." in Hackett, *Revolt of the Pueblo Indians,* pt. 1, pp. 24–25.

50. "[Opinion of the Cabildo of Santa Fe]," in Hackett, *Revolt of the Pueblo Indians,* pt. 1, p. 180.

51. Ibid., p. 182.

52. "[Memorandum and List of the Things . . . Needed for the New Conquest of New Mexico, El Paso, 12 October, 1680]," in Hackett, *Revolt of the Pueblo Indians,* pt. 1, pp. 200–202.

53. "The March to Isleta and the Capture of that Pueblo," in "General Introduction," in Hackett, *Revolt of the Pueblo Indians,* pt. 1, pp. cxxi-cxxiv; "Auto for Passing Muster, [Place of El Ancon de Fray García, 7 November, 1681]" and "Muster Roll, November 7–10, 1681," in Charles Wilson Hackett, *Revolt of the Pueblo Indians of New Mexico and Otermín's Attempted Reconquest, 1680–1682,* pt. 2 (Albuquerque: University of New Mexico Press, 1942) pp. 190–201; "[Proclamation of Antonio Otermín, San Lorenzo, 23 October, 1681]," in Hackett, *Revolt of the Pueblo Indians,* pt. 2, pp. 181–82.

54. "[March of the Army from El Paso to La Isleta, 5 November-8 December, 1681]," in Hackett, *Revolt of the Pueblo Indians,* pt. 2, pp. 202–12.

55. "Copy of the Order That was Given to the Lieutenant General of Cavalry, Juan Domínguez de Mendoza, [La Isleta, 8 December 1681]," in Hackett, *Revolt of the Pueblo Indians,* pt. 2, pp. 215–16.

56. "Declaration [of the Indian, Juan, Place on the Río del Norte, 18 December, 1681]," in Hackett, *Revolt of the Pueblo Indians,* pt. 2, p. 236; "[Auto of Antonio de Otermín, Place of the Río del Norte, 20 December, 1681]," in ibid., p. 254; "Declaration of Don Fernando de Chávez, [Place of the Río del Norte, 21 December, 1681]," in Hackett, *Revolt of the Pueblo Indians,* pt. 2, p. 276.

57. "Declaration of the Lieutenant General of Cavalry, [Place of the Río del Norte, 20 December, 1681]," in Hackett, *Revolt of the Pueblo Indians,* pt. 2, pp. 257–65.

58. "Declaration [of the Indian Juan]," in Hackett, *Revolt of the Pueblo Indians,* pt. 2, pp. 236–37; "Declaration [of Lucas, Piro Indian, Place of the Río del Norte, 19 December, 1681]," in Hackett, *Revolt of the Pueblo Indians,* pt. 2, p. 244; "Declaration of Josephe, Spanish-speaking Indian, [Place of the Río del Norte, 19 December 1681]," in Hackett, *Revolt of the Pueblo Indians,* pt. 2, pp. 240–41; "Declaration of Juan Lorenzo and Francisco Lorenzo, Brothers, [Place of the Río del Norte, 20 December 1681]," in Hackett, *Revolt of the Pueblo Indians,* pt. 2, pp. 251–52; "Declaration of Captain Pedro Márquez, [Place of the Río del Norte, 21 December 1681]," in Hackett, *Revolt of the Pueblo Indians,* pt. 2, p. 28; [Declaration] of Captain Roque de Madrid, [Place of the Río del Norte, 21 December, 1681]," in Hackett, *Revolt of the Pueblo Indians,* pt. 2, p. 283; "Declaration of Sargento Mayor Luis de Quintana, [Hacienda of Luis de Carbajal, 22 December 1681]," in Hackett, *Revolt of the Pueblo Indians,* pt. 2, p. 287.

59. Ibid.

60. "Declaration of the Lieutenant General of Cavalry," in Hackett, *Revolt of the Pueblo Indians,* pt.2, p. 263; "Declaration of Don Fernando de Chávez, [Place of the Río del Norte, 21 December, 1681]," in Hackett, *Revolt of the Pueblo Indians,* pt. 2, p. 277; "[Reply of the Fiscal, Don Martín de Solís Miranda, Mexico, 25 June 1682]," in Hackett, *Revolt of the Pueblo Indians,* pt. 2, pp. 386–87, 400; [Declaration] of Diego López [Sambrano, Hacienda of Luis de Carbajal, 22 December, 1681]," in Hackett, *Revolt of the Pueblo Indians,* pt. 2, p. 296.

61. "[Reply of the Fiscal]," in Hackett, *Revolt of the Pueblo Indians,* pt. 2, p. 400.

62. "Declaration of Don Fernando de Chávez, in Hackett, *Revolt of the Pueblo Indians,* pt. 2, p. 277.

63. "[Declaration] of Diego López, in Hackett, *Revolt of the Pueblo Indians,* pt. 2, p. 296.

64. Ibid., p. 298; "[Reply of the Fiscal]," in Hackett, *Revolt of the Pueblo Indians,* pt. 2, p. 396.

65. "Declaration of Sargento Mayor Luis de Quintana," in Hackett, *Revolt of the Pueblo Indians,* pt. 2, p. 291; "[Declaration] of Diego Lopéz [Sambrano]," in Hackett, *Revolt of the Pueblo Indians,* pt. 2, p. 302.

66. "[Declaration] of Diego López [Sambrano]," in Hackett, *Revolt of the Pueblo Indians,* pt. 2, p. 298.

67. "[Opinion of Fray Francisco de Ayeta, Hacienda of Luis de Carbajal, 23 December 1681]," in Hackett, *Revolt of the Pueblo Indians*, pt. 2, pp. 309–10.

68. Ibid., pp. 310–11.

69. "Auto for the Conclusion of the Opinions of the Junta, [Place Opposite La Isleta, 1 January 1682]," in Hackett, *Revolt of the Pueblo Indians*, pt. 2, pp. 354–56; "[Certifications of Francisco Javier, Place Opposite La Isleta, 1 January, 1682," in Hackett, *Revolt of the Pueblo Indians*, pt. 2, pp. 357–58.

70. "Declaration [of Jerónimo, A Tigua Indian, Place Opposite La Isleta, 1 January 1861]," in Hackett, *Revolt of the Pueblo Indians*, pt. 2, p. 361; "[Reply of the Fiscal]," in Hackett, *Revolt of the Pueblo Indians*, pt. 2, p. 394.

71. Hubert Howe Bancroft, *History of Arizona and New Mexico, 1530–1888*, vol. 17 in *The Works of Hubert Howe Bancroft* (San Francisco: History Company, 1889), pp. 192–94; Hallenbeck, *Land of the Conquistadores*, pp. 174–76; *The Mercurio Volante of Don Carlos de Sigüenza y Góngora: An Account of the First Expedition of Don Diego de Vargas into New Mexico in 1692*, vol. 3 (Los Angeles: Quivira Society, 1932), pp. 57–58.

72. *Mercurio Volante*, pp. 57–58; Hodge et al., *Benavides' Revised Memorial*, p. 263, n. 77. Forbes, *Apache, Navaho, and Spaniard*, p. 208, also cites a letter written by Diego de Vargas, 14 August 1691, as a source of information about the attack. Forbes states that "Reneros saw fit to make a raid into New Mexico which appears suspiciously like a slaving expedition. The Spaniards attacked and destroyed the Keres pueblo of Santa Ana, which was apparently the most vulnerable Pueblo Indian settlement, since all of the Tiwa and Piro towns had been depopulated by previous Spanish campaigns. Reneros subsequently attacked Zía but was forced to retreat by the great numbers of Keres defenders. He managed, however, to carry off his human booty from Santa Ana and returned to El Paso." Both Bancroft, *History*, p. 194, and Ralph Emerson Twitchell, *The Leading Facts of New Mexican History*, vol. 1 (Cedar Rapids, Iowa: Torch Press, 1911), p. 379, cite Juan M. Mange, "Historia de la Pimería Alta," which states that the attack occurred 8 October 1687, and that ten captives were "sentenced to 10 years in the mines of Nueva Viscaya" (Twitchell, *Leading Facts*, pp. 379–80, n. 385).

73. Ellis, "Anthropological Evidence Supporting the Land Claim," pp. 29–30; Adolf F. Bandelier, *Final Report of Investigations among the Indians of the Southwestern United States Carried on Mainly in the Years from 1880 to 1885*, Archaeological Institute of America Papers, American Series, no. 4, pt. 2 (Cambridge: John Wilson and Son, University Press, 1892), p. 195 (with note) describes the campaign and suggests that the pueblo destroyed was on Black Mesa.

74. *Mercurio Volante*, pp. 57–58.

75. Ibid., pp. 57–58, says simply that Reneros "succeeded in getting back from the village of Zía"; Twitchell, *Leading Facts*, p. 378; Bancroft, *History*, p. 194, n. 34; Forbes, *Apache, Navaho, and Spaniard*, p. 208.

76. The date of this second attack on Zía is sometimes given as 1688; Spicer, *Cycles*

of Conquest, p. 163; Bancroft, *History,* p. 194; Twitchell, *Leading Facts,* pp. 379–80; Beck, *New Mexico,* p. 84; Forbes, *Apache, Navaho, and Spaniards,* p. 217, adds that "this barbarous raid had a tremendous impact upon the other Keres, and the pueblos of Santo Domingo, San Felipe, Cochiti, and others were abandoned in favor of more easily defended settlements in the sierras." The *Mercurio Volante,* pp. 57–58, states that Cruzat "subdued" Zía "by force of arms, about six-hundred rebels dying in the fight," not counting "many others who were burned alive in their own houses because they would not give themselves up." This document dates the event 29 August 1689.

77. Interview with Porfirio Montoya et al., 4 February 1980, Santa Ana Pueblo Oral History Project, Tape no. 8, pp. 8–12; Old Man of Santana, "Account of the Spanish Grant to the Holy Ghost Springs Canyon Grant," n.d., incl. in H. Carrick, Memorandum, 27 December 1951, SPA; Ellis, "Anthropological Evidence Supporting the Land Claim," pp. 29–31, 34–36, summarizes a slightly different version of this tradition, naming the Zía man as Bartolomé Ojeda. According to this version, the pueblo of Cochití was also involved, and the men were slow in returning to their pueblos because a young boy sent them the wrong signals. The people of Tamaya met Kastera's leader "at his camp just below the crest of the long hill crossed by highway 44 between the Rio Grande and Tamaya," p. 35. In Tape no. 8, Santa Ana Pueblo Oral History Project, the name of the Zía man is unintelligible. A Zía man of the same name appears in the Spanish records shortly after the attack on Zía: A document dated 20 September 1689, recorded at the Pueblo of Mi Señora de Guadalupe del Paso del Río del Norte, reports that "There was saved from shipwreck an Indian, Bartolomé de Ojeda, native of the Pueblo of Zía, said native being one who had especially distinguished himself in battle. . . ." Ojeda, described as 21 or 22 at the time, was questioned by Domingo Jironza Petriz de Cruzate, in the presence of Don Pedro Ladron de Guitar, the Secretary of Government and War, about the boundaries of Santo Domingo Pueblo. See D.V. Whiting, Translator's Summary of Communication, Government Printing Office, 27 January 1937, encl. in H. H. Wright, Chief Clerk, GPO, to C. E. MacEachran, Chief Clerk and Admin. Asst., Dept. of State, 8 March 1937 (Translation Request 5408, 5409), encl. in MacEachran to Floyd E. Dotson, Chief Clerk, ID, 9 March 1937, encl. in J. M. Stewart, Dir. of Lands, to Dr. S. D. Aberle, Gen. Supt., UPA, 15 March 1937, CF 1907–1939, UP 1939-311-7938, RG 75, BIA.

78. Interview with Porfirio Montoya et al., Tape no. 8, pp. 10–11.

79. Ibid. p. 13.

80. Spicer, *Cycles of Conquest,* pp. 164–65; Hallenbeck, *Land of the Conquistadores,* pp. 177–86; Beck, *New Mexico,* pp. 85–89; Forbes, *Apache, Navaho, and Spaniard,* pp. 235–74; José Manuel Espinosa, *The First Expedition of Diego de Vargas into New Mexico, 1692* (Albuquerque: University of New Mexico Press, 1940), pp. 170–76, 181, 285–86.

81. Interview with Porfirio Montoya et al., 4 February 1980, Santa Ana Pueblo

Oral History Project, Tape no. 8, pp. 11–15; Interview with Porfirio Montoya, Donna Pino, Thomas Leubben, and Floyd Montoya, 16 January 1980, Santa Ana Pueblo Oral History Project, Tape no. 2. pp. 8–11, 13.

82. Fray Angelico Chávez, *Archives of the Archdiocese of Santa Fe, 1678–1900* (Washington, D.C.: Academy of American Franciscan History, 1957), pp. 241, 246, 251, 257, lists the friars who served at Santa Ana from January 1694 to June 1699; see Appendix 4 for a complete listing.

83. Although Bandelier, *Final Report*, pt. i, p. 126, and pt. ii, p. 194, stated that there was a church and convent at the Tamayame village on Santa Ana (Black) Mesa in 1680, there is no corroborating evidence. W. S. Stallings, Jr., obtained tree-ring dates of 1729+ and 1733+ at the existing Santa Ana church, but these are regarded as uncertain; see Terah L. Smiley, *A Summary of Tree-Ring Dates from Some Southwestern Archaeological Sites, Laboratory Bulletin of Tree-Ring Research*, no. 5 (Tucson: University of Arizona, 1952), Table of Dates, no. 30, following p. 13. Ellis, "Anthropological Evidence Supporting the Land Claim," p. 36, states that "the church services of the late 17th century were held in the open" at the "west end of the south plaza," according to Santa Ana tradition. See also interview with Porfirio Montoya et al., 4 February 1980, Santa Ana Pueblo Oral History Project, Tape no. 8, p. 12.

Chapter 5

1. John Francis Bannon, *The Spanish Borderlands Frontier, 1512–1821* (New York: Holt, Rinehart and Winston, 1970), pp. 92–107, 169–71, and passim; Marc Simmons, *New Mexico: Bicentennial History* (New York: W. W. Norton and Co., 1977), pp. 77–100; David Lavender, *The Southwest* (New York: Harper and Row, 1980), pp. 70–98; and Noel M. Loomis and Abraham P. Nasatir, *Pedro Vial and the Roads to Santa Fe* (Norman: University of Oklahoma Press, 1967), pp. 9–15, and passim, all discuss European movements toward New Spain in the late seventeenth and the eighteenth centuries as well as the effects of the perceived threat on the borderlands colonies, including New Mexico. A fuller discussion of Russian expansion may be found in Arrell Morgan Gibson, *The American Indian: Prehistory to the Present* (Lexington, Mass.: D. C. Heath and Co., 1980), pp. 162–81. In addition to protecting the mines of New Spain from potential European competitors, the northern colonies also served as a buffer from the attacks of hostile Indians, who presented, through much of this period, a greater and far more direct threat to New Spain. For a discussion of the role of New Mexico's non-Pueblo Indians in this period, see Chapter 6.

2. Hubert Howe Bancroft, *History of Arizona and New Mexico, 1530–1888*, vol. 17 in *The Works of Hubert Howe Bancroft* (San Francisco: The History Company, 1889), p. 279.

3. D. W. Meinig, *Southwest: Three Peoples in Geographical Change, 1600–1700* (New York: Oxford University Press, 1971), figure 2-1, p. 10. For a description of Spanish settlements and towns in 1776, see Eleanor B. Adams and Fray Angelico Chávez,

trans. and ed., *The Missions of New Mexico, 1776: A Description by Fray Atanasio Dominguez with Other Contemporary Documents* (Albuquerque: University of New Mexico Press, 1956); of particular interest are p. 144 and p. 145, n. 1, which discuss the founding and history of Bernalillo. See also Oakah L. Jones, Jr., *Los Paisanos: Spanish Settlers on the Northern Frontier of New Spain* (Norman: University of Oklahoma Press, 1979), pp. 109–35, for descriptions of population and settlement in New Mexico.

4. Myra Ellen Jenkins, "The Baltasar Baca 'Grant': History of an Encroachment," *El Palacio* 68, no. 1 (Spring 1961): 47–49; the passage quoted, from book 14, title 12, law 18, vol. 2, p. 104 of the *Recopilacíon,* appears on p. 49. See also Herbert O. Brayer, *Pueblo Indian Land Grants of the "Rio Abajo," New Mexico* (Albuquerque: University of New Mexico Press, 1939).

5. Jenkins, "Baltasar Baca 'Grant'," p. 49, n. 11.

6. Testimony of Santa Ana Governor Antonio Esculla, in Report to Accompany H.R. Bill no. 1343, "Pueblo of Santa Ana." H. Rept. 70, 40th Cong., 2nd sess., s.s. no. 1358 (Washington, D.C.: GPO, 1868), p. 1. Esculla, who was "about 60," noted that it had "been searched for diligently for a long time."

7. Testimony of José Sarracino, Lt. Gov. of Santa Ana, in H. Rept. 70, 40th Cong., 2nd sess., p. 2. Sarracino, who was "about 50" in 1868, noted that the "old men of the pueblo" remembered the grant.

8. For archaeological evidence of the farming villages used by the Tamayame, see Florence Hawley Ellis, "Anthropological Evidence Supporting the Land Claim of the Pueblos of Zia, Santa Ana, and Jemez," manuscript, University of New Mexico, Library of Anthropology, Department of Anthropology, n.d., pp. 16, 30, 46–47.

9. Fray Francisco Atanasio Domínguez, in Adams and Chavez, *Missions of New Mexico,* p. 170.

10. "Geographical Descriptions of New Mexico by the Reverend Preacher Fray Juan Agustín de Morfi, Reader Jubilado and Son of this Province of Santo Evangelico of Mexico, Year of 1782," in Alfred Barnaby Thomas, ed., *Forgotten Frontiers: A Study of the Spanish Indian Policy of Juan Bautista de Anza, Governor of New Mexico, 1777–1787* (Norman: University of Oklahoma Press, 1932), pp. 90–91, 98.

11. Ellis, "Anthropological Evidence Supporting the Land Claim," pp. 46–47.

12. Ibid.

13. Adams and Chávez, *Missions of New Mexico,* pp. 144–45, n. 1; A. J. O. Anderson, "Spanish Cities of New Mexico," in V. Salas, ed., *Spanish Culture in the United States* (Madrid: Revista Geográfica Española, n.d.), p. 92.

14. Ibid.; Ward Alan Minge, "The Pueblo of Santa Ana's El Ranchito Purchase, and the Adjudication of the Boundary with San Felipe: A Report Prepared for the Pueblo of Santa Ana," 31 October 1983, manuscript, p. 5 and n. 2 (all page references to handwritten numbers), files of Rothstein, Walther, Donatelli, Hughes, Dahlstrom & Cron, Attorneys for the Pueblo of Santa Ana, Santa Fe, New Mexico.

15. Translation of Deed of Sale dated 27 June, 1709, Exhibit D, Lucius C. Embree et al., Pueblo Lands Board, "Santa Ana Pueblo, El Ranchito Grant or Purchase:

Report on Title to Land Purchased by Pueblo Indians," 19 July 1927, SPA; Will M. Tipton, Summary of Deed of 27 June 1709, by Manuel Baca to Nine Indians of the Pueblo of Santa Ana, for a Tract of Land in a Bend at the Mouth of Santa Ana River, leaf 53, p. 2, in "Memoranda of Content of Documents Relating to Lands of Pueblo Indians: Book 'C'—Kearny Code Land Records," manuscript prepared by order of the Secretary of the Interior for the Use of the Special Attorney for the Pueblo Indians of New Mexico, 1911–1912, UP-df-2, AB, RG 75, BIA, FRCD, cited hereafter as Tipton, "Book 'C'—Kearny Code Land Records." Boundary description translated and quoted by Will M. Tipton.

16. Minge, "The Pueblo of Santa Ana's El Ranchito Purchase, and the Adjudication of the Boundary with San Felipe: A Report Prepared for the Pueblo of Santa Ana, p.6.

17. Summary of Deed by Juan Gonzalez to the Indians of Santa Ana, n.d., in Tipton, "Book 'C'—Kearny Code Land Records," leaf 56, p. 1; boundary as described by Minge, " The Pueblo of Santa Ana's El Ranchito Purchase and the Adjudication of the Boundary with San Felipe: A Report Prepared for the Pueblo of Santa Ana," p. 7.

18. Adams and Chavez, *Missions of New Mexico*, p. 171 n.; the editors note that the date of sale (1734) testified to must be inaccurate since Magdalena Baca was not married to Juan Márquez until the following year; the sale must have taken place between that year and 1741, when he killed her. Adams and Chavez cite SANM documents 570 and 572; the latter, according to notes prepared by David Snow for the tribal attorneys, is now missing. See David H. Snow, compiler, "Inventory of Historic Documents Pertaining to Title to Real Property in Re Santa Ana Pueblo," manuscript, January 1992, p. 7, in the files of Rothstein, Walther, Donatelli, Hughes, Dahlstrom & Cron, Attorneys for the Pueblo of Santa Ana, Santa Fe, New Mexico.

19. Translation of Deed of Sale dated 4 June 1742, Exhibit F, Lucius C. Embree et al., Pueblo Lands Board, "Santa Ana Pueblo, El Ranchito Grant or Purchase: Report on Title to Lands Purchased by Pueblo Indians," 19 July 1927, SPA; Summaries of Deed dated 14 October 1713 for Land Sold by Juan Gonzalez Bas to Doña Josefa Baca; Statement of Chief Alcalde Ignacio Sánchez Vergara, 11 August 1812, Santa Ana; Certificate by Gov. Juan Domingo Bustamante, 14 November 1724, Bernalillo; and Deed dated 4 June 1742, by Doña Josefa Baca to the Indians of Santa Ana, all in Tipton, "Book 'C'—Kearny Code Land Records," leaves 56–57; boundary as translated in Minge, "The Pueblo of Santa Ana's El Ranchito Purchase, and the Adjudication of the Boundary with San Felipe: A Report Prepared for the Pueblo of Santa Ana," p. 6.

20. Myra Ellen Jenkins, Summary of Deed from Baltazar Romero to Santa Ana Pueblo, Annulled by Governor, in "Summary of Spanish Archives of New Mexico and Land Grant Records Concerning the Pueblos of Santa Ana and San Felipe," manuscript, 8 February 1976, p. 1, SANM no. 1345 (hereafter cited as Jenkins, "Summary"); Will M. Tipton, Summary of Annulment of a Sale of Land by Baltazar Romero to Indians of the Pueblo of Santa Ana by Governor Gervasio Cruzat y

Góngora, 1 March 1734, Archive 1345, in "Memoranda of the Contents of those Spanish Archives in the U.S. Surveyor General's Office at Santa Fe, New Mexico, that Relate to Lands of the Pueblo Indians," manuscript, 1912, UP-df-2, AB, RG 75, BIA, FRCD (hereafter cited as Tipton, "Spanish Archives").

21. Summaries of Letter from Alcalde Antonio Baca to Gov. Vélez Cachupín, 9 May 1753; Gov. Cachupín, Authorization of Sale, 13 May 1753; Deed from Alejandro Mora to the Indians of the Pueblo of Santa Ana, 24 May 1753; Memorandum of the Names of Thirty-five Indians Who Contributed to the Purchase; List of 43 Persons to Whom the Lands were Partitioned; Deed by Pedro Romero, Son of Baltazar Romero, to Javier Miranda, 20 November 1739; Approval of Foregoing Proceedings by Governor Vélez Cachupín, 28 May 1753; and Receipt by Alejandro Mora for Money Received from Captain Don Antonio Baca for a Ranch Sold to the Indians of Santa Ana, 25 May 1755, all in Tipton, "Book 'C'—Kearny Code Land Records," leaves 22–23, 25, 26; Minge, "The Pueblo of Santa Ana's El Ranchito Purchase, and the Adjudication of the Boundary with San Felipe," p. 7.

22. Minge, "The Pueblo of Santa Ana's El Ranchito Purchase, and the Adjudication of the Boundary with San Felipe: A Report Prepared for the Pueblo of Santa Ana," p. 8.

23. Ellis, "Anthropological Evidence Supporting the Land Claim," pp. 45–47, gives a range of dates from c. 1750 to c. 1850 for these sites.

24. Ward Alan Minge, "Outline for History of Santa Ana Pueblo during Spanish and Mexican Periods," manuscript, December 1980, Santa Ana Tribal Archive, pp. 41–42.

25. Summaries of Record of Proceedings, Santa Ana Petition to Purchase Farmlands, prepared by Alcalde Mayor Don Bernardo Miera y Pacheco, 5 July 1763; Record of Proceedings, Appointment of Appraisers, prepared by Miera y Pacheco, 6 July 1763; Record of Proceedings, Appraisals, prepared by Miera y Pacheco, 7 July 1763; Record of Proceedings, Santa Anas Deliver Payment of 3,000 pesos in Kind, prepared by Miera y Pacheco, 7 July 1763; Record of Proceedings, Record of Sales and Boundaries, prepared by Miera y Pacheco, 7 July 1763; Letter from Don Bernardo Miera y Pacheco to Governor Tomás Vélez Cachupín, 8 July 1763; Letter from Governor Cachupín to Miera y Pacheco, 9 July, 1763, all in SANM no. 1349, summarized in both Tipton, "Spanish Archives," and Jenkins, "Summary"; see also Minge, "Outline for History of Santa Ana Pueblo," pp. 42–45, and Minge, "The Pueblo of Santa Ana's El Ranchito Purchase, and the Adjudication of the Boundary with San Felipe: A Report Prepared for the Pueblo of Santa Ana," pp. 8–9, 64–70, from which translations of boundaries and estimates of distances and areas are taken.

26. Tipton, "Spanish Archives"; Jenkins, "Summary"; Minge, "Outline for History of Santa Ana Pueblo," pp. 42–45. Individual documents listed in previous note.

27. Statement of Porfirio Montoya, 16 May 1952, SPA files; Interview with Valencio García, 26 February 1980, Santa Ana Pueblo Oral History Project, Tape no. 1.

28. Adams and Chávez, *Missions of New Mexico*, pp. 170–71.

29. "Geographical Descriptions of New Mexico Written by the Reverend Preacher Fray Juan Agustín de Morfi," in Thomas, *Forgotten Frontiers,* p. 98.

30. Floyd Montoya, "Short History of Santa Ana," manuscript, Santa Ana Tribal Archives 1980, pp. 15–16; see also Porfirio Montoya, interview with Floyd Montoya, Donna Pino, and Tom Leubben, 11 February 1980, Santa Ana Pueblo Oral History Project, Tape no. 12.

31. Floyd Montoya, "Short History," p. 16; Ellis, "Anthropological Evidence Supporting the Land Claim," pp. 56–57, 44.

32. Minge, "The Pueblo of Santa Ana's El Ranchito Purchase, and the Adjudication of the Boundary with San Felipe: A Report Prepared for the Pueblo of Santa Ana," pp. 6–7 and n. 5.

33. Brayer, *Pueblo Indian Land Grants,* p. 107; Frank D. Reeve, "The Navajo-Spanish Peace, 1720s-1770s," *New Mexico Historical Review* 34, no. 1 (January 1959): 29–38, discusses Spanish settlement of the Río Puerco region, but does not include the Espiritu Santo.

34. Brayer, *Pueblo Indian Land Grants,* p. 107; H. Pierce to Dr. Aberle, 28 September 1943, SPA, includes translations of the original documents as well as copies of the pueblo brief filed in the Court of Private Land Claims, the surveyor general's opinion, and the patent issued to T. B. Catron.

35. Brayer, *Pueblo Indian Land Grants,* p. 107.

36. Interview with Porfirio Montoya, Donna Pino, Floyd Montoya, and Tom Leubben, 4 February 1980, Santa Ana Pueblo Oral History Project, Tape no. 8, pp. 11–12.

37. Fray Angelico Chávez, *Archives of the Archdiocese of Santa Fe, 1678–1900* (Washington, D.C.: Academy of American Franciscan History, 1957), pp. 241, 246, 251, 257; George Kubler, *The Religious Architecture of New Mexico in the Colonial Period and Since the American Occupation* (Colorado Springs, Colo.,: Taylor Museum, 1940), pp. 109–10; Terah L. Smiley, *A Summary of the Tree-Ring Dates from Some Southwestern Archaeological Sites, Laboratory Bulletin of Tree-Ring Research,* no. 5 (Tucson: University of Arizona, 1952), Table of Dates, no. 30, following p. 13, dates the existing church from 1729+ to 1733+; "Declaration of Father Fray Juan Alvarez [Nambe, 12 January, 1706]" in Charles Wilson Hackett, ed., *Historical Documents Relating to New Mexico, Nueva Viscaya, and Approaches thereto, to 1773* (Washington, D.C.: Carnegie Institute, 1923), 3: 376.

38. Chávez, *Archives,* pp. 25–26.

39. Minge, "Outline for History of Santa Ana Pueblo," p. 31; Adams and Chávez, *Missions of New Mexico,* p. 329; Chávez, *Archives,* pp. 25–26.

40. Declaration of Fray Miguel de Menchero, Santa Barbara, 10 May 1744, in Hackett, *Historical Documents* 3: 404.

41. Chávez, *Archives,* pp. 25–26.

42. Ibid.; Chávez lists visitations in 1712, 1714, 1716, 1718, 1721, 1722, and 1724, as well as several undated ones in this period.

43. Letter of Bishop Benito Crespo to Viceroy, 25 September 1730, in Eleanor B. Adams, ed., *Bishop Tamaron's Visitation of New Mexico, 1760* (Albuquerque: Historical Society of New Mexico, 1954), p. 102; Chávez, *Archives,* p. 161; Bishop Tamaron y Romerol, Report of 11 July 1765, in Adams, *Bishop Tamaron's Visitation,* pp. 78–79; Adams, ibid., p. 66; Bancroft, *History,* pp. 240–41 and passim.

44. Chávez, *Archives,* pp. 28, 29, 32, 33.

45. Chávez, *Archives,* p. 222.

46. Adams, *Bishop Tamaron's Visitation,* pp. 95–106.

47. Adams and Chávez, *Missions of New Mexico,* p. 329; Bancroft, *History,* pp. 240–42 and n. 35; Edgar L. Hewett and Reginald G. Fisher, *Mission Monuments of New Mexico* (Albuquerque: University of New Mexico Press, 1943), p. 244, calls Father Araoz a martyr; Earle R. Forrest, *Missions and Pueblos of the Old Southwest: Their Myths, Legends, Fiestas, and Ceremonies, with Some Accounts of the Indian Tribes and their Dances; and of the Penitentes* (Cleveland: Arthur H. Clark Co., 1929), p. 29, says that the friar was "poisoned by the Indians at Santa Ana in 1631."; Theodosius Meyer, *St. Francis and Franciscans in New Mexico* (n.p.: n.p., 1926), p. 51, claims Araos was poisoned in 1731 and adds that he was a "renowned preacher and was very forcible and frank in his utterances." Araoz is variously listed as Arauz, Araos, and Saraoz.

48. Chávez, *Archives,* pp. 29, 32, 34, 150; Kubler, *Religious Architecture of New Mexico,* p. 109; Minge, "Outline for History of Santa Ana Pueblo," p. 31. If the church was dedicated at the time of Menchero's first visit, its dates would correspond with those obtained by tree-ring dating in Smiley, *Summary of the Tree-ring Dates,* table of dates no. 30, following p. 33.

49. Chávez, *Archives,* pp. 25, 34.

50. Letter of Father Trigo Istacalco to Father Procurador General Fray José Miguel de los Ríos, 23 July 1754, in Chávez, *Archives,* 3:463.

51. Adams, *Bishop Tamaron's Visitation,* pp. 66, 76.

52. Adams and Chávez, *Missions of New Mexico,* pp. 166–70.

53. Ibid., p. 169; Dominguez actually lists the number of Indian workers at the Cochití mission; subsequently he notes that Santa Ana mission service was the same as that reported for Cochití, pp. 157, 167.

54. Interview with Porfirio Montoya et al., 4 February 1980, Santa Ana Pueblo Oral History Project, Tape no. 8, p. 12.

55. Adams and Chávez, *Missions of New Mexico,* pp. 157, 167.

56. Ibid., p. 171.

57. Ibid., p. 170.

58. Ibid., p. 171.

59. Ibid., p. 167.

60. Ibid., p. 169.

61. Oakah L. Jones, Jr., *Pueblo Warriors and Spanish Conquest* (Norman: University of Oklahoma Press, 1966), pp. 80–81, notes the confirmation of various pueblo officials, including those of Santa Ana, in November 1708; Hackett, *Historical*

Documents, 3:369, describes the reception of the governors in 1706; Marc Simmons, *Spanish Government in New Mexico* (Albuquerque: University of New Mexico Press, 1968), p. 179, describes the *bastón de justicia,* or staff of office, carried by the alcaldes and other Spanish officials. Chester E. Faris, "Pueblo Governor's Canes" (Albuquerque: BIA Area Office, 1952), manuscript, RF, RG 75, BIA, NA, recounts the history of the canes given to pueblo officers by the Spanish, Mexican, and American governments; interview with Porfirio Montoya et al., 4 February 1980, Santa Ana Pueblo Oral History Project, Tape no. 8, p. 12, discusses Tamaya's Spanish canes, but Montoya states that he does not know when or how they were first presented to pueblo officials.

62. Simmons, *Spanish Government,* pp. 170–91, includes the alcalde's relations with the pueblos in his discussion of the alcalde's appointment, duties, and authority; Minge, "Outline for History of Santa Ana Pueblo," pp. 45–52, summarizes the documentary records of Tamaya's contacts with the alcaldes in this period; Albert H. Schroeder, "Rio Grande Ethnohistory," in *New Perspectives on the Pueblos,* ed. Alfonso Ortiz (Albuquerque: University of New Mexico Press, 1972), pp. 64–65, describes the role of Spanish civil institutions in the pueblos from 1696 to 1821 and notes that some Tamayame "went to the Plains to hunt buffalo without a license"; Jones, *Los Paisanos,* p. 250.

63. Minge, "Outline for History of Santa Ana Pueblo," pp. 51–52; Simmons, *Spanish Government,* pp. 167–68 and passim; Morfi in Thomas, *Forgotten Frontiers,* pp. 90–91.

64. Simmons, *Spanish Government,* pp. 187–92; Jenkins, "Baltasar Baca 'Grant,'" pp. 52–53; and Bancroft, *History,* p. 273, summarize the alcalde's powers and the charges made against unjust alcaldes.

65. Minge, "Outline for History of Santa Ana Pueblo," pp. 51–52; Appointment Made by Don Mariano Mendiola Velarde, Guadalajara, 21 June 1817, SANM 2692, cited in Minge, ibid., p. 52; Sánchez Vergara acted for the Tamayame on several occasions, but he also supported San Felipe in the land dispute at times, and Ralph E. Twitchell, *The Spanish Archives of New Mexico* (Cedar Rapids, Iowa: Torch Press, 1914) 2:525, lists an 1808 suit between Santa Ana and Sánchez Vergara for "extortion" and "forced personal service."

66. Minge, "Outline for History of Santa Ana Pueblo," pp. 45–48; Miera y Pacheco's records of the 1763 purchase are cited in n. 25, above; Bancroft, *History,* pp. 240–42.

67. Simmons, *Spanish Government,* pp. 187–92; Jenkins, "Baltasar Baca 'Grant,'" pp. 52–53; Bancroft, *History,* p. 273.

68. Adams and Chávez, *Missions of New Mexico,* pp. 339, 313, n. 6.; "The Form of Government Used at the Missions of San Diego de los Jémez, and San Agustín de la Isleta by Father Fray Joaquín de Jesus Ruiz, Their Former Minister," c. 1773, in Hackett, *Historical Documents,* 3:504.

69. Adams and Chávez, *Mission of New Mexico,* p. 313, n. 6; p. 314, n. 7.

70. Bancroft, *History*, p. 273, n. 39, summarizes the complaints against the alcaldes presented by Serrano, Lezaun, and Morfi from 1760 to 1792. Sanz de Lezaun spent much of his time in New Mexico from 1748 to 1758 at Santa Ana, Zía, Jémez, and San Felipe; Chávez, *Archives*, p. 256.

71. Simmons, *Spanish Government*, pp. 66–67, 79–80, 176–77, 190–91.

72. Jenkins, "Summary," p. 4, José Mariano de la Peña, Alcalde of Albuquerque, to Governor of New Mexico Facundo Melgares, 8 May 1819, examines deeds by San Felipes to Spaniards, dated 1782 to 1816; Tipton, "Spanish Archives," no. 1365, summarizes the same document; Jenkins, "Summary," p. 3, report of Arze, 6 June 1813, Archive 1356; Tipton, "Spanish Archives," no. 1356; Statement by Nerio Antonio Montoya, Chief Alcalde of the Queres, 14 July 1779, in Tipton, Book 'C'—Kearny Code Land Records," leaf 62, p. 2; SANM 1356 documents also translated by Ward Alan Minge, Plaintiff's Exhibit No. 9 in Pueblo of Santa Ana v. Alfredo Baca and Mary Lou Baca, US District Court, District of New Mexico, filed 30 April 1985, in the files of Rothstein, Walther, Donatelli, Hughes, Dahlstrom & Cron, Attorneys for the Pueblo of Santa Ana, Santa Fe, New Mexico.

73. Eusebio Mairo, Governor of Santa Ana, Petition to Felipe Sandoval, Protector of the Indians, 5 May 1813, SANM no. 1356, in Jenkins, "Summary," p. 1; same document is summarized in Tipton, "Spanish Archives" and translated by Minge, Plaintiff's Exhibit No. 9.

74. Protector of the Indians Felipe Sandoval, Referring Petition of Eusebio Mario to Acting Governor of New Mexico José Manrique, 10 May 1813, SANM no. 1356, summarized in Jenkins, "Summary," p. 2; Tipton, "Spanish Archives," no. 1356; and Minge, Plaintiff's Exhibit 9; Minge's narrative summary of the 1813 and 1819 adjudications, in "The Pueblo of Santa Ana's El Ranchito Purchase, and the Adjudication of the Boundary with San Felipe: A Report Prepared for the Pueblo of Santa Ana," pp. 12–13, is in error in stating that Alcalde José Mariano de la Peña was appointed in 1813 to handle the adjudication; the documents—including Minge's translations—clearly indicate that the 1813 adjudication was conducted by Alcalde José Pino and that Peña took charge of the review in 1819.

75. José Pino, Alcalde of Albuquerque, Proceedings, 13 May 1813, SANM no. 1356, in Jenkins, "Summary," p. 2; Tipton, "Spanish Archives," no. 1356; and Minge, Plaintiff's Exhibit 9; Boundaries as defined in Minge, "The Pueblo of Santa Ana's El Ranchito Purchase, and the Adjudication of the Boundary with San Felipe: A Report Prepared for the Pueblo of Santa Ana," p. 13.

76. Alcalde Pino to Governor of New Mexico, 14 May 1813, SANM no. 1356, in Jenkins, "Summary," p. 2; Tipton, "Spanish Archives," no. 1356; and Minge, Plaintiff's Exhibit 9, pp. 2–3.

77. Protest from Governor and Lieutenant Governor of San Felipe Pueblo to Felipe Sandoval, Protector of the Indians, 21 May 1813, in Jenkins, "Summary," p. 3; Tipton, "Spanish Archives," no. 1356; and Minge, Plaintiff's Exhibit 9, pp. 3–4.

78. Felipe Sandoval, Protector of the Indians, Statement Appended to San Felipe

Petition, 29 May 1813, in Jenkins, "Summary," SANM 1356, p. 2; Tipton, "Spanish Archives," no. 1356; and Minge, Plaintiff's Exhibit 9, p.4, which shows the date as 19 May, presumably an error since the note was in response to San Felipe's request of 21 May.

79. Reports of José María de Arze, Alfarez of the Santa Fe Presidial Company, 5, 6, and 7 June 1813, in Jenkins, "Summary," SANM 1356, p. 3; Tipton, "Spanish Archives," no. 1356; and Minge, Plaintiff's Exhibit 9, pp. 4–8.

80. Ibid.

81. Ibid.; Acting Governor of New Mexico José Manrique, Approval of Arze's Proposal, in Jenkins, "Summary," SANM 1356, p. 3; Tipton, "Spanish Archives," no. 1356; and Minge, Plaintiff's Exhibit 9, p. 8.

82. Tipton, "Spanish Archives," no. 1363, p. 1, leaf 3.

83. Letter from Ignacio María Sánchez Vergara, Protector of the Indians, to Lt. Col. Facundo Melgares, 14 April 1819, with marginal note, 22 April 1819, by Governor of New Mexico, summarized in Tipton, "Spanish Archives," no. 1364; Letter from José Mariano de la Peña, Alcalde of Albuquerque, to Governor Melgares, 8 May 1819, summarized in Jenkins, "Summary," SANM 1365, p. 3, and Tipton, "Spanish Archives," no. 1365; Statements of Josef Mariano de la Peña, 8 May 1819, and Letter from Sánchez Vergara to Melgares, 9 May 1819, SANM 1365, translated by Ward Alan Minge, Plaintiff's Exhibit 10, Pueblo of Santa Ana v. Alfredo Baca and Mary Lou Baca, filed 30 April 1985, US District Court, District of New Mexico, pp. 1–4.

84. Ibid.; Letter from Governor Melgares to Alcalde Peña, 11 May 1819, in Jenkins, "Summary," p. 4, and Tipton, "Spanish Archives," SANM 1365.

85. Protector of the Indians Sánchez Vergara to Governor Melgares, 4 June 1819, in Jenkins, "Summary," SANM 1366, p. 4; Tipton, "Spanish Archives," no. 1366.

86. Letter from Alcalde Peña to Governor Melgares, 13 August 1819, in Jenkins, "Summary," SANM 1234, p. 5; Tipton, "Spanish Archives," no. 1234; Ralph Emerson Twitchell, *Spanish Archives of New Mexico* (Cedar Rapids: Torch Press, 1914), 1:358–59, adds the comment that "The style of this man Peña is such as to make it very difficult in many instances to understand what he meant, and practically impossible to make an intelligible translation of much that he said."

87. Statement by Ignacio María Sánchez Vergara, 1 October 1819, in Tipton, "Book 'C'—Kearny Code Land Records," leaf 64, p. 1.

88. Petition by Andrés Mayguas, n.d. [1822], on behalf of the Indians of Santa Ana, summarized in Tipton, "Book 'C'—Kearny Code Land Records," leaf 63, p. 1.

Chapter 6

1. Fray Angelico Chávez, *Archives of the Archdiocese of Santa Fe, 1678–1900* (Washington, D.C.: Academy of American Franciscan History, 1957), pp. 79, 179, 180, 183.

2. Oakah L. Jones, Jr., *Los Paisanos: Spanish Settlers on the Northern Frontier of New Spain* (Norman: University of Oklahoma Press, 1979), p. 128.

3. Chávez, *Archives*, p. 153. The license was granted in 1829.

4. Albert H. Schroeder, "Rio Grande Ethnohistory," in *New Perspectives on the Pueblos*, ed. Alfonso Ortiz (Albuquerque: University of New Mexico Press, 1972), pp. 57–60; Albert H. Schroeder, "Shifting for Survival in the Spanish Southwest," in *New Spain's Far Northern Frontier, —Essays on Spain in the American West, 1540–1821*, ed. David J. Weber (Albuquerque: University of New Mexico Press, 1979), pp. 239–45; Edward H. Spicer, *Cycles of Conquest: The Impact of Spain, Mexico, and the United States on the Indians of the Southwest, 1533–1960* (Tucson: University of Arizona Press, 1962), pp. 153–55.

5. Dates ranging from A.D. 900 to A.D. 1525 or later have been assigned to the Navajo arrival in the Southwest. For a brief discussion of Navajo prehistory and a list of the major sources that deal with the question see Peter Iverson, *The Navajos: A Critical Bibliography* (Bloomington and London: Indiana University Press 1976), p. 13.

6. Porfirio Montoya, Interview with Floyd Montoya, Tom Leubben, and Donna Pino, 16 January 1980, Santa Ana Pueblo Oral History Project, Tape no. 3, p. 3.

7. For a brief discussion and a list of sources related to Apache migrations, see Michael E. Melody, *The Apaches: A Critical Bibliography* (Bloomington and London: Indiana University Press, 1977), pp. 2–3.

8. For a discussion of Uto-Aztecan prehistory, see Earl J. Swanson, Jr., ed., *Utaztecan Prehistory* (Pocatello, Idaho: Idaho State University Museum, 1968), which includes papers by James Goss, William H. Jacobsen, Jr., and Jeremiah F. Epstein; see also Warren L. d'Azevedo et al., eds., *The Current Status of Anthropological Research in the Great Basin: 1964* (Reno: Desert Research Institute, 1966); Jesse D. Jennings, *Prehistory of Utah and the Eastern Great Basin*, University of Utah Anthropological Papers, no. 98 (Salt Lake City: University of Utah Press, 1978), pp. 235–38, briefly summarizes the arrival of Athapascan and Shoshonean speakers in the region; E. Adamson Hoebel, *The Plains Indians: A Critical Bibliography* (Bloomington and London: Indiana University Press, 1977), pp. 12–18, 45, includes the Comanche; Ernest Wallace and E. Adamson Hoebel, *The Comanches: Lords of the South Plains* (Norman: University of Oklahoma Press, 1952), pp. 3–12, summarizes Comanche movements.

9. Schroeder, "Shifting for Survival," pp. 246–50; Schroeder, "Rio Grande Ethnohistory," pp. 57–60; Albert H. Schroeder, "Pueblos Abandoned in Historic Times," in *Southwest*, ed. Alfonso Ortiz, vol. 9 of *Handbook of North American Indians*, ed. William C. Sturtevant (Washington, D.C.: Smithsonian Institution, 1979), pp. 236–54, describes the pueblos of the 1500s in detail and includes maps showing those abandoned, as well as the modern locations of the surviving pueblos.

10. Schroeder, "Shifting for Survival," pp. 246–50; Schroeder, "Rio Grande Ethnohistory," pp. 57–60; Schroeder, "Pueblos Abandoned in Historic Times." Opinions of the relative importance of three factors in this dislocation—Spanish intru-

sion, raiding by Apaches and Navajos, and pre-Spanish intertribal and interpueblo rivalries—vary widely. Among those who discuss the causes of population decline, relocation, and the shifting alliances of the period are Spicer, *Cycles of Conquest,* pp. 162–67, 491, 493–95; Jack D. Forbes, *Apache, Navaho, and Spaniard* (Norman: University of Oklahoma Press, 1960), pp. 237–43, 281–84; Marc Simmons, *New Mexico: A Bicentennial History* (New York: W. W. Norton and Co., 1977), pp. 71–76; and Oakah L. Jones, Jr., *Pueblo Warriors and the Spanish Conquest* (Norman: University of Oklahoma Press, 1966), pp. ix, 61, and passim. De Vargas's accounts of the pueblos at the time of the Reconquest may be found in José Manuel Espinosa, *The First Expedition of Diego de Vargas into New Mexico, 1692* (Albuquerque: University of New Mexico Press, 1940).

11. Forbes, *Apache, Navajo, and Spaniard,* p. 284; S. Lyman Tyler, "Some Economic Aspects of Indian Contacts in the Spanish Southwest," in *The Changing Ways of Southwestern Indians: A Historic Perspective,* ed. Albert H. Schroeder (Glorieta, NM: Rio Grande Press, 1973), pp. 35–45, discusses trade in goods and captives among the tribes and with the Spaniards; Paul M. Raczka, "Traditions of Northern Plains Raiders in New Mexico," in ibid., pp. 47–53, describes pre-horse trade routes between the plains tribes and the pueblos, as well as later raids by tribes as distant as the Cheyenne, Yakima, Nez Percé, Blackfoot, Gros Ventre, and Assiniboine.

12. Schroeder, "Rio Grande Ethnohistory," pp. 57–60; Schroeder, "Shifting for Survival," pp. 246–50; Spicer, *Cycles of Conquest,* 546–51; Wallace and Hoebel, *Comanches,* pp. 37–40; Alfred Barnaby Thomas, ed. and trans., *After Coronado: Spanish Exploration Northeast of New Mexico, 1696–1727,* 2nd ed. (Norman: University of Oklahoma Press, 1966); Alfred Barnaby Thomas, *The Plains Indians and New Mexico, 1751–1778: A Collection of Documents Illustrative of the History of the Eastern Frontier of New Mexico* (Albuquerque: University of New Mexico Press, 1940); Alfred Barnaby Thomas, *Forgotten Frontiers: A Study of the Spanish Indian Policy of Don Juan Bautista de Anza, Governor of New Mexico, 1777–1787* (Norman: University of Oklahoma Press, 1932); Forbes, *Apache, Navajo and Spaniard,* pp. 279–80.

13. Ibid.

14. Jones, *Pueblo Warriors,* explains the organization of this system of alliances and auxiliary troops.

15. Espinosa, *First Expedition,* p. 286.

16. Jones, *Pueblo Warriors,* p. 65.

17. Frank D. Reeve, "Navaho-Spanish Wars, 1680–1720," *New Mexico Historical Review* 33, no. 3 (July 1958):216.

18. Jones, *Pueblo Warriors,* pp. 77, 79.

19. Ibid., pp. 79–80.

20. Thomas, *Plains Indians,* p. 8.

21. Ibid., pp. 7, 16.

22. Letter of Bishop Benito Crespo to Viceroy Juan Vázquez de Acuna, Marquis de Casafuerte, Bernalillo, 8 September 1730, in *Bishop Tamaron's Visitation of New Mex-*

ico, 1760, ed. Eleanor B. Adams (Albuquerque: Historical Society of New Mexico, 1954), p. 98.

23. Ward Alan Minge, "Outline for History of Santa Ana Pueblo During Spanish and Mexican Periods," manuscript, December 1980, Santa Ana Tribal Archive, p. 47.

24. Lansing B. Bloom, ed., *Antonio Barriero's "Ojeada Sobre Nuevo Mexico"* (Santa Fe: El Palacio Press, 1928), pp. 18–19.

25. Thomas, *Plains Indians*, pp. 17–18.

26. Minge, "Outline for History of Santa Ana Pueblo," p. 47.

27. Jones, *Pueblo Warriors*, pp. 128–29.

28. Ralph Emerson Twitchell, *The Spanish Archives of New Mexico* (Cedar Rapids: Torch Press, 1914), 1:90–92, #277; Frank D. Reeve, "The Navaho-Spanish Peace: 1720s–1770s," *New Mexico Historical Review* 34, no. 1 (January 1959): 29–38, discusses the settling and later abandonment of the Río Puerco region and Nuestra Señora de La Luz, but does not mention the Espiritu Santo holdings of Tamaya, Zía, and Jémez.

29. Herbert O. Brayer, *Pueblo Indian Lands of the "Rio Abajo," New Mexico* (Albuquerque: University of New Mexico Press, 1939), p. 107.

30. Jones, *Pueblo Warriors*, p. 133.

31. Thomas, *Plains Indians*, pp. 172–73.

32. Chávez, *Archives*, p. 234; Thomas, *Forgotten Frontiers*, p. 351; Eleanor B. Adams and Fray Angelico Chávez, trans. and eds., *The Missions of New Mexico, 1776: A Description by Fray Atanasio Dominguez with Other Contemporary Documents* (Albuquerque: University of New Mexico Press, 1956), p. 143.

33. Chávez, *Archives*, pp. 44–45; Thomas, *Plains Indians*, p. 228; Thomas, *Forgotten Frontiers*, pp. 267–69.

34. Jones, *Pueblo Warriors*, p. 162.

35. Chávez, *Archives*, p. 222.

36. Ibid., p. 234.

37. Jones, *Los Paisanos*, pp. 139–40.

38. Chávez, *Archives*, p. 234.

39. Ibid., p. 238.

40. Ibid., p. 236.

41. Jones, *Los Paisanos*, pp. 140–41.

42. Chávez, *Archives*, p. 69.

43. Jones, *Los Paisanos*, pp. 140–41.

44. Warren A. Beck, *New Mexico: A History of Four Centuries* (Norman: University of Oklahoma Press, 1962), p. 98.

45. Ibid., pp. 103–4.

46. Chávez, *Archives*, pp. 87; Myra Ellen Jenkins and Albert H. Schroeder, *A Brief History of New Mexico* (Albuquerque: University of New Mexico Press, 1974), pp. 26–30.

47. Chávez, *Archives*, pp. 41, 82.

48. Ignacio Sánchez Vergara to Governor José Manrique, 25 April 1809, SANM no. 2224, cited in Minge, "Outline for History of Santa Ana Pueblo," p. 49.

49. Jenkins and Schroeder, *Brief History*, pp. 33–34, 37; Brayer, *Pueblo Indian Lands*, pp. 19–20.

50. Thomas James, *Three Years among the Indians and Mexicans* (1846; reprint, Philadelphia and New York: J. P. Lippincott and Co., 1962), pp. 88–89.

51. Chávez, *Archives*, pp. 85, 178.

52. Jenkins and Schroeder, *Brief History*, p. 34.

53. Bloom, *Antonio Barriero's Ojeada*, p. 16.

54. Chávez, *Archives*, p. 178.

55. Chester E. Faris, "Pueblo Governor's Canes" (Albuquerque: BIA Area Office, 1952), manuscript, RF, RG 75, BIA, NA.

56. Jenkins and Schroeder, *Brief History*, pp. 34, 41; Lansing B. Bloom, "New Mexico Under Mexican Administration 1822–1846," *Old Santa Fe* 1, no. 2 (1913): 157–58; Minutes of the Junta Departmental, Santa Fe, 22 May 1837, MANM, cited in Minge, "Outline for History of Santa Ana Pueblo," p. 55; *Mariano Martínez de Lejanza to the Inhabitants of New Mexico, 17 June 1844*, no. 220 in Ritch Collection, Huntington Library, Pasadena, Calif., cited in ibid., p. 60.

57. Chávez, *Archives*, p. 75.

58. Ibid, p. 210; Minge, "Outline for History of Santa Ana Pueblo," p. 55.

59. Chávez, *Archives*, p. 179.

60. Ibid., p. 97.

61. Ibid., pp. 194, 247.

62. "Table of Missions of the Custodia de la Conversión de San Pablo, 1821" in Bloom, "New Mexico Under Mexican Administration," p. 28; Chávez, *Archives*, p. 259; Jenkins and Schroeder, *Brief History*, pp. 37, 40.

63. Chávez, *Archives*, p. 185; Jenkins and Schroeder, *Brief History*, pp. 37, 40.

64. Bloom, *Antonio Barriero's Ojeada*, p. 16.

65. Jenkins and Schroeder, *Brief History*, pp. 33–44; Myra Ellen Jenkins, "The Baltasar Baca 'Grant': History of an Encroachment," *El Palacio* 68, no. 1 (Spring 1961): 60–61.

66. Ignacio María Sánchez Vergara, 28 February 1821, Resolution of Dispute involving claims of Pablo Montoya and José García against the Pueblo of Santa Ana, in the files of Rothstein, Walther, Donatelli, Hughes, Dahlstrom & Cron, Attorneys for the Pueblo of Santa Ana, Santa Fe, New Mexico, indicates that García "apparently . . . was to give back the money to individuals" from Santa Ana; see also item number 141, Snow, "Inventory of Historic Documents Pertaining to Title to Real Property in re Santa Ana Pueblo," which indicates that Pablo Montoya received a judgement against Santa Ana in 1821.

67. Summary of Petition (n.d.) by Andres Maygua on behalf of the Indians of Santa Ana, in Will M. Tipton, "Memoranda of Contents of Documents Relating to Lands of Pueblo Indians: Book 'C'—Kearny Code Land Records," manuscript prepared by

order of the Secretary of the Interior for the Use of the Special Attorney for the Pueblo Indians of New Mexico, 1911–1912, UP-df-2, AB, RG 75, BIA, FRCD; see also documents dated 27 April 1822 and 5 May 1822, in the files of Rothstein, Walther, Donatelli, Hughes, Dahlstrom & Cron, Attorneys for the Pueblo of Santa Ana, Santa Fe, New Mexico.

68. Summaries of Order of 27 April 1822, from Governor Melgares to Alcalde of Alameda, Reply of Alcalde Baltazar Perea, 1 May or 5 May 1822, and Order of Governor Melgares, 9 May 1822, in Tipton, "Book 'C'—Kearny Code Land Records." Various suits, complaints, and hearings are recorded in SANM, JSC docs.

69. Statement of Don Ignacio María Sánchez [Vergara], 1 April 1822; Statements signed by Pedro Jose Perea, Jurisdiction of San Carlos of Alameda, the council of San Felipe (signed by Jose Mariano Valencia), and San Felipe Indians Andres Chavez, El Capitán Don Arsenio Sanchez, Miguel Reaño, Victoria Candelaria (wife of Jose Antonio), and witnesses, at Bernalillo, 1 June 1823, all summaries in English of materials in JSC, in the files of Rothstein, Walther, Donatelli, Hughes, Dahlstrom & Cron, Attorneys for the Pueblo of Santa Ana, Santa Fe, New Mexico.

70. "Summary of Santa Fe Land Document Number 1, 1826," in the files of Rothstein, Walther, Donatelli, Hughes, Dahlstrom & Cron, Attorneys for the Pueblo of Santa Ana, Santa Fe, New Mexico, includes references to judgements in 1826 and 1837, the first of which would suggest that the dispute may have preceded the change in the river's course, which occurred in 1828.

71. Water rights data from manuscripts by Richard Frost, Michael Myers, William Taylor, and Larry Kelly, "Colonial Land and Water Rights of New Mexico Indian Pueblos," pp. 38–41, and "Water Rights in Spanish Law and Practice," p. 4, New Mexico State Engineer's Office.

72. Chávez, *Archives*, p. 61.

73. Twitchell, *Spanish Archives*, 2:525.

74. Ibid., 2:577.

75. Chávez, *Archives*, p. 78.

76. Bloom, "New Mexico," *Old Santa Fe* 1, no. 1 (July, 1914): 39; Josiah Gregg, *Commerce of the Prairies*, ed. Max L. Moorhead (Norman: University of Oklahoma Press, 1954) p. 105; Ralph Emerson Twitchell, *The Leading Facts of New Mexican History* (Cedar Rapids, Iowa: Torch Press, 1911–17), 2:449.

77. James, *Three Years*, pp. 82–83.

78. Chávez, *Archives*, pp. 179, 180, 183.

79. Gregg, *Commerce of the Prairies*, p. 106; Ezra B. W. Zubrow, *Population, Contact, and Climate in the New Mexican Pueblos*, Anthropological Papers, no. 24 (Tucson: University of Arizona Press, 1974), p. 11, describes widespread drought in New Mexico from 1776 to 1785 and again from 1841 to 1850; the period from 1826 to 1840, contrary to the friars' reports, seems to have been a time of "better than average moisture" according to Zubrow.

80. Letter from José Antonio Sandoval, Jusgado de Jémes, to Governor of the

Territory, 3 August 1821, MANM, cited in Minge, "Outline for History of Santa Ana Pueblo," p. 61.

81. Chávez, *Archives*, p. 182.

82. Blas Antonio Chaves, Alcalde de Jémes, to Governor Don Francisco Sarracino, 6 February 1834, MANM, cited in Minge, "Outline for History of Santa Ana Pueblo," p. 61.

83. Circular by Governor Manual Armijo, Santa Fe, 23 November 1839, MANM, cited in Minge, "Outline for History of Santa Ana Pueblo," p. 60; Militia Surveys Conducted During the First Week in March 1839, MANM, cited in ibid., p. 61.

84. Minge, "Outline for History of Santa Ana Pueblo," p. 61.

85. Commandant General to the Prefect of the First District, Captain Don Antonio Sava, 22 May 1845; Commandant General to the Military Commander at the Pueblo of Jémez, Captain Don Francisco Sandoval, 31 May 1845, both in Letter Book of the Commandancia General of the Department of New Mexico, 1844, MANM, cited in Minge, "Outline for History of Santa Ana Pueblo," p. 62.

Chapter 7

1. Pauline Turner Strong, "Santa Ana Pueblo," in *Southwest,* ed. Alfonso Ortiz, vol. 9 in *Handbook of North American Indians,* ed. William C. Sturtevant (Washington, D.C.: Smithsonian Institution, 1979), p. 403; Larry Frank and Francis C. Harlow, *Historic Pottery of the Pueblo Indians, 1600–1880* (Boston: New York Graphic Society, 1974), pp. 97–115.

2. David H. Snow, "Some Economic Considerations of Historic Rio Grande Pueblo Pottery," in *The Changing Ways of Southwestern Indians: A Historic Perspective,* ed. Albert Schroeder (Glorieta, NM: Rio Grande Classics, 1973), pp. 63–64, 68.

3. Porfirio Montoya, interview with Floyd Montoya, Dona Pino, and Tom Leubben, 11 February 1980, Santa Ana Pueblo Oral History Project, Tape no. 12, pp. 1–3.

4. Ibid.

5. Florence Hawley Ellis, "Anthropological Evidence Supporting the Land Claim of the Pueblos of Zia, Santa Ana, and Jemez," manuscript, University of New Mexico, Library of Anthropology, Anthropology Department, n.d., p. 48.

6. Porfirio Montoya, interview with Floyd Montoya et al., 11 February 1980, Santa Ana Pueblo Oral History Project, Tape no. 12, pp. 5–6.

7. See chapter 6.

8. Lansing B. Bloom, ed., *Antonio Barriero's "Ojeada Sobre Nuevo Mexico"* (Santa Fe: El Palacio Press, 1928), pp. 18–19.

9. Strong, "Santa Ana Pueblo," p. 403; Ellis, "Anthropological Evidence Supporting the Land Claim," p. 57.

10. Strong, "Santa Ana Pueblo," pp. 402–3.

11. Ellis, "Anthropological Evidence Supporting the Land Claim," p. 56.

12. Warren A. Beck, *New Mexico: A History of Four Centuries* (Norman: University

of Oklahoma Press, 1962), pp. 99–102; Max L. Moorhead, *New Mexico's Royal Road: Trade and Travel on the Chihuahua Trail* (Norman: University of Oklahoma Press, 1958), pp. 58, 49–52.

13. Beck, *New Mexico*, pp. 109–16; Moorhead, *New Mexico's Royal Road*, pp. 59–61.

14. Moorhead, *New Mexico's Royal Road*, pp. 62–65; Josiah Gregg, *Commerce of the Prairies*, ed. Max L. Moorhead (Norman: University of Oklahoma Press, 1954), p. 332; Hubert Howe Bancroft, *History of Arizona and New Mexico, 1530–1888*, vol. 17 in *The Works of Hubert Howe Bancroft* (San Francisco: The History Company, 1889), p. 332; Moorhead's annotation of Gregg's journal includes an analysis of the available statistics relating to the value and volume of the New Mexico trade, all of which he considers unreliable.

15. Bloom, *Antonio Barriero's Ojeada*, p. 24.

16. Gregg, *Commerce of the Prairies*, p. 80; Moorhead, *New Mexico's Royal Road*, p. 80–81; Bloom, *Antonio Barriero's Ojeada*, pp. 24–25; Augustus Storrs, "Trade between Missouri and Mexico," in *Southwest on the Turquoise Trail: The First Diaries on the Road to Santa Fe*, ed. Archer Butler Hulbert (n.p.: Stewart Commission of Colorado College and the Denver Public Library, 1933), pp. 83–84.

17. Gregg, *Commerce of the Prairies*, pp. 80, 212–14; Moorhead, *New Mexico's Royal Road*, pp. 63–66; Storrs, "Trade between Missouri and Mexico," pp. 84–85; Richard Graham, "On the Southwestern Trade: Answers to Questions of Thomas H. Benton," in Hulbert, *Southwest on the Turquoise Trail*, p. 99; Alphonso Wetmore's Diary, in ibid., p. 178.

18. Moorhead, *New Mexico's Royal Road*, pp. 3–54, 95–122.

19. Gregg, *Commerce of the Prairies*, p. 269.

20. Susan Shelby Magoffin, *Down the Santa Fe Trail and into Mexico*, ed. Stella M. Drumm (New Haven and London: Yale University Press, 1962), p. 149; James Ohio Pattie, *The Personal Narrative of James Ohio Pattie of Kentucky*, ed. Timothy Flint (Chicago: Lakeside Press, R. R. Donnelly and Sons, 1930), pp. 72, 127; Gregg, *Commerce of the Prairies*, pp. 135, 269.

21. James H. Simpson, *Navaho Expedition: Journal of a Military Reconnaissance from Santa Fe, New Mexico, to the Navaho Country Made in 1849 by Lieutenant James H. Simpson*, ed. Frank McNitt (Norman: University of Oklahoma Press, 1964), pp. 154, 158; Gregg, *Commerce of the Prairies*, p. 268.

22. Gregg, *Commerce of the Prairies*, p. 268.

23. Ibid., p. 191.

24. Ibid., p. 187.

25. Ibid., p. 188.

26. Magoffin, *Down the Santa Fe Trail*, p. 153.

27. Moorhead, *New Mexico's Royal Road*, pp. 109, 195.

28. Pattie, *Personal Narrative*, pp. 71–72.

29. Simpson, *Navaho Expedition*, p. 154.

30. Pattie, *Personal Narrative*, p. 57.

31. Gregg, *Commerce of the Prairies,* pp. 161–62.

32. Ibid., p. 190.

33. "Proclamation by Stephen Watts Kearny, Brigadier-General, U.S.A., Santa Fe, New Mexico, August 22, 1846," and "Bill of Rights as Declared by Brigadier General Stephen W. Kearny, September 22, 1946," in *New Mexico Historic Documents,* ed. Richard N. Ellis (Albuquerque: University of New Mexico Press, 1975), pp. 4–5, 8.

34. Chester E. Faris, "Pueblo Governor's Canes" (Albuquerque: BIA Area Office, 1952), RF, NA, RG 75, BIA, p. 3; Major W. H. Emory, Notes from a Military Reconnaissance, HED 7, 309th Cong., 1st sess., 1848, quoted in Faris, "Pueblo Governor's Canes," p. 3; Dwight L. Clarke, ed., *The Original Journals of Henry Smith Turner, with Stephen Watts Kearny to New Mexico and California, 1846–1847* (Norman: University of Oklahoma Press, 1966), pp. 75–76.

35. Clarke, *Original Journals,* p. 75.

36. Ibid., pp. 75–78.

37. Philip St. George Cooke et al., *Exploring Southwestern Trails, 1846–1854,* ed. Ralph P. Bieber with Averam B. Bender (Glendale, Calif.: Arthur H. Clark Co., 1938), pp. 72–74.

38. HED 41, 30th Cong., 1st sess., 1848, p. 39, 567–68, quoted in Cooke et al., *Exploring Southwestern Trails,* pp. 72–73, includes these comments made by Lieutenant W. H. Emory and Captain Abraham R. Johnston in 1846.

39. J. W. Abert, "Report to W. L. Marcy, Secretary of War, 4 February 1848," in *Report of the Secretary of War,* SED 23, 30th Cong., 1st sess., 1848; reprinted as *Abert's New Mexico Report, 1846–47* (Albuquerque: Horn and Wallace, 1962), p. 62.

40. Ibid., pp. 46, 63.

41. Ibid., pp. 64–66, 71.

42. Ibid., p. 71.

43. Ibid.

44. Ibid., p. 73.

45. Ibid., p. 74.

46. Ibid., pp. 76–77.

47. Ibid., pp. 77–78, 81; "Poblazón," the name that Abert states the Mexicans used to describe one of the ruins, might be a variant form of "población" (population), "poblachón" (a large collection of houses, more than a village and less than a town), or "poblado" (town or village); no Spanish town of that name appears elsewhere in the records. The boundaries of the town of Nuestra Señora de la Luz, abandoned in the late eighteenth century, adjoined those of the Espiritu Santo along the Río Puerco at the base of Mesa Prieta. Abert's text gives no precise measure of how far north the party traveled. The map (endpapers) that he and Peck prepared shows Poblazón at approximately lat. 35°14–15', lon. 107°5', east and slightly north of the site near Paguate (measured at lat. 35°13', lon. 107°20'), where Abert made the drawing included in the journal on p. 75. The latitude shown would intersect the Río

Puerco near the base of Mesa Prieta; on the other hand, the longitude given lies five to ten miles south of that point. It can be argued that the course of the stream that the explorers followed west the next day, as drawn on the map, more closely resembles the route of Salado Creek, with its branches, than the Cañada de los Canoncitos farther south (USGS, Albuquerque, 1963). This would tend to support the more northerly location proposed for the site.

48. Porfirio Montoya, interview with Floyd Montoya et al., 11 February 1980, Santa Ana Pueblo Oral History Project, Tape no. 12, p. 5; Ellis, "Anthropological Evidence Supporting the Land Claim," p. 47, identifies two Tamayame sites along the Río Puerco, P2–5 (five miles north of the Puerco bridge on Highway 66), which lay "ten miles or more south of the lands near the southern tip of Mesa Prieta, where other Santa Anas were struggling to make a living," and P3-BSW, a much larger site "seven miles up the Puerco from the bridge." The first site included "Puname polychrome sherds representing 18th or early 19th century." Montoya notes that, even in the process of gathering material for the claim, no evidence emerged that Zía people farmed in this region.

49. Porfirio Montoya, interview with Floyd Montoya, Donna Pino, and Thomas Leubben, 16 January 1980, Santa Ana Pueblo Oral History Project, Tape no. 3, includes the migration story and discusses the location of the village; Porfirio Montoya, interview with Floyd Montoya and Tom Leubben, 25 March 1980, Santa Ana Pueblo Oral History Project, Tape no. 16, pp. 1, 7–8, also describes the route, noting that the people sought shelter on the mesa top at night. According to tradition, the village was built on the south (or west) side of the river, where it winds around the base of the mesa. If the tradition is accurate and this is the village Abert found, this description would suggest that the Río Puerco has since changed course.

50. Abert, "Report," p. 95.

51. Ibid., p. 96.

52. Ibid., p. 137.

53. Simpson, *Navaho Expedition*, p. 24; Annie Heloise Abel, ed., *The Official Correspondence of James S. Calhoun while Indian Agent at Santa Fe and Superintendent of Indian Affairs in New Mexico* (Washington, D.C.: GPO, 1915), p. 38.

54. Simpson, *Navaho Expedition*, p. lxxvii, describes Beale as "probably a Navajo" who held no office at Santa Ana.

55. Simpson, *Navaho Expedition*, p. lxxviii; Abel, *Official Correspondence*, p. 38.

56. Simpson, *Navaho Expedition*, p. lxxix.

57. James S. Calhoun, IA, SF, NM, to [Orlando Brown], CIA, 1 October 1849, AP I, *ARCIA 1849*, SED 1, 31st Cong., 1st sess. (Washington, D.C.: Wm. Belt, 1850), p. 1001; Abel, *Official Correspondence*, p. 38.

58. George Archibald McCall, *New Mexico in 1850: A Military View*, ed. Robert W. Frazer (Norman: University of Oklahoma Press, 1968), p. 178.

59. Ibid., pp. 84, 180.

60. Ibid., p. 156.

61. Calhoun to Brown, 1 October 1849; E. A. Graves, IA, Albiquen Ag., to D. Meriwether, Gov., eo SIA, NM, 31 August 1853, incl. in Meriwether to George W. Manypenny, CIA, 31 August 1853, AP no. 80, NMS, *ARCIA 1853*, SED 1, 33d Cong., 1st sess. (Washington, D.C.: Beverly Tucker, Senate Printer, 1854), pp. 434–41; D. Meriwether, Gov., eo SIA, NM, to Geo. W. Manypenny, CIA, 1 September 1854, AP no. 84, NMS, *ARCIA 1854*, HED 1, 33d Cong., 2nd sess. (Washington, D.C.: A. O. P. Nicholson, Printer, 1854), pp. 374–85; Meriwether to Manypenny, September 1855, AP no. 94, NMS, *ARCIA 1855*, SED 1, 34th Cong., 1st sess. (Washington, D.C.: A. O. P. Nicholson, Senate Printer, 1856), pp. 506–10. These reports illustrate the general impression of the pueblos that developed quickly and remained constant through much of the century. Although the description was generally accurate, the individual reports often include erroneous details. For example, Indian Agent Graves, just before resigning his post, submitted a report arguing that the pueblos had been nomadic until Spaniards persuaded them to settle in farms; see E. A. Graves, IA, to George W. Manypenny, CIA, 8 June 1854, AP no. 85, NMS, *ARCIA 1854*, HED 1, 33d Cong., 2nd sess. (Washington, D.C.: A. O. P. Nicholson, Printer, 1854), pp. 385–92.

62. Almost all of the annual reports for these years include, either in the narrative or in the statistical charts, the figure of eight to ten thousand people for total pueblo population—a figure based largely on estimate. Santa Ana population is listed as 399 in James S. Calhoun, IA, SF, NM, to Luke Lea, CIA, 16 February 1851, AP no. 58, NMS, *ARCIA 1851*, HED 2, 32d Cong., 1st sess. (Washington, D.C.: A. Boyd Hamilton, Printer, 1851), pp. 190–92.

63. David Meriwether, Gov., eo SIA, NM, to George W. Manypenny, CIA, 30 September 1856, AP no. 72, NMS, *ARCIA 1856* HED 1, 34th Cong., 3d sess. (Washington, D.C.: Cornelius Wendell, Printer, 1856), pp. 731–35.

64. James S. Calhoun, Gov., eo SIA, NM, to Luke Lea, CIA, 30 June 1851, AP no. 61, NMS, *ARCIA 1851*, HED 2, 32d Cong., 1st sess. (A. Boyd Hamilton, Printer, 1851), pp. 197–98.

65. "Compendium of the Report of the Commissioner of Indian Affairs, 1859," *ARCIA 1859*, SED 1, 36th Cong., 1st sess. (Washington, D.C.: George W. Bowman, Printer, 1860), p. 393; Michael Steck, SIA, NM, to William P. Dole, CIA, 19 September 1863, AP no. 41, NMS, *ARCIA 1863*, HED 1, 38th Cong., 1st sess. (Washington, D.C.: GPO, 1864), pp. 225–30; again, virtually every annual report in these years contains references to problems with hostile tribes and to the peaceable disposition of the pueblos.

66. [William P. Dole], CIA, to [James P. Usher], SI, 31 October 1863, *ARCIA 1863*, HED 1, 38th Cong., 1st sess. (Washington, D.C.: GPO, 1864), pp. 136–37.

67. J. S. Calhoun, IA, SF, NM, extract from a letter, 12 October 1850, AP no. 32, *ARCIA 1850*, SED 1, 31st Cong., 2nd sess. (Washington, D.C.: Union Office, 1851), pp. 139–41.

68. Michael Steck, SIA, NM, to William P. Dole, CIA, 11 October 1864, AP no. 71, NMS, *ARCIA 1864*, HED 1, 38th Cong., 2nd sess. (Washington, D.C.: GPO, 1865) p. 325 [ID ed., p. 181].

69. Brig. Gen. James H. Carleton, Cmdg. Dept. of NM, to Brig. Gen. Lorenzo Thomas, Adj. Gen., U. S. Army, 6 September 1863, AP no. 42, NMS, *ARCIA 1863*, HED 1, 38th Cong., 1st sess. (Washington, D.C.: GPO, 1864), pp. 230–31; Annie Heloise Abel, ed., "The Journal of John Greiner," *Old Santa Fe* 3, no. 11 (July 1916):204.

70. Calhoun, 12 October 1850; Luke Lea, CIA, to A. H. H. Stuart, SI, 27 November 1850, *ARCIA 1850*, SED 1, 31st Cong., 2nd sess. (Washington, D.C.: Union Office, 1851), pp. 42–43; James S. Calhoun, IA, SF, NM, to Luke Lea, CIA, 2 February 1851, AP no. 56, NMS, *ARCIA 1851*, HED 2, 32d Cong., 1st sess. (Washington, D.C.: A. Boyd Hamilton, Printer, 1851), pp. 186–90; D. V. Whiting to James S. Calhoun, IA, SF, NM, 10 February 1851, incl. in Calhoun to Lea, 16 February 1851; J. S. Calhoun, IA, SF, NM, to Luke Lea, CIA, 4 February 1851, AP no. 57, NMS, *ARCIA 1851*, p. 190; James S. Calhoun to Luke Lea, CIA, 31 March 1851, AP No. 59, NMS, *ARCIA 1851*, pp. 193–94; James S. Calhoun to Luke Lea, CIA, 4 May 1851, AP No. 60, NMS, *ARCIA 1851*, pp. 195–97; Jas. L. Collins, SIA, NM, to Charles E. Mix, CIA, 27 September 1858, AP no. 73, NMS, *ARCIA 1858*, HED 2, 35th Cong., 2nd sess. (Washington: James B. Steadman, Printer, 1859), p. 544; James L. Collins, SIA, NM, to Alfred B. Greenwood, CIA, 17 September 1859, AP no. 167, NMS, *ARCIA 1859*, SED 1, 36th Cong., 1st sess. (Washington, D.C.: George W. Bowman, Printer, 1860), p. 708.

71. James S. Calhoun, IA, NM, to Orlando Brown, CIA, 1 October 1849, *ARCIA 1849*, SED 1, 31st Cong., 1st sess. (Washington, D.C.: GPO, 1850), pp. 994–1102; James S. Calhoun, IA, NM to Orlando Brown, CIA 29 March 1850, *ARCIA 1850*, SED 1, 31st Cong., 2nd sess. (Washington, D.C.: GPO, 1851), pp. 128–31; Hugh N. Smith to Orlando Brown, CIA, 9 March 1850, *ARCIA 1850*, SED 1, 31st Cong., 2nd sess. (Washington, D. C.: GPO, 1851), pp. 141–43; James S. Calhoun, IA, NM, to Luke Lea, CIA, 31 March 1851, *ARCIA 1851*, HED 2, 32nd Cong., 1st sess. (Washington, D.C.: GPO, 1852), pp. 193–94; E. A. Graves, IA, to Governor D. Meriwether, SIA, NM, 31 August 1853, *ARCIA 1853*, SED 1, 33d Cong., 1st sess. (Washington, D.C.: GPO, 1854), pp. 434–41; George W. Manypenny, CIA, to Robert McClelland, SI, 22 November 1856, *ARCIA 1856*, HED 1, 34th Cong., 3d sess. (Washington, D.C.: GPO, 1857), pp. 566–75; S. M. Yost, IA, to J. W. Denver, CIA, 30 August 1857, NMS Report No. 121, *ARCIA 1857*, HED 2, 35th Cong., 1st sess. (Washington, D. C.: GPO, 1858), pp. 569–72; James W. Denver, CIA, to Jacob Thompson, SI, 30 November 1857, *ARCIA 1857*, p. 297.

72. John Ward, IA, PA, to M. Steck, SIA, SF, NM, 30 June 1864, AP No. 72, *ARCIA 1864*, HED 1, 38th Cong., 2nd sess. (Washington, D.C.: GPO, 1865), pp. 331–39; Ward notes that Santa Ana and several other pueblos had a disproportionate number of blind residents.

73. [William P. Dole], CIA, to [John P. Usher], SI, 15 November 1864, *ARCIA 1864,* HED 1, 38th Cong., 2nd sess. (Washington, D.C.: GPO, 1865), pp. 161–64; Steck to Dole, 11 October 1864; Calhoun to Brown, 1 October 1849; Lea to Stuart, 27 November 1850; Calhoun to Lea, 30 June 1851; Samuel Gorman, Missionary to Pueblos, Laguna, NM, to James L. Collins, SIA, NM, 2 October 1858, incl. in Collins to Mix, 27 September, 1858; J. S. Calhoun, IA, SF, NM, to Orlando Brown, CIA, 30 March 1850, AP no. 29, *ARCIA 1850,* SED 1, 31st Cong., 2nd sess. (Washington, D.C.: Union Office, 1851), pp. 131–35; Hugh N. Smith to Orlando Brown, CIA, 9 March 1850, AP no. 33, *ARCIA 1850,* pp. 141–43.

74. James S. Calhoun to Luke Lea, CIA, 1 October 1851, AP no. 65, NMS, *ARCIA 1851,* HED 2, 32nd Cong., 1st sess. (Washington, D.C.: A. Boyd Hamilton, Printer, 1851), pp. 204–5; J. S. Calhoun to Col. E. V. Sumner, Cmdg. 9th Mil. Dept., Ft. Union, NM, 4 August 1851, incl. in Calhoun to Luke Lea, CIA, 31 August 1851, AP no. 64, NMS, *ARCIA 1851,* pp. 200–204; Calhoun to Lea, 4 May 1851 and 30 June 1851; Meriwether to Manypenny, 1 September 1854.

75. Clarke, *Original Journals,* p. 74.

76. Abel, "Journal."

77. See for example Testimony of Ignacio María Sánchez Vergara, 1 October 1819, summarizing the actions of Mariano de la Peña to restore to Santa Ana lands sold by San Felipe, marked on the obverse, "[Re]gistrado en el Libro [?], folio 64 . . . 1850" and signed by Donaciano Vigil, Registrador, in the files of Rothstein, Walther, Donatelli, Hughes, Dahlstrom & Cron, Attorneys for the Pueblo of Santa Ana, Santa Fe, New Mexico; Memorandum form Richard W. Hughes to Ward Alan Minge re Baca Case Testimony, 26 February 1984, p. 7, in the files of Rothstein, Walther, Donatelli, Hughes, Dahlstrom & Cron, Attorneys for the Pueblo of Santa Ana, Santa Fe, New Mexico; David Snow, "Inventory of Historic Documents Pertaining to the Title to Real Property in Re Santa Ana Pueblo," p. 1; Richard Hughes, "Inventory of Historic Documents—Pueblo of Santa Ana," in the files of Rothstein, Walther, Donatelli, Hughes, Dahlstrom & Cron, Attorneys for the Pueblo of Santa Ana, Santa Fe, New Mexico, notes certifications throughout and includes, in item 1R, a description of the 16-leaf document that "contains certified transcriptions of, apparently, all or nearly all of Santa Ana's principal land documents, certified and transcribed by John Greiner, Secretary of the Territory of New Mexico," 6 December 1852, with "notations apparently added during Court of Private Land Claims proceedings."

78. Abel, "Journal," p. 205.

79. Ibid., p. 206.

80. Ibid., p. 207.

81. Ibid., p. 242.

82. Ibid., p. 218.

83. Ibid., p. 233.

84. Ibid., p. 236.

85. Ibid., p. 238.

86. Ibid., p. 197.

87. Ibid., p. 207.

88. Ibid., p. 225.

89. Ibid., pp. 234–35.

90. For example, see ibid., pp. 213, 215, 219, 220.

91. Edward H. Spicer, *Cycles of Conquest: The Impact of Spain, Mexico, and the United States on the Indians of the Southwest, 1533–1960* (Tucson: University of Arizona Press, 1962), pp. 343–57, briefly summarizes America's Indian policy and its application in the Southwest; for a more general history and description, see S. Lyman Tyler, *A History of Indian Policy* (Washington, D.C.: US Dept. of Interior, BIA, 1973).

92. Myra Ellen Jenkins and Albert H. Schroeder, *A Brief History of New Mexico* (Albuquerque: University of New Mexico Press, 1974), pp. 50–51; Alvin R. Sunseri, *Seeds of Discord: New Mexico in the Aftermath of the American Conquest, 1846–1861* (Chicago: Nelson Hall, 1979); Lynn I. Perrigo, *The American Southwest: Its People and Cultures* (Albuquerque: University of New Mexico Press, 1971), pp. 178–241.

93. Perrigo, *American Southwest,* pp. 210–11; Frank D. Reeve, "The Federal Indian Policy in New Mexico, 1858–1880," *New Mexico Historical Review* 12 (1937) and 13 (1938), focuses on policy related to non-pueblo tribes.

94. Calhoun to Lea, 1 October 1851.

95. Abel, "Journal," p. 238; Herman J. Viola, *Diplomats in Buckskins: A History of Indian Delegations in Washington City* (Washington, D.C.: Smithsonian Institution Press, 1981), p. 55.

96. Abel, "Journal."

97. Meriwether to Manypenny, 30 September 1856.

98. Dole to Usher, 15 November 1864.

99. Collins to Mix, 27 September 1854, p. 544.

100. Calhoun to Lea, 4 May 1851.

101. Abel, "Journal."

102. James L. Collins, SIA, NM, to William P. Dole, CIA, 10 October 1862, AP no. 50, NMS, *ARCIA 1862,* HED 1, 37th Cong., 3d sess. (Washington, D.C.: GPO, 1862), p. 385.

103. Viola, *Diplomats in Buckskins,* p. 106. Faris "Pueblo Governor's Canes," p. 6; *Santa Fe New Mexican,* 27 May 1864, quoted in Faris, ibid., p. 6; H. R. Whiting, Commissioner, Dept. of Justice, Albuquerque, NM, to CIA, 6 July 1911, P-1911-044-60120, RF, RG 75, BIA, NA; C. F. Hauke, 2nd Asst. CIA, to H. R. Whiting, 20 July and 20 October 1911, P-1911-044-60120, RF, RG 75, BIA, NA; Sylvanus Griswold Morler, School of American Archaeology, MNM, to CIA, 18 August 1913, P-1911-044-60120, RF, RG 75, BIA, NA; Cato Sells, CIA, to Senator J. H. Gallinger, 17 November 1913, P-1911-044-60120, RF, RG 75, BIA, NA; C. F. Hauke, 2nd Asst. CIA, to Sylvanus Griswold Morler, MNM, 14 October 1913, P-1911-044-60120, RF, RG 75, BIA, NA; J. H. Gallinger, Memorandum, received 13 November 1913, P-1911-044-60120, RF, RG 75, BIA, NA.

Chapter 8

1. James F. Meline, *Two Thousand Miles on Horseback: Santa Fe and Back, A Summer Tour through Kansas, Nebraska, Colorado, and New Mexico, in the Year 1866* (1868; reprint, Albuquerque: Horn and Wallace, 1966), p. 254.

2. Ibid., pp. 155–56.

3. Ibid., pp. 230–31, describes threshing at San Felipe; W. H. Emory, "Notes of a Military Reconnaissance from Fort Leavenworth in Missouri to San Diego in California," SED 7, 30th Cong., 1st sess. (Washington, D.C.: Wendell and Van Benthuysen, 1848), pp. 38–40, describes the process at Sandía.

4. Meline, *Two Thousand Miles on Horseback*, pp. 118–19.

5. James S. Calhoun, in *The Official Correspondence of James S. Calhoun while Indian Agent at Santa Fe and Superintendent of Indian Affairs in New Mexico*, ed. Annie Heloise Abel (Washington, D.C.: GPO, 1915), p. 31.

6. Meline, *Two Thousand Miles on Horseback*, p. 254.

7. Ibid., pp. 178, 181.

8. Ibid., p. 223.

9. For a discussion of the historical roots and development of American Indian policy, see S. Lyman Tyler, *A History of Indian Policy* (Washington, D. C.: U. S. Dept. of Interior, BIA, 1973); Francis Paul Prucha, *American Indian Policy in the Formative Years: The Indian Trade and Intercourse Acts, 1790–1834* (Cambridge, Mass.: Harvard University Press, 1962); and Ronald N. Satz, *American Indian Policy in the Jacksonian Era* (Lincoln: University of Nebraska Press, 1975).

10. The complex legal issues of sovereignty, wardship, trust status, identity, and jurisdiction which underlie this discussion have been discussed primarily in legal and technical sources. They are summarized and outlined in Floyd A. O'Neil and Gregory C. Thompson, *A History of the Indians of the United States: A Syllabus*, ed. Laura Bayer, American West Center Occasional Papers, no. 12 (Salt Lake City: American West Center, 1979), pp. 536–85. For more detailed studies, see Hank Adams et al., *Report on Trust Responsibilities and the Federal-Indian Relationship, including Treaty Review*, Task Force One, Final Report to the American Indian Policy Review Commission (Washington, D.C.: GPO, 1976); Sherwin Broadhead et al., *Report on Federal, State, and Tribal Jurisdiction*, Task Force Four, Final Report to the American Indian Policy Review Commission (Washington, D.C.: GPO, 1976); Felix S. Cohen, *Handbook of Federal Indian Law* (Washington, D.C.: GPO, 1941); Theodore W. Taylor, *The States and Their Indian Citizens* (Washington, D.C.: Department of the Interior, Bureau of Indian Affairs, 1972); and Wilcomb E. Washburn, *Red Man's Land—White Man's Law: A Study of the Past and Present Status of the American Indian* (New York: Charles Scribner's Sons, 1971).

11. After the mid-eighteenth century, American policymakers placed increasing emphasis on the need to assimilate, educate, and "civilize" Indians; as a result, the concept of wardship gained an increasingly prominent position in theory.

12. Hubert Howe Bancroft, *History of Arizona and New Mexico, 1530–1888,* vol. 17 in *The Works of Hubert Howe Bancroft* (San Francisco: History Company, 1889), n. 10, pp. 637–40, summarizes the bills passed by the New Mexico legislature through 1862.

13. Hugh N. Smith to Orlando Brown, CIA, 9 March 1850, AP no. 33, *ARCIA 1850,* SED 1, 31st Cong., 2nd sess. (Washington, D.C.: Union Office, 1851), p. 142.

14. J. S. Calhoun to Orlando Brown, 16 November 1849, in Abel, *Official Correspondence,* pp. 78–81.

15. J. S. Calhoun, IA, to Orlando Brown, CIA, 30 March 1850, AP no. 29, *ARCIA 1850,* SED 1, 31st Cong., 2nd sess. (Washington, D.C.: Union Office, 1851), pp. 131–35.

16. J. S. Calhoun, Gov., eo SIA, NM, to Luke Lea, CIA, 30 June 1851, AP no. 61, NMS, *ARCIA 1851,* HED 2, 32d Cong., 1st sess. (Washington, D.C.: A. Boyd Hamilton, Printer, 1851), pp. 197–98.

17. D. Meriwether, Gov., eo SIA, NM, to Geo. W. Manypenny, CIA, 1 September 1854, AP no. 84, NMS, *ARCIA 1854,* HED 1, 33d Cong., 2nd sess. (Washington, D.C.: A. O. P. Nicholson, Printer, 1854), pp. 374–85.

18. S. M. Yost, IA, PA, to J. W. Denver, CIA, 30 August 1857, AP no. 121, NMS, *ARCIA 1857,* HED 2, 35th Cong., 1st sess. (Washington, D.C.: Cornelius Wendell, Printer, 1857), pp. 569–72.

19. L. Lea, CIA, to A. H. H. Stuart, SI, 27 November 1850, *ARCIA 1850,* SED l, 31st Cong., 2nd sess. (Washington, D.C.: Union Office, 1851), pp. 42–43.

20. George W. Manypenny, CIA, to R. McClelland, SI, 26 November 1855, *ARCIA 1855,* SED 1, 34th Cong., 1st sess. (Washington, D.C.: A. O. P. Nicholson, Senate Printer, 1856), pp. 331–34, 341.

21. R. H. Stanton, U. S. House Committee on Elections, "Report on Contested Election, Lane v. Gallegos," 24 February 1854, H. Rept. 121, 33d Cong., 1st sess. (Washington, D.C.: A. O. P. Nicholson, Printer, 1854), pp. 1–4.

22. For example, [Eli S. Parker], CIA to [Jacob D. Cox], SI, 23 December 1869, *ARCIA 1869,* HED 1, 41st Cong., 2nd sess. (Washington, D.C.: GPO, 1870), pp. 463–65, noted that since 1857 only ten thousand dollars had been appropriated for the pueblos; five years earlier [William P. Dole], CIA, to [John P. Usher], SI, 15 November 1864, *ARCIA 1864,* HED 1, 38th Cong., 2nd sess. (Washington, D.C.: GPO, 1865), pp. 161–64, had pointed out that few of the tools purchased under that appropriation had actually reached the pueblos. See also John Ward, Sp. IA, P, to [N. G. Taylor, CIA?], 7 September 1868, AP no. 36, NMS, *ARCIA 1868,* HED 1, 40th Cong., 3d sess. (Washington, D.C.: GPO, 1869), pp. 636–38; John Ward, S. IA, P, to Col. A. B. Norton, SIA, N.M., 18 September 1866, AP no. 44, NMS, *ARCIA 1866,* HED 1, 39th Cong., 2nd sess. (Washington, D.C.: GPO, 1867), p. 148; 1st Lt. George E. Ford, Sp. IA, P, to Maj. Wm. Clinton, SIA, NM, 8 September 1869, AP no. 57, NMS, *ARCIA 1869,* HED 1, 41st Cong., 2nd sess. (Washington, D.C.: GPO, 1870), pp. 693–96.

23. Chester E. Faris, "Pueblo Governors' Canes" (Albuquerque: BIA Area Office, 1952), RF, NA, RG 75, BIA, p. 6; William P. Dole, CIA, to W. F. M. Henry [*sic.* should be W. F. M. Arny], Sec., Actg. Gov., New Mexico Territory, 26 June 1863, AP no. 49, *ARCIA 1863,* HED 1, 38th Cong., 1st sess. (Washington, D.C.: GPO, 1864), pp. 238–39.

24. Dole to Henry [Arny], 26 June 1863.

25. [Dole], CIA, to [Usher], SI, 15 November 1864.

26. A. B. Norton, SIA, NM, to D. N. Cooley, CIA, 28 September 1866, AP no. 43, *ARCIA 1866,* HED 1, 39th Cong., 2nd sess. (Washington, D.C.: GPO, 1867), pp. 146–47.

27. J. K. Graves, Sp. IA, NM, to D. M. Cooley, CIA, 1866, AP no. 40, NMS, *ARCIA 1866,* HED 1, 39th Cong., 2nd sess. (Washington, D.C.: GPO, 1867), pp. 131–35.

28. [John P.] Slough, Chief Justice, 1st Judicial District, New Mexico Territory, Opinion in *U.S. v. Benigno Ortiz,* 1867, AP no. 59, NMS, *ARCIA 1867,* ID ed. (Washington, D.C.: GPO, 1868), pp. 217–21.

29. John Ward, Sp. IA, P, to Col. A. B. Norton, SIA, NM, 2 August 1867, AP no. 54, NMS, *ARCIA 1867,* ID ed. (Washington, D.C.: GPO, 1868), pp. 207–8.

30. W. F. M. Arny, IA, AA, NM, to Chas E. Mix, ACIA, 11 August 1867, AP no. 58, NMS, *ARCIA 1867,* ID ed. (Washington, D.C.: GPO, 1868), pp. 215–17.

31. A. B. Norton, SIA, NM, to N. G. Taylor, CIA, 24 August 1867, AP no. 49, NMS, *ARCIA 1867,* ID ed. (Washington, D.C.: GPO, 1868), pp. 189–95.

32. [Charles E. Mix], ACIA, to [Orville H. Browning], SI, 15 November 1867, *ARCIA 1867,* ID ed. (Washington, D.C.: GPO, 1868), pp. 11–13.

33. Henry Stanbery, US Atty. Gen., to S. B. Elkins, US Atty. for NM, 23 November 1867, AP no. 60, NMS, *ARCIA 1867,* ID ed. (Washington, D.C.: GPO, 1868), pp. 221–22.

34. J[ohn] Ward, IA, PA, Reply, 24 August 1865, typed excerpt from "Report of the Joint Special Committee on Condition of Indian Tribes," S. Rept. 156, 39th Cong., 2nd sess. (Washington, D.C.: GPO, 1867), SPA, p. 457.

35. Ford to Clinton, 8 September 1869.

36. Jno. Orme Cole, IA, P, to Col. Nathaniel Pope, SIA, NM, 19 August 1872, AP no. 55, NMS, *ARCIA 1872,* HED 1, 42d Cong, 3d sess. (Washington, D.C.: GPO, 1873), pp. 693–94.

37. Edwin C. Lewis, IA, PA, to E. P. Smith, CIA, 15 September 1874, *ARCIA 1874,* HED 1, 43d Cong., 2nd sess. (Washington, D.C.: GPO, 1875), pp. 616–18.

38. Ford to Clinton, 8 September 1867.

39. Edwin C. Lewis, IA, P, to L. Edwin Dudley, SIA, NM, 25 September 1873, AP no. 52, NMS, *ARCIA 1873,* HED 1, 43d Cong., 1st sess. (Washington, D.C.: GPO, 1874), p. 646.

40. L. Edwin Dudley, SIA, NM to Edw. P. Smith, CIA, 15 November 1873, AP no. 46, *ARCIA 1873,* HED 1, 43d Cong., 1st sess. (Washington, D.C.: GPO, 1874), pp. 637–38;

somewhat curiously, Dudley gave that as the reason he was "opposed to any effort to secure any decision by the Supreme Court of the United States upon this question."

41. Ben M. Thomas, IA, PA, to E. P. Smith, CIA, 8 September 1875, *ARCIA 1875,* ID ed. (Washington, D.C.: GPO, 1875), pp. 332–33, Ben M. Thomas IA, P, to [John O. Smith], CIA, 24 August 1876, *ARCIA 1876,* HED 1, 44th Cong., 2nd sess. (Washington, D.C.: GPO, 1877), p. 515.

42. 1st Lt. Charles L. Cooper, IA, P, to Maj. William Clinton, SIA, NMT, 8 September 1869, AP no. 56, NMS, *ARCIA 1869,* HED 1, 41st Cong., 2nd sess. (Washington, D.C.: GPO, 1870), pp. 691–92.

43. Ford to Clinton, 8 September 1869.

44. [Parker], CIA, to [Cox], SI, 23 December 1869.

45. Vincent Colyer, Sp. I. Com., "Report on the Indian Tribes and Reservations of Eastern Kansas, Indian Territory, Northern Texas, New Mexico, Northeastern Arizona, and Southeastern Colorado, Outlined by Personal Observation and Inspection among These Tribes during the Year 1869," Appendix C3, *ARCIA 1869,* HED 1, 41st Cong., 2nd sess. (Washington, D.C.: GPO, 1870), pp. 530–31.

46. W. F. M. Arny, IA, P, to Col. Nathaniel Pope, SIA, 18 August 1871, AP no. 37, NMS, *ARCIA 1871,* ID ed. (Washington, D.C: GPO, 1872), pp. 380–95.

47. Land Division, UPA, Albuquerque, NM, "Pueblo of Santa Ana Land Status," 1 April 1940, SPA, p. 4.

48. Ibid., pp. 4–5.

49. Lt. A. W. Whipple et al., "Report Upon the Indian Tribes," SED 78, 33d Cong., 2nd sess. (Washington, D.C.: n.p., 1855), p. 12.

50. William W. Morrow, *Spanish and Mexican Private Land Grants* (1923; reprint, New York: Arno Press, 1974), pp. 20–23.

51. Act of 22 July 1854, in ibid., p. 21; Lynn I. Perrigo, *The American Southwest: Its Peoples and Cultures* (New York: Holt, Rinehart & Winston, 1971), pp. 214–15.

52. Quoted in "Pueblo of Santa Ana Land Status," p. 3.

53. [G. S.] Orth, Chairman, House Committee on Private Land Claims, "Report on the Pueblo of Santa Ana, to Accompany H.R. No. 1343," 1 July 1868, H. Rept. 70, 40th Cong., 2nd sess. (Washington, D.C.: GPO, 1868), pp. 1–3.

54. "Pueblo of Santa Ana Land Status," p. 3; Wm. Pelham, NM Surveyor General, "Schedule of Pueblo Grants," 12 January 1858, incl. in Pelham to Hendricks, 23 March 1858, HED 89, 35th Cong., 1st sess. (Washington, D.C.: James B. Steedman, Printer, 1858), p. 3; J. Thompson, SI, to Jas. L. Orr, Speaker, US House, 23 March 1858, HED 89, 35th Cong., 1st sess. (Washington, D.C.: James B. Steedman, Printer, 1858), p. 1; Thomas A. Hendricks, CGLO, to J. Thompson, SI, 2 March 1858, incl. in Thompson to Orr, 23 March 1858, HED 89, 35th Cong., 1st sess. (Washington, D.C.: James B. Steedman, Printer, 1858), pp. 1–2; Pelham, NM Surveyor General, to Thomas A. Hendricks, CGLO, 15 September 1858, AD, Section G, RCGLO, *ARSI 1858,* SED 1, 35th Cong., 2nd sess. (Washington, D.C.: Wm. Harris, Printer, 1859), pp. 296–300.

55. Faris, "Pueblo Governors' Canes," p. 6; "Papers on the Pueblo of Santa Ana," 1867–68, HED 13, 40th Cong., 1st sess. (Washington, D.C.: GPO, 1868), microcard copy.

56. [James W. Denver], CIA, to [Jacob Thompson], SI, 30 November 1857, *ARCIA 1857,* HED 2, 35th Cong., 1st sess. (Washington, D.C.: Cornelius Wendell, Printer, 1857), p. 297; Wm. G. Pelham, NM Surveyor General, "Schedule of Pueblo Grants Examined and Approved by the Surveyor General of New Mexico, and Transmitted for the Final Action of Congress in the Premises," 12 January 1858, encl. in Pelham to Hendricks, 12 January 1858, encl. in Hendricks to Thompson, 2 March 1858, encl. in Thompson to Orr, 23 March 1858, HED 89, 35th Cong., 1st sess. (Washington, D.C.: James B. Steedman, Printer, 1858), p. 3; Thos. A. Hendricks, CGLO, to Jacob Thompson, SI, 30 November 1858, *ARSI 1858,* SED 1, 35th Cong., 2nd sess. (Washington, D.C.: Wm. Harris, Printer, 1859), pp. 106, 125, 130–32, 135, 140–41; [Charles E. Mix], CIA, to [Jacob Thompson], SI, 6 November 1858, *ARCIA 1858,* SED 1, 35th Cong., 2nd sess. (Washington, D.C.: Wm. Harris, Printer, 1859), p. 359; John Ward, IA, PA, "Statistics of the Indian Pueblos of New Mexico," 30 June 1864, encl. in Ward to Steck, 30 June 1864, AP no. 74, *ARCIA 1864,* HED 1, 38th Cong., 2nd sess. (Washington, D.C. GPO, 1865), P. 343.

57. Toribio Romero, IA, P, to A. B. Norton, SIA, NM, August 1866, Appendix, NM No. 2, *ARCIA 1866,* HED 1, 39th Cong., 2nd sess. (Washington, D.C.: GPO, 1867), pp. 314–15.

58. "Papers on the Pueblo of Santa Ana"; Orth, "Report on the Pueblo of Santa Ana"; "Pueblo of Santa Ana Land Status," p. 17.

59. W. F. M. Arny, IA, to Col. Nathaniel Pope, SIA, 18 August 1871, AP no. 37, NMS, *ARCIA 1871,* ID ed. (Washington, D.C.: GPO, 1872), p. 390.

60. "Transcript of Grant of Land to the Indian Pueblos of Zía, Santa Ana, and Jémez, Reported as Pueblo Claim T," in "Private Land Claims in New Mexico." HED 206, 43d Cong., 1st sess. (Washington, D.C.: GPO, 1874), pp. 2–3, 12.

61. Will M. Tipton, Insp., ID, "Memoranda in Regard to Indian Pueblo Grants in New Mexico," c. 1912, UP-df-2, AB, RG 75, BIA, FRCD, p. 8.

62. Stephen C. McElroy, US Dept. Surveyor, "Plat of the Zía, Santa Ana, and Jémez Grant," October-November 1877, RG 75, BIA, NA.

63. Bancroft, *History,* pp. 758–59; General Supt., UPA, "Report on the Ancient Claim of the Pueblo of Jémez and the Present Status of the Espiritu Santo Grant, together with a Classified Schedule of the Land Holdings and Permitted Areas of the Pueblo of Jémez," 5 May 1945, encl. in John C. Evans, Gen. Supt., UPA, to Juan Luis Pecos, Gov., Jémez P., 4 May 1945, SPA; Sophie D. Aberle, "The Pueblo Indians of New Mexico: Their Land, Economy, and Civil Organization," American Anthropological Association, Memoir no. 70, *American Anthropologist* 50, no. 4, pt. 2 (October 1948):10; Herbert O. Brayer, *Pueblo Indian Lands of the "Río Abajo," New Mexico* (Albuquerque: University of New Mexico Press, 1939), dates the confirmation of this grant to 1877.

64. M. C. Williams, IA, PA, to [John H. Oberly], CIA, 1 September 1888, *ARCIA 1888,* ID ed. (Washington, D.C.: GPO, 1888), pp. 197–99; "The Upper Rio Puerco Drainages: Brief History of Land Use," SCS, Section of Human Surveys, January 1937, SPA.

65. M. C. Williams, IA, PA, to CIA, 18 June 1888, MLS, FRCD, Reel 9, cited in James Vlasich, "Pueblo Indian Irrigation, Agriculture and Water Rights" (Ph.D diss., University of Utah, 1980), p. 166, no. 96; Vlasich states that the grant was confirmed by Congress in 1874.

66. T. J. Anderson, Asst. CGLO, to A. B. Upshaw, ACIA, 18 July 1888, P-1888-18100, LR, 1887–1907, RG 75, BIA, NA.

67. "Transcript of Grant of Land to the Indian Pueblos of Zía, Santa Ana, and Jémez"; Oliver LaFarge, with Arthur N. Morgan, *Santa Fe: The Autobiography of a Southwestern Town* (Norman: University of Oklahoma Press, 1959), p. 112.

68. Henry R. Poore, "Condition of Sixteen New Mexico Indian Pueblos, 1890," in ID, Census Office, *Report on Indians Taxed and Indians Not Taxed in the United States (Except Alaska) in the Eleventh Census: 1890* (Washington, D.C.: GPO, 1894), p. 430.

69. Ibid.; M. C. Williams IA, PA, to [Thomas J. Morgan], CIA, 10 June 1889, P-1889-15807, LR, 1881–1907, RG 75, BIA, NA.

70. Poore, "Condition," p. 432.

71. Robert W. Larson, *New Mexico Populism: A Study of Radical Protest in a Western Territory* (Boulder, Colo.: Colorado Associated University Press, 1974), p. 24.

72. Ibid., p. 16.

73. Benjamin M. Read, *Illustrated History of New Mexico* (Santa Fe, 1912, p. 378, cited in Larson, *New Mexico Populism,* p. 33, n. 37.

74. Larson, *New Mexico Populism,* pp. 79–80.

75. Ibid., p. 68.

76. Ibid., p. 69.

77. Ibid., pp. 77–78 and passim; Frederick W. Nolan, *The Life and Death of John Henry Tunstall* (Albuquerque: University of New Mexico Press, 1965), pp. 370, 385, 419, 441; Howard Roberts Lamar, *The Far Southwest, 1846–1912: A Territorial History* (New Haven and London: Yale University Press, 1966), pp. 146–50; Perrigo, *American Southwest,* pp. 310–12; William A. Keleher, *The Fabulous Frontier: Twelve New Mexico Items,* rev. ed. (Albuquerque: University of New Mexico Press, 1962), pp. 117–40, 212.

78. Lamar, *Far Southwest,* p. 149.

79. Keleher, *Fabulous Frontier,* p. 130.

80. Lamar, *Far Southwest,* p. 150.

81. Morrow, *Spanish and Mexican Private Land Grants,* pp. 22–27; Calvin Horn, *New Mexico's Troubled Years: The Story of the Early Territorial Governors* (Albuquerque: Horn & Wallace, 1963), pp. 138–42, discusses the disposal of papers cleared from an office intended for Attorney General Thomas B. Catron in 1870. According to Arie W. Poldervaart, *Blacked Robed Justice* (n.p.: Historical Society of New Mexico, 1948), pp. 8–9, New Mexico court files were "not always in the best of order."

82. John H. Robertson, IA, P&JA, to [Thomas J. Morgan], CIA, 2 March 1892, P&JA-1892-8738, LR, 1881–1901, RG 75, BIA, NA.

83. Robertson to CIA, 12 March 1892, P&JA-1802-10144, LR, 1881–1907, RG 75, BIA, NA.

84. Julian Japatero, Gov., Jémez P. et al., by E. M. Fenton, Teacher, Presbyterian School, to J. W. Noble, SI, 28 March 1892, P&JA-1892-12691, LR, 1881–1907, RG 75, BIA, NA.

85. W. H. H. Miller, US Atty. Gen. to SI, 28 July 1891, *Official Opinions of the Attorneys-General of the United States,* ed. Edward A. Hibbard, Esq., HMD no. 44, Vol. 20, 53d Cong., 3d sess. (Washington, D.C.: GPO, 1895), pp. 215–17.

86. Eugene A. Fiske, US Atty. for NM, to William A. Maury, A. Atty. Gen., US, 29 March 1892, in Maury to SI, 16 April 1892, P&JA-1892-14519, LR, 1881–1907, RG 75, BIA, NA.

87. Maury to SI, 16 April 1892.

88. Robertson to E.M. Fenton, 20 March 1892, MLS, AB, RG 75, BIA, FRCD.

89. Robertson to Gov. and Officials, Jémez P., 23 April 1892, MLS, RG 75, BIA, AB, NA.

90. "Report on the Ancient Claim of the Pueblo of Jémez"; Aberle, "Pueblo Indians of New Mexico," p. 10; both sources list the date of filing incorrectly as 1883, ten years before the actual date and eight years before the Court of Private Land Claims was established.

91. Capt. John L. Bullis, A.IA, P&JA, to M. S. Otero, 26 April 1894, MLS, RG 75, BIA, AB, FRCD.

92. Capt. John L. Bullis, A.IA, P&JA, to Governor of Jémez Pueblo, 2 October 1894, MLS, RG 75, BIA, AB, FRCD.

93. G. Hill Howard, Solicitor for Plaintiff, *Pueblo of Santa Ana and Its Inhabitants v. U.S., Amended Petition,* Court of Private Land Claims, Santa Fe, NM, May 1896, SAPRG; Pueblo files include copies of the agreement authorizing Howard to represent the pueblo, as well as various receipts for payments made to him; see Richard Hughes, "Inventory of Historic Documents—Pueblo of Santa Ana," in the files of Rothstein, Walther, Donatelli, Hughes, Dahlstrom & Cron, Attorneys for the Pueblo of Santa Ana, Santa Fe, New Mexico, items 5D, 5E, 5F, and 5G.

94. Capt. [John L. Bullis], A.IA, P&JA, to Governor of Santa Ana Pueblo, 28 November 1896, MLS, RG 75, BIA, AB, FRCD.

95. Capt. John L. Bullis, A.IA, P&JA, to Governor of Santa Ana Pueblo, 17 December 1896, and to G. Hill Howard, 28 November 1896, both in MLS, RG 75, BIA, AB, FRCD.

96. Minge, "The Pueblo of Santa Ana's El Ranchito Purchase, and the Adjudication of the Boundary with San Felipe: A Report Prepared for the Pueblo of Santa Ana," pp. 21–22; Sketch Map Showing Location of Río Grande Purchase Lands, Prepared for the Court of Private Land Claims Hearings, marked "Santa Ana Petition, Exhibit F," in the files of Rothstein, Walther, Donatelli, Hughes, Dahlstrom &

Cron, Attorneys for the Pueblo of Santa Ana, Santa Fe, New Mexico; see also items 1S and 1T in Hughes, "Inventory of Historic Documents—Pueblo of Santa Ana."

97. Minge, "The Pueblo of Santa Ana's El Ranchito Purchase, and the Adjudication of the Boundary with San Felipe: A Report Prepared for the Pueblo of Santa Ana," pp. 23–24; Joseph R. Reed, Chief Justice, Court of Private Land Claims, "Pueblo of Santa Ana and the Inhabitants Thereof, vs. United States: no. 157: El Ranchito Case," copy by James Reecer, Clerk, and Ireno L. Chavez, Deputy, 31 May 1897, SPA.

98. Minge, "The Pueblo of Santa Ana's El Ranchito Purchase, and the Adjudication of the Boundary with San Felipe: A Report Prepared for the Pueblo of Santa Ana," pp. 22–24.

99. "Report on the Ancient Claim of the Pueblo of Jémez."

100. Henry M. Atkinson, NM SG, Patent to Santa Ana Pueblo Land Claim, 25 April 1883, approved and sealed by Chester A. Arthur, SPA; William H. Taft, US Pres., by M. W. Young, Sec., and T. W. Sanford, Recorder, GLO, Grant to the Pueblo of Santa Ana, in Accordance with Court of Private Land Claims Docket no. 190, NM no. 84386, 18 October 1909, SPA.

101. For example, see N. S. Walpole, IA, P&JA, to [William A. Jones], CIA, 10 August 1899, *ARCIA 1899,* HED 5, 56th Cong., 1st sess., pt. 1 (Washington, D.C.: GPO, 1899), pp. 245–55.

102. Dolores Romero, IA, PA, to [John D. C. Atkins], CIA, 10 September 1885, *ARCIA 1885,* HED 1, 49th Cong., 1st sess. (Washington, D.C.: GPO, 1886), pp. 382–85; Pedro Sánchez, IA, PA, to Jno. D. C. Atkins, CIA, 15 April, 1885, P-1885-8606, LR, 1881–1907, RG 75, BIA, NA, also discusses attempts to defraud the pueblos.

103. Edmund G. Ross, NM Gov., to L. Q. C. Lamar, SI, 21 October 1885, *ARCIA 1885,* HED 1, 49th Cong., 1st sess. (Washington, D.C.: GPO 1886), p. 1011.

104. Poore, "Condition," p. 436; Poore, however, also noted the effects of trespass on the pueblos, stating that not one had "preserved its grant as confirmed by the Congress of 1858" (p. 425) and that "their present need is legal protection" (p. 436).

105. Romero to [Atkins], CIA, 10 September 1885; John D. C. Atkins, CIA, to [Lucius Q. C. Lamar], SI, 5 October 1885, *ARCIA 1885,* HED 1, 49th Cong., 1st sess. (Washington, D.C.: GPO, 1886), pp. 65–67.

106. Blandina Segale, *At the End of the Santa Fe Trail* (Milwaukee: Bruce Publishing Co., 1948), p. 227.

107. Atkins to Lamar, 5 October 1885; [Atkins], CIA, to [Lamar], SI, 21 September 1887, *ARCIA 1887,* HED 1, 50th Cong., 1st sess. (Washington, D.C.: GPO, 1889), p. 72.

108. [William A. Jones], CIA, to [Ethan A. Hitchcock], SI, 1 October 1900, *ARCIA 1900,* HED 5, 56th Cong., 2nd sess. (Washington, D.C.: GPO, 1900), pp. 171–72.

109. Ibid.

110. W. H. Pope, Sp. Atty. for Pueblos, to [William A. Jones], CIA, 3 May 1902, P-1902-27627, LR, 1881–1907, RG 75, BIA, NA.

111. "Unique Pueblo Indian Congress," Santa Fe *New Mexican,* 7 April 1904, in LaFarge, *Santa Fe,* pp. 181–83.

112. LaFarge, *Santa Fe,* pp. 183–84.

113. "Unique Pueblo Indian Congress," in ibid., pp. 181–83; Atty. Abbott and Supt. Crandall, telegram to [Francis E. Leupp], CIA, 6 April 1904, P-1907-63661, LR, 1881–1907, RG 75, BIA, NA.

114. Abbott and Crandall to CIA, 6 April 1904; C. J. Crandall, Supt. SFIS, to [Francis E. Leupp], CIA, 17 August 1904, *ARCIA 1904,* pt. 1, HED 5, 58th Cong., 3d sess. (Washington, D.C.: GPO, 1905), pp. 258–62; Governors, Lieutenant Governors, and Principal Men of Isleta, Laguna, Acoma, Santa Ana, and San Felipe Pueblos to CIA, 27 May 1904, SAPRG.

115. D. G. Dwyre, Clerk and Principal, AIS, Receipt, in Burton B. Custer, Supt. AIS, to Governor of Santa Ana Pueblo, 24 September 1907, SAPRG.

116. "Indian Legislation of Fifty-eighth Congress: Miscellaneous," 1905, *ARCIA 1905,* pt. 1, HED 5, 59th Cong., 1st sess. (Washington, D.C.: GPO, 1906), p. 465.

117. "Enabling Act for New Mexico," 20 June 1910, in *New Mexico Historic Documents,* ed. Richard N. Ellis (Albuquerque: University of New Mexico Press, 1975), sec. 2, p. 76.

118. "Meeting of the Pueblo Indians of New Mexico, Held at the Santa Fe Indian School, Santa Fe, New Mexico," 24 July 1912, SP-df-45, RG 75, BIA, AB, FRCD; for the decision in the case, issued the previous day, see W. H. Pope, US Dist. Judge, NM, Opinion and Syllabus of the Court in *U.S. v. Felipe Sandoval,* no. 12, 23 July 1912, SP-df-45, RG 75, BIA, AB, FRCD.

119. [Cato Sells], CIA, to [Franklin K. Lane], SI, 14 September 1914, *ARCIA 1914,* HED 1475, 63d Cong., 3d sess. (Washington, D.C.: GPO, 1915), pp. 45–46, 71; "Pueblo of Santa Ana Land Status."

120. H. Pierce to Dr. Aberle, 28 September 1943, SPA; E. Adams Whyte, Recorder, GLO, Certification of Patent Copy, 28 June 1940, encl. in J. M. Stewart, Dir. of Lands, BIA, to Dr. Sophie D. Aberle, Supt., UPA, 9 July 1940, attached to Pierce to Aberle, 28 September 1943; the patent was dated 12 October 1916.

121. For example, see N. S. Walpole, IA, P&JA, Notice to Whom It May Concern, 28 January 1899, MLS, RG 75, BIA, AB, FRCD; J. D. Henderson, IA, PA, Statement, 27 June 1867, SAPRG; José C. Estrada, JP, Copy of the Book of Judicial Record of the Archives of the Justice of the Peace of Precinct no. 1 of Bernalillo County, Territory of New Mexico, SAPRG; Capt. John L. Bullis, A.IA., P&JA, to Remedio Trujillo and others, 13 March 1894, MLS, RG 75, BIA, RG 75, FRCD; Bullis to Metro Montoya, 14 September 1894, MLS, RG 75, BIA, AB, FRCD.

122. N. S. Walpole, IA, P&JA, to Gov. José Enrique, Lt. Gov. José León, and Capt. of War Jesús Moya, Santa Ana Pueblo, 11 February 1900, MLS, RG 75, BIA, AB, FRCD; Walpole to Pres., Albq. Land and Irrigation Co., 14 February 1900, MLS,

RG 75, BIA, AB, FRCD; Walpole to Governors and Headsmen, Santo Domingo, San Felipe, Santa Ana, Sandía, and Isleta Pueblos, 24 February 1900, MLS, RG 75, BIA, AB, FRCD; Walpole to Sheriff Hubbell, 22 March 1900, MLS, RG 75, BIA, AB, FRCD; José Enrique, Governor of Santa Ana, et al., to Albuquerque Low Line Ditch Co., 6 February 1900, Exhibit B, Plaintiff's "Complaints and Exhibits," *Albuquerque Land and Irrigation Co. v. Pueblo of Santa Ana et al.*, 2nd Judicial District Court, Bernalillo County, 3 March 1900, P&JA-1900-15143, LR, 1881–1907, RG 75, BIA, NA; Gov. Juan Montaño, San Felipe Pueblo, et al., to Agent Walpole, c. 1900, P&JA-1900-15143, LR, 1881–1907, RG 75, BIA, NA; J. W. Crumpacker, Assoc. Justice, New Mexico Supreme Court, and Judge, 2nd Judicial District, Bernalillo County, NM, by Harry P. Owen, Clerk, Injunction against José Manuel Enrique, Governor of Santa Ana Pueblo, et al., in *Albuquerque Land and Irrigation Co. v. Pueblo of Santa Ana et al.,* no. 5526, 2nd Judicial District Ct., Bernalillo County, 5 March 1900, P&JA-1900-15143, LR, 1881–1907, RG 75, BIA, NA.

Chapter 9

1. Henry R. Poore, "Condition of Sixteen New Mexico Indian Pueblos, 1890," in US ID, Census Office, *Report on Indians Taxed and Indians Not Taxed in the United States (Except Alaska) at the Eleventh Census: 1890* (Washington, D.C.: GPO, 1894). pp. 431–32; Charles H. Lange and Carroll L. Riley, eds., *The Southwestern Journals of Adolph F. Bandelier, 1880–1882* (Albuquerque and Santa Fe: University of New Mexico Press and Museum of New Mexico Press, 1966), pp. 111, 117, 126, 186, describes the times and methods of planting various crops at Santo Domingo.

2. Poore, "Condition," pp. 431–32; Porfirio Montoya, interview with Floyd Montoya, Donna Pino, and Tom Leubben, 11 February 1980, Santa Ana Pueblo Oral History Project, Tape no. 12, p. 7, describes the areas in which the Tamayame herded when Montoya was about ten years old, during the first decade of the twentieth century.

3. Agents' reports throughout the late nineteenth century often refer to crop damage caused by insects and floods. See Felipe Delgado, NMSIA, to W. P. Dole, CIA, 20 August 1865 and 10 September 1865, and CIA to SI, 1865, all in *ARCIA 1865,* ID ed. (Washington, D.C.: GPO, 1865), pp. 160–64, 168–69, 18–23; Felipe Delgado, NMSIA, to J. K. Graves, Sp. IC, 9 January 1866, J. K. Graves, Sp. IA, NM, Report to D. N. Cooley, CIA, 1866; and Toribio Romero, PIA, to A. B. Norton, NMSIA, August 1866, all in *ARCIA 1866,* HED 1, 39th Cong., 2nd sess. (Washington, D.C.: GPO, 1867), pp. 138–39, 131–35, 314–15, which notes that some pueblos lost all of their crops the previous year and that the agent had to "relieve the urgent wants" of Santa Ana, Santo Domingo, and Isleta; John Ward, Sp. PIA., to Col. A. B. Norton, NMSIA, 2 August 1867, AP no. 54, NMS, *ARCIA 1867,* ID ed. (Washington, D.C.: GPO, 1868), pp. 207–8; John Ward, Sp. PIA, to CIA, 7 September 1868, and "Statement Showing the Farming Operations for 1868 of the Different Indian

Tribes," both in *ARCIA 1868,* HED 1, 40th Cong., 3rd sess. (Washington, D.C.: GPO, 1869), pp. 636–38, 826; L. Edwin Dudley, NMSIA, to Edw. P. Smith, CIA, 15 November 1873, AP no. 46, *ARCIA 1873,* HED 1, 43d Cong., 1st sess. (Washington, D.C.: GPO, 1974), pp. 637–38; Ben M. Thomas, IA, P&AA, to CIA, 4 September 1878, *ARCIA 1878,* HED 1, 45th Cong., 3rd sess. (Washington, D.C.: GPO, 1879), p. 605–6; Ben M. Thomas, IA, P&AA, to CIA, 1 September 1880, *ARCIA 1880,* HED 1, 46th Cong., 3rd sess. (Washington, D.C: GPO, 1881), pp. 255–56; Dolores Romero, IA, to CIA, 27 August 1886, *ARCIA 1886,* HED 1, 49th Cong., 2nd sess. (Washington, D.C.: GPO, 1887), pp. 423–24. For a discussion of drought in the region, see W. M. Denevan, "Livestock Numbers in Nineteenth Century New Mexico and the Problem of Gullying in the Southwest," *Annals of the Association of American Geographers* 57 (1967); Ezra B. W. Zubrow, *Population, Contact, and Climate in the New Mexican Pueblos,* Anthropological Papers, no. 24 (Tucson: University of Arizona Press, 1974); Carl Hodge and Peter C. Duisberg, eds., *Aridity and Man,* Publications of the American Association for the Advancement of Science, no. 74 (Washington, D.C.: American Association for the Advancement of Science, 1963), p. 508.

4. Among the diseases reported by the pueblo agent were smallpox, a contagious eye disease, diphtheria, spinal meningitis, tuberculosis, and trachoma. In addition to the agent's annual reports, see [Ben M.] Thomas, IA, Telegram to CIA, 5 December 1882, P-1882-21943, LR, 1881–1907, RG 75, BIA, NA; Thomas, Telegram to CIA, 13 January 1883, P-1883-935, LR, 1881–1907, RG 75, BIA, NA; Pedro Sánchez, IA, Telegram to H. Price, CIA, 19 August 1883, P-1883-15227, LR, 1881–1907, RG 75, BIA, NA; Pedro Sánchez, IA, Telegram to H. Price, CIA, 17 September 1883, P-1883-17278, LR, 1881–1907, RG 75, BIA, NA; "Consolidated Report of Sick and Wounded, United States Indian Service, for Year Ending June 30, 1883," *ARCIA 1883,* HED 1, 48th Cong., 1st sess. (Washington, D.C.: GPO, 1884), pp. 362–69; George R. Milburn, Sp. IA, to H. Price, CIA, 25 February 1884, P-1884-4033, LR, 1881–1907, RG 75, BIA, NA; "Consolidated Report of Sick and Wounded . . . 1884," *ARCIA 1884,* HED 1, 48th Cong., 2nd sess. (Washington, D.C.: GPO, 1885), pp. 382–89; W. P. McClure, IA, To CIA, 26 August 1889, *ARCIA 1889,* HED 1, 51st Cong, 1st sess. (Washington, D.C.: GPO, 1890), pp. 262–64, which notes many deaths from smallpox and diphtheria at various pueblos, including Santa Ana; John L. Bullis, A.IA, to CIA, 22 April 1895, P&JA-1895-18129, LR, 1881–1907, RG 75, BIA, NA; Charles L. Cooper, A.IA, to CIA, 30 March 1898, P&JA-1898-15051, LR, 1881–1907, RG 75, BIA, NA; A. C. Tonner, ACIA, to Samuel L. Taggart, Sp. IA, 8 February 1898, encl. in Cooper to CIA, 30 March 1898; N. S. Walpole, IA, to Governors of the Various Pueblos, c/o Indian School Teacher, 19 November 1898, MLS, RG 75, BIA, FRCD; N. S. Walpole, IA, Telegram to CIA, 22 December 1898, P&JA-1898-57700, LR, 1881–1907, RG 75, BIA, NA; N. S. Walpole, IA, P&JA, to CIA, 14 January 1899, P&JA-1899-3074, LR, 1881–1907, RG 75, BIA, NA: Charles E. Burton, Supervising Teacher, P&JA, to IA, 31 December 1898, encl. in Walpole

to CIA, 14 January 1899; N. S. Walpole, IA, to Dr. R. Lund, Bernalillo, 10 February 1899, MLS, RG 75, BIA, FRCD; N. S. Walpole, IA, to CIA, 28 January 1899, P&JA-1899-5262, LR, 1881–1907, RG 75, BIA; [N. S. Walpole], IA, to the Governor of Sandía Pueblo, c. 20 January 1899, MLS, RG 75, BIA, FRCD; [N. S.] Walpole, IA, Telegrams to Dr. Lund, Bernalillo, 16 January 1899, MLS, RG 75, BIA, FRCD; Edgar A. Allen, Supt. AIS, to CIA, 24 August 1899, *ARCIA 1899,* HED 5, 56th Cong., 1st sess. (Washington, D.C.: GPO, 1899), pp. 409–10; S. M. Brosius, Indian Rights Assn., to CIA, 14 November 1899, P&JA-1899-54703, LR, 1881–1907, RG 75, BIA, NA, which charges that the agent's negligence contributed to the pueblo death rate during the smallpox epidemic; Ralph P. Collins, A.IA, to CIA, 5 August 1902, *ARCIA 1902,* HED 5, 57th Cong., 2nd sess. (Washington, D.C.: GPO, 1903). pp. 254–56; "Table 20.—Prevalence of Tuberculosis and Trachoma among Indians, Fiscal Year Ended June 30, 1912," *ARCIA 1912,* HED 933, 62d Cong., 3rd sess. (Washington, D.C.: GPO, 1913), p. 170.

5. Miguel Antonio Otero, *My Nine Years as Governor of New Mexico, 1897–1906,* ed. Marion Dargan (Albuquerque: University of New Mexico Press, 1940), p. 24; Otero also entertained the pueblo officers at his home after the official meeting.

6. Poore, "Condition," p. 432; Kirby Benedict, NM Chief Justice, to W. P. Dole, CIA, 12 June 1865, AP no. 39, *ARCIA 1865,* ID ed. (Washington, D.C.: GPO, 1865), p. 168.

7. J. S. Calhoun, IA, to Orlando Brown, CIA, 17 November 1849, AP no. 27, *ARCIA 1850,* SED 1, 31st Cong., 2nd sess. (Washington, D.C.: Union Office, 1851), pp. 125–28.

8. John Ward, Sp. IA, to [Col. A. B. Norton, SIA], 10 June 1867, AP no. 54 ½, NMS, *ARCIA 1867,* ID ed. (Washington, D.C.: GPO, 1868), pp. 208–9.

9. William H. Goetzmann, *Army Exploration in the American West, 1803–1863* (New Haven: Yale University Press, 1959), provides a summary of the major explorations and surveys; see also the explorers' journals cited in Chapter 7, above.

10. Emmanuel H. D. Domenech, *Seven Years Residence in the Great Deserts of North America* (London, 1860), as cited in Lansing B. Bloom, "The Emergence of Chaco Canyon in History," Appendix 1 in Edgar L. Hewett, *The Chaco Canyon and its Monuments* (Albuquerque: University of New Mexico Press and School of American Research, 1936), p. 148.

11. Hubert Howe Bancroft, *History of Arizona and New Mexico, 1530–1888,* vol. 17 in *The Works of Hubert Howe Bancroft* (San Francisco: History Company, 1889), p. 773; Myra Ellen Jenkins and Albert H. Schroeder, *A Brief History of New Mexico* (Albuquerque: University of New Mexico Press, 1974), pp. 48, 51.

12. Oliver LaFarge, with Arthur N. Morgan, *Santa Fe: The Autobiography of a Southwestern Town* (Norman: University of Oklahoma Press, 1959), pp. 40–41.

13. Ibid., p. 38.

14. Ibid., pp. 90–91.

15. Jenkins and Schroeder, *Brief History,* p. 53.

16. Jack D. Rittenhouse, *Cabezón: A New Mexico Ghost Town* (Santa Fe: Stagecoach Press, 1965), pp. 16–17, 31, 33, 36–39, 64–67, 70.

17. Ibid., p. 79.

18. Jenkins and Schroeder, *Brief History*, pp. 64–65; see also Keith L. Bryant, *A History of the Atchison, Topeka, and Santa Fe Railroad* (New York: n.p., 1974); and David F. Myrick, *New Mexico's Railroads: An Historical Survey* (Golden, CO: Colorado Railroad Museum, 1970).

19. Lillian Whiting, *The Land of Enchantment: From Pikes Peak to the Pacific* (Boston: Little, Brown, and Co., 1909), p. 196.

20. George A. Dorsey, *Indians of the Southwest* (n.p.: George T. Nicholson, with the Passenger Department of the Atchison, Topeka and Santa Fe Railway System, 1903), pp. 67, 72–75; Frank McNitt, *The Indian Traders* (Norman: University of Oklahoma Press, 1962), p. 315.

21. Bancroft, *History*, p. 723; Howard Roberts Lamar, *The Far Southwest: 1846–1912: A Territorial History* (New Haven and London: Yale University Press, 1966), p. 107.

22. Bancroft, *History*, p. 723.

23. Lamar, *Far Southwest*, p. 176.

24. Frank H. Jonas, ed., *Politics in the American West* (Salt Lake City: University of Utah Press, 1969), p. 263.

25. Bancroft, *History*, p. 788.

26. Ibid., p. 789.

27. Lamar, *Far Southwest*, p. 175.

28. Poore, "Condition," p. 430.

29. Bancroft, *History*, p. 787; Lionel A. Sheldon, NM Gov., to S. J. Kirkwood, SI, 31 October 1881, *ARCIA 1881*, HED 1, 47th Cong., 1st sess. (Washington, D.C.: GPO, 1882), p. 992.

30. Bancroft, *History*, pp. 748–56, 787; Linda S. Cordell, ed., *Tijeras Canyon: Analyses of the Past* (Albuquerque: Maxwell Museum of Anthropology and University of New Mexico Press, 1980), pp. 48–50; Sheldon to Kirkwood, 31 October 1881, p. 992.

31. Warren A. Beck and Ynez D. Haase, *Historical Atlas of New Mexico* (Norman: University of Oklahoma Press, 1969), Map 39.

32. Bancroft, *History*, p. 787.

33. Lamar, *Far Southwest*, p. 175.

34. Denevan, "Livestock Numbers," p. 696.

35. Hodge and Duisberg, *Aridity and Man*, p. 510.

36. *The Resources of New Mexico: Prepared under the Auspices of the Territorial Bureau of Immigration for the Territorial Fair to Be Held at Albuquerque, N.M., October 3rd to 8th, 1881* (1881; reprint, Santa Fe: William Gannon, 1973), pp. 49–52; Bancroft, *History*, p. 774; Ralph Emerson Twitchell, *The Leading Facts of New Mexican History* (Cedar Rapids, Iowa: Torch Press, 1911–17), 2:482–84, 492, 568; William S. Greever, *Arid*

Domain: The Santa Fe Railway and Its Western Land Grant (Stanford, Calif.: Stanford University Press, 1954), pp. 43–52.

37. J. D. Henderson, IA, P. Statement, 27 June 1867, SAPRG.

38. Lange and Riley, *Southwestern Journals,* p. 187.

39. Clarence Gary [?], Atty, Western Union Telegraph Co., to Leonard Whitney, General Manager, 27 September 1881, P-1881-17279, LR, 1881–1907, BIA, NA: L. C. Baker, Superintendent, 21 September 1881, encl. in Gary to Whitney; R. B. Gemmell, Superintendent of Telegraph, AT&SFRR, Telegrams to L. C. Baker, 20 September 1881, encl. in Baker to Clowsy encl. in Gary to Whitney.

40. J. D. Henderson, IA, P. Statement, 27 June 1867, SAPRG.

41. José Perea, Petition against Governor Pedro Pino of Santa Ana Pueblo, in José C. Estrada, Justice of the Peace, Copy of the Book of Judicial Record of the Archives of the Justice of the Peace of Precinct no. #1 of Bernalillo, Territory of New Mexico, SAPRG.

42. Ben M. Thomas to Candelario Estrada, 22 August 1877, MLS (mic. copy), FRCD, Roll 941, reel 2, cited in James A. Vlasich, "Pueblo Indian Agriculture, Irrigation and Water Rights" (Ph.D. diss., University of Utah, 1980), p. 161, n. 73.

43. Ben M. Thomas, IA, to Josea L. Perea, 24 April 1879, MLS (mic. copy), FRCD, roll 941, reel 3, cited in Vlasich, "Pueblo Indian Agriculture," p. 162.

44. Ben M. Thomas, IA, P&AA, to [Ezra A. Hayt], CIA, 14 August 1879, *ARCIA 1879,* ID ed. (Washington, D.C.: GPO, 1879), pp. 118–20.

45. Charles H. Lange and Carroll L. Riley, eds., *The Southwestern Journal of Adolph F. Bandelier, 1880–1882* (Albuquerque: University of New Mexico Press, 1966), p. 230.

46. Agent Bewmstromar to Don Pedro Yunague, Governor of Santa Ana, 19 July 1882, SAPRG.

47. Pedro Sánchez, IA, to Jno. D. C. Atkins, CIA, 15 April 1885, P-1885-8606, LR, 1881–1907, RG 75, BIA, NA.

48. C. F. Gildersleeve, Telegram to Anthony Joseph, 28 April 1885, p-1885-9541, LR, 1881–1907, RG 75, BIA, NA.

49. M. C. Williams, IA, to Henry L. Waldo, 12 March 1887, MLS (mic. copy), FRCD, roll 941, reel no. 9, cited in Vlasich, "Pueblo Indian Agriculture," p. 170, n. 112; Williams to CIA, 18 June 1888, MLS (mic. copy), FRCD, roll 941, reel no. 9, cited in Vlasich, ibid., p. 166, n. 96; Poore, "Condition," p. 425.

50. Poore, "Condition," p. 430.

51. Ibid.

52. Ibid., Rittenhouse, *Cabezon,* pp. 63–76 and passim; T. M. Pearce, ed., *New Mexico Place Names: A Geographical Dictionary* (Albuquerque: University of New Mexico Press, 1965), p. 28.

53. Poore, "Condition," p. 432.

54. M. C. Williams, IA, to Henry L. Waldo, 12 March 1887, MLS (mic. copy), FRCD, roll 941, reel no. 9, cited in Vlasich, "Pueblo Indian Agriculture," p. 170,

n. 112; Williams to CIA, 18 June 1888, MLS (mic. copy), FRCD, roll 941, reel no. 9, cited in Vlasich, ibid., p. 166, n. 96.

55. John H. Robertson, IA, Notice, 21 February 1893, SAPRG.

56. John L. Bullis, A.IA, to H. H. Brodie, Walsenburg, CO, 21 July 1894, MLS, RG 75, BIA, FRCD.

57. John L. Bullis, A.IA, to Remedio Trujillo and others, 13 March 1894, MLS, RG 75, BIA, FRCD.

58. John L. Bullis, A.IA, to Juan Gurule, Santa Ana Pueblo, 10 July 1894, MLS, RG 75, BIA, FRCD.

59. John L. Bullis, A.IA, to Metro Montoya, Bernalillo, 14 September 1894, MLS, RG 75, BIA, FRCD.

60. N. S. Walpole, IA, Notice to Whom It May Concern, 28 January 1899, MLS, RG 75, BIA, FRCD.

61. N. S. Walpole, IA, to CIA, 10 August 1899, *ARCIA 1899*, HED 5, 56th Cong., 1st sess. (Washington, D.C.: GPO, 1899), pt. 1, p. 252.

62. James T. Newhall, Clerk, to Governor of Santa Ana Pueblo, 1 February 1898, MLS, RG 75, BIA, FRCD; Charles L. Cooper, A.IA, to Pedro Perea, Bernalillo, 3 March 1898, MLS, RG 75, BIA, FRCD.

63. N. S. Walpole, IA, to Governor of Santa Ana Pueblo, 20 February 1899, MLS, RG 75, BIA, FRCD.

64. N. S. Walpole, IA, to Governor of Santa Ana Pueblo, 17 July 1899, MLS, RG 75, BIA, FRCD.

65. N. S. Walpole, IA, to CIA, 10 August 1899, *ARCIA 1899*, HED 5, 56th Cong., 1st sess. (Washington, D.C.: GPO, 1899), pt. 1, pp. 252–53.

66. N. S. Walpole, IA, to Governor of Santa Ana Pueblo, 4 November 1899, MLS, RG 75, BIA, FRCD.

67. Pedro Llonagua, Governor of Santa Ana Pueblo, to Wm. McKinley, US Pres., 7 November 1899, P&JA-1899-55522, LR, 1881–1907, RG 75, BIA, NA; Ambrisio Tenorio, Chief, Pedro Yollanagua, Governor, and Other Officials and Principals of Santa Ana Pueblo, Petition to William McKinley, 30 October 1899, encl. in Llonagua to McKinley, 7 November 1899.

68. "Proceedings of the Board of Indian Commissioners at the Eighteenth Lake Mohonk Indian Conference," 17 October 1900, Appendix D, *RBIC, ARCIA 1900*, HED 5, 56th Cong., 2nd sess. (Washington, D.C.: GPO, 1900), pt. 2, pp. 724–25.

69. W. A. Richards, Asst. CGLO, to CIA, 21 December 1899, P&JA-1899-60990, LR, 1881–1907, RG 75, BIA, NA.

70. N. S. Walpole, IA, to Governor of Santa Ana Pueblo, 8 December 1899, MLS, RG 75, BIA, FRCD.

71. Plaintiff's Complaint, *Albuquerque Land and Irrigation Co. v. Pueblo of Santa Ana et al.,* 5 March 1900, encl. in Walpole to CIA, 24 March 1900, P-1900-15143, LR, 1881–1907, RG 75, BIA, NA.

72. N. S. Walpole, IA, to Governor José Enrique, Lieutenant Governor José León,

and Captain of War Jesús Moya, Santa Ana Pueblo, 11 February 1900, MLS, RG 75, BIA, FRCD.

73. N. S. Walpole, IA, to President, Albuquerque Land and Irrigation Co., 14 February 1900, encl. in Walpole to Governors and Headmen of Santo Domingo et al., 24 February 1900, MLS, RG 75, BIA, FRCD.

74. N. S. Walpole, IA, to the Governors and Headmen of Santo Domingo, San Felipe, Santa Ana, Sandía, and Isleta Pueblos, 24 February 1900, MLS, RG 75, BIA, FRCD.

75. José Enrique, Governor of Santa Ana Pueblo, et al., to Albuquerque Low Line Ditch Co., 6 February 1900, Exhibit B, Plaintiff's Complaint and Exhibits, *Albuquerque Land and Irrigation Co. v. Pueblo of Santa Ana et al.,* 2nd Judicial District Court, Bernalillo, 5 March 1900, encl. in Walpole to CIA, 24 March 1900, P&JA-1900-15143, LR, 1881–1907, RG 75, BIA, NA.

76. Attorneys for the Albuquerque Land and Irrigation Co., Plaintiff's Complaint and Exhibits, *Albuquerque Land and Irrigation Co. v. Pueblo of Santa Ana et al.,* 5 March 1900, encl. in Walpole in CIA, 24 March 1900, P&JA-1900-15143, LR, 1881–1907, RG 75, BIA, NA.

77. Ibid.

78. J. W. Crumpacker, Assoc. Justice, New Mexico Supreme Court, and Judge, 2nd Judicial District, Bernalillo County, by Harry P. Owen, Clerk, Injunction to José Manuel Enrique, Governor of Santa Ana Pueblo, et al., in *Albuquerque Land and Irrigation Co. v. Pueblo of Santa Ana et al.,* no. 5526, 2nd Judicial District Court, Bernalillo, 5 March 1900, encl. in Walpole to CIA, 24 March 1900.

79. N. S. Walpole, IA, to J. W. Crumpacker, Judge, 2nd Judicial District, 20 March 1900, MLS, RG 75, BIA, FRCD.

80. N. S. Walpole, IA, to [Thomas] Hubbell, Sheriff, 22 March 1900, MLS, RG 75, BIA, FRCD.

81. N. S. Walpole, IA, to Ambrisio Tenorio, Cacique of Santa Ana Pueblo, 24 March 1900, MLS, RG 75, BIA, FRCD.

82. N. S. Walpole, IA, to [William A. Jones], CIA, 24 March 1900, P&JA-1900-15143, LR, 1881–1907, RG 75, BIA, NA.

83. Ibid.; N. S. Walpole, IA, to J. W. Crumpacker, Judge, 2nd Judicial District, Bernalillo, 4 April 1900, MLS, RG 75, BIA, FRCD.

84. [William A. Jones], CIA, to SI, 1 October 1900, *ARCIA 1900,* HED 5, 56th Cong., 2nd sess. (Washington, D.C.: GPO, 1900), pp. 171–72.

85. N. S. Walpole, IA, To Whom It May Concern, 3 April 1900, MLS, RG 75, BIA, FRCD; James K. Allen, Supt., AIS, to Ealaiso Badiaz, Bernalillo, 17 September 1904, SAPRG.

86. William H. Taft, US Pres., by M. W. Young, sec., and T. W. Sanford, Recorder, GLO, Grant to Pueblo of Santa Ana, in accordance with CPLC, Docket no. 190, NM, no. 84368, 18 October 1909, SPA.

87. R. Perry, Supt., AIS, to Francis C. Wilson, Sp. Atty. for Pueblo Indians, 9 June 1910, SAPRG.

88. Juan Venancio, Affidavit, 28 April 1910, SAPRG.

89. [P. T. Lonergan], Supt., AIS, to CIA, 31 July 1912, SP-df-67, RG 75, BIA, FRCD; Supt., AIS, to CIA, 29 July 1913, SP-df-67, RG 75, BIA, FRCD.

90. R. G. Valentine, CIA, to SI, 8 April 1912, SF-1912-308.2-46847-10-3, LR, 1881–1907, RG 75, BIA, NA.

91. A. D. O., Algodones, NM, to G. H. [*sic*] Lonergan, 25 September 1912, SP-df-67, RG 75, BIA, FRCD.

92. Supt., AIS, to CIA, 29 July 1913, SP-df-67, RG 75, BIA, FRCD.

93. Francis C. Wilson, Sp. Atty. for Pueblos, Plaintiff's Complaint, *Pueblo of Santa Ana v. Diego Gutiérrez,* 25 June 1913, SPA.

94. M. C. de Baca, Atty., Defendants' Answer, *Pueblo of Santa Ana v. Diego Gutiérrez et al.,* no. 283, Sandoval County District Court, 16 July 1913, SPA.

95. M. C. de Baca, Atty., for José C. de Baca et al., Separate Answer of Defendants Diego Gutiérrez et al., *Pueblo of Santa Ana v. Diego Gutiérrez et al.,* no. 283, Sandoval County District Court, 16 July 1913, SPA.

96. [Francis C. Wilson], Special Atty. for Pueblos, Plaintiff's Reply, *Pueblo of Santa Ana v. Diego Gutiérrez et al.,* no. 285, Sandoval County District Court, c. July 1913, SPA.

97. E. Adams Whyte, Recorder, GLO, Certification of Patent Copy, 28 June 1940, encl. in J. M. Stewart, Dir. of Lands, BIA, to Dr. Sophie D. Aberle, Supt., UPA, 9 July 1940, attached to H. Pierce to Dr. Aberle, 28 September 1943, SPA.

98. Hodge and Duisberg, *Aridity and Man,* p. 508; Zubrow, *Population, Contact, and Climate,* p. 11; Rittenhouse, *Cabezon,* pp. 79, 82–83, 38–40; Denevan, "Livestock Numbers," p. 701.

99. Rittenhouse, *Cabezon,* pp. 82–83; Denevan, "Livestock Numbers," p. 693.

100. Rittenhouse, *Cabezon,* pp. 82–83.

101. Porfirio Montoya, interview with Floyd Montoya, Dona Pino, and Tom Leubben, 11 February 1980, Santa Ana Pueblo Oral History Project, Tape no. 12, p. 5.

102. Several sources chronicle the general changes in America's Indian policy in the nineteenth century. For an overview, see S. Lyman Tyler, *A History of Indian Policy* (Washington, D.C.: ID, BIA, 1973), and Francis Paul Prucha, *American Indian Policy in Crisis: Christian Reformers and the Indian, 1865–1900* (Norman: University of Oklahoma Press, 1976). The changing attitudes of officials responsible for the pueblos emerge clearly in the annual reports of New Mexico's agents and superintendents.

103. In addition to the sources above, several accounts describe the development of assimilation policies and the allotment program; see Henry E. Fritz, *The Movement for Indian Assimilation, 1860–1890* (Philadelphia: University of Pennsylvania Press, 1963); Loring Benson Priest, *Uncle Sam's Stepchildren: The Reformation of United States Indian Policy, 1856–1887* (Lincoln: University of Nebraska Press, 1942); and Wilcomb E. Washburn, *The Assault on Indian Tribalism: The General Allotment Law (Dawes Act) of 1887,* ed. Harold M. Hyman (New York: J. B. Lippincott Co., 1975).

104. The early reports of agents such as Calhoun, Greiner, and others generally reflect this view, as do travelers' journals and letters.

105. Though the changing attitudes varied somewhat from agent to agent, the annual reports in the years after the Civil War generally tended to condemn pueblo ways and traditions. See the annual reports of agents Arny, Ward, Romero, Ford, Cooper, Cole, and Lewis, and the specific incidents discussed below.

106. From Agent Calhoun on, the annual reports usually requested funds, teachers, and equipment for pueblo schools; many agents presented detailed proposals, such as the one suggested in First Lt. George E. Ford, Sp.IA, PA, to Major William Clinton, NMSIA, 8 September 1869, AP no. 57, NMS, *ARCIA 1869*, HED 1, 41st Cong., 2nd sess. (Washington, D.C.: GPO, 1870), pp. 693–96.

107. Samuel Gorman, Missionary to Pueblos, Laguna, NM, to J. L. Collins, NMSIA, 2 October 1858, encl. in Collins to C. E. Mix, CIA, 27 September 1858, AP no. 76, NMS, *ARCIA 1858*, HED 2, 35th Cong., 2nd sess. (Washington, D.C.: James B. Steadman, Printer, 1959), pp. 551–53.

108. John Ward, PIA, "Statistics of the Indian Pueblos of New Mexico . . . ," 30 June 1864, encl. in Ward to Steck, 30 June 1864, AP no. 74, *ARCIA 1864*, HED 1, 38th Cong., 2nd sess. (Washington, D. C.: GPO, 1865), p. 343.

109. John Ward, PIA, to M. Steck, NMSIA, 30 June 1864, HED 1, 38th Cong., 2nd sess. (Washington, D.C.: GPO, 1865), pp. 331–39.

110. First Lt. Charles L. Cooper, PIA, to Maj. William Clinton, NMSIA, 1 September 1870, AP no. 48, NMS, *ARCIA 1870*, HED 1, 41st Cong., 3rd sess. (Washington, D.C.: GPO, 1871), pp. 625–26.

111. W. F. M. Arny, PIA, to Col. Nathaniel Pope, NMSIA 18 August 1871, AP no. 37, NMS, *ARCIA 1871*, ID ed. (Washington, D.C.: GPO, 1872), pp. 380–95.

112. W. F. M. Arny, PIA, to Col. Nathaniel Pope, NMSIA, 23 August 1872, AP no. 56, NMS, *ARCIA 1872*, HED 1, 42nd Cong., 3rd sess. (Washington, D.C.: GPO, 1873), pp. 684–85.

113. Jno. Orme Cole, IA, to Col. Nathaniel Pope, NMSIA, 29 August 1872, AP no. 55, NMS, *ARCIA 1872*, HED 1, 42nd Cong., 3rd sess. (Washington, D.C.: GPO, 1873), pp. 693–94.

114. "Table Showing Number of Indians within the Limits of the United States, Exclusive of Those in Alaska, &c.," 1873, *ARCIA 1873*, HED, 1, 43rd Cong., 1st sess. (Washington D.C.: GPO, 1874), pp. 710–11.

115. Edwin C. Lewis, PIA, to L. Edwin Dudley, NMSIA, 25 September 1873, AP no. 52, NMS, *ARCIA 1873*, HED 1, 43rd Cong., 1st sess. (Washington, D.C.: GPO, 1874), pp. 645–47; L. E. Dudley, Late NMSIA, to Edw. P. Smith, CIA, 27 October 1874, *ARCIA 1874*, HED 1, 43rd Cong., 2nd sess. (Washington, D.C.: GPO, 1875), pp. 610–12; Edwin C. Lewis to E. P. Smith, CIA, 15 September 1874, *ARCIA 1874*, pp. 616–18; Ben M. Thomas, IA, to E. P. Smith, CIA, 8 September 1875, *ARCIA 1875*, ID ed. (Washington, D.C.: GPO, 1875), pp. 332–33; Thomas to CIA, 24 August 1876, *ARCIA 1876*, HED 1, 44th Cong., 2nd sess. (Washington, D.C.: GPO, 1877); Thomas to

CIA, 20 August 1877, HED 1, 45th Cong., 2nd sess. (Washington, D.C.: GPO, 1878), pp. 557–58; and J. M. Shields, Teacher, JIS, to Dr. B. M. Thomas, IA, 9 August 1882, *ARCIA 1882,* HED 1, 47th Cong., 2nd sess. (Washington, D.C.: GPO, 1883), p. 192.

116. Prucha, *American Indian Policy in Crisis,* pp. 270–71, 288; [E. M. Marble], ACIA, to [Carl Schurz], SI, 1 November 1880, *ARCIA 1880,* HED 1, 46th Cong., 3rd sess. (Washington, D.C.: GPO, 1881), p. 87; [C. M. Semple, Principal], CIS, to Capt. R. H. Pratt, Supt., 20 August 1883, *ARCIA 1883,* HED 1, 48th Cong., 1st sess. (Washington, D.C.: GPO, 1884), pp. 220–22; Herman J. Viola, *Diplomats in Buck-skins: A History of Indian Delegations in Washington City* (Washington, D.C.: Smithsonian Institution Press, 1981), pp. 50–51, and passim, discusses the experiences of Indian delegations to Carlisle during this period.

117. Ben M. Thomas, IA, P&JA, to Hiram Price, CIA, 1 September 1882, *ARCIA 1882,* HED 1, 47th Cong., 2nd sess. (Washington, D.C.: GPO, 1883), pp. 189–91.

118. "Table of Statistics Relating to Indian Education," "Average Attendance at Day Schools for 1881 and 1882," "List of Boarding Schools, 1881–1882," "List of Day Schools," and "Table of Statistics Relating to Population, Industries, and Sources of Subsistence of Various Indian Tribes, Together with Religious, Vital, and Criminal Statistics," 1882, *ARCIA 1882,* HED 1, 47th Cong., 2nd sess. (Washington, D.C.: GPO, 1883), pp. 382–83, 1022, 1021, and 398–99 respectively.

119. Pedro Sánchez, IA, to CIA, August 1884, *ARCIA 1884,* HED 1, 48th Cong., 2nd sess. (Washington, D.C.: GPO, 1885), pp. 182–83.

120. In addition to the sources above, several accounts describe boarding school education; see Margaret Szasz, *Education and the American Indian: The Road to Self-Determination, 1928–73* (Albuquerque: University of New Mexico Press, 1974); and Evelyn C. Adams, *American Indian Education: Government Schools and Economic Programs* (New York: King's Crown Press, 1946).

121. R. H. Pratt, CIS, to CIA, 7 September 1887, *ARCIA 1887,* HED 1, 50th Cong., 1st sess. (Washington, D.C.: GPO, 1889), pp. 338–39.

122. R. W. D. Ryan, Supt., AIS, to CIA, 1 August 1885, *ARCIA 1885,* HED 1, 49th Cong., 1st sess. (Washington, D.C.: GPO, 1886), pp. 480–82.

123. Ben M. Thomas, IA, P&JA, to CIA, 1 September 1881, and H. Price, CIA, to SI, 24 October 1881, *ARCIA 1881,* HED 1, 47th Cong., 1st sess. (Washington, D.C.: GPO, 1882), pp. 198–99 and 25–26 respectively.

124. John Menaul, Teacher, LIS, to Dr. B. M. Thomas, IA, 4 September 1882, *ARCIA 1882,* HED 1, 47th Cong., 2nd sess. (Washington, D.C.: GPO, 1883), p. 191.

125. Charles S. Lusk, Sec., BCIM, to J. D. C. Atkins, CIA, 18 October 1885, P-1885-24704, LR, 1881–1907, RG 75, BIA, NA: J. B. Salpointe, Archbishop of Santa Fe, to BCIM, Washington, D.C., 18 October 1885, encl. in Lusk to Atkins, 18 October 1885, P-1885-24705, LR, 1881–1907, RG 75, BIA, NA.

126. "Table B: Government and Contract Schools under Supervision of Indian Agents: Location, Attendance, etc.," 1885, *ARCIA 1885,* HED 1, 49th Cong., 1st sess. (Washington, D.C.: GPO, 1886), pp. 196–97.

127. Dolores Romero, PIA, to J. D. C. Atkins, CIA, 6 May 1886, P-1885-12802, LR, 1881–1907, RG 75, BIA, NA.

128. P. F. Burke, Supt., AIS, to CIA, 31 August 1887, *ARCIA 1887*, HED 1, 50th Cong., 1st sess. (Washington, D.C.: GPO, 1889), pp. 330–34; Exhibit No. 5, "Reports of the Superintendents," Albuquerque Indian School, *ARCIA 1887*, p. 837 includes a slightly different version; quoted material is from p. 330.

129. William B. Creager, Supt, AIS, to CIA, 15 August 1890, *ARCIA 1890*, HED 1, 51st Cong., 2nd sess. (Washington, D.C.: GPO, 1891), p. 300; Daniel Dorchester, SIS, to SI, 11 November 1890, *ARCIA 1890*, p. 260.

130. Wm. B. Creager, Supt., AIS, to CIA, 1 September 1889, *ARCIA 1889*, HED 1, 51st Cong., 1st sess. (Washington, D.C.: GPO, 1890), pp. 361–62.

131. Ibid.

132. M. C. Williams, PIA, Report, 1887, *ARCIA 1887*, HED 1, 50th Cong., 1st sess. (Washington, D.C.: GPO, 1889), p. 903; William B. Creager, Supt., AIS, to CIA, 15 August 1890, *ARCIA 1890*, HED 1, 51st Cong., 2nd sess. (Washington, D.C.: GPO, 1891), pp. 297–301.

133. CIA to SI, 1 October 1891, *ARCIA 1891*, HED 1, 52d Cong., 1st sess. (Washington, D.C.: GPO, 1892), pp. 25–37; George H. Shields, US Asst. Atty. Gen., to SI, 4 May 1891, *ARCIA 1891*, pp. 149–51; P. L. Chapelle, Vice Pres., BCIM, to John W. Noble, SI, 6 May 1891, P-1891-17072, LR, 1881–1907, RG 75, BIA, NA; J. B. Salpointe, Archbishop of Santa Fe, to the Governor, the Principal Men, and Neighbors of the Pueblo of Ildefonso, 31 May 1891, *ARCIA 1892*, HED 1, 52nd Cong., 2nd sess. (Washington, D.C.: GPO, 1893), p. 164; Capt. John L. Bullis, A.IA, to CIA, 25 September 1896, P&JA-1896-37088, LR, 1881–1907, RG 75, BIA, NA.

134. José Atencio Calabasa, Governor of Santo Domingo, and the Mayores, to Rev. Father Antonio, Supt., St. Catherine's School, 16 April 1891 [Translation], encl. in J. B. Salpointe, Archbishop of Santa Fe. to Rev. J. A. Stephan, Director, BCIM, 16 April 1891, encl. in P. L. Chappelle, Vice President, BCIM, to T. J. Morgan, CIA, 9 May 1891, *ARCIA 1892*, HED 1, 52nd Cong., 2nd. sess. (Washington, D.C.: GPO, 1893), p. 161.

135. T. J. Morgan, CIA, to Rev. P. L. Chappelle, Coadjutor Bishop of Santa Fe, 15 August 1892, *ARCIA 1892*, HED 1, 52nd Cong., 2nd sess. (Washington, D.C.: GPO, 1893), pp. 165–66; Charles F. Lummis, *Mesa, Cañon, and Pueblo: Our Homeland of the Southwest* (New York and London: Century Co., 1925), pp. 403–4.

136. Mariano Martin et al., Governor, Officers, and Principals of Zía Pueblo, to President Benjamin Harrison, 5 January 1891, P-1891-14607, LR, 1881–1907, RG 75, BIA, NA; John H. Robertson, IA, to CIA, 13 January 1892, P&JA-1892-2051, LR, 1881–1907, RG 75, BIA, NA.

137. [Daniel Dorchester, Superintendent of Indian Schools], to [Daniel M. Browning, CIA], 20 September 1893, *ARCIA 1893*, HED 1, 53rd Cong., 2nd sess. (Washington D.C.: 1895), pp. 366–77; Lummis, *Mesa, Cañon, and Pueblo*, pp. 403–4; Blandina Segale, *At the End of the Santa Fe Trail* (Milwaukee: Bruce Publishing Co., 1948), pp. 215–16.

138. Capt. John L. Bullis, A.IA, to CIA, 25 August 1896, *ARCIA 1896*, HED 5, 54th Cong., 2nd sess. (Washington, D.C.: GPO, 1897), pp. 213–15.

139. José Segura, IA, to CIA, 25 August 1890, *ARCIA 1890*, HED 1, 51st Cong., 2nd sess. (Washington, D.C.: GPO, 1891), pp. 172–74; Juan José Alonzo, Lt. Gov., Laguna Pueblo, to W. P. McClure, IA, 12 November 1889, P-1889-33317, LR, 1881–1907, RG 75, BIA NA; John Charlton, BIC, to Merrill E. Gates, Chairman, BIC, 1890, *ARCIA 1890*, pp. 810–13; T. J. Morgan, CIA, to SI, 27 August 1892, *ARCIA 1892*, HED 1, 52nd Cong., 2nd sess. (Washington, D.C.: GPO, 1893), pp. 26–29; [Daniel Dorchester], Superintendent of Indian Schools, to [Thomas J. Morgan, CIA], 16 August 1892, *ARCIA 1892*, pp. 526–63; [John H. Robertson], IA, to [T. J. Morgan, CIA], 30 August 1892, *ARCIA 1892*, pp. 333–36; Capt. C. E. Nordstrom, A.IA, to CIA, 16 August 1897, *ARCIA 1897*, HED 5, 55th Cong., 2nd sess. (Washington, D.C.: GPO, 1897), pp. 194–203; Edgar A. Allen, Supt., AIS, to CIA, 23 August 1898, *ARCIA 1898*, HED 5, 55th Cong., 3rd sess. (Washington, D.C.: GPO, 1898), pp. 380–81; Ralph P. Collins, Supt., AIS, to CIA, 27 September 1900, *ARCIA 1900*, HED 5, 56th Cong., 2nd sess. (Washington, D.C.: GPO, 1900), pp. 494–95.

140. Nordstrom to CIA, 16 August 1897, *ARCIA 1897*, p. 198.

141. Capt. John L. Bullis, A.IA, to Governor of—Pueblo, 11 September 1893, MLS, RG 75, BIA, AB, FRCD; Dorchester to CIA, 16 August 1892; from 1889 on, The Sisters of Loretto regularly submitted quarterly bills to the pueblo agent for Indian students at the Bernalillo contract school, but their requests and reports do not indicate the pueblos from which the students came; an 1889 report states that Keres students attended the school; see W. P. McClure, IA, to CIA, 20 September 1889, P-1889-26915, LR, 1881–1907, RG 75, BIA, NA; McClure to CIA, 3 December 1889, P-1889-35260, LR, 1881–1907, RG 75, BIA, NA; McClure to CIA, 5 December 1889, P-1889-35260, LR, 1881–1907, RG 75, BIA, NA; Sister Mary M., Report to W. P. McClure, IA, 10 September 1889, P-1889-26915, LR, 1881–1907, RG 75, BIA, NA; Sisters of Loretto, Bill Submitted to John W. Robertson, IA, 21 November 1891, MLS, RG 75, BIA, AB, FRCD; Sisters of Loretto, School Statistics Accompanying Annual Report, 1892, P&JA-1892-27783, LR, 1881–1907, RG 75, BIA, NA; Capt. John L. Bullis, A.IA, to CIA, 17 August 1893, MLS, RG 75, BIA, AB, FRCD; Sister Margaret Mary, Request for Payment, 30 September 1893, MLS, RG 75, BIA, AB, FRCD; Bullis to CIA, 9 November 1893, P&JA-1893-42360, LR, 1881–1907, RG 75, BIA, NA; Sister Margaret Mary, Request for Payment, 31 December 1893, MLS, RG 75, BIA, AB, FRCD; Sister Margaret Mary, Request for Payment, 30 September 1895, MLS, RG 75, BIA, AB, FRCD: Sister Margaret Mary, School Statistics, 1896, P&JA-1896-33189, LR, 1881–1907, RG 75, BIA, NA; A.IA to CIA, 10 October 1896, MLS, RG 75, BIA, AB, FRCD; Sister Margaret Mary, Request for Payment, 30 June 1896, MLS, RG 75, BIA, AB, FRCD; Sisters of Loretto, School Statistics, 1898, P&JA-1898-38351, LR, 1881–1907, RG 75, BIA, NA; Charles E. Burton to Charles L. Cooper, A.IA, 20 May 1898, MLS, RG 75, BIA,

AB, FRCD; and Sister Margaret Mary, Report, 30 June 1905, *ARCIA 1905*, pt. 1, HED 5, 59th Cong., 1st sess. (Washington, D.C.: GPO, 1906), p. 264.

142. Capt. John L. Bullis, A.IA, to Gov. of—Pueblo, 8 August 1894, MLS, RG 75, BIA, AB, FRCD.

143. B. F. Perea, County Schools, "Application for Contract with Pueblo School District No. One, Bernalillo County," 19 September 1896, P&JA-1896-36405, LR, 1881–1907, RG 75, BIA, NA, with endorsement by Capt. John L. Bullis, A.IA; Capt, John L. Bullis, A.IA, to Governor of Santa Ana Pueblo, 31 August 1896, MLS, RG 75, BIA, AB, FRCD; Capt. John L. Bullis, A.IA, to CIA, 6 June 1896, MLS, RG 75, BIA, AB, FRCD; Capt. John L. Bullis, A.IA, to CIA, 20 April 1896, P&JA-1896-15506, LR, 1881–1907, RG 75, BIA, NA.

144. N. S. Walpole, IA, P&JA, to CIA, 11 August 1898, *ARCIA 1898*, HED 5, 55th Cong., 3rd sess. (Washington, D.C.: GPO, 1898), pp. 206–11; N. S. Walpole, IA, P&JA, to CIA, 7 April 1899, P&JA-1899-16905, LR, 1881–1907, RG 75, BIA, NA; N. S. Walpole, to CIA, 22 April 1899, P&JA-1899-19762, LR, 1881–1907, RG 75, BIA, NA; N. S. Walpole, IA, to CIA, 27 July 1899, P&JA-1899-36365, LR, 1881–1907, RG 75, BIA, NA; Sketch Map Showing Location of Proposed Santa Ana School, Old Santa Ana Pueblo, and Other Schools, drawn on Walpole to CIA, 7 April 1899; N. S. Walpole, IA, to Governor of Santa Ana Pueblo, 14 April 1899, MLS, RG 75, BIA, AB, FRCD.

145. N. S. Walpole, IA, to Rev. Father J. M. Condert, Bernalillo, 18 August 1899, MLS, RG 75, BIA, AB, FRCD; N. S. Walpole, IA, to Governor of Santa Ana Pueblo, 18 August 1899, MLS, RG 75, BIA, AB, FRCD.

146. N. S. Walpole, IA, to Messrs. Milton, Bradley and Co., 9 September 1899, MLS, RG 75, BIA, AB, FRCD; N. S. Walpole, IA, to Railroad Agent, Bernalillo, 29 November 1899, MLS, RG 75, BIA, AB, FRCD.

147. N. S. Walpole, IA, to Railroad Agent, Bernalillo, 25 June 1900, MLS, RG 75, BIA, AB, FRCD; N. S. Walpole, IA, to CIA, 14 August 1900, *ARCIA 1900*, HED 5, 56th Cong., 2nd sess. (Washington, D.C.: GPO, 1900), pp. 292–97; "Statistics as to Indian Schools" and "Employed in the Indian School Service," *ARCIA 1900*, pp. 626–27, 730; M. E. Dissette, Supervising Teacher, to Ralph P. Collins, Supt., AIS, 6 September 1901, *ARCIA 1901*, HED 5, 57th Cong., 1st sess. (Washington, D.C.: GPO, 1902), pp. 548–49; W. A. Jones, CIA,, to SI, 16 October 1902, *ARCIA 1902*, pt. 1, HED 5, 57th Cong., 2nd sess. (Washington, D.C.: GPO, 1903), p. 37; "Statistics as to Indian Schools" and "List of Persons Employed in the Indian School Service," *ARCIA 1902*, pp. 620–21, 670; W. A. Jones, CIA, to SI, 14 October 1903, *ARCIA 1903*, pt. 1, HED 5, 58th Cong., 2nd sess. (Washington, D.C.: GPO, 1904), pp. 43–44; "List of Persons Employed in the Indian School Service" and "Statistics as to Indian Schools," *ARCIA 1903*, pp. 553, 496–97; A. W. Wright, Supervisor, "Papers Read and Discussed, Albuquerque Institute," 24–25 April 1903, *ARCIA 1903*, pp. 388–89; "List of Persons Employed in the Indian School Service" and "Statistics as to Indian Schools," *ARCIA 1904*, pt.1, HED 5, 58th Cong., 3rd sess.

(Washington, D.C.: GPO, 1905), pp. 655, 584–85; James K. Allen, Supt., AIS, to CIA, 7 August 1905, *ARCIA 1905*, pt. 1, HED 5, 59th Cong., 1st sess. (Washington, D.C.: GPO, 1906), pp. 260–64; CIA to SI, 30 September 1905, *ARCIA 1905*, p. 44.

148. Agreement between the Governor and Principals of Santa Ana Pueblo and P. Bourgade, Archbishop of Santa Fe, 17 March 1903, SAPRG.

149. Dorchester to CIA, 16 August 1892, *ARCIA 1892*, pp. 537, 546–47.

150. [George Manypenny], CIA, to SI, 26 November 1853, *ARCIA 1853*, SED 1, 33d Cong., 1st sess. (Washington, D.C.: Beverly Tucker, Senate Printer, 1854), pp. 251–60; Nathaniel Pope, SIA, to Committee on Indian Affairs, Washington, D.C., 1871, AP no. 34, NMS, *ARCIA 1871*, ID ed. (Washington, D.C.: GPO, 1872), pp. 371–75; Nathaniel Pope to Francis A. Walker, CIA, 10 October 1872, AP no. 49, NMS, *ARCIA 1872*, HED 1, 42nd Cong., 3rd sess. (Washington, D.C.: GPO, 1873), pp. 686–87; Capt. C. E. Nordstrom, A.IA, to CIA, 10 November 1897, encl. in Capt. Frank D. Baldwin, A.IA, Kiowa Agency, to [A. C. Tonner, A.CIA], 3 January 1898, P&JA-1897-48080 and P&JA-1898-1174, LR, 1881–1907, RG 75, BIA, NA; Lange and Riley, *Southwestern Journals* pp. 98–102, 162.

151. Pedro Sánchez, IA, to H. Price, CIA, 17 October 1883, P-1883-19554, LR, 1881–1907, RG 75, BIA, NA; Pedro Sánchez, IA, "To the Pueblo Indians within the Territory of New Mexico," 2 September 1883, encl. in Sánchez to Price, 17 October 1883; Pedro Sánchez, IA, to Hiram Price, CIA, 26 June 1883, P-1883-11891, LR, 1881–1907, RG 75, BIA, NA.

152. Capt. R. H. Pratt, Supt., CIS, 10 September 1889, encl. in Morgan to Pratt, 3 December 1889, P-1889-35101, LR, 1881–1907, RG 75, BIA, NA; Frank D. Lewis, Sp. IA, to CIA, 16 November 1889, P-1889-33625, LR, 1881–1907, RG 75, BIA, NA; W. P. McClure, IA, to CIA, 23 September 1889, P-1889-27261, LR, 1881–1907, RG 75, BIA, NA; McClure to CIA, 20 September 1889, P-1889-27123, LR, 1881–1907, RG 75, BIA, NA; Solomon Bibo to Capt. R. H. Pratt, Supt., CIS, 3 September 1889, encl. in Pratt to CIA, 10 September 1889, encl. in Morgan to Pratt, 3 December 1889, P-1889-35101, LR, 1881–1907, RG 75, BIA, NA; John H. Robertson, IA, to CIA, 9 March 1892, MLS, RG 75, BIA, AB, FRCD.

153. [A. O. Wright, Supervisor], Synopsis of Report to Superintendent of Indian Schools, 1903, *ARCIA 1903*, pt. 1, HED 5, 58th Cong., 2nd sess. (Washington, D.C.: GPO, 1904), p. 406.

154. Capt. John L. Bullis, A.IA, to Governor of Santa Clara Pueblo, 30 January 1894, MLS, RG 75, BIA, AB, FRCD; Burton B. Custer, Supt., AIS, to Governor of Santa Ana Pueblo, 22 March 1907, SAPRG.

Chapter 10

1. John B. Harper, Irrigation Supt., to CIA, 5 September 1901, encl. in W. H. Pope, Sp. Atty., to CIA, 3 May 1902, P-1901-49767 and P-1902-27627, LR, 1881–1907, RG 75, BIA, NA.

2. C. J. Crandall, Supt., SFIS, to CIA, 24 August 1902, *ARCIA 1902*, pt. 1, HED 5, 57th Cong., 2d sess. (Washington, D.C.: GPO, 1903), pp. 256–58.

3. Pope to CIA, 3 May 1902.

4. "Indian Legislation Passed during the Second Session of the 56th Congress: Miscellaneous," 1901, *ARCIA 1901*, HED 5, 57th Cong., 1st sess. (Washington, D.C.: GPO, 1902), p. 615; Darwin R. James, Chmn., BIC, "Thirty-Second Annual Report of the Board of Indian Commissioners," 31 January 1901, *ARSI 1900*, HED 5, 56th Cong., 2d sess., pt. 2 (Washington, D.C.: GPO, 1900), p. 648; C. J. Crandall, Supt., SFIS, to CIA, 17 August 1904, *ARCIA 1904*, pt. 1, HED 5, 58th Cong., 3d sess. (Washington, D.C.: GPO, 1905), pp. 258–62; see also chapter 8, nn. 105–13, above.

5. A. D. O., Algodones, NM, to G. H. Lohnergan [*sic*, P. T. Lonergan], 25 September 1912, SP-df-67, RG 75, BIA, AB, FRCD.

6. Supt., AIS, to CIA, 29 July 1913, SP-df-67, RG 75, BIA, AB, FRCD.

7. Francis O. Wilson, Sp. Atty., Plaintiff's Complaint, *Pueblo of Santa Ana v. Diego Gutiérrez et al.*, NM Dist. Ct., Sandoval Cty., 25 June 1913, SPA; P. T. Lonergan, Supt., to Francis O. Wilson, July 1913, SPA.

8. George Vaux, Jr., Chmn., BIC, et al., to SI, 30 September 1914, *RBIC, ARCIA 1914*, HED 1475, 63d Cong., 3rd sess. (Washington, D.C.: GPO, 1915), pp. 316, 322.

9. Leo Crane, Supt., SPA, to Chairman and Members, US House Committee on Indian Affairs, 15 May 1920, SP-df-4, RG 75, BIA, AB, FRCD.

10. F. L. Myres, Supt., AT&SFRR, NM Division, to José Cruz Montoya, Governor of Santa Ana Pueblo, 8 June 1918, SAPRG; José Garcia, Governor, Santa Ana Pueblo, Agreement with AT&SFRR, 18 May 1918, encl. in Myres to Montoya, 8 June 1918, SAPRG.

11. "Land Disputes," Santa Fe *New Mexican*, 17 May 1920, in Oliver LaFarge, with Arthur N. Morgan, *Santa Fe: The Autobiography of a Southwestern Town* (Norman: University of Oklahoma Press, 1959), p. 264.

12. SI to Pres., 20 Nov. 1920, *ARSI 1920*, vol. 1, HED 849, 66th Cong., 3rd sess. (Washington, D.C.: GPO, 1920), p. 48.

13. Ibid.; Crane to Chairman and Members, US House Committee on Indian Affairs, 15 May 1920.

14. Atty. Abbot and C. J. Crandall, Supt., SFIS, Telegram to CIA, 6 April 1904, P-1904-63661, LR, 1881–1907, RG 75, BIA, NA.

15. Juan Rey Juancho, Governor of Isleta Pueblo, et al., by Leo Crane, Supt., SPA, Telegram to Indian Office, Washington, D.C., 19 April 1920, SP-df-4[?], RG 75, BIA, AB, FRCD.

16. J. A. Chavez, Govt. Stockman, to Leo Crane, Supt., SPA, 15 December 1920, SP-df-4[?], RG 75, BIA, FRCD.

17. Supt., SPA, to Four Delegates Selected by Seven Pueblos, 9 December 1920, SP-df-4[?], RG 75, BIA, AB, FRCD.

18. CIA to SI, 30 September 1921, *ARCIA 1921*, ID ed. (Washington, D.C.: GPO, 1921), pp. 31–32.

19. Sp. Asst. to Atty Gen. to SI, 29 December 1921, SP-df-67, RG 75, BIA, AB, FRCD.

20. Albert B. Fall, SI, to Senator Reed Smoot, Chmn., US Senate Committee on Public Lands and Surveys, 31 July 1922, SP-29, RG 75, BIA, AB, FRCD; Holm O. Bursum, US Senator, "A Bill to Ascertain and Settle Land Claims," S.B. 3855, 67th Cong., 2d sess., 20 April (calendar day 20 July) 1922, encl. in Fall to Smoot, 31 July 1922, SP-29, RG 75, BIA, AB, FRCD; SI, Report, 1922, *ARCIA 1922,* ID ed. (Washington, D.C.: GPO, 1922) pp. 46–51; CIA to SI, 1 September 1922, *ARCIA 1922,* ID ed. (Washington, D.C.: GPO, 1922), pp. 1–27.

21. "The Indian Bill," Santa Fe *New Mexican,* 20 September 1922, in LaFarge, *Santa Fe,* pp. 274–75.

22. "Effect of Indian Bill," Santa Fe *New Mexican,* 25 September 1922, in LaFarge, *Santa Fe,* p. 275.

23. "Indian Bill Will Destroy," Santa Fe *New Mexican,* 6 November 1922, in LaFarge, *Santa Fe,* pp. 277–78.

24. "From Headquarters," Santa Fe *New Mexican,* 12 December 1922, in LaFarge, *Santa Fe,* pp. 278–79.

25. "The Terrible White Man," Albuquerque *Morning Journal,* 19 December 1922, SP-29, RG 75, BIA, AB, FRCD.

26. "Origin of the Bursum Bill Explained by Santa Fean," unidentified Washington, D. C., newspaper, 6 February 1923, SP-29, RG 75, BIA, FRCD.

27. Guthdie Smith, Staff Correspondent, "Pueblo Lands Act Caught by Filibuster," Washington *Herald,* 3 March 1923, SP-29, RG 75, BIA, AB, FRCD.

28. Leo Crane, *Desert Drums: The Pueblo Indians of New Mexico, 1540–1928* (Boston: Little, Brown and Co., 1928), pp. 70–73.

29. Mary Austin, Santa Fe, to S. J. Crandall, 26 September 1923, SP-df-20, RG 75, BIA, AB, FRCD; Supt. to Mary Austin, 28 September 1923, SP-df-20, RG 75, BIA, AB, FRCD.

30. "An Act to Quiet the Title to Lands within Pueblo Indian Land Grants, and for Other Purposes," 7 June 1923, Stat. at Lg. 43, pt. 1, chap. 331, sec. 1–19, SP-df-82, RG 75, BIA, AB, FRCD; "Legislation Relating to Indian Affairs," 1923, *ARCIA 1924,* ID ed. (Washington, D.C.: GPO, 1924), p. 28.

31. Ibid.

32. Ibid.

33. SI, Report, *ARSI 1924,* ID ed. (Washington, D.C.: GPO, 1924), pp. 48–51; George Vaux, Jr., et al., BIC, to SI, 1 September 1925, *RBIC 1925,* ID ed. (Washington, D.C.: GPO, 1925), pp. 1–15.

34. Charles H. Burke, CIA, to SI, *ARCIA 1925,* ID ed., pp. 21, 27, typed excerpts, SPA.

35. CIA to SI, 1 September 1924, *ARCIA 1924,* pp. 1927.

36. H. J. Hagerman, "Report to the President in Compliance with the Instructions Contained in Commissioner Burke's Letter of 9 September 1926," SPA.

37. John Collier, Indian Defense Assn., to Governor of Santa Ana Pueblo, 8 November 1926, SAPRG.

38. "Proceedings of the United States Indian Pueblo Council Held at Santa Fe, New Mexico," 15–17 November 1926, SP-064-490273-19, RG 75, BIA, AB, FRCD.

39. Pueblo Lands Board, "Santa Ana Pueblo: Report on Title to Lands Granted or Confirmed to Pueblo Indians Not Extinguished," c. 19 July 1927, SPA; Pueblo Lands Board, "Santa Ana Pueblo: Report under Section 6 of Act of June 7, 1924," c. 9 July 1927, SPA.

40. Pueblo Lands Board, "Proceedings to Quiet Title of Charles F. Brown to PC 18, p. 1, and PC 19, p. 1, El Ranchito, Santa Ana, Abstract No. 2," 18 April 1927 (afternoon sess.), SPA; Pueblo Lands Board, "Proceedings to Quiet Title of Sostones Jaramillo to PC 20, p. 1, El Ranchito, Santa Ana, Abstract No. 1," 18 April 1927, SPA; Pueblo Lands Board, "Proceedings to Quiet Title of Atilano Gallegos, Administrator, et al., to PC 17, p. 1, El Ranchito, Santa Ana, Abstract No. 3," 19 April 1927, SPA; "Chart Showing Private Claims in the Santa Ana Ranchitos Purchase Brought up in Hearings before the Pueblo Lands Board," 18–21 April 1927, SPA.

41. E. Otero, Governor of Santa Ana Pueblo, "Notice of Withdrawal and Replacement of El Ranchito Grant Documents," 21 April 1927, SAPRG.

42. H. J. Hagerman, Pueblo Lands Board, and Mark Radcliffe, "Memorandum in re Certain Features of Santa Ana Situation with a View of Santa Ana Reports," 16 May 1927, SPA.

43. Lucius C. Embree et al., Pueblo Lands Board, "Santa Ana Pueblo, El Ranchito Grant or Purchase: Report on Title to Lands Purchased by Pueblo Indians," 19 July 1927, SPA.

44. Ibid.; H. J. H[agerman], Pueblo Lands Board, to Malcolm McDowell, Sec., BIC, 20 July 1927, SPA; Appraisers to Charles H. Jennings et al., Pueblo Lands Board, 25 June 1927, SPA; Lucius C. Embree et al., Pueblo Lands Board, "Santa Ana Pueblo: Concerning the Indian Titles Extinguished, El Ranchito Grant (Purchase)," 19 July 1927, SPA; "Memorandum to Be Put with the File in Connection with the Basis for Finding the Loss," c. July 1927, SPA; Lucius C. Embree et al., Pueblo Lands Board, "Santa Ana Pueblo, El Ranchito Grant (Purchase): Report of Valid Non-Indian Titles and Desirability of Removal of Non-Indian Occupants," 19 July 1927, SPA.

45. George A. H. Fraser, Sp. Asst. to Atty Gen. and Atty for Plaintiff, Plaintiff's Bills of Complaint in *U.S. as Guardian of the Pueblo of Santa Ana v. Charles F. Brown et al.,* No. 1814, US Dist. Ct., NM, filed 25 November 1927, SPA.

46. Lists of Documents Submitted to Pueblo Lands Board by Claimants for Santa Ana Pueblo Lands, pp. 20–28, 40–44, returned to claimants January 1928, SPA.

47. Louis H. Warner, Chairman, et al., Pueblo Lands Board, "Santa Ana Pueblo: Amendment to Reports under Act of June 7, 1924," submitted to SI 27 January 1930, SPA; "Santa Ana Case, Sostones Jaramillo Claim: Excerpts from the Testimony of C. B. Thompson," n.d., encl. in George A. H. Fraser, SP. Asst. to Atty Gen., to

Dudley Cornell, c/o Hanna and Wilson, 13 May 1929, SPA; Dudley Cornell to George A. H. Fraser, Sp. Asst. to Atty Gen., 22 May 1929 and 25 May 1929, SPA; George A. H. Fraser to Dudley Cornell, c/o Hanna and Wilson, 28 May 1929, SPA; Dudley Cornell, Telegram to George A. H. Fraser, 23 May 1929, SPA.

48. Guy P. Harrington, Cadastral Engineer, to Lem Towers, Supt., SPA, 6 August 1930, SPA; Lem A. Towers, Supt., SPA, to Guy P. Harrington, District Cadastral Engineer, 9 August 1930, SPA; Guy P. Harrington, Cadastral Engineer, to Lem A. Towers, Supt., SPA, 17 February 1931, SPA.

49. "Minutes of the United States Pueblo Council, Santa Fe, New Mexico, E. B. Merritt, Asst. CIA, Presiding," 9–10 November 1927, SP-064-490273-19, RG 75, BIA, AB, FRCD.

50. Jessie Johnson, Reporter, "Pueblo Lands Board: Transcript of Evidence, Santa Ana-San Felipe Controversy," 20 March 1931, SPA.

51. [Walter C. Cochrane, Sp. Atty. for Pueblos], to H. J. Hagerman, Special Commissioner, 27 June 1931, SPA; Pueblo Lands Board, "Supplemental Report upon Conflict between San Felipe Pueblo and Santa Ranchitos Purchase," [draft form], c. 27 June 1931, encl. in Cochrane to Hagerman, 27 June 1931; Louis H. Warner, Chairman, et al., Pueblo Lands Board, "Supplemental Report of Pueblo Lands Board, Organized under Act of Congress of June 7, 1924, upon a Conflict between the San Felipe Pueblo and Ranchitos Purchase of the Santa Ana Pueblo," 30 June 1931, encl. in Hagerman to Cochrane, 30 June 1931, SPA; for a discussion of the problems with surveys, see interview with Porfirio Montoya et al., 25 January 1980, Santa Ana Pueblo Oral History Project, Tape nos. 6 and 7.

52. H. J. Hagerman, Special Commissioner, to Ray Lyman Wilbur, SI, 30 June 1931, encl. in Hagerman to Cochrane, 30 June 1931, SPA.

53. J. Henry Scattergood, Asst. CIA, to H. J. Hagerman, NM Governor and Special Commissioner, 25 August 1931, encl. in Hagerman to Cochrane, 4 September 1931, SPA.

54. H. J. Hagerman, Special Commissioner, to Walter C. Cochrane, Special Atty. for Pueblos, 4 September 1931, SPA.

55. George A. H. Fraser, Sp. Atty., "Report on Two-Hundred-Acre [sic] Conflict between the Pueblo of San Felipe Grant and El Ranchito Purchase of Santa Ana," 1 October 1932, SPA.

56. George A. H. Fraser, Sp. Atty., to C. J. Rhoads, CIA, 8 November 1932, SPA.

57. C. J. Rhoads, CIA, to George A. H. Fraser, Sp. Asst. to Atty Gen., 15 November 1932, SPA.

58. Crampton and Dodd, "Compensation to Pueblo Indians of New Mexico," c. 1931, SPA; "Awards to Non-Indians in the Following Pueblos," 29 April 1931, SPA; H. J. Hagerman, Sp. Commissioner, to Charles J. Rhoads, CIA, 7 January 1932, UP-df-82, RG 75, BIA, AB, FRCD.

59. Lem A. Towers, Supt., SPA, to John Collier, CIA, 27 June 1933, SP-df-82, RG 75, BIA, AB, FRCD.

Chapter 11

1. Leslie A. White, "The Cultivation of Cotton by the Pueblo Indians of New Mexico," *Science* 94, no. 2433 (1941): 162.

2. Loren F. Jones, UPA Agricultural Extension Agent, "A Canning Demonstration on Wheels," *Indians at Work* 4, no. 22 (1 July 1937): 17–24; "Fourteen Pueblos to Care for Own Needy Members through Donations of Canned Goods," *Indians at Work* 5, no. 4 (1 December 1937): 14.

3. Pauline Turner Strong, "Santa Ana Pueblo," in *Southwest*, ed. Alfonso Ortiz, vol. 9 of *Handbook of North American Indians*, ed. William C. Sturtevant (Washington, D.C.: Smithsonian Institution, 1979), pp. 398–406; Statement of Porfirio Montoya, 16 May 1952, SPA.

4. Ralph T. Collins, Supt,. AIS, to CIA, 30 June 1901, *ARCIA 1901*, HED 5, 57th Cong., 1st sess. (Washington, D.C.: GPO, 1902), pp. 546–47; CIA to SI, 30 September 1907, *ARCIA 1907*, HED 5, 60th Cong., 1st sess. (Washington, D.C.: GPO, 1907), pp. 8–51; CIA to SI, 30 September 1908, *ARCIA 1908*, HED 1046, 60th Cong., 2nd sess. (Washington, D.C.: GPO, 1908), pp. 30–31; CIA to SI, 15 September 1909, *ARCIA 1909*, HED 107, 61st Cong., 2nd sess. (Washington, D.C.: GPO, 1910), pp. 7–60, CIA to SI, 1 November 1910, *ARCIA 1910*, HED 1006, 61st Cong., 3rd sess. (Washington, D.C.: GPO, 1911), pp. 8–13; CIA to SI, 2 October 1911, *ARCIA 1911*, HED 120, 62d Cong., 2nd sess. (Washington, D.C.: GPO, 1912), pp. 13–16; Charles H. Burke, CIA, to SI, 1 September 1923, *ARCIA 1923*, ID ed. (Washington, D.C.: GPO, 1923), pp. 6–21; throughout the 1930s, *Indians at Work* reported regularly on the IECW, WPA, and CCC programs involving the Indians of the Southwest; Eric T. Hagberg, Chief Clerk, UPA, to Manuel Gonzales, Governor, Santa Ana Pueblo, 14 June 1946, SAPRG; William A. Brophy, CIA, to Manuel Gonzales, Governor, Santa Ana Pueblo, 8 July 1946, SAPRG: Pueblo Agency to Mrs. John T. McLaughlin, Bernalillo County Chapter, Red Cross, 11 July 1918, SP-108, RG 75, BIA, FRCD; SI, Report, 20 November 1917, *ARSI 1917*, vol. 1. HED 915, 65th Cong., 2nd sess. (Washington, D.C.: 1919), pp. 62–63; S. D. Aberle, Supt., UPA, to Eligio Montoya, Governor, Santa Ana Pueblo, 21 February 1941, SAPRG; Aberle to José Rey León, Governor, Santa Ana Pueblo, 5 January 1942, SAPRG.

5. The schools' changing attitudes and programs are described in the annual reports of agents, school superintendents, and BIA officials through the 1920s, as well as in the issues of *Indians at Work* published in the 1930s and early 1940s; Lem A. Towers, Supt., SPA, "School Census of Indian Children, Santa Ana Pueblo," 31 July 1935, SP-054.1-490272-16, RG 75, BIA, AB, FRCD; Attendance Report, Santa Ana Day School, 31 May 1935, SP-df-145-RG 75, BIA, FRCD; Attendance Report, Santa Ana Day School, 26 May 1933, SP-df-45, RG 75, BIA, AB, FRCD; "Miscellaneous Information Regarding the Pueblo Indians and the United Pueblos Agency," 1939, encl. in Gen. Supt., UPA, to Dr. Ruth Underhill, 11 December 1939, UP-df-11, RG 75, BIA, AB, FRCD; Mary McDonald, Supt., Santa Ana Day School, et al.,

"Advance Estimate of Funds for Educational Needs, Fiscal Year 1941, Santa Ana Day School," 2 April 1940, UP-1936-220-40900-5, CF, 1907–1939, RG 75, BIA, NA; Mary Sell, Supt., Santa Ana Day School, et al., "Advance Estimate of Funds," 24 March 1943, UP-1936-220-40900-6, CF, 1907–1939, RG 75, BIA, NA; SPA; "List of Positions under Various Educational Branches," 1 October 1975, SPA; S. D. Aberle, Supt., UPA, to Ewa Marie Manuel, Santa Ana Pueblo, 25 May 1938, SAPRG; S. D. Aberle, Supt., UPA, to Evelyn M. García, Santa Ana Pueblo, 25 May 1938, SAPRG; Map (Doc. File), "Layout of the Santa Ana Day School Buildings," February 1939, SAPRG: Virgil K. Whitaker, Supt. of Education, AIS, to Jesús Manuel, Governor, Santa Ana Pueblo, 16 December 1943, SAPRG; Guy C. Williams, Supt., UPA, to Joe Y. García, Governor, Santa Ana Pueblo, 3 June 1960, SAPRG; Walter O. Olson, Asst. Area Director, Gallup Area Office, Revocable Permit, 28 August 1960, SAPRG; F. D. Shannon, Agency Realty Officer, UPA, to Joe Y. García, Governor, Santa Ana Pueblo 4, October 1960, SAPRG; Miguel Armijo, Governor, Santa Ana Pueblo, Pueblo Council Resolution, 7 December 1965, SAPRG; UPA, Adult Vocational Training Program, Santa Ana Pueblo, 17 June 1965, SAPRG; Patrick L. Wehling, A. Supt., UPA, to Vicente Armijo, Governor, Santa Ana Pueblo, 11 September 1968, SAPRG; Evaluation Survey of the Santa Ana Day School, November 1944, SAPRG: United Pueblos Agency Day School Enrollment, 1945–1946 and 1946–1947, SAPRG; Fred Williams, for Bernon L. Beggs, Supt. of Education, UPA, to all Governors and Educational Personnel, 7 October 1948, SAPRG; Joe García, Governor, Santa Ana Pueblo, Statement of Council on Closing of Santa Ana School, 21 April 1960, SAPRG.

6. Anna Wilmarth Ickes, *Mesa Land: The History and Romance of the American Southwest* (Boston and New York: Houghton Mifflin Co., 1933), p. 133; Strong, "Santa Ana Pueblo," p. 406, summarizes Tamaya's population figures; Statement of Porfirio Montoya, 16 May 1952; Statement of José Peina, 30 April 1952, SPA; see also the census figures and medical reports compiled by the superintendent in charge of Santa Ana during these years, SPA.

7. Statement of Porfirio Montoya, 16 May 1952; Statement of José Peina, 30 April 1952; Statement of José Manuel, 30 April 1952; Statement of Manuel Peina, 29 April 1952, SPA; Statement of José León, 29 April 1952, SPA; Porfirio Montoya, interview with Floyd Montoya, Dona Pino, and Tom Leubben, 11 February 1980, Santa Ana Pueblo Oral History Project, Tapes no. 12 and 13; Porfirio Montoya, interview with Floyd Montoya and Tom Leubben, 25 March 1980, Santa Ana Pueblo Oral History Project, Tape no. 16.

8. Statements of Porfirio Montoya, José Peina, José Manuel, Manuel Peina, and José León, 29–30 April 1952; Interviews with Porfirio Montoya, 11 February and 25 March 1980, Santa Ana Pueblo Oral History Project, Tape nos. 12 and 16; Cristo García, interview, 4 February 1980, Santa Ana Oral History Project, Tape no. 9; Leo Pena, interview with Floyd Montoya, 5 January 1980, Santa Ana Oral History Project, Tape no. 10; José Raymond Sánchez, interview with Floyd Montoya, 7 February 1980, Santa Ana Oral History Project, Tape no. 11.

9. "Pueblo Children Represent the United States in an International Art Exhibit," *Indians at Work* 2, no. 13 (15 February 1935): 27–28; Clara Lee Tanner, *Southwest Indian Art* (Tucson: University of Arizona and Arizona Silhouettes, 1957), p. 43.

10. Ibid.; "Education Notes," *Indians at Work* 2, no. 19 (15 May 1935): 46; Rose K. Brandt, Supervisor of Elementary Education, "The North American Exhibit of Children's Art," *Indians at Work* 3, no. 12 (1 February 1936): 20–21; Anne Raymond, Field Rep., SCS, "Students at Albuquerque Indian School Write and Present Puppet Show," *Indians at Work* 4, no. 22 (1 July 1937): 33–34.

11. Pueblo Art in the Modern Home," *Indians at Work* 6, no. 8 (April 1939): 23; "Indian Children Exhibit Paintings and Drawings in Washington," *Indians at Work* 6, no. 12 (August 1939): 33; Margaret Breen and Ralph Murphy, "Indian Day and the Indian Exhibit at the New Mexico Fair," *Indians at Work* 7, no. 4 (December 1939): 15–18; see also the annual reports of the commissioner of Indian affairs for the 1890s and early 1900s, which discuss pueblo contributions to expositions and fairs throughout the country.

12. Dama Margaret Smith (Mrs. White Mountain Smith), *Indian Tribes of the Southwest* (Stanford, Calif.: Stanford University Press, 1933), p. 91.

13. John Adair, *The Navajo and Pueblo Silversmiths* (Norman: University of Oklahoma Press, 1944), pp. 97, 187.

14. John Collier to Indian Arts and Crafts Boards, encl. in S. D. Aberle, Supt., UPA, to Governor Leo Pena, Santa Ana Pueblo, 21 May 1937, SAPRG; "Old Art in New Forms," *Indians at Work* 4, no. 8 (1 December 1936): 12–16.

15. John L. Sinclair, "Progress of Pottery-Making and Handicraft Revival at Santa Ana Pueblo," *El Palacio* 56, no. 5 (May 1949); "Santa Ana Man Drumming for Tourists at Coronado Monument, 1948," Photograph STA no. 126, 1948, NMSRCA, SAPRG; Strong, "Santa Ana Pueblo," pp. 403–4.

16. Strong, "Santa Ana Pueblo," pp. 403–4; CIA to SI, 14 September 1914, *ARCIA 1914*, HED 1475, 63d Cong., 3rd sess. (Washington, D.C.: GPO 1915), pp. 10–46; Samuel Elliot, Chairman, BIC, et al., to SI, 1 September 1930, *RBIC 1930*, ID ed. (Washington, D.C.: GPO, 1930), pp. 3–4.

17. [Walter C. Cochrane, Sp. Atty.], to Jo Eduvigen, c/o Bernalillo Mercantile Co., 16 July 1930, SPA; L. R. McDonald, Government Farmer, Bernalillo, to Walter C. Cochrane, Sp. Atty., 13 July 1930, SPA; [Cochrane] to Mariano G. Montoya, Sheriff, Sandoval County, 21 June 1930, SPA; J.C. Littlefield, Post Service Officer, American Legion Post No. 9, Ogden, Utah, to Supt., SPA, 8 January 1931, SP-2, RG 75, BIA, AB, FRCD; Manuel Gonzales, "Veteran's Note," Form 115, 10 January 1931, encl. in Littlefield to Supt., 8 January 1931, SP-2, RG 75, BIA, AB, FRCD; A. C. Cooley, Director of Extension and Industry, to Manuel Gonzales, Santa Ana Pueblo, 25 September 1935, UP-1935-255-52053, CF, 1907–1939, RG 75, BIA, NA; Lem A. Towers, Supt., SPA, to J. C. Littlefield, 16 January 1931, SP-2, RG 75, BIA, AB, FRCD; Manuel Gonzales to John Collier, CIA, 19 September 1935, UP-1935-255-52053, CF, 1907–1939, RG 75, BIA, NA; "Information Concerning Loans Made by

United States Veterans Bureau under the World War Adjusted Compensation Act, c. 1931," SP-2, RG 75, BIA, AB, FRCD.

18. "CCC-ID Work Program, Section C & D, Presentation of Projects, Fiscal Year 1942," p. 4, c. 1942, UP-df-87, RG 75, BIA, AB, FRCD; F. G. Healy, by Ina Sizer Cassidy, State Director, Writers' Project, Santa Fe, to Dr. Sophie D. Aberle, Supt., UPA, 11 April 1938, encl. in Healy by Cassidy to John Collier, CIA, 11 April 1938, UP-1938-033-22547, CF, 1907–1939, RG 75, BIA, NA; Alan Laflin, A. Supt., UPA, to Manuel Gonzalez, Governor, Santa Ana Pueblo, 22 January 1940, SAPRG; M. K. McCarty, Jr. Range Examiner, Memorandum to the Files, 11 May 1940, UP-df-88, RG 75, BIA, AB, FRCD; E. R. Smith, District Manager, Río Grande SCS, USDA, Working Agreement with the Pueblo of Santa Ana, 4 April 1939, SAPRG; Dewey Dismuke, Range-Forestry Supervisor, UPA, to Hilario Otero, Governor, Santa Ana Pueblo, 3 April 1944, SAPRG; Sophie D. Aberle, Supt., UPA, to CIA, attn. D. E. Murphy, 8 August 1941, UP-df-87, RG 75, BIA, AB, FRCD; UPA, "Annual Relief Program: Extent of and Plans for Meeting Relief Needs for the Fiscal Year 1942, Santa Ana Pueblo," 6 September 1941, UP-df-1, RG 75, BIA, AB, FRCD.

19. *Chronological Landmarks in American Agriculture,* Dept. of Agriculture, Economics, Statistics, and Cooperative Service, Agriculture Information Bulletin no. 425, compiled by Maryanna S. Smith, rev. ed. (Washington, D.C.: Department of Agriculture, 1980), pp. 10, 32, 54.

20. Charles L. Cooper, Capt. and A.IA, by James T. Newhall, Clerk, to Jesús María Antonio Moya, Governor, Santa Ana Pueblo, 23 May 1898, MLS, RG 75, BIA, AB, FRCD; Hilario Sánchez, Governor, Santa Ana Pueblo, to Lem A. Towers, Supt., SPA, 4 April 1935, UP-1936-255-32500E, CF, 1907–1939, RG 75, BIA, NA.

21. S. D. Aberle, Supt., UPA, Agreement to Reimburse, 6 May 1938, SAPRG; Montie S. Carlisle, Deputy Special Officer, UPA, "Santa Ana Reimbursable Loans," encl. in Carlisle to Governor Montoya, Santa Ana Pueblo, 15 February 1938, SAPRG; William Zimmerman, Jr., Asst. CIA, to Dr. Aberle, UPA, 13 May 1939, SAPRG; Ingebert G. Fauske, A. Extension Agt., UPA, for S. D. Aberle, Supt., to Santiago Tenorio, Governor, Santa Ana Pueblo, 26 May 1939, SAPRG; Lorin F. Jones, Agriculture Extension Agent, UPA, to Porfirio Montoya, Governor, Santa Ana Pueblo, 24 May 1938, SAPRG; Manuel Gonzales, Governor, Santa Ana Pueblo, and José Rey León, Lt. Gov., Application for Tribal Loan for Industry Among Indians, 15 March 1940, SAPRG; Santiago Tenorio, Governor, Santa Ana Pueblo, Memorandum to the Extension Department of the UPA, 15 December 1939, SAPRG; Ingebert G. Fauske, A. Ext. Agt., UPA, for S. D. Aberle, Supt., to Santiago Tenorio, Governor, Santa Ana Pueblo, 7 June 1939, SAPRG; Santiago Tenorio, Gov., and Emiliano Otero, Councilman, Santa Ana Pueblo, to S. D. Aberle, Supt., UPA, 22 December 1939, UP-1939-255-32500-E, CF, 1907–1939, RG 75, BIA, NA; Leo Pena, Governor, Santa Ana Pueblo, to Dr. S. D. Aberle, Supt., UPA, 31 July 1937, UP-1936-255-32500-E, CF, 1907–1939, RG 75, BIA, NA; Ingebert G. Fauske, A. Ext. Agt., UPA, to Santiago Tenorio, Governor, Santa Ana Pueblo, 30 January 1939, SAPRG; Manuel Gonzales,

Governor, Santa Ana Pueblo, Plans for Santa Ana Pueblo Community Farm Equipment Fund, SAPRG; Anna R. Masci, A. Chief Clerk and DDA, UPA, Receipt for Funds Transferred to the Governor of Santa Ana Pueblo, 18 January 1944, SAPRG; Jesús Manuel, Gov., et al., Santa Ana Pueblo, to Dr. S. D. Aberle, Supt., UPA, 16 June 1943, UP-1936-255-32500-E, CF, 1907–1939, RG 75, BIA; S. D. Aberle, Supt., UPA, to CIA, Chicago, 17 October 1942, UP-df-21, RG 75, BIA, AB, FRCD; José Rey León, Governor, Santa Ana Pueblo, et al., to Dr. S. D. Aberle, Supt., UPA, 16 October, 1942, encl. in Aberle to CIA, 17 October 1942, UP-df-21, RG 75, BIA, AB, FRCD; "Santa Ana Compensation Fund, Authorities Issued to June 30, 1940, Amount of Disbursements to Feb. 1941," 1941, UP-df-21, RG 75, BIA, AB, FRCD; Donald G. Schuler, A.CIA, to Dr. S. D. Aberle, Supt., UPA, 8 December 1942, UP-df-21, RG 75, BIA, AB, FRCD; S. D. Aberle, Supt., UPA, to CIA, 8 July 1940, UP-df-21, RG 75, BIA, AB, FRCD; "Tribal Council Resolution Authorizing the Cashing of Savings Bonds for Purchase of Combine," 4 June 1949, SAPRG; Walter V. Woehlke, Asst. to CIA, to Dr. Sophie D. Aberle, Supt., UPA, 11 July 1940, UP-df-21, RG 75, BIA, AB, FRCD; Governor and Lt. Governor, Santa Ana Pueblo, to Dr. S. D. Aberle, Supt., UPA, 8 July 1940, encl. in Aberle to CIA, 8 July 1940, UP-df-21, RG 75, BIA, AB, FRCD; Albert Montoya, Gov., Santa Ana Pueblo, Pueblo Council Resolution, 23 March 1959, encl. in Guy C. Williams, Supt., UPA, Memorandum to Area Director, Gallup Area Office, 25 March 1959, SAPRG; Albert Montoya, Governor, Santa Ana Pueblo, Pueblo Council Resolution, March 1959, SAPRG.

22. "Summary of Activities of the United Pueblos Agency in Developing Improved Agriculture Practices Among the Pueblo Indians of New Mexico," 1939, encl. in Gen. Supt., UPA, to Dr. Ruth Underhill, 11 December 1939, UP-df-1, RG 75, BIA, AB, FRCD; L. B. Liljenquist, A. Extension Agt., UPA, for S. D. Aberle, Supt., to Manuel Gonzales, Governor, Santa Ana Pueblo, 4 December 1940, SAPRG; F. B. Harmon, Disbursing Officer, UPA, to Santa Ana Indians c/o Governor, Santa Ana Pueblo, encl. Receipt for Earnings in 1939 AAA Program, 11 April 1940, SAPRG; Eric T. Hagberg, A. Chief Clerk, for S. D. Aberle, Gen. Supt., UPA, to Eligio Montoya, Governor, Santa Ana Pueblo, 5 November 1941, SAPRG.

23. R. H. Shipmen, Farm Agt., Statistical Summary, *ARIEW* 1935, UP-1939-031-13416, CF, 1907–1939, RG 75, BIA, NA; S. D. Aberle, Supt., et al., "Annual Report of Extension Workers, From B, Santa Ana Pueblo," 31 December 1936, UP-1937-031-38155, CF, 1907–1939, RG 75, BIA, NA; S. D. Aberle, Supt., UPA, to All Governors under United Pueblo Jurisdiction, 24 September 1935, SP-26, RG 75, BIA, AB, FRCD; S. D. Aberle, "The Pueblo Indians of New Mexico: Their Land, Economy, and Civil Organization," *American Anthropologist* 50, no. 4, pt. 2 (October 1948).

24. "Information Pertaining to Range Rider's Headquarters at Santa Ana," 10 April 1942, UP-df-19, RG 75, BIA, AB, FRCD; John G. Evans, Supt., UPA, Lease Between the Pueblo of Santa Ana and the United States, 12 July 1944, SAPRG; H. L. Gardner, Administrative Officer, UPA, to Eligio Montoya, Governor, Santa Ana Pueblo, 13 June 1949, SAPRG; John G. Evans, Supt., UPA, to Manuel Gonzales,

Governor, Santa Ana Pueblo, 26 April 1946, SAPRG; Eric T. Hagberg, Supt., UPA, to Howard H. Sheets, 8 June 1950, SAPRG; Unelio Menchego, A. Governor, Santa Ana Pueblo, and Emiliano Otero, Pueblo Council Resolution, 14 March 1950, SAPRG; Eric T. Hagberg, Area Director, UPA, to Howard H. Sheets, 4 August 1950, SAPRG; José Bobe Pino, Governor, Santa Ana Pueblo, "Surface and Borrow Permit for New Mexico State Highway Department," 28 August 1957, SAPRG; Agency Realty Officer, UPA, to Ted Boyd Co., 29 January 1958, SAPRG; F. D. Shannon, Agency Realty and Property Officer, UPA, to Ted Boyd Co., 6 January 1958, SAPRG; Longino Otero, Governor, Santa Ana Pueblo, 14 February 1950, SAPRG; Santa Ana Pueblo and Miller, Smith, and O'Hara, Sand and Gravel Permit Agreement, 2 April 1959, SAPRG; Albert Montoya, Governor, Santa Ana Pueblo, Pueblo Council Resolution, 14 September 1959, SAPRG; Bruce H. Eastman, Realty Officer, SPA, to Perry and Lowrey, 12 April 1960, SAPRG; Bruce H. Eastman to W. L. Davidson, 12 April 1960, SAPRG; C. M. McConnell, Deputy Regional Mining Supervisor, ID Geological Survey, 12 April 1960, SAPRG; Pueblo of Santa Ana and the State Highway Commission of New Mexico, Sand and Gravel Permit, 29 December 1960, SAPRG; F. D. Shannon, Agency Realty Officer, UPA, to W. L. Davidson, Mid-West Clay Products, 3 February 1961, SAPRG; F. D. Shannon to Joe Y. García, Governor, Santa Ana Pueblo, 4 October 1960, SAPRG; Joe García, Governor, Santa Ana Pueblo, "Mining Lease, Indian Lands," 26 August, 1960, SAPRG; Bruce H. Eastman to Clarence Huff, Bernalillo, 10 June 1960, SAPRG; Bruce H. Eastman to Joe Y. García, Governor, Santa Ana Pueblo, 4 August 1960, SAPRG; Bruce H. Eastman to Telesfor Castillo, Bernalillo, 27 June 1960, SAPRG; Farming Lease, 7 August 1961, SAPRG; Farming Pasture Lease to Telesfor Castillo, 28 April 1961, SAPRG; Bruce H. Eastman to Telesfor Castillo, Bernalillo, 28 January 1964.

25. José Bobe Pino et al., Council, Santa Ana Pueblo, to John Collier, CIA, 28 April 1936; S. D. Aberle, Supt., UPA, and V. W. Balderson, UPA, to County Chairman, Range Conservation Program, Sandoval County, Bernalillo, 21 September 1937, SAPRG; A. F. Apodaca, County Extension Agt., Bernalillo, to Governor, Santa Ana Pueblo, 22 September 1937, SAPRG; Annual Forestry Report, Santa Ana Reservation, 30 June 1939, UP-1939-031-39189, CF, 1907–1939, RG 75, BIA, NA; L. G. Boldt, Memorandum to Dewey Dismuke on Santa Ana Responsibility for Taylor Place Corrections in Fencing and Watering Facilities for Stock, 2 May 1950, UP-df-19, RG 75, BIA, AB, FRCD; Santa Ana Pueblo by Eligio Montoya and U. S. by H. L. Gardner, Administrative Officer, "Lease Between Pueblo of Santa Ana and the United States of America," 2 May 1949, attached to Boldt, Memorandum to Dismuke, 2 May 1950, UP-df-19, RG 75, BIA, AB, FRCD.

26. Wesley Calef, *Private Grazing and Public Lands: Studies of Local Management of the Taylor Grazing Act* (Chicago: University of Chicago Press, 1960), pp. 49–90; Aberle, "Pueblo Indians of New Mexico," p. 20; Nathan R. Margold, Solicitor, to SI, 13 February 1937, SAPRG; "The Taylor Grazing Act," encl. in Barnett to Governor Pena, 12 November 1937, SAPRG.

27. José Bobe Pino et al., Council, Santa Ana Pueblo, to John Collier, CIA, 28 April 1936, SPA; Collier to Council of the Pueblo of Santa Ana, through Supt., UPA, 29 April 1926, SPA.

28. Application for Grazing Permit, encl. in C. W. Wright to Governor Bobe, 4 May 1936, SAPRG; S. D. Aberle, Supt., UPA, to Leo Pena, Governor, Santa Ana Pueblo, 7 October 1937, SAPRG: Joseph Y. Barnett, for S. D. Aberle, Supt., UPA, to Leo Pena, Governor, Santa Ana Pueblo, 12 November 1936, SAPRG; Felix S. Cohen, A. Solicitor, to SI, 14 May 1938, UP-1937-301-12681 and UP-1937-919-418521; William A. Brophy, Nite Letter to John Collier, CIA (copy), 5 April 1938, UP-1937-301-12681, CF, 1907–1939, RG 75, BIA, NA; Joseph Y. Barnette, Asst. Field Aide, for S. D. Aberle, Supt., UPA, to Governor, Pueblo of Santa Ana, 4 January 1938, SAPRG; S. D. Aberle, Supt., UPA, to Porfirio Montoya, Governor, Santa Ana Pueblo, 30 March 1938, SAPRG; Joe H. Leech, Chief Hearings Officer, Division of Grazing, to Director, Division of Grazing, 18 July 1938, UP-1937-301-12681, CF, 1907–1939, RG 75, BIA, NA; S. D. Aberle, Supt., UPA, to Lee Muck, Dir. of Forestry, BIA, 20 August 1938, UP-1937-301-12681, CF, 1907–1939, RG 75, BIA, NA; Julian A. Territt, A. Director, Division of Grazing, Memorandum for Mr. Muck, 20 August 1938, UP-1937-301-12681, CF, 1907–1939, RG 75, BIA, NA; Lee Muck, Director of Forestry, to S. D. Aberle, Supt., UPA, 22 August 1938, UP-1937-301-12681, CF 1907–1939, RG 75, BIA, NA; Photographs (duplicated copy) no. 62, 70, 60, "Survey of Water Holes for Santa Ana Pueblo Division of Grazing Applications," 19 May 1938, UP-1937-301-12681-1-A; Porfirio Montoya, Governor, Santa Ana Pueblo, "Application for Grazing Permit, Supplementary to Original Application of March 5, 1937," 21 May 1938, encl. in "IV. Appendix: Report on Grazing Application of Santa Ana Pueblo," c. 28 May 1938, UP-1937-301-12681-1-D, CF, 1907–1939, RG 75, BIA, NA; "Report of Grazing Application of Santa Ana Pueblo, c. 28 May 1938"; C. F. Dierking, Regional Grazier, NM, "Notice to Applicants of Grazing Fees Due," 28 May 1938, UP-1937-301-12681-1-D, encl., in "IV., Appendix: Report on Grazing Application," 28 May 1938; W. V. Woehlke, "Memorandum to Mr. Collier: Subject, Pueblo Grazing Applications," 14 June 1938, UP-1937-301-12681, CF, 1907–1939, RG 75, BIA, NA; William A. Brophy, Atty. for Appellant, "Appeal for Adjudication of Regional Grazier, and Specification of Error Therefor, in the Matter of the Appeal of the Pueblo of Santa Ana," 17 June 1938, UP-1938-301-44601, CF, 1907–1939, RG 75, BIA.

29. J. H. Leech, Chief Hearings Officer, Division of Grazing, to C. F. Dierking, Regional Grazier, 1 July 1938, UP-1937-301-12681, CF, 1907–1939, RG 75, BIA, NA; Porfirio Montoya, Governor of Santa Ana Pueblo, et al., "United States, Department of the Interior, Division of Grazing: Stipulation," 6 September 1938, SPA; "Notes for Hearing of Santa Ana Grazing Appeal," c. 6 September 1938, SPA.

30. C. F. Dierking, Regional Grazier, ID, to Pueblo of Santa Ana, c/o UPA, 6 February 1939, SAPRG; S. D. Aberle, Supt., UPA, to Eligio Montoya, Governor of Santa Ana Pueblo, 8 October 1941, SAPRG; Hilario Otero, Governor of Santa Ana

Pueblo, and H. R. Rodgers, NM State Land Office Committee on Lands, "Temporary Grazing Permit on State Land #23," 1 October 1943, encl. in Virgil K. Whitaker to Governor Hilario Otero, 11 February 1944, SAPRG; S. D. Aberle, Supt., UPA, to Jesús Manuel, Governor of Santa Ana Pueblo, 23 June 1943, SAPRG; H. M. Salmon, Acting Regional Grazier, ID, "Ten Year Grazing Permit," 1 July 1944, SAPRG, with maps showing allotment lines in Grazing Districts no. 1 and no. 2-A; Lloyd M. Elston, Range Examiner, UPA, to Hilario Otero, Governor of Santa Ana Pueblo, 16 May 1944, SAPRG; Virgil K. Whitaker, A. Supt., UPA, to Hilario Otero, Governor of Santa Ana Pueblo, 11 February 1944, SAPRG; Virgil K. Whitaker, A. Supt., UPA, to Floyd N. Lee, Chmn., Grazing Service Advisory Board, San Ysidro District no. 1, 11 March 1944, SAPRG; Hilario Otero, Governor of Santa Ana Pueblo, to H. R. Rodgers, Commissioner of Public Lands, State Lands Office, 12 September 1944, SAPRG; Dewey Dismuke for Eric T. Hagberg, Supt., UPA, to Eligio Montoya, Governor of Santa Ana Pueblo, 15 July 1949, SAPRG; Hazel G. Carrick, Land Field Clerk, UPA, Receipt for Cashier's Check, 29 July 1949, SAPRG; Dewey Dismuke, Chief of Tribal Affairs Division, UPA, to Elijio Montoya, Governor of Santa Ana Pueblo, 12 December 1949, SAPRG; José Bobe Pino, Governor of Santa Ana Pueblo, to Donald I. Bailey, Dist. Range Manager, BLM, 15 May 1957, SAPRG; F. D. Shannon, UPA Realty Officer, to Albert Montoya, Governor, Santa Ana Pueblo, to BLM, attn. Charles Hodgins, 5 November 1968, SAPRG; Patrick L. Wehling, A. Supt., UPA, to Porfirio Montoya, Governor of Santa Ana Pueblo, 18 October 1966, SAPRG; Patrick L. Wehling, A. Supt., UPA, to Vicente Armijo, Governor of Santa Ana Pueblo, 9 August 1968, SAPRG.

31. F. C. Abbott, Jr., Range Examiner, "Range Management Plan for Zía Pueblo Grant, Santa Ana Pueblo Grant including El Ranchito Grant, San Felipe Pueblo Grant and Indian Reservation, and Santo Domingo Pueblo Grant," AD, SCS-TC-BIA, 20 April 1937, UP-1936-341-9159-A and duplicate UP-1937-301-00, CF, 1907–1939, RG 75, BIA, NA; "Location Map," 4 November 1936, encl. in Abbott, "Range Management Plan"; E. A. Johnson, Asst. Dir., SCS, TC-BIA, 16 September 1938, UP-1938-021.5-55388; John Herrick, Asst. to CIA, to E. A. Johnson, SCS, TC-BIA, 21 September 1938, UP-1938-021.5-55388; John Herrick, Asst. to CIA, to Dr. Sophie D. Aberle, Supt., UPA, 1 October 1938, UP-1938-021.5-55388, CF, 1907–1939, RG 75, BIA, NA; Alan G. Harper, Director, SCS, TC-BIA, to John Herrick, Asst. to CIA, 10 October 1938, UP-1938-021.5-55388; CF, 1907–1939, RG 75, BIA, NA; E.A. Johnson, Asst. Dir., SCS, TC-BIA, to John Collier, CIA, attn. John Herrick, 16 August 1938, UP-1938-021.5-55388; John Herrick, Asst. to CIA, to E. A. Johnson, Asst. Dir., SCS, TC-BIA, 24 August 1938, UP-1938-021.5-55388; Alan G. Harper, Dir., SCS, TC-BIA, to John Herrick, Asst. to CIA, 31 August 1938, UP-1938-021.5-55388. CF, 1907–1939, RG 75, BIA, NA.

32. S. D. Aberle, Supt., and Lorin F. Jones, Supervisor of Extension Work, UPA, "Annual Report of Extension Workers," 31 December 1937, UP-1938-031-16435, CF, 1907–1939, RG 75, BIA, NA.

33. Forest Service, Annual Report, 1937; Longinio Otero, Governor of Santa Ana Pueblo, and John B. Pino, Governor of Zía Pueblo, Land Management Proposal, 1950, SAPRG; Lonnie E. Sussett, Agency Land Operations Officer, Memorandum to José Bobe Pino, Governor of Santa Ana Pueblo, c. 1956, SAPRG.

34. John Collier, CIA, to Council of Santa Ana Pueblo through Supt., SPA, 29 April 1936, SAPRG; S. D. Aberle, Supt., UPA, to José Bobe, Governor of Santa Ana Pueblo, 4 May 1946, SAPRG; Dewey Dismuke, Chief Agricultural Aide, UPA, to Porfirio Montoya, Governor of Santa Ana Pueblo, 27 July 1938, SAPRG; Santiago Tenorio, Governor of Santa Ana, and the Governors and Principal Men of Zía, Santa Ana, and Jémez, Petition to Harold L. Ickes et al., c. 1939, SPA; Alan Laflin, A. Supt., UPA, to CIA, 30 July 1940, SPA; George Toledo, Governor of Jémez, et al., to CIA, 27 July 1940, encl. in Laflin to CIA, SPA; James M. Gray, DLALU, SCS, to J. M. Stewart, Director of Lands, BIA, 26 January 1939, UP-1936-310-75700-F-LI-NM-6, CF, 1907–1939, RG 75, BIA; Everett M. Grantham, US Atty., by A. Gilberto Espinosa, Asst., to Attorney General, Washington, D. C., attn. Carl McFarland, 10 March 1939, UP-1939-308.2-15220, CF, 1907–1939, RG 75, BIA, NA; Supt., UPA, to C. F. Dierking, Regional Grazier, 3 May 1939, UP-1939-308.2-31239, CF, 1907–1939, RG 75, BIA, NA; Walter V. Woehlke, Memorandum to CIA on the M. L. Wilson Conference, 26 September 1939, UP-1936-341-9159-A, CF, 1907–1939, RG 75, BIA; John G. Evans, Supt., UPA, to Juan Luis Pecos, Governor of Jémez, 4 May 1945, SPA; John G. Evans, Supt., UPA, "Report on the Ancient Claim of the Pueblo of Jémez and the Present Status of the Espiritu Santo Grant, together with a Classified Schedule of the Land Holdings and Permitted Areas of the Pueblo of Jémez," 15 May 1945, encl. in Evans to Pecos, 4 May 1945, SPA; Men of Jémez, Zía, and Santa Ana, Statements about Pueblo History and the Espiritu Santo Grant, 23 May 1949, SAPRG; H. Pierce to S. D. Aberle, 28 September 1943, SPA.

35. Opinion of the Indian Claims Commission, Docket No. 137, *Pueblos of Zía, Santa Ana, and Jémez v. U.S.,* 7 May 1968, SAPRG; Renewal of Contract with Attorneys Claud S. Mann and M. J. Claybourgh, 29 September 1966, SAPRG; Claud S. Mann and Mark Claybourgh, Attys., to Santiago Armijo, Governor of Santa Ana Pueblo, 2 March 1964, SAPRG; Claud S. Mann, Atty., to CIA, 9 March 1964, SAPRG; Homer B. Jenkins, Chief, Branch of Tribal Programs, to W. Wade Head, Area Director, BIA, Gallup, 7 November 1957, SAPRG; Expense Lists, Jémez, Zía, and Santa Ana Pueblos, 9 March 1957, SAPRG; "Information Taken at Meeting with the Three Indian Pueblos held 14 January 1951 at Zía Pueblo," SAPRG; H. Carrick, Memorandum, 27 December 1951, SPA; Old Man of Santana, "Account of Spanish Grant to the Holy Ghost Springs Canyon Grant," n.d., encl. in Carrick, 27 December 1951; Copy of the Ojo del Espiritu Santo Grant, n.d., encl. in Carrick, 27 December 1951; Claud S. Mann and Dudley Cornell, Attys., and Richard M. Krannawitter, Notary Public, Contract with the Pueblos of Zía, Santa Ana, and Jémez, 30 November 1950, SAPRG; Eric T. Hagberg, Supt., UPA, to Governors of Zía, Santa Ana, and Jémez, 10 October 1950, SAPRG; Henry Weihegen, University of New

Mexico College of Law, to Longino Otero, Governor of Santa Ana Pueblo, et al., 12 October 1950, SAPRG.

36. A. W. Simington, Land Field Agt., to J. M. Stewart, Dir. of Lands, BIA, 30 September 1939, UP-1936-310-986-16, CF, 1907–1939, RG 75, BIA, NA; Leo Pena, Governor of Santa Ana Pueblo, et al., Pueblo Council Resolution, 1 August 1937, UP-1939-310-986-16, CF, 1907–1939, RG 75, BIA, NA, and SAPRG; Ernest Sallee, Asst. Land Field Agent, BIA, to Leo Pena, Governor of Santa Ana Pueblo, 21 December 1937, SAPRG and SPA; Sophie D. Aberle, Supt., UPA, to SI, attn. Asst. Sec. Chapman, 5 August 1937, SPA; Carolina Garcia and David B. García, "Offer to Sell Lands to the United States," 24 July 1937, encl. in Aberle to SI, 5 August 1937; M. J. McGuinness et al. and the Pueblo of Santa Ana, Warranty Deed, 6 April 1939, encl. in Simington to Stewart, 30 September 1939; "Abstract of Title, No. 11, 230, to the Following Described Real Estate Situated in Sandoval County, New Mexico," c. May 1939, encl. in Simington to Stewart, 30 September 1939; Map, "Sketch Showing Lands Proposed for Purchase by Pueblo of Santa Ana," 15 October 1940, encl. in A. W. Simington, Land Field Agt., Memorandum to Mr. Formhals, 16 October 1940, SPA; Land Division, UPA, "Pueblo of Santa Ana Land Status," 1 April 1940, SPA; Robert K. Taylor, "Offer to Sell Lands to the United States," 1 May 1939, UP-1936-310-986-16, CF, 1907–1939, RG 75, BIA; S. D. Aberle, Supt., UPA, to Santiago Tenorio, Governor of Santa Ana Pueblo, 12 July 1939, SAPRG; Pueblo of Santa Ana, by Santiago Tenorio, Governor, Resolution, 16 February 1939, UP-1936-310-986-16, CF, 1907–1939, RG 75, BIA, UPA; Journal Voucher, 1946, SAPRG, David Dozier, Area Supt., to Hazel [Carrick?], c. September 1946, SPA; Eric T. Hagberg, Supt., UPA, to A.W. Simington, Land Field Agt., BIA, 9 September 1946, SPA; "Plan of Land Belonging to Mariano Montoya, El Ranchito Grant, T 13N, R 4E, Sec. 30 NMPM," 31 October 1946, SPA; P. V. Archibal to Governor of Santa Ana Pueblo, 30 June 1948, SAPRG; J. M. Stewart, Chief, BIA Land Division, "Submarginal Land Purchase—New Mexico," c. 1934, UP-1936-310-75700-F-LI-NM-6, CF, 1907–1939, RG 75, BIA, NA; Richard Hughes, Attorney, "Inserts into Santa Ana Historical Study," encl. in letter to Laura Bayer, 23 July 1992, p. 1.

37. Hughes, "Inserts into Santa Ana Historical Study," pp. 2–5.

38. Ibid., pp. 6–8; Act of 8 June 1940, Ch. 283, 54 Stat. 253; United States v. University of New Mexico, 731 F.2d 7003 (10th Cir. 1984); Act of 28 October 1986, Pub.L. 99–575.

39. Hughes, "Inserts into Santa Ana Historical Study, pp. 3–5, 8.

40. S. D. Aberle, Supt., UPA, to CIA, 12 March 1940, SPA; Jesse D. Crawford, Memorandum to the Files on the Santa Ana-San Felipe Overlap Dispute, 10 February 1941, SPA; J. A. Wagner, Jr., Range Examiner, UPA, Memorandum to Mr. O'Neill, 19 April 1939, SPA; R. H. Rupkey, Senior Engineer, Irrigation Service, Colorado River Project, to L. G. Boldt, UPA, 13 January 1941, SPA; Dan T. O'Neill, UPA, Memorandum to Dr. Aberle, 23 May 1949, SPA; Meeting to Discuss the Santa Ana-San Felipe Overlap, Santa Ana Pueblo Community Center, 25 January 1980, Santa Ana Pueblo Oral History Project, Tape nos. 6 and 7.

41. Santiago E. Campos, District Judge, "Court's Findings of Fact and Conclusions of Law," *Pueblo of Santa Ana v. Alfredo Baca and Mary Lou Baca,* filed 30 April 1985, US Dist. Court, Santa Fe, New Mexico, copy in the files of Rothstein, Walther, Donatelli, Hughes, Dahlstrom & Cron, Attorneys for the Pueblo of Santa Ana, Santa Fe, New Mexico; Pueblo of Santa Ana, Plaintiff-Appellee, v. Alfredo Baca and Mary Lou Baca, Defendants-Appellants, No. 86-1337, 844 F.2d 708, US Circuit Court of Appeals, 10th Circuit, 25 March 1988, in *Federal Reporter,* 2nd series, pp. 708–13, copy marked "Santa Ana Petition Exhibit C," in the files of Rothstein, Walther, Donatelli, Hughes, Dahlstrom & Cron, Attorneys for the Pueblo of Santa Ana, Santa Fe, New Mexico.

42. Pueblo of Santa Ana and the Santa Fe Northwestern Railway Co., 22 March 1927, SAPRG; E. N. Sanderson, President, New Mexico Power Co., to SI, 18 October 1928; Lem A. Towers, Supt., SPA, to H. R. McKee, Supt., AT&SFRR, 8 August 1933, SPA; McKee to Towers, 11 December 1933, encl. in Towers to Judge R. H. Hanna, 22 December 1933, SPA; William A. Brophy, Sp. Atty. for PI, to Ernest Sallee, UPA, 12 June 1936; M. Limbaugh, State Highway Engineer, to SI, 29 November 1937, encl. in S. D. Aberle, Supt., UPA, to John Collier, CIA, 8 December 1937, UP-1937-375-75819, CF, 1907–1939, RG 75, BIA, NA; Santa Ana Pueblo, by Leo Pena, Governor, Board of County Commissioners, by Leopold Martínez, Chairman, and New Mexico, through the State Highway Commission, by M. Limbaugh, Engineer, Agreement for Highway Right-Of-Way, 22 November 1937, encl. in Aberle to Collier, 8 December 1937; Leo Pena and Fabiano López, Governor and Lt. Governor of Santa Ana Pueblo, Agreement with NM State Highway Commission, 22 November 1937, SAPRG; H. M. Knutson, Chief Clerk, for S. D. Aberle, Supt., UPA, to Porfirio Montoya, Governor of Santa Ana Pueblo, 30 March 1938, SAPRG; William Zimmerman, Jr., Asst. CIA, to SI, 21 February 1938, UP-1936-375-75819, CF, 1907–1939, RG 75, BIA, NA; J. M. Stewart, Dir. of Lands, to S. D. Aberle, Supt., UPA, 22 March 1938, UP-1937-375-75819, CF, 1907–1939, RG 75, BIA, NA; John Collier, CIA, to Commissioner Johnson, GLO, 16 March 1938, UP-1937-375-75819, CF, 1907–1939, RG 75, BIA, NA; S. D. Aberle, Supt., UPA, to Porfirio Montoya, Governor of Santa Ana Pueblo, 18 February 1938, encl. in Knutson to Montoya, 1 April 1938; Donald I. Bailey, Dist. Range Manager, by Keith J. Finley, to José Bobe Pino, Governor of Santa Ana Pueblo, 28 October 1957, SAPRG; Pueblo Council Resolution, c. 1957, SAPRG [Atrisco Canal Right-of-Way]; José Bobe Pino, Governor of Santa Ana Pueblo, Pueblo Council Resolution, 27 August 1957, encl. in Agreement between the Pueblo of Santa Ana and the US, 4 November 1957, SAPRG; Guy C. Williams, Supt., UPA, to José Bobe Pino, Governor of Santa Ana Pueblo, 12 November 1957, SAPRG; F. D. Shannon, Agency Realty Officer, to José Bobe Pino, Governor of Santa Ana Pueblo, 24 December 1957, SAPRG; Guy C. Williams, Supt., UPA, to Hood D. Kizziar[?], Supervisor of Right-of-way and Claims, Texas-New Mexico Pipeline Co., 9 April 1957, SAPRG; Santiago Armijo, Governor of Santa Ana Pueblo, Pueblo Council Resolution, 18 July 1958, SAPRG; Albert Montoya, Gover-

nor of Santa Ana Pueblo, Pueblo Council Resolution, 4 April 1959, SAPRG; Albert Montoya, Governor of Santa Ana Pueblo, Pueblo Council Resolution, 14 September 1959, SAPRG; *State of New Mexico ex. rel. State Highway Commission v. U.S. and the Pueblo of Santa Ana,* 7 March 1957, SAPRG; Guy C. Williams, Supt., UPA, to L. D. Wilson, Chief Highway Engineer, 11 March 1957, SAPRG; L. D. Wilson, Chief Highway Engineer, by Robert W. de la Rue, to the Governor and Council of Santa Ana Pueblo, 18 March 1957, SAPRG; Santiago Armijo, Governor of Santa Ana Pueblo, Pueblo Council Resolution, 3 September 1958, SAPRG; Santiago Armijo, Governor of Santa Ana Pueblo, Pueblo Council Resolution, 29 October 1958, SAPRG; Albert Montoya, Governor of Santa Ana Pueblo, Pueblo Council Resolution, 2 March 1959, SAPRG; Kenneth L. Payton, Supt., SPA, to New Mexico State Highway Commission, 13 June 1969, encl. map and grant of easement, SAPRG; Pueblo of Santa Ana and the New Mexico State Highway Commission, Drainage Agreement, 30 April 1968, SAPRG; Albert Montoya, Governor of Santa Ana Pueblo, and W. L. Davidson, Use Agreement, 14 September 1959, SAPRG; Bruce H. Eastman, Realty Officer, UPA, to W. L. Davidson, 12 April 1960, SAPRG; Santiago Armijo, Governor of Santa Ana Pueblo, Pueblo Council Resolution, 24 September 1964, SAPRG; Eugene Foster, R/W Agent, UPA, to UPA, 8 November 1968, SAPRG.

43. José Bobe Pino, Governor of Santa Ana Pueblo, by M. G., to C. W. Wright, UPA, 16 June 1936, SPA; Manuel Gonzales, Lt. Governor of Santa Ana Pueblo, to E. R. Fryer, UPA, 23 March 1936, of SPA; Manuel Gonzales, Lt. Governor of Santa Ana Pueblo, to F. M. Stevens, UPA, c. 1936, SPA; William A. Brophy, Sp. Atty. for Pueblos, to Charles F. Brown, Bernalillo, 5 October 1936, SAPRG; Brophy to Ted M. Formhals, Road Supervisor, UPA, 5 October 1936, SAPRG; Ted M. Formhals, UPA, Memorandum to Mr. Brophy, 3 November 1942, SPA; L. G. Boldt, UPA, Memorandum to Judge Hanna, 12 March 1946, SPA; Eric T. Hagberg, A. Supt., UPA, to Amado Shije, Governor of Zía Pueblo, 20 December 1946, SAPRG; John G. Evans, Supt., UPA, to Mariano Montoya, Bernalillo, 21 April 1945, SAPRG; David C. Dozier, Area Supervisor, UPA, Memorandum to John G. Evans, Dewey Dismuke, and L. G. Boldt, 23 June 1946, SAPRG; Eric T. Hagberg, A. Supt., UPA, to Juan Lucero, Bernalillo, 11 March 1947, SAPRG; Hagberg to Manuel Gonzales, Governor of Santa Ana Pueblo, 23 December 1946, SAPRG; Dewey Dismuke et al., Memorandum, 10 December 1948, SPA; J. W. Young, District Manager, BLM, to Santa Ana Pueblo, c/o UPA, 6 December 1960, SAPRG; Cooperative Agreement for Stock Water from the Borrego Grant Well No. 4, March 1964, SAPRG.

44. Excerpts from CIA to SI, 2 October 1911, *ARCIA 1911,* HED 120, 62d Cong., 2nd sess., pp 14–16; CIA to SI, 12 September 1912, *ARCIA 1912,* HED 933, 62d Cong., 3rd sess. (Washington, D.C.: GPO, 1913), pp. 3–70; "Table 37—Miles of Ditches on Reservations," 1912, *ARCIA 1912,* pp. 226–29; CIA to SIA, 1914, 1915, and 1916, typed excerpts from *ARCIA, SPA;* Tables 24, 25, and 39, *ARCIA 1918,* HED 409, 65th Cong., 3rd sess. (Washington, D.C.: GPO, 1919), pp. 186–87, 184–85, 214; Table 25, *ARCIA 1919,* HED 1455, 66th Cong., 2nd sess. (Washington,

D.C.: GPO, 1920), pp. 174–75; SI, Report, 20 November 1919, *ARSI 1919,* vol. 1, HED 1455, 66th Cong., 2nd sess. (Washington, D.C.: GPO, 1919), pp. 41, 75; CIA to SI, 30 September 1920, *ARCIA 1920,* HED 849, 66th Cong., 3rd sess. (Washington, D.C.: GPO, 1920), pp. 28–29, 54–55.

45. CIA to SI, 8 December 1913, *ARCIA 1913,* HED 1009, 63d Cong., 2nd sess. (Washington, D.C.: GPO, 1914), pp. 3–45.

46. R. H. Hanna, Sp. Atty. for Pueblos, to H. F. Robinson, Supervising Engineer, 29 March 1920, SPA; Charles F. Brown, Secretary, Bernalillo Community Ditch, to H. F. Robinson, US Indian Irrigation Service, 23 March 1921, encl. sketch maps, SPA; H. F. Robinson, Supervising Engineer, to R. H. Hanna, Sp. Atty., 25 March 1920, SPA; Bernalillo Community Ditch and Santa Ana Pueblo, Agreement, April 1920, SPA.

47. Minutes of the Council of Pueblo Indians, General Sessions, 24 March 1928, SP-df-20, RG 75, BIA, AB, FRCD; "Area of Lands Included in the Middle Rio Grande Conservancy District, c. 1928," SP-26 [?], RG 75, BIA, AB, FRCD.

48. Ibid.

49. [Walter C. Cochrane] to H. J.Hagerman, NM Governor and Special Commissioner of the Pueblo Lands Board, 27 October 1930, SPA; Cochrane to Hagerman, 15 November 1930, SPA.

50. H. Rupkey, Asst. Engineer, Fifth Irrigation Dist., to Daniel Otero, Governor, Santa Ana Pueblo, 25 June 1931, SAPRG; Wilfred W. Baker, Div. Eng., MRGCD, Copy of Verbal Agreement with Governor Otero, Santa Ana Pueblo, encl. in Rupkey to Otero; Walter C. Cochrane, Sp. Atty. for Pueblos, to H. J. Hagerman, NM Gov., 27 October 1930, SPA; L. C. Bammet, Vice Pres., MRGCD, to Hilario Sánchez, Governor, Santa Ana Pueblo, 9 April 1930, SAPRG; John Collier, Ex Sec., American Indian Defense Assn., to Officers of the Conservancy, Pueblos, 21 May 1930, SAPRG; John Collier to the Several Pueblo Delegates, 23 April 1930, SAPRG; Bunkholder, MRGCD, to Governor, Santa Ana Pueblo, 1 March 1930, SAPRG: R. H. Rupkey, Asst. Engineer, Fifth Irrigation Dist., to C. H. Neuffer, Supervising Engineer, 17 February 1931, SAPRG; D. W. Lomberg, NM Highway Commission, and the Pueblo of Santa Ana, Agreement, 23 June 1930, SAPRG: Lem A. Towers, Supt., SPA, to Hilario Sánchez, Governor of Santa Ana Pueblo, 9 September and 23 September 1930, SAPRG; Santa Ana Pueblo and the Middle Río Grande Conservancy District, Agreement, 19 December 1930, encl. in Towers to Sánchez, 23 September 1930.

51. C. A. Anderson, Chief Engineer, MRGCD, to R. H. Rupkey, Engineer, 15 April 1936, SAPRG; S. D. Aberle, Supt., UPA, and Engineer Rupkey, to C. A. Anderson, Chief Engineer, MRGCD, 16 April 1936, SAPRG; Rupkey to Carl Anderson, Chief Engineer, MRGCD, 25 September 1936, SAPRG; Leo Pena, Governor of Santa Ana Pueblo, et al., and Chairman of the Board of Directors, Middle Rio Grande Conservancy District, Agreement, 23 June 1937, SAPRG; S. D. Aberle, Supt., to P. J. Flickinger, BIA, 16 July 1936, UP-1936-341-9159, CF, 1907–1939, RG 75, BIA, NA; A. L. Wathen, Director of Irrigation, to Dr. S. D. Aberle, Supt., UPA,

27 July 1937, UP-1936-341-9159, CF, 1907–1939, RG 75, BIA, NA; Stanley Phillippi, Asst. Chief Engineer, MRGCD, to Leo Pena, Governor of Santa Ana Pueblo, 14 September 1937, SAPRG; Phillippi to Porfirio Montoya, Lt. Governor, 9 February 1938, SAPRG; Phillippi to Governor of Santa Ana Pueblo, 8 December 1939, SAPRG; Phillippi to Manuel Gonzalez, Governor of Santa Ana Pueblo, 13 September 1940, SAPRG.

52. "Lands Irrigated in 1931," SPA; US Indian Irrigation Service, "Project Monthly Summary Cost Report," January 1939, UP-1936-341-9159-M-11, CF, 1907–1939, RG 75, BIA, NA; "Balance Sheet; Santa Ana Project," January 1939, UP-1936-341-9159-M-11, CF, 1907–1939, RG 75, BIA, NA; "Project Monthly Summary Cost Report" and "Balance Sheet, Santa Ana Project," December 1938, UP-1936-341-9159-M-11, CF, 1907–1939, RG 75, BIA, NA; Robert H. Rupkey, Irrigation Division, "Progress and Cost Report," October 1937, UP-1936-341-9159-M-7, CF, 1907–1939, RG 75, BIA, NA; Completed Forms for Santa Ana Irrigation Project, January and March 1937, UP-1936-341-9159-M-4 and M-5, CF 1907–1939, RG 75, BIA, NA; John Collier, CIA, to Sophie D. Aberle, Gen. Supt., UPA, 31 October 1935, UP-1935-341-55407, CF, 1907–1939, RG 75, BIA, NA; Charles W. Eliot II, Executive Officer, National Resource Committee, to John Collier, CIA, 10 July and 4 October 1935, UP-1935-341-55407; H. A. Wallace to SI, 3 September 1935, UP-1938-021.5-55388, CF, 1907–1939, RG 75, BIA, NA; R. G. Tugwell, A. SA, to SI, 1 August 1935, UP-1938-021.5-55388, CF, 1907–1939, RG 75, BIA, NA; Harold L. Ickes, SI, to SA, 11 July 1935, UP-1938-021.5-55388, CF, 1907–1939, RG 75, BIA, NA; C. W. Wright and S. D. Aberle, UPA, to José Bobe Pino, Governor, Santa Ana Pueblo, 2 May 1936, SAPRG: "Pueblos: Construction Program as Submitted by Agency and as Presented to Public Works Administration," c. 1936, UP-1936-341-9159-A, CF, 1907–1939, RG 75, BIA, NA; Robert H. Rupkey, Irrigation Division, UPA, "Progress and Cost Report, Fiscal Year 1936," UP-1936-341-9159-A, CF, 1907–1939, RG 75, BIA, NA; C. M. Chilson, UPA, Memorandum to Dr. Aberle, 29 May 1939, UP-df-88, RG 75, BIA, AB, FRCD.

53. *Indians at Work* 8, no. 10 (June 1941):10 and no. 11 (July 1941):4–10 and cover.

54. "Army Due to Start Rio Grande Levee Work Next Month," *Albuquerque Journal*, 7 December 1943, pp. 1, 12, UP-1936-341-9159-X, CF, 1907–1939, RG 75, BIA, NA. Among those who wrote to Commissioner Collier and Secretary Ickes were Frances Connelly of the American Association of Indian Affairs, M. W. Postelthwaite of the Museum of Colorado College, Congressman Clinton P. Anderson, Natacha Rambova, the Rev. Eric Tasman of South Orange, NJ, Irene S. Ebenhack of the Illinois Federation of Women's Clubs, J. O. Brew of the Peabody Museum, Ida Milliman of NJ, George W. Coffin of Denver, Eleanor L. Reindollar of the Maryland Academy of Sciences, Rena Maverick Green of the San Antonio Conservation Society, and Max Rutter of Comfort, TX; their letters, the mailing lists for the printed hearings, and the official replies may be found in UP-1936-341-9159-X, CF, 1907–1939, RG 75, BIA, NA, which also contains copies of related articles from the

Washington Post, the *Santa Fe New Mexican, Life,* the *Christian Science Monitor,* the *Albuquerque Tribune,* the *Albuquerque Journal, P.M., Indian Truth,* and the *Philadelphia Inquirer,* as well as letters from the pueblos of San Felipe and San Ildefonso, records of the delegation that went to Washington, and newsletters of the American Association on Indian Affairs and the New Mexico Association on Indian Affairs. Collier stated his position in a series of letters, including one to Mrs. Charles S. Dietrich of the NM Association on Indian Affairs, 24 March 1943, in that file, and one to the Governors of the New Mexico Pueblos, 6 March 1943, SAPRG. A copy of the bill sponsored by NM Representative Clinton Anderson, "A Bill to Authorize the Exploration of Proposed Dam Sites Located on Indian Lands within the State of New Mexico," H.R. 323, 78th Cong., 1st sess., 17 March 1943, committee reports, and related letters can be found in UP-1936-341-9159-A, CF, 1907–1939, RG 75, BIA, NA.

55. Able Paisano, Secretary, All Pueblo Council, to Jesús Manuel, Governor, Santa Ana Pueblo, 5 April 1943, SAPRG; Walter O. Olson, Acting Supt., UPA, Memorandum for the Files on the All Pueblo Council Meeting of 31 March 1943, 5 April 1943, UP-1936-341-9159-X, CF, 1907–1939, RG 75, BIA, NA; Olson, Memorandum to Dr. Aberle: Comments on the All Pueblo Council Meeting of 31 March 1943, UP-1936-341-9159-X, CF, 1907–1939, RG 75, BIA, NA; David Dozier, Farm Agent, UPA, Confidential Memorandum to the Files on the All Pueblo Council Meeting of 31 March 1943, 5 April 1943, UP-1936-341-9159-X, CF, 1907–1939, RG 75, BIA, NA; John Collier, CIA, to Able Paisano, Secretary of the All Pueblo Council, 8 April 1943, UP-1936-341-9159-X, CF, 1907–1939, RG 75, BIA, NA.

56. Engineers Start Flood Survey," *Albuquerque Journal,* 16 October 1943, UP-1936-341-9159-X, CF, 1907–1939, RG 75, BIA, NA; John G. Evans, Acting Supt., UPA, to John Collier, CIA, 20 May 1944, UP-1936-341-9159-X, CF, 1907–1939, RG 75, BIA, NA; C.H. Southworth, A.Dir., Irrigation, to Virgil K. Whitaker, A. Supt., UPA, 16 July 1945, UP-1936-341-9159-A; Whitaker to CIA, attn. E. C. Fortier, 27 June 1945, UP-1936-341-9159-A, CF, 1907–1939, RG 75, BIA, NA; Memorandum of a Meeting of Representatives from SCS, War Department Corps of Engineers, USGS Water Quality Division, and Bureau of Reclamation, with Sketch Map of Río Grande Watershed, 25 May 1945, encl. in Whitaker to CIA, attn. Fortier; "We Must Get it," editorial, *Albuquerque Tribune,* 14 December 1945, and "Río Grande Project," editorial, *Albuquerque Journal,* 16 December 1945, both encl. in John G. Evans, Gen. Supt., UPA, to CIA, attn. A. L. Wathen, 17 December 1945, UP-1936-341-9159-A, CF, 1907–1939, RG 75, BIA, NA; "Santa Ana Pueblo, El Ranchito Grant, Proposed Floodway," 1944, SAPRG.

57. E. C. Fortier, Dir. of Irrigation, Interior Dept., to Manuel Gonzales, Spokesman, Santa Ana Pueblo, 18 October 1944, SAPRG; Governors and Representatives of the Six New Mexico Pueblos, Resolution to Congress through the Committee on Indian Affairs, 1944, SAPRG; MRGCD, Records of Pueblo Acreage, Operation, and Maintenance, September 1944, SAPRG; Unelio Menchego, Ditch Boss, Santa Ana

Pueblo, and MRGCD Ditch Rider, Statement concerning Santa Ana Water Shortage, 18 October 1946, SPA; Abel Paisano, Secretary, All Pueblo Council, to Manuel Gonzales, Governor, Santa Ana Pueblo, 18 September 1946, SAPRG; Porfirio Montoya, Statement about a Meeting to Discuss Indian Water Rights, 18 October 1946, SAPRG; Francisco Tenorio et al., Statement concerning Pueblo Water Rights, Shortages, and Delivery, 1946, SPA; Eric T. Hagberg, A. Supt., UPA, to Governor, Santa Ana Pueblo, 31 December 1946, SAPRG; E. T. H. [Hagberg?] to CIA, drafts 17 and 28 October 1949, SPA; L. G. Boldt, Irrigation Eng., "Report to E. T. H. on the Effect of Proposed AEC Water Diversions on Pueblo Irrigation," 28 October 1949, SPA; Dewey Dismuke, UPA, to Lojenio Otero, Governor, Santa Ana Pueblo, 16 May 1950, SAPRG; Albert Montoya, Governor, Santa Ana Pueblo, Council Resolution, 1959, SAPRG; W. M. Whipple, Brig. Gen. and Div. Eng., US Army, "Interim Survey Report for Flood Control on Main Stem of the Rio Grande," 18 March 1959, SAPRG; "Location Map—Santa Ana Pueblo, El Ranchito Grant," 21 August 1959, SAPRG; Guy C. Williams, Supt., UPA, to Santiago Armijo, Governor, Santa Ana Pueblo, 31 January 1964, SAPRG; Governor Armijo, Santa Ana Pueblo, Remarks on Silting Problem, Minutes of Six Middle Rio Grande Pueblos Irrigation Committee Meeting, 14 December 1964, SAPRG; "Rio Grande Tributary Projects: Jemez," 24 August 1964, SAPRG; Map, "Jemez Project, New Mexico, Plan of Development," 27 June 1964, SAPRG; Patrick L. Wehling, A. Supt., UPA, Memorandum to Area Director, attn. Land Operations, 8 May 1968, SAPRG; Vicente Armijo, Governor, Santa Ana Pueblo, Memorandum of Agreement between the United States and the Pueblo of Santa Ana, 5 September 1968, SAPRG; Paul A. Howdyshell, Field Sanitary Engineer, Division of Indian Health, "Project Summary, Santa Ana Domestic Water and Sewerage Facilities, Santa Ana Pueblo, Public Law 86-121," 1968, SAPRG; Abel Paisano, Chmn., All Pueblo Council, and the Governors of the Six Middle Río Grande Pueblos, to MRGCD, 14 July 1950, SAPRG; M. C. Hinderlider et al., Rio Grande Compact Commission, "Minutes of Special (Twenty-third) Meeting," 10–11 April 1951, SPA; M. C. Hinderlider et al., Río Grande Compact Commission, "Rio Grande Compact," 18 March 1938, encl. as Exhibit A in Price Daniel, AG, TE, Plaintiff's Motion, Statement, and Complaint in *State of Texas v. State of New Mexico et al.,* US Supreme Court, October 1951, SPA; Diego Abeita, Chmn,. Middle Río Grande Pueblo Irrigation Committee, to Porfirio Montoya, Santa Ana Pueblo, 25 April 1952, SPA; Mastin G. White, ID Solicitor, to US AG, 14 December 1951, SPA; William A. Brophy, Sp. Atty. for Pueblos, Memorandum to Diego Abeita et al., Irrigation Committee, 29 April 1952, SPA; BIA Area Director, Albuquerque, to CIA, 17 April 1952, SPA; W. A. Brophy, Memorandum on a Meeting at the Dept. of Justice, 24 April 1952, encl. in Brophy to Abeita et al.; Bill Brophy, Teletype Message to Charles L. Graves, Area Director, BIA, 25 April 1952, SPA; C. H. Southworth, Consultant, Phoenix Area Office, to Alan G. Harper et al., Area Directors, 24 February 1943, SPA; Ralph M. Gelvin, Phoenix Area Director, to J. M. Stewart et al., Supt., 24 February 1952, encl. in Southworth to Harper et al.;

Southworth, Memorandum to Ralph M. Gelvin et al., Area Directors, 27 January 1953, SPA; Harry A. Sellery, Jr., Chief Counsel, to Murray L. Crosse, Area Counsel, Window Rock, 9 March 1953, SPA; Orme Lewis, Asst. SI, to Representative Arthur V. Watkins, 28 April 1953, SPA; E. J. Otz, for the CIA, Memorandum to R. C. Price, Director, Division of Water and Power, 16 March 1953, SPA; A. R. Fife, Albuquerque Area Irrigation Engineer, BIA, to C. H. Southworth, Consultant, Indian Field Service, 21 September 1953, SPA; "Summary Indian Irrigation Projects—Upper Colorado River Basin," September 1953, encl. in Fife to Southworth; William A. Brophy, Memorandum to Mr. Fife, 4 August 1953, SPA; Diego Abeita, Chmn., Irrigation Committee, "Resolution of Middle Rio Grande Pueblos of Cochití, Santo Domingo, San Felipe, Santa Ana, Sandía, and Isleta and Their Irrigation Committee" [certified copy], 8 November 1955, SPA; Abeita to Governors and Irrigation Committee Members, Middle Río Grande Pueblos, 9 February and 8 March 1960, SAPRG: Governors, Six Middle Río Grande Pueblos, to Edwin L. Meecham, US Senate, 10 March 1964, SAPRG; Abeita to Vicente Armijo, Governor, Santa Ana Pueblo, 13 December 1968, SAPRG; Abeita, Six Middle Río Grande Pueblos Irrigation Committee Resolution, 19 December 1968, encl. in Abeita to Armijo.

58. Hughes, "Inserts into Santa Ana Historical Study," p. 9; Act of 30 June 1948, Ch. 771, 62 Stat. 1171.

59. Hughes, "Inserts into Santa Ana Historical Study," p. 9.

Appendix 1

1. Jesse D. Jennings, "Origins," in *Ancient Native Americans,* (San Francisco: W. H. Freeman and Co., 1978), pp. 1–43; Jesse D. Jennings, *Prehistory of North America,* 2d ed. (New York: McGraw-Hill Book Co., 1974), pp. 47–52; George A. Agogino and Michael L. Kunz, "The Paleo-Indian: Fact and Theory of Early Migration to the New World," *Indian Historian* 4, no. 1 (1971): 21–27.

2. William D. Lipe, "The Southwest," in *Ancient Native Americans,* ed. Jennings, p. 332; Jennings, *Prehistory of North America,* pp. 80–94.

3. Lipe, "Southwest," pp. 332–35; Jennings, *Prehistory of North America,* pp. 81–125.

4. Lipe, "Southwest," pp. 335–36, 339–40; Cynthia Irwin-Williams, *The Oshara Tradition: Origins of Anasazi Culture,* Eastern New Mexico University Contributions in Anthropology, vol. 5, no. 1 (1973). For a discussion of the general features of Archaic cultures, see Jennings, *Prehistory of North America,* pp. 127–91.

5. Lipe, "Southwest," pp. 335–36, 339–40.

6. Ibid.

7. Ibid., pp. 335–36, 339–43, 366–38; Jennings, *Prehistory of North America,* pp. 302–3; Jesse D. Jennings, *Prehistory of Utah and the Eastern Great Basin,* University of Utah Anthropological Papers, no. 98 (Salt Lake City: University of Utah Press, 1978), pp. 95–99.

8. Lipe, "Southwest," pp. 363–69; Jennings, *Prehistory of North America,* p. 303; Jennings, *Prehistory of Utah,* p. 98.

9. Lipe, "Southwest," p. 369; Jennings, *Prehistory of North America,* p. 306.

10. Jennings, *Prehistory of North America,* p. 293, has maps showing Anasazi extent as two-hundred-year intervals.

11. Lipe, "Southwest," pp. 370–75; Jennings, *Prehistory of North America,* pp. 307–8; John C. McGregor, *Southwestern Archaeology,* 2d ed. (Urbana: University of Illinois Press, 1965), pp. 279–95; R. Gwinn Vivian, "An Inquiry into Prehistoric Social Organization in Chaco Canyon, New Mexico," in *Reconstructing Prehistoric Pueblo Societies,* ed. William A. Longacre, (Albuquerque: University of New Mexico Press, 1975), p. 68.

12. Lipe, "Southwest," p. 375.

13. Ibid., p. 377–78; James Schoenwetter and Alfred E. Dittert Jr., "An Ecological Interpretation of Anasazi Settlement Patterns," in *Anthropological Archaeology in the Americas,* ed. B. J. Meggers (Washington, D.C.: Anthropological Society of Washington, 1968), p. 41; Stephen J. Kunitz and Robert C. Euler, *Aspects of Southwestern Paleoepidemiology,* Anthropological Reports, no. 2 (Prescott, Ariz.: Prescott College Press, 1972), pp. 3–7, 39–40.

14. Lipe, "Southwest," pp. 278–79; Schoenwetter and Dittert, "Ecological Interpretation," pp. 41–44, 58–59; Jennings, *Prehistory of North America,* p. 311; Kirk Bryan, "Pre-Columbian Agriculture in the Southwest as Conditioned by Periods of Alluviation," *Annals of the Association of American Geographers* 31, no. 4 (December 1941): 328–40.

15. Lipe, "Southwest," p. 375.

16. Ibid., pp. 376–77; McGregor, *Southwestern Archaeology,* pp. 389, 394; Fred Wendorf and Erik K. Reed, "An Alternative Reconstruction of Northern Rio Grande Prehistory," *El Palacio* 62 (1955): 146, 161–62.

17. Fred Eggan, *Social Organization of the Western Pueblos* (Chicago and London: University of Chicago Press, 1950), pp. 2–3; Harold E. Driver, *Indians of North America* (Chicago and London: University of Chicago Press, 1961), p. 576.

18. Irvine Davis, "Linguistic Clues to Northern Rio Grande Prehistory," *El Palacio* 66, no. 3 (June 1959): 77–79.

19. Adolph L. Bandelier, *Final Report of Investigations among the Indians of the Southwestern United States Carried on Mainly in the Years from 1880 to 1885,* Archaeological Institute of America Papers, America Series, nos. 3, 4, (Cambridge: John Wilson and Son, University Press, 1892), p. 32; Edgar L. Hewett, *Antiquities of the Jemez Plateau,* pp. 12–13, cited in Ralph Emerson Twitchell, *The Leading Facts of the New Mexico History* (Cedar Rapids, Iowa: Torch Press, 1911), p. 39, n. 23, and pp. 40–42, n. 24.

20. Edward S. Curtis, *The North American Indian,* vol. 16 (1926; reprint, New York: Johnson Reprint, 1970), pp. 65–68; Edgar L. Hewett, *Pajarito Plateau and Its Ancient People,* 2d ed., revised by Bertha P. Dutton (Albuquerque: University of New Mexico Press, 1953), pp. 41–52.

21. Edward Sapir, "Central and North American Languages," in *Encyclopedia Britannica,* 14th ed., vol. 5, pp. 139–41, cited in Davis, "Linguistic Clues," p. 84.

22. Florence M. Hawley, "Pueblo Social Organization as a Lead to Pueblo History," *American Anthropologist,* new series 39, no. 3, pt. 1 (July-September 1937): 520–21.

23. Florence Hawley Ellis, "Keresan Patterns of Kinship and Social Organization," *American Anthropologist* 52, no. 4, pt. 1 (1950): 511.

24. H. P. Mera, *Ceramic Clues to the Prehistory of North Central New Mexico,* Archaeological Survey Technical Series Bulletin no. 8 (Santa Fe: Laboratory of Anthropology, 1935), p. 39.

25. Elsie Clews Parsons, "Relations Between Ethnology and Archaeology in the Southwest," *American Antiquity* 5, no. 3, (1940): 220.

26. Davis, "Linguistic Clues," p. 79; Stanley Newman, "American Indian Linguistics in the Southwest," *American Anthropologist* 56, no. 4, pt. 1 (August 1954): 631; Alfonso Ortiz, ed., *New Perspectives on the Pueblos* (Albuquerque: University of New Mexico Press, 1972), p. 20, notes a recent attempt to revive the Keres-Hokan link.

27. Wendorf and Reed, "Alternative Reconstruction," p. 159.

28. Ibid., pp. 138–139, 147, 161; Schoenwetter and Dittert, "Ecological Interpretation," p. 55.

29. "The Significance of Skull Deformation in the Southwest," *El Palacio* 56, no. 4 (April 1949): 106–19; "Sources of Upper Rio Grande Pueblo Culture and Population," *El Palacio* 56, no. 6 (June 1949): 163–84; "East Central Arizona Archaeology in Relation to the Western Pueblos," *Southwestern Journal of Anthropology* 6, no. 2 (Summer 1950): 120–39.

30. Ellis, "Keresan Patterns of Kinship," p. 522; Florence M. Hawley, "Big Kivas, Little Kivas, and Moiety Houses in Historical Reconstruction," *Southwestern Journal of Anthropology* 6, no. 3 (1950): 286–302; Fred Wendorf, "A Reconstruction of Northern Rio Grande Prehistory," *American Anthropologist* 56, no. 2, pt. 1 (April 1954): 221.

31. Wendorf, "Reconstruction," pp. 213, 220–22; Wendorf and Reed, "Alternative Reconstruction," pp. 160–61.

32. Wendorf and Reed, "Alternative Reconstruction."

33. Ibid., pp. 163–164; Richard L. Ford et al., "Three Perspectives on Puebloan Prehistory," in *New Perspectives on the Pueblos,* ed. Ortiz, p. 20; Florence Hawley Ellis, *A Reconstruction of the Basic Jemez Pattern of Social Organization with Comparisons to other Tanoan Social Structures,* University of New Mexico Publications in Anthropology, no. 11 (Albuquerque: University of New Mexico Press, 1964), pp. 7–8.

34. Ford et al., "Three Perspectives," pp. 20, 23–24, 26–29, 33–36, 39.

35. Davis, "Linguistic Clues," pp. 77–81, 83.

36. Florence Hawley Ellis, "Where Did the Pueblo People Come From?" *El Palacio* 74, no. 3 (Autumn 1967).

37. Ibid.

38. Florence Hawley Ellis, "Anthropological Evidence Supporting the Land Claim of the Pueblos of Zia, Santa Ana, and Jemez," manuscript, University of New Mexico, n.d., pp. 13–15.

39. Ibid.

40. Ibid., pp. 16, 30.

41. Ibid.

42. H. P. Mera, *Population Changes in the Rio Grande Glaze-Paint Area,* Archaeological Survey Technical Series Bulletin no. 9 (Santa Fe: Laboratory of Anthropology, 1940), pp. 26–27, identified this as a Keres site and noted that some Santa Anas claimed it was a seventeenth-century Santa Ana settlement. Adolph F. Bandelier, *Final Report,* pt. 2, p. 193, noted that Santa Anas claimed the ruin at Cangelon on the volcanic mesa about four miles north of Bernalillo.

43. Herbert E. Bolton, *Coronado on the Turquoise Trail: Knight of the Pueblos and Plains* (Albuquerque: University of New Mexico Press, 1949), pp. 184–88, 192–94, 197–98, 210–30; George P. Hammond and Agapito Rey, eds., *Narratives of the Coronado Expedition, 1540–1542* (Albuquerque: University of New Mexico Press, 1940), pp. 182–84, 220–27, 233–34, 254, 258–60, 299–300.

44. Ibid.

45. Ellis, "Anthropological Evidence Supporting the Land Claims," pp. 9–11, 13, 16, 44–46; Florence Hawley Ellis, "The Immediate History of Zía Pueblo as Derived from Excavation in Refuse Deposits," *American Antiquity* 31, no. 6 (October 1966); Larry Frank and Francis H. Harlow, *Historic Pottery of the Pueblo Indians, 1600–1880* (Boston: New York Graphic Society, 1974), pp. 97–115.

46. Ellis, "Anthropological Evidence Supporting the Land Claim," p. 55.

47. George P. Hammond and Agapito Rey, *Don Juan de Oñate, Colonizer of New Mexico, 1595–1628,* pt. 1 (Albuquerque: University of New Mexico Press, 1953), pp. 337–41, 345. The Tamaya mentioned here may have been the pueblo on top of Black Mesa identified by Adolph F. Bandelier in *Final Report,* pt. 2, p. 194.

Index

Index

Index

Index

Index